Designing Interactive Speech Systems:
From First Ideas to User Testing

Springer

London
Berlin
Heidelberg
New York
Barcelona
Budapest
Hong Kong
Milan
Paris
Santa Clara
Singapore
Tokyo

Niels Ole Bernsen, Hans Dybkjær and
Laila Dybkjær

Designing Interactive Speech Systems:

From First Ideas to User Testing

Springer

Niels Ole Bernsen
Laila Dybkjær
Maersk Mc-Kinney Moller Institute for Production Technology
Odense University, Denmark

Hans Dybkjær
Prolog Development Center A/S, Copenhagen, Denmark

ISBN 3-540-76048-2 Springer-Verlag Berlin Heidelberg New York

British Library Cataloguing in Publication Data
Designing interactive speech systems : from first ideas to user testing
   1. Speech processing systems   2. Interactive computer systems
   I. Bernsen, Niels Ole   II. Dybkjær, Hans   III. Dybkjær, Laila
   006.4'54
   ISBN 3540760482

Library of Congress Cataloging-in-Publication Data
Designing interactive speech systems : from first ideas to user testing / Niels Ole Bernsen, Hans Dybkjær, and Laila Dybkjær.
   p.   cm.
   Includes bibliographical references and index.
   ISBN 3-540-76048-2 (alk. paper)
   1. Human–computer interaction.   2. Automatic speech recognition.   3. Electronic
   digital computers--Input–output equipment..
   I. Bernsen, Niels Ole, 1947-   . II. Dybkjær, Hans, 1961-   . III. Dybkjær, Laila, 1959-   .
   QA76.9.H85D49 1998
                          97-46543

Typesetting: Gray Publishing, Tunbridge Wells, Kent
Printed and bound at the Athenæum Press Ltd., Gateshead, Tyne and Wear
34/3830-543210 Printed on acid-free paper

Contents

Preface

When we began the Danish Dialogue Project, back in 1991, it was felt that the ultimate in basic speech recognition technologies, i.e. robust, marketable speaker-independent continuous speech recognition, would have become reality by the end of the project. We are delighted that this is the case and that advanced speech technologies are now finding their way into a multitude of practical applications in a growing number of languages. In the same period, user-oriented spoken interaction model design has developed from a rather esoteric subject into a focal area of research and practical interest.

This book describes our experiences from developing and evaluating the interaction model for the Danish Dialogue System. Although selected results from this work have been presented in a number of publications over the years, we believe that it takes a book to really get the "feel" of a complex interactive speech system. When re-reading our own papers, or reading those of others, there is often the impression that much information of importance to the understanding of the actual, down-to-earth and practical development and evaluation process has been left out because it was not deemed of sufficient importance to the particular point of novelty being presented.

Throughout our work we have tried to stick to the agenda of application-oriented research. "Application orientation" means a focus on real users, real-time and real tasks for which interactive speech systems could provide solutions. "Research" means that the work not only aims at demonstrating a working solution but also aims at generalizing results to the extent possible at the time. It is too early to entertain the ambition of creating a textbook on the subject. At this stage, the best one can offer is a comprehensive description of an individual development effort coupled with modest or tentative generalizations in terms of concepts, theories, methods and tools, and spiced with concrete and "dirty" examples and references to similar efforts by other developers.

We hope that some of the many computer scientists, engineers and others who are starting to develop interactive speech systems might find some of our observations and results useful to their own work. Graduate students specializing in natural interactive systems more generally, or interactive speech systems in particular, might also use the book to form a concrete idea of what it means to develop and evaluate interactive speech systems. Finally, fellow researchers might at least derive the pleasure of seeing some of the wrong turns reported, which they themselves have been unwilling to put into print.

The book has a simple structure. *Chapter 1* discusses interactive speech systems, tools and techniques from a structural as well as a state-of-the-art point of view, and presents the "rationalized development" approach adopted in this book. *Chapter 2* presents a theory of the elements of advanced interactive speech systems which, in our view, should be considered by today's developers. *Chapter 3* is the first in a series of chapters which apply a standard software engineering life-cycle model to the development and evaluation of interactive speech systems. In particular, Chapter 3 looks at completeness and consistency of requirement specifications and presents prototools for design space development and speech functionality analysis. *Chapter 4* describes how to design the first interaction model and presents a set of guidelines for interaction model design. *Chapter 5* provides a detailed discussion of the Wizard of Oz system simulation technique. *Chapter 6* describes implementational issues. *Chapter 7* is an introduction to the increasingly important subject of corpus handling during the development and evaluation of interactive speech systems. *Chapter 8* discusses interactive speech system evaluation based on a distinction between performance evaluation, diagnostic evaluation and adequacy evaluation. Finally, *Chapter 9* takes a look ahead, in two directions. One is towards what we call advanced mixed initiative interactive speech systems. The other is towards multimodal systems that include speech as one of their input/output modalities.

Acknowledgements

The Danish Dialogue Project received generous support from the Natural Sciences and Technical Sciences Research Councils. We gratefully acknowledge their support. Our colleagues in the Danish Dialogue Project from the Centre for PersonKommunikation, Aalborg University, and the Centre for Language Technology, Copenhagen, developed the system's platform, speech recognizer, speech telephone interface, player, grammar and parser. Discussions during project meetings no doubt influenced our work on interaction model development in many subtle ways. Tove Klausen and Judith Ramsay contributed to the Design Space Development approach in the Esprit Long-term Research project AMODEUS-2. Dimitris Papazachariou contributed to the simulation and analysis of advanced mixed initiative dialogue in the Human Capital and Mobility Research Network in Spoken Dialogue and Discourse. Funded by the Nordic Council, Vytautas Zinkevicius participated in recent studies on how to transfer skills in the use of the co-operativity guidelines. Norman Fraser might be able to find snippets of his contributions to the DISC proposal in the state-of-the-art sections in Chapter 1. Our partners in the Esprit Long-term Research Project, DISC, have consented to use the software engineering life-cycle approach to interactive speech systems adopted in this book as one of the points of departure for the project. And we look forward to extending and revising our understanding of corpus handling through learning from our partners in the upcoming Telematics MATE Project. Many thanks to you all!

1. *Interactive Speech Systems*

1.1 Introduction

Natural Human–Computer Interaction

When we use a computer system to perform a certain task, the computer system acts both as a tool and as a partner in communication. It would be stretching the sense of the term "communication" beyond reasonable limits to say that one communicates with a spade when using it. The computer is different to the spade in important ways. The user must input information in some form in order to make the system execute. Similarly, to inform the user of its state, processes and their results, the computer must output information to the user. The information which is being exchanged between user and system during task performance can be represented in different forms, or modalities, using a variety of different input/output devices. For a wide range of tasks, the system can achieve task adequacy as a tool by exchanging information with its users in ways that are completely different to those of human–human communication, such as through a keyboard and mouse as input devices, the screen as an output device and typed command notation as the key modality for representing input information. With or without the inclusion of typed command input notation, this form of interaction is called the graphical user interface (GUI) paradigm. Within limits of various kinds, users are able to adapt to such highly artificial styles of communication as long as the input/output devices used for the purpose are reasonably ergonomical in their design. In the ideal world, however, and whenever desirable, there is no reason why the exchange of information with computer systems should not be done in ways that are much more natural to the users. Arguably, the most natural form of situated human–human communication is two-way, face-to-face discourse using speech, facial expression and gesture, and incorporating other modalities of information representation and exchange as needed, such as written text, maps, drawings, graphs, animation, video, soundscapes, etc. Even if such ideal communication with the computer system were to become reality, the computer would not completely loose its spade-like (or tool) aspects. "Direct" manual or bodily interaction, as exemplified by the GUI paradigm, would remain useful for many purposes. But even those aspects could be made much more natural and ergonomic than is currently the case, and they would become reduced to serving the task aspects for which they can demonstrate superiority with respect to usability.

What is an Interactive Speech System?

Interactive speech systems represent one step towards fully natural communication with computer systems. For the purpose of this book, *interactive speech systems* will be characterized as computer systems which allow people to perform at least part of their tasks through some form of spoken language dialogue. The computer is able to understand a person's spoken input utterances and generate appropriate spoken output to the user. Interactive speech systems, in this sense, are *unimodal I/O* systems. That is, they use information represented as speech and nothing else in their two-way communication with users. The class of unimodal interactive speech systems may be sub-divided into systems which take continuous, speaker-independent spoken input (Figure 1.1, area 4) and systems which do not (Figure 1.1, area 3). We call the former *advanced interactive speech systems*. To locate interactive speech systems in the space of interactive systems more generally, interactive speech systems may be contrasted with two other families of systems: *interactive systems which do not use speech* (Figure 1.1, area 1), such as graphical user interfaces; and *interactive systems which do not use speech interactively* (Figure 1.1, area 2). The latter class of systems includes all speech systems that either do not understand speech input or do not generate speech output. Speech-to-text systems, text-to-speech systems, telephone-based voice response systems (also called touch-tone or DTMF systems) that allow navigation among pre-recorded or synthesized messages, input command systems for car phones, graphical screen execution, cockpit equipment operation, etc., in which the system's feedback is not spoken output but simply an execution of the spoken command, systems that merely record spoken input, as well as systems, such as standard multimedia systems or systems equipped with pre-recorded speech alarms, that merely replay speech as output – all exemplify interactive systems which do not use speech interactively.

Unimodal interactive speech systems may be contrasted with *multimodal interactive speech systems* (Figure 1.1, area 5) which use additional modalities in exchanging information with their users. Examples of multimodal interactive speech systems are interactive speech systems coupled with a graphical speaking face aimed to facilitate the comprehension of synthetic speech (Bertenstam *et al.,* 1995; Cole *et al.,* 1996) or – as yet non-existent – intelligent multimedia presentation systems that generate as output a coordinated combination of spoken language and graphical images. Only very advanced and as yet non-existent intelligent multimodal systems which combine spoken language input understanding and spoken language output generation with many other input and output modalities would begin to approach the human–human face-to-face paradigm of natural communication mentioned above.

Scope of Interactive Speech Systems

Systems which satisfy the above definition of interactive speech systems are of at least two types. The *first* type includes systems which act as a dialogue partner in a restricted domain, often serving as domain experts. Examples are information and reservation systems, such as the flight and train timetable inquiry systems developed in the European Sundial Project (Peckham, 1993), the Philips (Aust *et al.,* 1995), Swiss Rail (Peng and Vital, 1996) and RailTel (Lamel *et al.,* 1995) train timetable

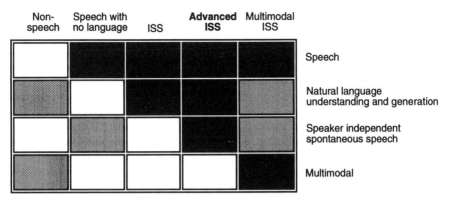

Figure 1.1: Advanced interactive speech systems as defined for the purpose of this book are unimodal speech systems (or speech-only systems) with speaker-independent spontaneous speech input and natural language understanding and generation. The figure contrasts such systems (AISS) with two other types of interactive speech systems (ISS and MISS), as well as with speech systems which lack understanding of what is being recognized or generated or both, and systems which do not use speech.

inquiry systems, the Danish Dialogue System for flight ticket reservation, telephone switchboard service systems, such as the Vocalis Operetta (http://www.vocalis.com/pages/products/operetta.htm), various telephone company service systems, such as telephone service disconnect ordering systems (Mazor *et al.*, 1994), voice-activated telephone extension systems (Naito *et al.*, 1995), systems which tell why a dialled number did not work (Ortel, 1995), systems for the partial automation of directory enquiries (Forssten, 1994), systems for providing information on weather and yellow pages (Cole *et al.*, 1994; Sadek *et al.*, 1996), systems for switchboard repair (Smith and Hipp, 1994), and appointment scheduling systems (Fanty *et al.*, 1995). The *second* type includes multilingual spoken dialogue translation systems, such as Janus (Lavie *et al.*, 1996; Zhan *et al.*, 1996), ΦDmDialog for conference registration (Kitano, 1991) and Verbmobil (Wahlster, 1993).

Commercial Advances: Speaker-independent, Spontaneous Speech Recognition

Although inferior with respect to the paradigm of fully natural human–human communication, interactive speech systems promise, on the one hand, substantive progress in naturalness of human–machine communication and, on the other, intelligent human–machine communication for tasks that do not easily lend themselves to other modes of interaction, such as stationary or mobile communication at a distance over the telephone or via various wireless devices, or heads-up control tasks in the cockpit or in the car. What makes interactive speech systems particularly interesting at the present time is that they have recently become commercially available in their most versatile and natural form, i.e. real-time systems that understand speaker-independent continuous speech. Acceptable-quality speech synthesis in several languages has already been in existence for some time. Moreover, the best speech recognizers now enable acceptable-quality understanding of over-the-telephone, speaker-independent continuous speech input of medium-size vocabularies of 1000–2000 words. As a result, the first commercial telephone-based interactive speech systems accepting speaker-independent continuous speech input have been installed around the world (see Section 1.3.2) and others are set to follow at what appears to be a rapidly increasing pace. Earlier commercial interactive speech systems either use speaker-dependent speech input, which requires that the system be trained to a particular user, and/or non-continuous speech input in the form of isolated words or connected speech. Speaker-dependent speech input severely restricts the systems' versatility. Isolated word input or connected speech input severely limits the naturalness of providing spoken input to computer systems. For these reasons, we will restrict the interactive speech systems discussed in the present book to systems that accept continuous, speaker-independent spoken input (Figure 1.1, area 4). These will be called *advanced interactive speech systems*, or just *interactive speech systems*, in what follows.

The Logical Process Model

Speech recognizers and speech generators still need improvement in many respects, including basic recognition rate; coping with spoken language specificities, such as hesitations, repetitions of words or syllables, ill-formed phrases, incomplete sentences, etc.; rejecting non-authorized words or interpreting them using the context of the sentence or dialogue; and dynamically adapting to the user's personal way of speaking (linguistic behaviour, own stereotypes, etc.); voice output quality; and ability to handle input prosody and output prosody in concatenated pre-recorded speech or speech synthesis. Meanwhile, the errors and misunderstandings that occur between user and system because of less-than-ideal speech recognition and generation can often be satisfactorily handled through spoken interaction. However, the facts that users can now speak to their computer systems in basically the same way as they speak to other humans, that is, by using continuous speaker-independent speech, and that they can understand the machine's spoken response without significant difficulty, especially when pre-recorded speech is being used, mean that two of the five logical steps that make up the information processing done by interactive speech systems are now in place for practical use (Figure 1.2).

The Linguistic Processing Steps

The linguistic processing done by today's advanced interactive speech systems consists of: (i) linguistic analysis of the spoken input produced by the speech recognizer; and (ii) generation from an underlying semantic representation of linguistic output to the speech generator. Natural language generation per se is often absent from current systems because the underlying output semantics, once chosen by the system, is directly linked to pre-designed system output phrases which simply have to be played to the user or passed through the speech synthesizer. When more advanced natural language generation becomes necessary there does not seem to be any reason why advanced interactive speech systems designers could not draw upon what is already known about language generation in the natural language processing community. The system's output will be decoded by humans. As long as the system's messages are clear and precise in the interactive context, it matters less whether they are being phrased somewhat too closely to the grammar of written language compared to spoken language. Humans are simply very good at decoding linguistic output phrases and utterances, However, they are also very good at modelling the system's output phrases, so this would have to be taken care of. The problem is more serious on the linguistic input side. Most advanced interactive speech

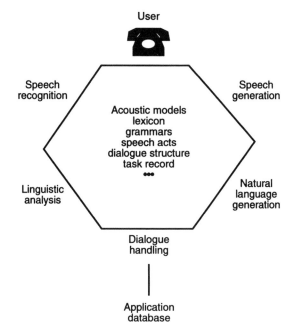

Figure 1.2: Typical logical structure of an interactive speech system.

systems need some form of linguistic analysis of the spoken input. However, spoken language behaves very differently to written language and its behaviour remains poorly understood. This means that there is no easy way of transferring linguistic progress in written language understanding to the understanding of spoken input. Thus, there is still no consensus whatsoever with respect to how to optimize grammar and parsing for advanced interactive speech systems. Full written language parsing techniques do not work. What actually works, more or less, is commonly called "robust parsing", but this term does not presently have any clear meaning apart from referring to less than full written language parsing. Other issues are: whether to use stand-alone grammar and lexicon(s) or build these into the speech recognizer; how to achieve spoken sub-language adequacy (lexicon and grammar) for language understanding and generation; whether to use morphology (declarative and principled, but slow processing) or a full-form lexicon (fast); how to integrate syntax and semantics; how to efficiently separate resources from the procedures which use them (modularity); how to add linguistic knowledge (grammar and vocabulary) to the system during or after development (extensibility); and how to build one shared grammar for analysis and generation (modularity).

Dialogue Processing is the Core of Interactive Speech Systems/Technologies

Despite the very real problems of designing grammars and parsing techniques for spoken input, it is probably in dialogue processing that current development of advanced interactive speech systems is furthest removed from theoretical and practical mastery in terms of best practice development and evaluation procedures, methods, tools, standards and supporting concepts and theory. The main reason appears to be the comparative novelty of the problems themselves rather than their unique difficulty. In a very real sense, the management by machine of spoken dialogue can only be investigated in running interactive speech systems or in realistic simulations of such systems. Investigations of this nature have only been possible during the last decade or so, whereas research on speech recognition and generation, and on (written) linguistic input analysis and (written) language generation, has a much longer history. Of course, many individual aspects of human–human conversation have been investigated for more than a decade but theoretical results have proven difficult to transfer to spoken human–machine interaction (see Chapter 4). This is because the machine is a highly inferior partner in dialogue compared to human interlocutors. We propose to attack the problem of human–machine spoken dialogue from a different perspective. Instead of attempting to transfer results from human–human conversation theory straight away, we attempt to lay the foundations of an incremental, application-oriented theory of human–machine dialogue from the bottom up, starting with the needs of current dialogue design and calling upon novel theory development and results from human–human conversation theory based on the demands of practical dialogue design.

The Interaction Model

In the terms introduced above, the present book addresses the subject of advanced interactive speech systems with a particular focus on the nature and practical development and evaluation of their dialogue component as part of the overall system. Despite this focus, it should be kept in mind that it is impossible to build a dialogue model without regard for the language model. Language is an inseparable part of dialogue and, hence, of the interaction between an interactive speech system and its users. We shall use the term *interaction model* to designate the combined model of language and dialogue needed for an interactive speech system. More generally speaking, an interaction model comprises models for input understanding, output production, dialogue management, and domain and other contextual knowledge.

Speech Functionality, Software System Development, Advanced Mixed Initiative Interaction and Intelligent Multimodal Systems

The development of interaction models for interactive speech systems happens in a larger context. We shall be addressing part of that context in what follows. First, any particular case of interactive speech system development assumes that speech is an appropriate modality for the exchange of information between user and system with respect to the system to be developed. Evidently, speech is not always appropriate. So there is a need for guidance on when to use or not to use, as the case may be, speech in interactive applications. We shall present an early version of a tool which may assist developers in deciding when (or not) to use speech in particular applications. Secondly, interactive speech system development is a particular sub-class of software system development more generally. As such it may benefit from tools for the support of the software system's development process. We shall present and illustrate our use of one such tool, i.e. the Design Space Development approach to software specification and development. Thirdly, current advanced interactive speech systems remain primitive and of restricted applicability when compared to expected future system generations. We shall take a look at two lines of approach which will have to succeed in order to radically improve system interactivity and versatility, and make real progress towards fully natural communication with computer systems. One approach is to solve the problems involved in achieving advanced mixed initiative dialogue between users and system. Another, to integrate speech understanding and production into intelligent multimodal systems (cf. Figure 1.1).

1.2 Background and Scope of This Book

Current ad hoc Practices

The accelerating industrial exploitation of advanced interactive speech technologies means that development and evaluation practices emerge locally in both research and industry. These practices are largely ad hoc and fragmented, and tend to emerge without benefiting from the accumulating but often unrecorded experience in the field as a whole. This means that errors are being duplicated and that the practice of each team of developers is likely to be sub-optimal compared to what is possible already. The remedy for this state of affairs is the sharing of experience and results among development teams in industry and academia, "results" meaning best practice procedures for advanced interactive speech system development and evaluation, novel sets of concepts, new methods and tools that can help in removing development uncertainties, speed up time-to-market, improve user acceptance and reduce development cost.

Our Approach

The main background for this book is our work during the past 5 years on specifying, designing, rapid prototyping, implementing and evaluating the interaction model of the Danish Dialogue System. During that work we encountered a large number of unsolved problems in the spoken interaction model and dialogue component development and evaluation, and we attempted to address some of them. The approach that we used in addressing the problems is illustrated by the "spiral model" in Figure 1.3. It consists of: first, encountering the problem and trying to solve it in practice; secondly, reflecting on the problem and proposing concepts, theories, procedures, methods and tools to solve the problem, always aiming at enabling a more general and principled approach to the problem in future development and evaluation tasks; thirdly, developing and testing, to the extent possible given limited resources in terms of personpower, accessible corpora, accessible development projects at other sites, etc., the proposed concepts, theories, procedures, methods and tools; and thereby, fourthly, improving the basis for future interactive speech system development and evaluation. Secondary background for the book has been provided by work done in representing design spaces for designer problem solving in large software projects, exploratory work on advanced mixed initiative spoken interaction, work on Modality Theory, i.e. the theory of which modalities to use in representing and exchanging information with computer systems given their early requirement specifications, and work on the specification of an intelligent multimodal system that integrates speech understanding and production.

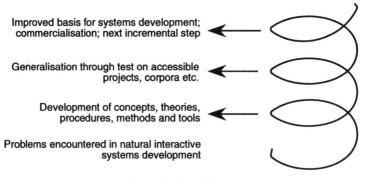

Improved basis for systems development; commercialisation; next incremental step ←

Generalisation through test on accessible projects, corpora etc. ←

Development of concepts, theories, procedures, methods and tools ←

Problems encountered in natural interactive systems development

Figure 1.3:. The spiral model.

A Rationalized Development Process

We can hardly claim to have produced *complete and general* solutions to any single unsolved problem in interaction model and dialogue component development and evaluation. To do so requires a very substantial effort in the investigation of several different, major advanced interactive speech system development tasks. Yet we believe to have made progress on several issues and believe that the best way to share results is to systematically describe what we have done in a book. Reflecting the approach shown in Figure 1.3, the description of results will take the form of a *rationalized development process* as shown in Figure 1.4. That is, instead of just describing what we actually did, we describe how we would develop an advanced interactive speech application were we to make use of the results of our completed project. Figure 1.4 roughly contrasts the rationalized development process we offer, including its series of limited generalizations (a), with a possible future "ideal textbook" view of spoken interaction model development and evaluation best practice supported by all the relevant generalizations (b). What Figure 1.4 fails to illustrate, however, is the very real possibility that future progress might *replace* the results that we are going to describe rather than just generalizing those results further and providing the many needed generalizations that are missing from our account. In describing a rationalized development process for advanced interactive speech systems, we shall illustrate the approaches proposed through numerous examples from actual development and evaluation experience.

The Danish Dialogue System

The Danish Dialogue System is a research prototype for Danish domestic flight ticket reservation. The prototype system was developed in the Danish Dialogue Project. The project was supported by the Danish Research Councils for the Technical and the Natural Sciences, and involved an effort of about 30 person/years by the Centre for PersonKommunikation at Aalborg University (speech recognition, grammar, player), the Centre for Language Technology, Copenhagen (grammar, parsing), and the Centre for Cognitive Science, Roskilde University (dialogue component and application design and implementation, interaction model aspects, output design).

The system runs on a PC and is accessed over the telephone. It is a speaker-independent continuous speech understanding system which speaks and under-

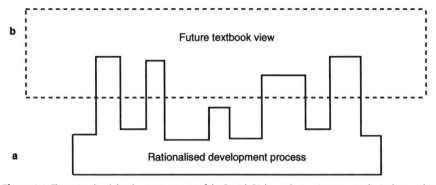

Figure 1.4: The rationalized development process of the Danish Dialogue System incorporates limited generalizations from the actual development process (a). Some of these generalizations might be included in an ideal future textbook presentation of the development process (b), providing fully generalized best practice procedures, methods and tools supported by underlying concepts and theory.

stands Danish with a vocabulary of about 500 words. The prototype runs in close-to-real-time. Its main components are shown in Figure 1.5.

When a user calls the system it is detected by the *telephone line interface*. The *speech recognizer* then receives the user's speech signal. The speech recognizer is based on Hidden Markov Models (HMMs) and represents a further developed version of the recognizer that was developed in the Esprit Sunstar Project (Lindberg *et al.*, 1992; Lindberg and Kristiansen, 1995). In addition to user input, the speech recognizer needs predictions from the dialogue management module (see below) on the particular sub-grammars and vocabulary to use at any given point during interaction. Predictions are needed because, to enable real-time performance, at most 100 words can be active in memory at a time. The sub-grammars used by the speech recognizer are word pair grammars represented as finite state transition networks in which transitions represent HMMs. Viterbi search is used to find a 1-best path through the network. This path represents a string of lexical references which constitutes the output of the speech recognition module.

The lexical string is input to the *parser*. The dialogue management module also provides predictions to the parser on which sub-grammars and vocabulary to use, and which semantic objects to fill in on the basis of the input string from the recognizer. The semantic objects are frame-like structures containing slots for domain-relevant information. The number of available slots varies depending on the expected input. The sub-grammars used for linguistic analysis are unification-based Augmented Phrase Structure Grammars (APSGs) implemented in a formalism which is a sub-set of the one used in the Eurotra Project (Copeland *et al.*, 1991). The parser module analyses the input based on the active sub-grammars using a chart data structure and an object-oriented implementation of the Earley parsing algorithm. The parser uses semantic mapping rules for assigning the semantic interpretations (Povlsen, 1994), which in turn are used for filling in the active semantic objects.

The *dialogue management module* consists of the Interpretation and Control Module (ICM) and the dialogue description. The dialogue management module interprets the contents of the semantic objects and decides on the next system action which may be to send a query to the database, send output to the user or wait for new input.

In the latter case, predictions on the next user input are sent to the recognizer and the parser. If no input is detected during a certain interval, new output is sent to the user.

The *database* contains information on timetables, flights, reservations and customers, as well as rules for managing the information and queries received. System output is produced by concatenation of pre-recorded phrases.

The output phrases are selected by the dialogue management module and replayed by a separate *reproductive speech module.*

The *text recognizer* is only used when the speech recognizer is disabled. This is useful during the debugging and testing of the system.

The *DDL-tool* does not form part of the running system but is a tool used to create the dialogue description, i.e. the implemented dialogue model.

The *Communication Manager* is a data bus which transfers messages between all other modules.

The interaction model for the system was iteratively designed by means of the Wizard of Oz experimental prototyping method. The model resulting from the last WOZ iteration was implemented and debugged, and the implemented system was tested with naive users. The WOZ experiments produced a corpus of transcribed dialogues, user questionnaires and interviews; the implementation and debugging phase produced log files; and the user test produced log files and a corpus of transcribed dialogues, user questionnaires and interviews. All these sources of information were subjected to in-depth analysis. Throughout the development process, the sources have served as a basis for evaluating the interaction model by identifying interaction problems and revealing unsatisfied design goals and constraints.

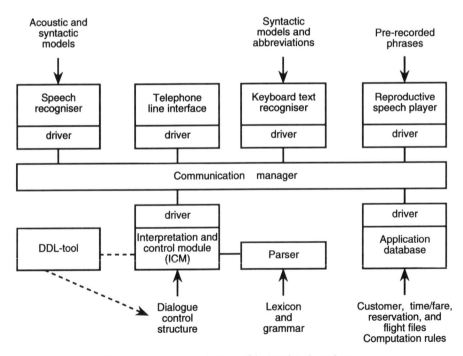

Figure 1.5: The overall architecture of the Danish Dialogue System.

The resulting system is representative of prototype advanced interactive speech systems developed in the 1990s. Although not (yet) a commercial system, the system has been developed as a realistic application through substantial interaction with potential end-users and their organizations. Based on the test results obtained, we believe that the system can be commercialized given an appropriate speech recognizer and appropriate grammars and parsing strategies.

Generalization

Our development of the dialogue control component (the dialogue description) and various other parts of the interaction model of the Danish Dialogue System formed the basis of a series of generalizations which may be useful to other developers of advanced interactive speech systems. The requirement specification phase and subsequent development phases were used to test an approach to design space representation and reasoning called Design Space Development. The Wizard of Oz simulation phase was used to collect detailed "how-to-do-what-and-when" information on the Wizard of Oz method. The Wizard of Oz simulation phase was also used to develop a first set of guidelines for the design of cooperative system interaction. These guidelines were subsequently refined and compared to a well-established theory of cooperative human–human conversation. Finally, the guidelines were validated as part of the final user test of the implemented system. It turned out that the guidelines could form the backbone of a rigorous method for diagnostic evaluation of spoken interactive system behaviour. In addition, the principles appear promising as guidelines for the design of cooperative system interaction prior to implementation. Evaluation of the implemented system led to a more general investigation of some of the problems involved in evaluating advanced interactive speech systems. Work on the many information sources produced during system development and evaluation led to experience with corpus handling and text markup methodology for advanced interactive speech system development and evaluation. Analysis of task-oriented human–human spoken dialogue and Wizard of Oz simulations of advanced mixed initiative dialogue led to ideas on how to machine-implement identification of the speech acts that are contextually relevant during task-oriented dialogue. Modality theory supported investigation of speech functionality, i.e. of when to use speech in an application and when not do so, leading to first ideas on a tool to support decision making during early design. Finally, throughout the development process we worked on systematizing a bottom-up approach to a theory of task-oriented spoken interaction. These are the generalizations in terms of theory, concepts, methods and tools that we propose to present as part of the rationalized development process to be described in the following chapters.

Related Publications

At the time of writing, no other comprehensive publication appears available with a focus similar to that of the present one. Related work by Smith and Hipp (1994) presents a theory of dialogue based on the implementation and testing of an application for the repair of electronic circuits. The authors focus on operational and implementational issues, such as dialogue processing and parsing, rather than on the dialogue design process, cooperativity and evaluation. Jönsson (1993) addresses how to manage coherent dialogue in natural language interfaces. He describes the use of a Wizard of Oz simulation environment for the investigation of written, multimodal natural language dialogue. The empirical results on, among other things, focus and dialogue act structures are used in the design of a dialogue manager for natural language interfaces, specialized for various database applications such as car and travel sales. Cole *et al.* (1996) surveys the vast field of language technologies and the opening vistas of multimodal systems incorporating language technologies. The book consists of 13 chapters written by 97 different authors. It is a very useful source of overviews and references.

EAGLES-I (the Expert Advisory Group on Language Engineering Standards) was an LRE project launched in 1993 and aimed at accelerating the provision of common functional specifications for the development of large-scale speech and language resources in Europe. One of the first activities in EAGLES-I was to conduct a survey of existing resources and standards. Based on the survey, a set of initial recommendations was disseminated to the speech and language communities for comments. The exercise was iterated, leading to the dissemination of a set of final recommendations and obtaining feedback on them. For more information on EAGLES-I see Calzolari and McNaught (1996) and Gibbon *et al.* (1997). EAGLES-II (1997–1998) aims at consolidating, extending and disseminating work done in EAGLES-I.

Useful source material on speech functionality is presented in Baber and Noyes (1993). Several books on various aspects of interactive speech systems are underway, including Peckham and Fraser (forthcoming).

1.3   State of the Art

In this brief overview of the state of the art we shall focus on research prototype and commercial advanced interactive speech systems which take speaker-independent continuous speech input and generate spoken output. Multimodal systems that include advanced interactive speech will be discussed in Section 9.3 of Chapter 9. We distinguish between *research systems,* i.e. running prototype systems built for research and demonstration purposes (Section 1.3.1), and *commercial systems* which are already on the market (Section 1.3.2). In addition, we describe some advanced tools and techniques in support of interactive speech system development and evaluation (Section 1.3.3).

1.3.1   Research Systems

Advanced interactive speech research systems have been, and continue to be, developed and implemented in Europe, the US and Japan since the late 1980s. These systems obviously did not emerge out of thin air, but had many precursors among less sophisticated applications using less, or no, speaker independence, having connected word input, lacking realistic domain specifications, simulating important parts of their functionality and/or having been developed for typed rather than spoken interaction. Examples are APHODEX (Haton, 1988) and EVAR (Niemann *et al.,*

1988). Since the late 1980s, valuable research on interactive speech systems has been done under the DARPA, later ARPA, spoken language systems programme which involves competitive evaluations and includes, among other participants, MIT, SRI, CMU, BBN and European laboratories, such as LIMSI in France. Papers on these systems can be found in a series of workshop proceedings published by Morgan Kaufmann (ARPA, 1994; DARPA, 1989, 1990, 1991, 1992). Young (1997) reviews the ARPA Programme. The common domain used by all the participants was that of Air Travel Information Systems (ATIS). CMU has developed the Janus system for speech-to-speech translation of meeting scheduling dialogue contributions in several languages, including English, German, Korean, Japanese and Spanish (Lavie et al., 1996; Zhan et al., 1996). In Europe, a strong base of expertise has been established through projects such as Esprit Sundial, the Danish Dialogue Project and the German Verbmobil. Sundial addressed air and train travel information systems. The Danish Dialogue Project addressed air travel reservation. The large Verbmobil Project, which began in 1993 and was continued for another 3-year period in 1996, is aimed at developing a spoken language conversation support system for German/English and Japanese/English human–human negotiation dialogues in face-to-face situations.

We shall look in more detail at Sundial and Verbmobil. The following descriptions are based on Peckham (1993), on information provided by Scott McGlashan from Sundial and on the Verbmobil information available at http://www.dfki.uni-sb.de/verbmobil/Vm.Infobrosch.Text.8.3.96.html.

Sundial

The Sundial (Speech UNderstanding in DIALogue) Project, 1989–1993, was one of the largest collaborative speech technology projects in Europe at the time. The goal of the project was to build real-time integrated dialogue systems capable of maintaining cooperative dialogues with users over standard telephone lines (Fraser and Thornton, 1995; Peckham, 1991, 1993; Peckham and Fraser, 1994, forthcoming). Systems were developed for four languages – French, German, Italian and English – within the task domains of flight reservation and information query (UK and France), and train information query (Germany and Italy). System functionality was partially specified on the basis of Wizard of Oz simulations and was evaluated with potential users under a variety of conditions. The vocabulary size is about 1000 words for each system.

In order to maintain spoken dialogues with users, each system carries out three principal functions: the interpretation of user utterances; the generation of system utterances; and management of the dialogue so that system utterances are natural and coherent in the light of user utterances. In each system these functions are distributed over five modules (compare Figure 1.2 above). Linguistic interpretation is dealt with by two modules: an acoustic processing module based on sub-word models using Hidden Markov Models (CDHMM) which take acoustic signals as input and outputs word or phoneme lattices (Kuhn et al., 1992), and a linguistic processing module which parses the input, extracts a plausible string, and provides syntactic and semantic representations of the utterance (Andry and Thornton, 1991). The dialogue manager module takes each linguistic representation and gives it an interpretation within the dialogue context (Eckert and McGlashan, 1993; McGlashan et al., 1992). Using this interpretation, the dialogue manager decides how the dialogue might continue and, if it is the system's turn to speak, plans a schematic linguistic representation for the system utterance. Generation of the system utterance is carried out by the message generation module which produces a detailed linguistic representation, and the speech synthesis module which synthesizes the representation for telephone output.

Each of the Sundial systems aims to engage in an unconstrained dialogue with (naive or expert) users in order to establish and, if possible, meet their information needs. To achieve this empirical data were collected and analysed. In addition to data from human–human dialogues, data were collected using the Wizard of Oz technique (Fraser and Gilbert, 1991a). Comparison between human–human and human-computer dialogue corpora revealed that with a computer (or what is perceived to be a computer), spoken interaction is significantly more constrained than interaction with a human (MacDermid, 1993). These findings were used to prioritize problems in system design and to inform the design of subsequent simulations.

It is typical of Wizard of Oz simulations that they are often used to perform focused experiments in addition to serving overall system development (cf. Chapter 5). In the first UK Wizard of Oz simulation study, all components of the Sundial system were simulated except for the text-to-speech synthesizer. The study examined naive subjects' response to masculine and feminine synthetic voice quality, different confirmation strategies used by the wizard, and the effect of breakdown and repair sequences on the dialogue. The second study examined naive subjects' response to standard and enhanced prosody in the synthetic speech. A multiple parameter confirmation strategy was used throughout. The main focus of the third study was to examine the formulation of requests by naive subjects, who were professional users of flight inquiry services, in comparison to a control group of members of the public. No constraining guidance for naive callers was given to subjects. However, following subjects' comments in the previous simulations, repetition of target parameters and telephone numbers in solutions were added. The final study examined the impact of printed user guidelines for prospective users of Sundial. These guidelines help callers use the UK demonstrator system in the most efficient way.

The Sundial systems have been evaluated in terms of both "blackbox" and "glassbox" metrics (Simpson and Fraser, 1993). Blackbox metrics assume that the internal workings of the system are invisible to the evaluator. Glassbox metrics assume that system-internal representations are available for inspection at key points during processing. In this way fine-grained evaluation of system sub-components can go hand-in-hand with a more general evaluation of the system as a whole. Blackbox metrics include contextual appropriateness (a measure of the appropriateness of a system utterance in its immediate dialogue context) and transaction success (a measure of the success of the system in providing users with the information they require, if such information is available in the database). Glassbox metrics include word and sentence accuracy, as well as information content which measures the system's ability to extract task-relevant information from user utterances. The results of evaluating the system based on 255 German intercity timetable inquiry dialogues are summarized in Figure 1.6.

By the end of Sundial real-time over-the-telephone conversational dialogues were being demonstrated in the laboratory with transaction success rates of up to 96%. For example, Figure 1.7 shows a very simple dialogue with the British system collected over a long-distance telephone line with an untrained user.

Contextual appropriateness	appropriate	98%
	inappropriate	2%
Transaction success	success	6%
	relaxed constraints	80%
	announcing no solution	14%
Accuracy	word accuracy	66.5%
	sentence accuracy	47.1%

Figure 1.6: Evaluation results from 255 dialogues with the German intercity timetable inquiry system.

System:	Welcome to British Airways flight information service. How can I help you?
User:	I wonder whether you could tell me what time the next flight from Paris to Heathrow gets in.
System:	Was that from Paris?
User:	Yes.
System:	Did you say to Heathrow Airport?
User:	Yes.
System:	That flight arrives at ten fifteen. Do you have another inquiry?
User:	No thank you.
System:	Thank you for calling. Good-bye.

Figure 1.7: Sundial dialogue over a long-distance telephone line with an untrained user (example provided by Norman Fraser).

Large-scale collaboration on advanced interactive speech systems for flight and train timetable inquiry and reservation, such as Sundial, has had lasting effects in Europe. The Danish Dialogue Project built on the Sunstar Project with respect to the speech recognizer (Lindberg *et al.*, 1992) and the DDL/ICM architecture (Bækgaard *et al.*, 1992). Sunstar ran in parallel with Sundial. A significant number of other subsequent projects, some of which aim at developing multimodal systems, should be mentioned, such as: RailTel for mixed initiative dialogue telephone access to French Rail's static timetable information, as well as to limited additional information about services offered on the trains, fare-related restrictions and supplements (Lamel *et al.*, 1995); MASK which developed a prototype multimodal multimedia service kiosk for train travel information and reservation (Chhor, 1997); MAIS which aimed to foster the deployment of multilingual inquiry systems, providing voice-controlled access to information and transaction services (http://guagua.echo.lu/langeng/ en/mlap94/mais.html); Waxholm, which is a multimodal system providing information on boat traffic in the Stockholm archipelago (Bertenstam *et al.*, 1995); and a recent project, ARISE, on train information services (http://www2.echo.lu/ langeng/en/le3/arise/arise.html). In addition, the Sundial process probably contributed to the establishment of companies such as Vocalis in Cambridge, and the rather massive general effort in the field helped produce the Philips commercial train timetable inquiry system (Section 1.3.2).

Verbmobil

Verbmobil (launched in 1993) is a very large-scale (95.9 million DM 1993–1996) R&D project sponsored by the German Federal Ministry of Science, Research and Technology. The project involved from early on 22 academic and seven co-financing industrial laboratories, but this number of participants now seems to have decreased. Most partners are from Germany but the consortium includes two US laboratories and one Japanese group. The aim is to develop a speaker-independent spontaneous spoken language translation support system for German/English, German/Japanese human–human negotiation dialogues in face-to-face situations. It is assumed that the dialogue partners communicate in English and that both of them have at least a passive knowledge of English. In making their dialogue contributions, the partners can use the Verbmobil system to translate utterances in their own language into spoken English. English contributions are processed by the system as well in order to gather contextual information and construct a discourse model. The system uses this knowledge to disambiguate utterances and improve the quality of its translations. The domain is in the first phase limited to dialogues aimed at agreeing on a meeting date, place, etc. (appointment scheduling). In this phase the vocabulary is approx. 2300 words. A research prototype was presented in the autumn of 1996 and plans exist for larger-scale applications after 1997.

The Verbmobil speech recognizer evaluates the probability of the words recognized and organizes these in a word hypothesis graph. An evaluation carried out in 1996 showed a recognition rate of 73.3% of words from non-trained spontaneous dialogues in the domain. The Verbmobil prosody module performs segmentation of phrase and sentence boundaries based on information about pauses, intonation, duration and signal strength. The module is able to distinguish 93% of the relevant phrase boundaries, thereby reducing the scope of syntactic interpretation by 70%.

In linguistic processing, Verbmobil combines syntactic and semantic constraints. Syntactically ambiguous input, such as whether an occurrence of "you" designates a person or a group of people, is presented as semantically underspecified for the semantic analysis which takes the dialogue context into account in attempting to disambiguate the input. The dialogue module also supports translation through the use of statistical models for the identification and prediction of dialogue acts. In 1996, 70% of the dialogue acts were identified in this way. Following dialogue act identification, a plan recognizer organizes the identified dialogue acts into phases which represent the course of the dialogue in abbreviated form. In future, this representation will be used in the production of a dialogue protocol that may serve as a summary of the dialogue. The results of syntactic–semantic processing are sent to the transfer module which translates the sentence into an abstract, foreign language semantic predicate representation. Based on this representation, the language generator constructs syntactically correct sentences. Finally, the speech synthesizer produces the English translation in as natural a form as possible, including relevant intonation.

To improve the robustness of Verbmobil "flat" processing techniques have been added to the above-mentioned, combined with in-depth syntactic–semantic analysis. Input which cannot be dealt with in the latter way is handled through a spotting technique which attempts to capture the central pieces of information from the word hypothesis graph, such as dialogue act and date. Foreign language schemata are then used to produce the translation.

The Verbmobil dialogue manager may tell users to speak louder and can initiate clarification dialogues with users when receiving, for instance, inconsistent user input, such as "30 February", or contradictory temporal information, such as "in the morning at 4 o'clock in the afternoon".

In the second phase of the project (1997–) the system's application domain is being extended, more language pairs are being added and the use of Verbmobil for distance working will be tested. An example dialogue is provided in Figure 1.8.

A: I guess we should meet in September. How about Friday the first of September.
B: (mouse click) Montag wäre mir lieber (mouse click).
Verbmobil: I would prefer Monday.
A: OK, so Monday the third. That's fine with me. What about 11 o'clock?
B: (mouse click) Gut, wir treffen uns dann in meinem Büro (mouse click).
Verbmobil: OK, so then we meet in my office.

Figure 1.8: Dialogue with Verbmobil.

1.3.2 Commercial Systems

Current commercial interactive speech systems are still highly limited in their interactive capabilities. Still, these systems are able to carry out routine tasks that were previously done by humans, thereby generating significant savings in the companies or public institutions that install them. Such systems are now achieving significant real-world applications in large markets such as banking, finance, insurance, travel, leisure, PTO markets and market research (Blyth and Piper, 1994).

Early Commercial Systems: Bell, AT&T

Let us first mention a number of commercial interactive speech systems which are not yet "advanced" in our sense but which show lines of development towards such systems. In 1989 Bell Northern Research began deploying "Automated Alternate Billing Services" through local telephone companies in the USA, with Ameritech being the first. The system rang customers, told them they had a collect call and asked whether they would accept the call. Using a very small vocabulary (yes/no and some synonyms) the system successfully completed about 95% of the calls that were candidates for automation (Bossemeyer and Schwab, 1991).

In 1992 AT&T introduced a service to automate the other end of the transaction, allowing customers to place collect calls, use a calling card, order a person-to-person call or place bill-to-third-number calls. User trials were considered successful, not just from a technical standpoint, but also because customers were willing to use the service (Franco, 1993). By the end of 1993, it was estimated that over 1 billion telephone calls each year were being automated by this service.

Key differences between the two systems are that the latter introduced word spotting and barge-in technologies. Word spotting allows keywords to be recognized in the midst of additional acoustic material. Barge-in (also known as talkover or echo cancellation) allows users to speak and be recognized while the system is playing a message. A small but growing number of interactive speech services using these technologies have now been trialled by PTOs, mostly in the USA. These have focused on areas such as voice dialling and directory assistance call completion. NYNEX thus has had a system called VOIS in their public telephone system since 1990. It uses automatic speech recognition to identify the number (the system asks for the number) that the customer has dialled but for some reason was not valid or working. The system gives a spoken message of why the connection did not occur (Ortel, 1995).

Advanced Interactive Speech Systems: SPEECHtel, Operetta, Philips

The following systems illustrate the gradual emergence of advanced interactive speech systems.

SPEECHtel, developed by Vocalis, partly demonstrates advanced interactive speech technology because it uses a combination of speaker-dependent and speaker-independent technology. SPEECHtel is a voice dialling system which allows telephone users to place calls by speaking the name of the person they want rather than keying in their telephone number. The system maintains personal directories for each subscriber. However, SPEECHtel also includes speaker-independent capabilities to allow users to speak the number they wish to dial or navigate through a range of value-added services, such as voice messaging and network feature control. The system works across both fixed and mobile telephone networks. SPEECHtel systems are currently being trialled by a number of European network operators (http://www.vocalis.com/pages/products/spchtel.htm).

As advanced interactive speech systems approach current limits, such as those of speech recognition technology or of manageable task complexity, human backup support becomes necessary to ensure user acceptability. Operetta from Vocalis combines automation with human fall-back. Operetta takes messages and handles and routes all incoming calls automatically. The system interrogates callers to find out who they wish to speak to and acts appropriately. Operetta allows callers to interact entirely through speech, with no pressing of telephone buttons, listening to long lists of extension numbers or remembering which extension number to press. Combining automation with human fall-back liberates receptionists or secretaries to perform other tasks. Operetta handles many simultaneous incoming calls and continues on its own when the receptionist has gone home (http://www.vocalis.com/pages/products/operetta.htm).

Perhaps the most impressive advanced interactive speech system in current operation in Europe is the Philips train timetable information system (Aust et al., 1995; Aust and Oerder, 1995). A demonstrator has been in operation and publicly available in Germany since February 1994 on telephone number +49 241 604020. Since January 1996 Swiss Rail have commercially operated a descendant of the Philips system on telephone number +41 157 0222. Another descendant of the Philips system is being developed in the Netherlands and is expected to be in operation before the end of 1997 (Strik et al., 1996).

The Philips system provides information on train connections between 1200 German cities. The system runs on a DEC AXP PC (275 MHz) and is accessed over the telephone. It is a real-time, speaker-independent continuous speech under-standing system which speaks and understands German with a vocabulary of about 1850 words. The system has five main components: speech recognition; speech understanding; dialogue control; database; and speech output generation.

The Philips PHICOS system is used for speech recognition. It uses Hidden Markov Models with continuous mixture densities, six-state left-to-right phoneme models for a total of 40 phonemes, and a tree-organized beam search. As output the speech recognizer produces a directed acyclic word graph whose nodes represent points in time and whose edges are labelled with a word and an accompanying acoustic score. Each path through the graph represents a sentence hypothesis. The word graph is passed on to the speech understanding module whose task it is to find the best path through the graph and determine its meaning. The meaning it attempts to determine is something which can serve as the basis for a database query, such as "from city A to city B". Other parts of the input utterance are not subjected to further processing. This makes it easier to deal with incorrect grammar or insufficiently recognized utter-ances. The understanding module transforms the word graph into a concept graph which has concepts along the edges instead of words. A stochastic context-free gram-mar is used to add probabilities and model the concepts. An attribute grammar is used to determine the meanings of concepts. In the dialogue control module, most aspects of automatic inquiry dialogues, such as questions, slot definitions and veri-fication phrases, are specified in a declarative way. An interpreter takes care of the selection of appropriate questions to the user in cases of ambiguity, contradiction, etc., handles the results from the speech understanding module and creates a data-base query. The database is the real one from German Rail, although the system is not connected to the official information service of German Rail. Results from the database and questions to users are passed to the speech output component in the form of complete written sentences. Speech output is produced by concatenating pre-recorded words and phrases corresponding to the input to this component.

By 1995 more than 10,000 dialogues had been collected. Approximately one third of these could not be used for evaluation because people only played with the sys-tem. Of the remaining two thirds, 10% seemed to consist of real requests while 40% had been performed by users who apparently just wanted to try the system. For the remaining 50% it cannot be decided which of these two possibilities are actually the case. The transaction success rate, i.e. the percentage of users who received the infor-mation they asked for, averages about 80% for these three groups. One quarter of the remaining calls failed due to poor recognition performance and the rest because of train stations that were not in the vocabulary. An example dialogue is provided in Figure 1.9.

Why Advanced Interactive Speech Systems Did Not Come Onto the Market Sooner

Many have speculated why advanced interactive speech has not become a commer-cial reality much earlier and faster than is actually the case. The linguistic problems involved have been addressed for decades with far more sophistication than is actually needed. Speech researchers have been claiming for more than a decade that sufficient-quality speech recognition was just around the corner. We do not profess to fully explain this phenomenon. However, it seems to be a fact that sufficient-

System:	Good morning. This is the automatic time-table information service. How can I help you?
Caller:	Good morning. I need a connection from Hamburg to Munich.
System:	When would you like to go from Hamburg to Munich?
Caller:	Next Friday, er, at eight o'clock.
System:	So you want to travel on Friday the 23rd of September at 8 am?
Caller:	Exactly.
System:	There is the following connection: with Intercity Express 793, departure from Hamburg at 8:02, arrival in Munich at 14:05. Would you like me to repeat the connection?
Caller:	No, but I need a train for the return trip on Sunday.
System:	At what time would you like to go from Munich to Hamburg on Sunday the 25th of September?
Caller:	I have to arrive in Hamburg late in the evening.
System:	So you want to arrive in Hamburg between 8 pm and 11 pm?
Caller:	Yes.
System:	There are three connections. This is the first one: with Intercity Express 880, departure from Munich at 15:54, arrival in Hamburg at 21:58. Would you like me to repeat the connection?
Caller:	No, thank you.
System:	Would you like the next connection?
Caller:	No, thanks, this one is fine.
System:	Do you need another connection?
Caller:	No.
System:	I wish you a pleasant journey. Thank you for calling. Good bye.

Figure 1.9: Dialogue from the field test of the Philips German train timetable information system. Translated from German.

quality, speaker-independent, continuous speech recognition was *not* just around the corner 10 years ago but has only recently become feasible in commercial applications. Many linguists still consider speech as a form of incorrect language, to the extent that the title of a panel at the COLING '96 conference was "Is Speech Language?" (Mariani and Krauwer, 1996). We have seen (Section 1.1) that there is still no consensus with respect to how to optimize grammars and parsing for advanced interactive speech systems. Moreover, building advanced interactive speech systems remains expensive and risky. Much will be gained when reasonably versatile hardware and software platforms, which could support the development and maintenance of larger families of applications, start to become available. For instance, it can be a difficult commercial proposition to first develop, at high cost, an interactive speech system that provides access to a database and then have to incur further high costs whenever the database is updated in ways that require modifications to be made of the interaction model.

Even given the advent of versatile platforms, and with the problem of sufficient-quality speech recognition practically solved, the absence of principled linguistic approaches to speech processing and many unsolved issues in interaction model development and evaluation will continue for some time to make life hard on commercial developers (see Section 1.4).

User familiarity is another important factor. Consumers are now getting used to voice response inquiry services. The next step may be that users become familiar with systems that replace the voice response technology with single-word commands, such as in some of the systems mentioned above or in the European Union's MAX system which had a vocabulary of 16 words and could inform users on ECU exchange rates, basic statistics, ECHO latest news, ECHO calendar, European Community programmes, concepts in information technology, European Community institutions and European Community press offices (MAX, 1991). As such interfaces become as common as they will ever be, consumers may well start demanding the kind of capabilities that only advanced interactive speech systems can provide. This demand could be the "user pull" that will be more successful than any "technology push" in getting advanced interactive speech systems to the market (Lyn Bates in Ostler (1996)). The fact that user acceptance depends on what customers are used to and like was highlighted in an investigation made by NYNEX Science and Technology (Basson *et al.*, 1996). Based on the Wizard of Oz simulation method, a number of field trials were carried out to assess the feasibility of speech recognition for telecommunications services. Several applications were explored including directory assistance call completion, partial automation of directory assistance, banking over the telephone and partial automation of a Customer Call Centre. The results suggested that speech applications would be most successful when deployed with novel services or with touch-tone services that had achieved only limited success, whereas the replacement of a successful touch-tone system with an interactive speech system tended not to be well received by users.

Another important point is that marketing is at least as important as, perhaps even more important than, technical capability. User acceptance depends heavily on many factors that have little to do with the interactive capabilities of the system, such as whether the time to produce an answer is predictable, or how easy the system is to configure and update (Lyn Bates in Ostler (1996)). This is also reflected in the following remark:

> From a commercial perspective, the success of a spoken dialogue system is only slightly related to technical matters. The key to commercial success is marketing: how a system is advertised to the end-users, how the system presents the company to those end-users and how smoothly errors are being handled. I have, for example, seen trial systems with a disgracefully low word accuracy score receiving a user satisfaction rating of around 95%. I have also seen technically excellent systems being removed from service due to negative user attitudes. (Fraser, personal communication.)

In view of the above, some hesitation among large end-user companies with respect to whether the time is ripe for introducing advanced interactive speech technologies is understandable. It seems likely that the commercial reality of advanced interactive speech systems, such as the Philips train timetable information application, could help convince those companies that the technology has become an option for serious and immediate consideration.

Who Prepares the Systems?

We believe that a considerable number of commercial advanced interactive speech systems are now well underway to the market place. For obvious reasons of commercial confidentiality, it is difficult to tell just how many and which systems are being built.

Indications are that systems are in preparation in companies such as IBM, Microsoft, BBN, Bell, AT&T, Canon, British Telecom, NTT, MITRE Corp., Philips, Lernout and Hauspie, and Vocalis.

1.3.3   Advanced Tools and Techniques

Development of the dialogue component and interaction model aspects of advanced interactive speech systems is currently undersupported in terms of tools and techniques. Useful support tools are few and this scarcity also characterizes well-described methodologies and techniques. We briefly describe a number of existing and emerging tools and techniques that we are aware of.

Wizard of Oz

Wizard of Oz is an experimental prototyping method in which a human (the wizard) simulates part or whole of the interaction model of the system to be developed and does so in interaction with users who are made to believe that they are interacting with a real system. The method is described in Chapter 5. To our knowledge, Wizard of Oz support tools have so far been developed for local use only. The following are examples of such tools. ARNE-3 is a simulation environment with the following main features (Jönsson, 1993): a response editor with canned texts and templates that are easily accessed through menus; provision of access to various background systems; presentation of graphical information; an editor for creating queries to database systems; and an interaction log with time stamps. In the Dutch SCHISMA Project a simulation environment was developed which supports the wizard through a multiwindow presentation of information. One window shows the dialogue between wizard and subject and has a pop-up menu that provides standard utterances; a second window has a form for querying the database and shows the result of the query. A menu in this window allows the wizard to select utterances containing slots that can be filled with data from the database query; a third window, the dialogue control window, allows the wizard to choose the states to go to from the current state of the dialogue (Andernach and Buis, unpublished paper, University of Twente, the Netherlands). Palantype is a special keyboard designed to increase the wizard's speed when keying in user input (Newell *et al.*, 1991). For the user test of the Danish Dialogue System we created a tool which enabled the wizard to use abbreviations for airports, for example, when keying in user input. A second tool corrected typos and turned the user's input into something that could be recognized by the real recognizer (see Section 8.2.2).

Corpus Handling

Several tools exist for corpus handling. The Text Encoding Initiative (TEI) is the most comprehensive tool in existence for the representation of text including transcribed speech. TEI includes a formalism and guidelines on how to use the formalism (see Chapter 7). Other software tools for corpus handling are: tools for editing; automatic tagging; viewing; and extracting data for statistical work and other evaluation purposes (see Chapters 7 and 8).

Dialogue Model Implementation

Several tools exist for the representation and implementation of dialogue management. DDLTool is a graphical editor which supports the representation of dialogue management software in the Dialogue Description Language (DDL). CSLUrp is a graphical rapid prototyping environment which in many respects is similar to DDLTool. CSLUrp is a major part of the OGI toolkit (see below). A third example of a tool for representing dialogue management is HDDL (Aust, 1996). In contrast to DDLTool and CSLUrp, HDDL supports textual dialogue representation. In particular DDL and DDLTool are discussed in more detail in Chapter 6.

Testing and Debugging

There are plenty of advanced techniques and tools for debugging and testing of software in general. These include techniques and tools for blackbox testing and glassbox testing, and various debuggers, such as DDLTool, part of CSLUrp, Gnu's C++ debugger and Purify. As debuggers are not specific to interactive speech systems, they will not be discussed in more detail in this book.

Evaluation

In the DARPA ATIS collaboration a software tool was developed to automatically compare a set of canonical answers to those produced by various systems (Bates *et al.*, 1990). The set of queries to which canonical answers were produced was chosen from a dialogue corpus. Only such queries were used to which clear and well-defined canonical answers could be constructed.

Toolkits

The Oregon Graduate Institute (OGI) has recently made a toolkit available on the Web called the CSLU toolkit. The CSLU toolkit is meant to support a wide range of activities related to the development of interactive speech systems, including data capture and analysis, corpus development, research in multilingual recognition and understanding, dialogue design, speaker recognition and language recognition. The toolkit consists of two main modules: CSLUsh and CSLUrp. CSLUsh is the programming shell and includes a collection of core libraries. CSLUrp is, as already mentioned, an authoring environment. The toolkit includes, among other things, a recognizer, software for answering the telephone and software for recording speech input. Incorporation of a text-to-speech synthesis system is promised (Sutton *et al.*, 1996).

Tool/Technique Development

The above list of tools and techniques is not exhaustive. Useful information on a range of hardware, software and resources for speech systems can be found at comp.speech (http://svr-www.eng.cam.ac.uk/comp.speech/FAQ.Packages.html).

In the following chapters, we present some candidate additions to the above list of tools and techniques. A point which merits emphasis is that transferring research results into practically useful tools and techniques is a non-trivial exercise in generalization. Usually, the exercise begins with: (i) an approach which has proved successful in a single development process; and (ii) an idea that the approach might be worth generalizing into something that could be useful to other developers. Generalization then follows a cycle of refinement and evaluation until the tool or technique in question is deemed sufficiently mature for transfer to other developers in industry or academia who should be able to use it without the personal support of its originators. Experience has shown that it is often useful to follow a cycle of in-house conceptual development and testing involving several development projects; followed by development and testing in "consultancy mode" at other partners' sites and in industry; followed again by real "transfer" testing and evaluation without interference from the originators of the tool or technique in question. Only when the latter test cycle yields satisfactory results can a novel method or tool be considered a validated improvement on current practice. Central problems in following the procedure just described are that it: (a) can be very demanding on resources; (b) assumes access to several development projects or at least to complete records of certain aspects of such projects. Such records rarely exist; and (c) assumes, at least in the final development stage of a tool or technique, collaboration by other developers, which can be difficult to attain in the real world.

1.4   Unsolved Problems

Despite unquestionable progress, particularly in those parts of the interactive speech system components field which have been delivering commercial applications for more than a decade, the design, development and evaluation of usable interactive speech systems is today as much of an art and craft as it is an exact science with established standards and procedures of good engineering practice. The route from initial idea through analysis, requirement specification, design–evaluation cycles, prototype development, in-house and field testing to the final product and its evaluation is replete with unknowns and development steps that are undersupported in terms of procedures, concepts, theory, methods and tools. Standard software practices can, of course, take the development teams some way forward with respect to domain and task analysis, development languages, platforms, architectures and modularity, off-the-shelf components and state of the art in some of the component technologies, such as speech recognizers and synthesizers, testing conformance with specifications, etc. Moreover, a consequence of the increasing commercialization of language technologies in general is that evaluation of language and speech systems is emerging as a scientific sub-discipline in its own right (Hirschmann and Thompson, 1996). Work on evaluation of interactive speech systems has received significant stimulation from the ARPA Spoken Language Technology initiative (ARPA, 1994; Jones and Galliers, 1996), and progress is being made in Europe as well (Calzolari and McNaught, 1996). A major effort in this area is foreseen under the European Union's 5th Framework Programme for Research and Technological Development which starts in 1998. However, the unknowns and undersupported development steps are evident from the following list of examples of unsolved problems that derive from considering primarily the interaction model development and evaluation cycle. Problems addressed in this book are marked with an asterisk.

Project Requirements and Realism

- Can a modular, extensible and reusable architecture be found that will ultimately warrant the development costs of the first application? What are the minimum requirements for computational resources of the application?
- How to develop a typology of interactive speech systems which can tell which type of system to use for which purpose?
- *When should interactive speech be included in an application given its task, domain, environment, user population, business requirements, etc.? Which input speech mode is needed for the application (single word versus connected word versus continuous speech)? Is word spotting sufficient? Which output speech mode is needed (speech synthesis, pre-recorded speech)?
- *Should spoken language modalities be combined with other modalities of information representation and exchange, such as graphics, and additional external devices, such as pointing devices, and how, i.e. what should be their respective roles given the task, domain, environment, user population, business requirements, etc., of the application? How useful is graphic lip movement and face synthesis for the enhancement of speech output understanding? How useful is lip movement interpretation for the enhancement of speech input understanding?
- How far is an integrated resource containing domain and semantic knowledge needed and feasible?

Development

- *How to efficiently develop the interaction model taking into account such aspects as dialogue type, dialogue strategies and minimal interaction model functionality needed for the application. For instance, should the application have system-directed dialogue, user-directed dialogue or mixed initiative dialogue; which type(s) of dialogue history should it have; does the application need a user model? Answering such questions requires an applied interactive speech theory which, based on early requirement specifications, can tell which interaction model aspects are needed for the application.
- *How to create tools for preventing dialogue design problems during early dialogue design, i.e. prior to implementation?
- *How to guide the choice of words in dialogue?
- How to handle awkward input?
- *How to design system feedback?
- *How to ensure usability and correctness of system communication with its users in context?
- *What are the efficient error handling mechanisms and strategies that may counterbalance a less than 100% recognition rate?
- How to make dynamic adaptation within the task structure to the course of the dialogue?
- *How to decide whether to develop the application using the Wizard of Oz method or through an implement–test–revise approach? What are the trade-offs?
- *What is needed for an efficient, cost-saving WOZ design?
- Which corpus techniques should be used for rapid characterization of the domain and identification of expression variants?

- *Which tools to use for the capture, viewing and analysis of data on user–system interaction during the performance evaluation and diagnostic evaluation anywhere in the development process?
- Which implementation formalisms to use?

Evaluation

- How to assess the effects of speech recognition errors on spoken language understanding and dialogue flow?
- *How to evaluate system wordings in dialogue?
- *How to perform diagnostic evaluation throughout the development process following a rigorous methodology (apart from traditional glassbox and blackbox evaluation)?
- *How to perform a systematic performance evaluation of the interaction model, i.e. measurements of the performance of the system in terms of a set of quantitative parameters, in particular dialogue management performance?
- *How to get beyond crude measures of interaction quality, such as duration, number of turns and error counts, and identify interaction problems, their types, severity and remedies?
- *How to evaluate user satisfaction and confidence through questionnaire/multiple scaling design?
- *How to objectively measure transaction success?
- *How to create general methods and criteria for adequacy evaluation of integrated interactive speech systems, i.e. methods and criteria for how well a particular system fits its purpose and meets actual user needs and expectations?
- How to make comparative performance and adequacy evaluation across interactive speech systems for different tasks?
- How to make a correlation of errors, speaker style, politeness, etc., with human ratings?
- How to evaluate portability of systems across application domains?

Issues such as the above are shared by all developers of interactive speech systems more or less, depending on the sophistication of the applications they are currently developing. Solutions to some of them are underway.

The Need For a Best Practice Scheme

Although we will only be dealing with aspects of spoken interaction such as those indicated above, what is ideally needed is a consolidated best practice scheme for the development and evaluation of advanced interactive speech systems and their components, thereby establishing the field as a sub-discipline of software engineering. These needs include optimizing the user friendliness of advanced interactive speech systems which will ultimately determine their rank among emerging input/output technologies. The lack of a consolidated best practice scheme continues to generate uncertainty about the potential of advanced interactive speech systems technologies, their proper domains of application, the user satisfaction they will create, the cost of producing them and the prospects of starting to do so, their development time, and the quality of products in both absolute and comparative terms. In June 1997 the authors and colleagues from KTH, Stockholm, LIMSI, Paris,

IMS, Stuttgart, Daimler-Benz, Ulm, Elsnet, Utrecht and Vocalis, Cambridge, started an Esprit Project (DISC) with the aim of establishing a first best practice methodology for the development and evaluation of interactive speech systems (http://www.elsnet.org/disc/).

2. *Speech Interaction Theory*

2.1 Introduction

With the spreading of interactive speech system technologies, a clear need arises for theory which may adequately support the development of increasingly sophisticated but still restricted interactive speech systems. A complete and applied theory of spoken human–machine interaction would rigorously support efficient interactive speech system development from initial requirements capture through to the test and maintenance phases. It would include support for interaction model development and implementation, appropriate functionality design, usability optimization, interactive speech system evaluation and maintenance. Above all, such a theory would have to be based on the fact that the interaction models of today's interactive speech systems are all *task-oriented*, they enable the system to carry out spoken interaction with users in limited application domains (Smith and Hipp, 1994). When combined with a basic level of meta-communication, or communication about the interaction itself, task-orientation is what enables current systems to successfully undertake spoken dialogue with humans despite their many limitations compared to human interlocutors. These comparative limitations may be briefly illustrated by taking a look at spoken human–human communication.

As humans we learn to perform spoken interaction fluently, effortlessly and efficiently about almost any topic and for almost any purpose. Human–human conversation serves both to organize social life in general and as the basis for more specific types of interaction, such as getting others to do something, obtaining information from them or solving problems together cooperatively. The ability to perform human–human-quality conversation requires a large number of skills and other characteristics, as illustrated in Figure 2.1. Spoken human–computer interaction, on the other hand, is constrained by the conversational limitations of the computer and rarely has any social function – at least not for the computer. This means that interaction models for interactive speech systems have to be very carefully crafted in order to work at all, even within limited domains. In interactive speech system development, usability considerations are not a luxury but a dire need. This is one more reason for developing interactive speech theory.

Most spoken or written language interaction theory has so far dealt with unrestricted human–human conversation and has not clearly focused on task-oriented dialogue. While no single, unified interaction theory has yet emerged from the various frameworks and approaches that have been proposed in the literature, parts of these theories and the aspects of dialogue they cover are potentially relevant to the

- Recognition of spontaneous speech, including the ability to recognise words and intonational patterns, generalizing across differences in gender, age, dialect, ambient noise level, signal strength etc.

- A very large vocabulary of words from widely different domains.

- Syntactic-semantic parsing of the complex, prosodic, non-fully-sentential grammar of spoken language, including characteristics of spontaneous speech input such as hesitations ("ah", "ehm"), repetitions ("could could I ..."), false starts ("on Saturday, no, Sunday") and non-words (coughs, the sound of keystrokes).

- Resolution of discourse phenomena such as anaphora and ellipsis, and tracking of discourse structure including discourse focus and discourse history.

- Inferential capabilities ranging over knowledge of the domain, the world, social life, the shared situation and the participants themselves.

- Planning and execution of domain tasks and meta-communication tasks.

- Dialogue turn-taking according to clues, semantics, plans etc., the interlocutor reacting in real time while the speaker still speaks.

- Generation of language characterised by complex semantic expressiveness and style adapted to situation, message and dialogue interlocutor(s).

- Speech generation including phenomena such as stress and intonation.

Figure 2.1: Some of the characteristics of human–human conversation. The list is not complete nor does it state how the listed capabilities are actually realized in the human cognitive system. Somehow, the human system is powerful enough to implement the listed phenomena.

more limited purpose of establishing a task-oriented theory of spoken human–computer interaction. This is true of Speech Acts Theory (Searle, 1969), Gricean theory of cooperativity in dialogue (Grice, 1975), discourse representation theory (Kamp and Reyle, 1993), plan-based approaches to dialogue (Carberry, 1990; Litman, 1985), Grosz and Sidner's (1986) intentional approach (Grosz *et al.*, 1989), relevance theory (Sperber and Wilson, 1987) and rhetorical structure theory (Mann and Thompson, 1987a, 1987b), among others. However, a theory of spoken interaction in support of interactive speech system development and evaluation cannot simply transfer results from interaction theories which deal with unrestricted human–human dialogue. Instead, it is necessary to define the level of interaction which current interactive speech systems are capable of, in order to be able to:

- precisely characterize each individual system including its limitations;
- precisely characterize similarities and differences between current systems;
- support the design and implementation of interactive speech systems;
- define the needs for research and technological development which might help to incrementally improve the capabilities of current interactive speech systems;
- facilitate the transfer of relevant results from human–human interaction theories.

A theory with these properties may be characterized as a *practical bottom-up theory of interactive speech systems.* It does not primarily synthesize the existing, often fragile and conflicting, results from spoken human–human interaction theories nor does it primarily aim at specifying the properties of the ideal interactive speech system which we will not be able to build in the foreseeable future anyway. Rather, the theory departs from the properties of current, comparatively simple, interactive speech systems; aims to make sure that these have been understood before proceeding towards more complex systems; incorporates results from existing human–human interaction theory only when relevant to the technological state of the art; and creates the elements of theory needed to support the design of high-level interaction models for specific interactive speech systems.

This chapter presents steps towards a practical bottom-up theory of spoken human–computer interaction. The theory provides a set of interaction elements and takes the form of an incremental task-oriented interaction theory which attempts to anticipate some of the problems to be addressed in developing successive system generations. Incrementality means that novel interaction elements can be added without the rest of the theory necessarily having to be revised.

Section 2.2 presents a model of the elements of the theory and illustrates these in a walk-through of a spoken human–computer dialogue. Sections 2.3–2.7 present the elements in more detail, grouped into the layers: context (Section 2.3); control (Section 2.4); language (Section 2.5); speech (Section 2.6); and performance (Section 2.7). Section 2.8 demonstrates how the theory may be used in characterizing interactive speech systems.

2.2   Elements of Interactive Speech Theory

The goal of interactive speech theory development is to describe the structure, contents and dynamics of spoken human–computer interaction from the point of view of the interactive speech system. On the one hand, users should have a pleasant and efficient conversation, on the other, the theory should have good computational properties and support system development.

The theory to be presented is far from complete. It is, rather, an organized conceptual toolbox of elements, at least some of which need to be taken into consideration when developing today's interactive speech systems. We are aware that the elements and their organization may be disputed on many points. There simply is no complete, general and accepted theory yet, and even a structured conceptual toolbox is bound to suffer from not fully analysed relationships between the elements and types of element it proposes. Conceivably, satisfactory analysis will have to wait until the problem space posed by interactive speech system development has been explored in much more depth than is currently the case.

Still, there is emerging consensus on several issues, and a number of concepts and techniques have proved useful to the building of interactive speech systems. Figure 2.2 shows a model of the elements of an interactive speech theory. The elements all appear important and sometimes necessary to the design and construction of interactive speech systems. The model will be used as reference throughout this book. The model is software-oriented, focusing on the objects or *elements* that go into the system. Hardware, including telephones and microphones, is not included and the same holds for the user's physical work environment. From the point of view of the model, these aspects belong to the many other constraints that have to be taken into account during interactive speech system specification (see Section 3.2). In explaining the model below, we will focus on the elements that are most relevant to the dialogue component and, more generally, to the interaction model of interactive speech systems.

The elements of Figure 2.2 may be used to construct high-level models of interactive speech systems and explain their behaviour. We will refer to the model in Figure 2.2 as the *basic speech interaction model*. The model exhibits two modes of organization:

First, the elements have been organized into five *layers*. At the bottom of the figure the *context* layer includes aspects of the history of interaction, domain model and user model. At the level above the context layer, the interaction *control* layer includes states of attention as well as the structures defined by the interlocutors' intentions and structural aspects of the linguistic exchanges. System control is largely based on structures at this level. The following *language* layer describes the linguistic aspects of interaction. Next is the *acoustic* layer which includes the transformations between speech signals and the symbolic expressions of language. Finally, the *performance* layer is a function of the other layers taken together and includes some general aspects of the system's behaviour.

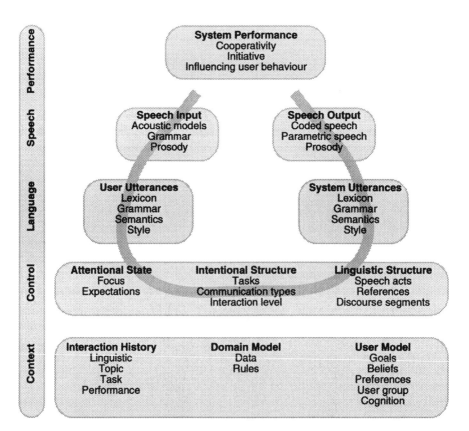

Figure 2.2: Elements of an interactive speech theory. Element types are shown in bold type. The grey band and grey boxes reflect the logical architecture of interactive speech systems (see Figure 1.2).

Secondly, the grey band in Figure 2.2 indicates the overall processing *flow* among the various types of element – input, intention and attention, output and performance – in a context defined by contextual elements. Developers often refer to elements or element types in terms of the corresponding system modules, such as the recognizer, parser, dialogue manager, inference engine, text generator and player, system performance being replaced by an abstraction of the (physical) user (cf. Figure 1.2).

It should be noted that some elements, such as lexicon size, user background and cooperativity, are in focus only at the time of design whereas other elements, such as linguistic structure, interaction history and user goals, are run-time constructs which are used dynamically by the system. In the present chapter, interactive speech theory will be presented primarily from an operational (or implementational) viewpoint. In Section 2.8 the theory will be used from a functional viewpoint as a vehicle for characterizing interactive speech systems. In the following chapters, the theory will be used to clarify and structure the development and evaluation process.

Figure 2.2 reflects a number of interactive speech system analyses and components from theories of spoken human–human interaction, including (Aust *et al.*, 1995; Bunt, 1994; Carberry, 1990, Figure 1.1; Eckert and McGlashan, 1993, Figures 1 and 2; Grau *et al.*, 1994, Figure 1; Grosz and Sidner, 1986; Jönsson, 1993, Figures 7.1 and 7.2; Smith and Hipp, 1994, Figure 3.3; Zue, 1994). Given these origins, it is clear that the concepts used in the model have been drawn from widely different disciplines, such as linguistics, computer science and cognitive science.

2.2.1 An Interaction Walk-through Illustrating the Elements

Following the flow organization of Figure 2.2, we begin by exemplifying the elements in a walk-through of a human–computer dialogue from the user test of the Danish Dialogue System (Figure 2.3). Throughout this section, *the system* refers to the Danish Dialogue System and not to interactive speech systems in general. Because the flow model links elements that are related in many different ways, a flow model walk-through might start at different points.

System Performance

The interaction model is task-oriented. It assumes that user and system have a common task, i.e. to make flight ticket reservations, and that the aim of user–system interaction is to perform this task in as rational a manner as possible. System performance should therefore be *cooperative,* i.e. the system should enable the interaction to proceed as efficiently as possible towards the common goal. We shall have more to say later on *cooperativity* in general and with respect to dialogues such as the one shown in Figure 2.3 in particular. For the moment, we leave it to the reader to judge the system's *cooperative* behaviour.

Initiative

It is clear from Figure 2.3 that the system has the overall initiative in the dialogue as shown in S2b, S3b, S4b, etc. The system preserves the initiative by concluding all of its turns with a closed question to the user, i.e. a question which asks for a well-defined piece of information, such as in S2b. However, the user may take the initiative in meta-communication. This sometimes works, as in U5a, but sometimes does not, as in U4a, cf. the linguistic structure and intentional structure below.

S1a	Hello, this is the DanLuft reservation system.	b	Where does the journey end?
b	Do you know this system?	U8a	Karup.
U1a	Nope, I don't. No.	S9a	To Karup.
S2a	The system can reserve tickets for Danish domestic flights. You use it by answering the system's questions. In addition you may use the two special commands *repeat* and *change* to have the most recent information repeated or corrected. The system will only understand you when you answer its questions briefly and one at a time.	b	Do you want a return ticket?
		U9a	No thanks.
		S10a	On which date will the journey start?
		U10a	The 11th of February.
		S11a	Saturday the 11th of February.
		b	At which time?
		U11a	Around noon.
		S12a	Sorry.
		b	I did not understand.
b	Please state your customer number.	U12a	Around noon, 11:50.
U2a	The customer number is 4.	S13a	11:50.
S3a	Customer number 4.	b	You have now booked one ticket for id-number 4, Marie Hansen, from Copenhagen to Karup on Saturday the 11th of February at 11:50. Your reference number is 49.
b	How many persons will travel?	
U3a	Two persons, one adult and one child.	
S4a	One person.	c	The total price is 680 kroner.
b	Please state the id-number of the person.	d	The tickets will be available at check-in desk number 19 in the airport. Tickets must be picked up at the latest 20 minutes before departure.
U4a	It was not one person, it was two persons, one adult and one child.	
S5a	Id-number 1, Jens Hansen.	e	Do you want more?
b	Where does the journey start?	U13a	Yes, please. I would like to book a similar ticket for one person.
U5a	Change.	
S6a	First person, id-number 1.	S14a	Customer number 4.
b	Is that correct?	b	Is that correct?
U6a	No, id-number 4.	U14a	Yes.
S7a	Id-number 4, Marie Hansen.	S15a	How many persons will travel?
b	Where does the journey start?	U15a	One person.
U7a	From Copenhagen.	•••	*(The user now books a ticket for the second person).*
S8a	From Copenhagen.		

Figure 2.3: A dialogue from the user test of the Danish Dialogue System (translated from Danish). The user interacts with the system for the first time. Turn numbers refer to the transcription of the dialogue with subject (or user) number 13 (Dybkjær et al., 1996). For ease of reference the turns are sub-divided into utterance units. For instance, "S1" is the first system turn which consists of two utterance units (S1a) and (S1b), and the user's answer is turn "U1" which consists of one utterance unit (U1a).

Influencing User Behaviour

The dialogue in Figure 2.3 shows some cases in which the system's choice of terms probably influenced the user's own choices, such as "persons" in S3b and U3a and "person" in S4a, S4b and U4a. The system persistently seeks to influence the user's linguistic behaviour through using words that belong to its input *lexicon*. In addition, the user's correct use of "change" in U5a is clearly based on the system's instruction in S2a.

Speech Input

An effect of the way the system's speech recognizer works can be seen in U4a–S5a. The speech recognizer expects the user to either provide an id-number (cf. S4b), i.e. a number, or to say "change" or "repeat". The recognizer misrecognizes U4a. The actual words used are not among its active *acoustic models* and the grammatical constructs are neither in the active nor in the passive part of its *grammar*. The misrecognized word string, however, still contains three of the four numbers provided but the parser only selects the final one of these, thus making its own contribution to the misunderstanding. The speech recognizer is not sensitive to *prosody* in the dialogue in Figure 2.3.

User Utterances

Although the recognizer gets U3a completely right, the *semantic* analysis fails by wrongly choosing the final "one" as the semantic value for the expected number of persons. The problem is caused by the *grammar* which does not accept conjunctions. In U3a it would also be difficult for the system to decide whether there are four or just two persons who are going to travel because the grammar does not handle coordinates. The word "noon" (U11a) is not in the *lexicon*. The general *style* of the user's utterances is rather terse as required by the system in S2a. Exceptions are U4a and U13a which are misrecognized or only partially recognized.

Attentional State

The system *focus set* comprises the current sub-task, i.e. the one addressed by the system in its latest question and which the user is expected to address in the next utterance, and the user-initiated meta-communication tasks. Based on the system focus, *expectations* concerning what the user will be saying next assist the system in choosing which sub-set of the acoustic models, the lexicon and the grammars will be used by the recognizer and the parser in decoding the subsequent user utterance. The misunderstanding following U4a was partly caused by inadequate system expectations.

Intentional Structure

The global structure of the dialogue is defined in terms of *tasks*, such as "reservation" (S2b–S13d), which in their turn include a number of sub-tasks, such as "customer" (S2b–S3a) and "route" (S5b–S9a). Note how some tasks, such as "delivery" (S13d), do not always require user turns. In the dialogue in Figure 2.3 the reason is that the user has no choice but must pick up the tickets at the airport. If the journey starts more than 3 days later the user may choose to have the tickets mailed.

Domain communication is communication about the task domain and occupies most of the dialogue in Figure 2.3. As we have seen, users may at any point initiate *meta-communication* to resolve misunderstandings or lack of understanding by using one of the keywords "repeat" and "change". Contrast, for instance, the system's reactions to U4a and U5a. The system ignores the user's meta-communication intention in U4a but recognizes that intention in U5a. The system may initiate meta-communication as well, for instance by telling the user that it did not understand what was said (S12a and S12b). In addition, the dialogue illustrates several phenomena which cannot be characterized as either domain communication or meta-communication, such as the opening greeting "Hello" (S1a), the information about the system itself (S1a, S1b and S2a), and the expressive "Sorry" (S12a). The dialogue in Figure 2.3 does not show many cases of the system deviating from its standard *level of interaction*. However, following the "change" command (U5a), the system descends to the more cumbersome, but safer, level of asking for explicit confirmation (S6a and S6b).

Linguistic Structure

At a primitive level, the system distinguishes between two types of user *speech acts*: commands and statements. User input in terms of one of the keywords "change" (U5a) and "repeat" is interpreted as commands. All other user input is considered as statements in response to factual system questions. With respect to *reference resolution,* the system handles simple ellipses, such as "From Copenhagen" (U7a) and "Karup" (U8a). The system does not use *discourse segmentation* information.

Interaction History

The *linguistic history* is primitive and only records the Boolean contents, i.e. the semantics but not the exact wording, of the latest system utterance in order to correctly interpret users' "yes" and "no" utterances. For instance, the analysis of U9a needs to establish whether "no" means one-way or return. In a different situation, the system might have asked "One-way ticket. Is that correct?". The *topic history* records the order of sub-tasks treated during the dialogue and is used in handling repair and clarification meta-communication as in U5a. The *task history* stores task-relevant information provided by the user, as well as information retrieved from the database. This information is used in the summarizing feedback (S13b) and when actually booking the ticket in the flight database, although the current system does not carry out any "real" booking. The system does not use a *performance history*.

Domain Model

The system's *data* are consulted after each task-relevant answer from the user. For instance, the system checks that the customer number (U2a–S3a) and the route (U7a–S9a) exist. Additional *rules* define world knowledge that is necessary to the semantic interpretation, such as how to infer the day of the week from a date (S11a).

User Model

The user is assumed to only have the *goal* of making a reservation as is made clear in S2b. The system models the user's *beliefs* via a status field for each information item. For instance, when starting the second reservation task (S14a), the system, using the task history, assumes that the user believes the customer number to be the same as in the previous reservation task and asks for confirmation (S14a and S14b) instead of asking anew as in S2b. Had the user's answer to the return ticket question (S9b) been "yes", the system would have asked if the user has a *preference* for discount fares and their associated departure times. A model of the user serves to guide adaptation to users during the dialogue. Thus, the system's introduction (S2a) provides information to the users who lack *expertise* with the system (S1b and U1a). In U4a the user forgets to use the keyword "change" for repair meta-communication, probably due to *cognitive overload* after the misrecognition in S4a.

System Utterances

These are constructed using a simple *grammar* that concatenates pre-defined words and phrases. For instance, S3a and S3b are a concatenation of the four words and phrases "Customer number", "four", "period" and "How many persons will travel?" ("period" inserts a short pause). No *lexicon* is used. The system uses a terse and direct *style* of expression.

Speech Output

The system's output speech is *coded* as references to pre-recorded phrases that are simply replayed. However, as a recording of system output would have shown, and despite the fact that care has been taken to record phrases uniformly and with an even voice, *prosodic* patterns are impossible to get completely right with today's concatenation technology.

We now proceed to presenting the elements in more detail, following the layered model in Figure 2.2. As said earlier, the layered elements concern development-time as well as run-time issues. We will focus on the topics that are central to this book and occasionally defer further discussion to the appropriate chapters.

2.3   Context

Context is of crucial importance to language understanding and generation, and plays a central role in interactive speech system development. The context provides constraints on lexicon, speech act interpretation, reference resolution, task execution and communication planning, system focus and expectations, the reasoning that the system must be able to perform and the utterances it should generate. Contextual constraints serve to remove ambiguity, facilitate search and inference, and increase the information contents of utterances as the more context, the shorter the messages need to be (Iwanska, 1995). Specification of context is closely related to the specific task and application in question. In a sense, each element is part of the context of each of the other elements.

In this section we review the three generic contextual elements of Figure 2.2: interaction history; domain model; and user model. The interaction history is primarily relevant to the local discourse and is used in the dynamic run-time model; the domain model represents the world context in the run-time model; part of the user model is used at run-time whilst other parts are used at development-time only.

2.3.1   Interaction History

An *interaction history* is a selective record of information which has been exchanged during interaction. It is useful to distinguish between at least four types of interaction history.

The *linguistic history* records the surface language, its semantics and possibly other linguistic aspects, such as speech acts and the order in which they occurred. The linguistic history encapsulates the linguistic context and is necessary in advanced systems in which the linguistic analysis is no longer context free. For instance, the capture of surface language is needed in cross-sentential reference resolution.

The *topic history* records the order in which sub-tasks have been addressed. The topic history encapsulates the attentional context and is used in guiding system meta-communication.

The *task history* stores the task-relevant information that has been exchanged during interaction, either all of it or that coming from the user or the system, or some of it, depending on the application. The task history encapsulates the task context. It is used in executing the results of the interaction and is necessary in most interactive speech systems. The task history may be used in providing summarizing feedback as in the Danish Dialogue System.

The *performance history* updates a model of how well interaction with the user is proceeding. The performance history encapsulates the user performance context and is used to modify the way in which the system addresses the user. Thus, the system may be capable of adapting to the user through changing the interaction level.

2.3.2   Domain Model

The domain of an interactive speech system determines the aspects of the world about which the system can communicate. The system usually acts as the front-end to some application, such as an e-mail system or a database. The domain model captures the concepts relevant to that application in terms of *data* and *rules*. For instance, during domain-related interaction the system evaluates each piece of user input by checking the input with the application database and/or already provided information stored in the task history. Information retrieved from the application, or provided earlier but to be used now, is checked with the user. The domain model usually has to include both facts and inferences about the application and general world knowledge. Among other things, the system's database contains explicit facts on flight departures, rules stating that the out date must be the same or earlier than the return date, and inference patterns enabling the system to infer dates from input such as "today" (date completion).

A vast literature of general relevance to domain modelling has been produced in disciplines such as artificial intelligence, knowledge bases and expert systems (see Russell and Norvig, 1995). The interested reader is referred to this literature. Clearly, domain modelling for a particular interactive speech system depends heavily on the application and domain in question (cf. Section 3.2). It may be noted that there is a tendency in the more recent literature (e.g. Christiansen *et al.*, 1996; Gasterland *et al.*, 1992) to relate application knowledge representation techniques more closely to interface development. Such integrated use of the domain model of an interactive speech system can be seen, for instance, in Smith and Hipp (1994). Their system, the Circuit-Fix-it-Shop, provides problem-solving assistance for the repair of electronic circuits. Domain model and tasks are described in declarative logic. Problem solving is executed via theorem proving and the dialogue is driven by the proofs. The spoken language interaction supplies missing actions. In this case, the entire interaction model is in some sense controlled by the domain model. Proofs may be interrupted, suspended and reopened, and the paradigm that proofs-are-tasks-are-dialogue issues the domain with a central and natural role in the interaction model.

2.3.3   User Model

User modelling is important in interactive speech system development. The better the system can take aspects, such as user goals, beliefs, skills, preferences and cognition, into account the more *cooperative* the system can be (Gasterland *et al.*, 1992). The general fragility of current speech systems means that they must be particularly carefully crafted to fit the behaviour of their users. Still, even if the subject of user modelling is huge in itself it represents only a single corner of speech interaction models.

At run-time, user *goals* determine which tasks and sub-tasks the system actually has to execute among those that the system is capable of performing. In the Swiss Rail system (Peng and Vital, 1996), for instance, the user is assumed to have just one overall goal, namely to obtain train timetable information. Other systems may be capable of satisfying several different general user goals, such as checking e-mails over the telephone and consulting an appointment schedule.

The system should model relevant user *beliefs*, i.e. what some or all users believe to be true of the system, the domain and relevant states of affairs in the world. Figure 2.4 illustrates how crucial a proper understanding of user beliefs can be. After the feedback in S26a, the Danish Dialogue System assumes that the user accepts the fed-back information unless the user subsequently applies the "change" command. However, the consternated user forgets about the command because the fed-back id-number is right but the name is wrong. The user then interprets the system's "Sorry" (S27a) as an acceptance of U26a, whereas what the system actually meant was "I did not get any relevant information from your utterance". The system should have said (in S27a), for instance, "Sorry, I did not understand. Where does the journey start?" to make sure that the user shares the system's beliefs about the exchange. A system introduction to interaction (cf. Figure 2.3) is a useful vehicle for modifying the user's expectations with respect to the interaction. More generally speaking, interaction model developers should be prepared to anticipate, sometimes even false, user expectations of many different kinds: concerning the interaction, domain facts, the world, etc.

S26a	Id-number 1, Jens Hansen.
b	Where does the journey start?
U26a	No, it is not Jens Hansen, id-number 1 is Lars Bo Larsen.
S27a	Sorry, where does the journey start?
U27a	In Ålborg.

Figure 2.4: The importance of taking relevant user beliefs into account illustrated from a dialogue with subject number 13. The user later reserved a correct ticket but the faulty one was not deleted.

User *preferences* are options preferred by all, or some, users, such as to let departure time depend on discount availability (domain related), to perform the interactive task in a certain order or to have the initiative during interaction (interaction related). The latter preference, like many user preferences, may be regarded as a soft constraint, i.e. a constraint that may be ignored at development time if harder constraints have to be satisfied.

User groups represent relevant classifications of potential users. The novice-expert distinction is one such classification. User *expertise* may be characterized along two dimensions: domain novice–expert and system novice–expert. With respect to systems for everyday use, most users can be considered experts to some degree. Thus, most users involved in the development of the Danish Dialogue System were used to book flight (or other forms of transport) tickets. In comparative terms, these users were domain experts although not at the level of travel agents, but they had never before interacted with an interactive speech system. As these users were representative of the intended user population, the system provided little domain help and sought instead to make clear how users should interact with it. In addition to these novice–expert distinctions among users, many other user groupings may have to be taken into account by interactive speech systems developers, for instance distinctions between users from different professional communities, between native and non-native speakers, or between speakers of different dialects. To deal with the latter, the recognizer may apply dialect and language adaptation/identification (Dobler and Ruehl, 1995, Hazen and Zue, 1994), or do as the Swiss Rail information system does when communication fails: ask the user "Bitte Hochdeutsch sprechen!" ("Please speak High German!").

In addition to user properties such as those mentioned above, developers should bear in mind that users have to perform rapid, situation-dependent *cognitive processing* during interaction and that users' capabilities of doing so are severely limited. In U26a (Figure 2.4), the user should have said "Change" according to the instructions provided in the system's introduction. The reason why the user apparently forgot the instruction is probably cognitive overload. This suggests that designer-designed keywords, such as "change", are a liability in interactive speech systems.

2.4   Interaction Control

Controlling the interaction is a core function in interactive speech systems. Interaction control determines what to expect from the user, how to interpret high-level input structures, consultation of the context elements, what to output to the user, and generally when and how to do what. Being done at run-time, control builds on structures determined at development time. The nature of these control tasks implies that control has to operate on superordinate interaction structures and states. Following Grosz and Sidner (1986), the interaction model distinguishes three types of superordinate interaction structure and state. The *attentional state* includes the entities in current interaction focus; the *intentional structure* addresses the purposes involved in interaction; and the *linguistic structure* includes characterization of high-level structures in the input and output discourse.

2.4.1 Attentional State

We use the term *attentional state* (Grosz and Sidner, 1986) to refer to the elements that concern what is going on in the interaction at a certain point in time. The attentional state is inherently dynamic, recording the important objects, properties and relations at any point during interaction. The system represents the attentional state as a *focus set*. The focus set includes the set of sub-tasks about which the system is currently able to communicate. The focus set may include all sub-tasks, as in the Philips timetable information system (Section 1.3.2), or only a sub-set thereof, as in the Danish Dialogue System. The latter strategy is used if only a sub-set of the system's input vocabulary and grammar can be active at any one time.

The *focus* is the topic which is most likely to be brought up in the next user utterance. For instance, if the system has asked for a departure airport, this topic will be in focus with respect to the next user utterance. If the user instead provides a destination airport this may still be understood if included in the focus set.

Expectations may be attributed to the system if not all sub-tasks are in the focus set. Then expectations serve as a basis for constraining the search space by selecting the relevant sub-set of the acoustic models, the lexicon and the grammars to be active during processing of the next user input. If the user chooses to address sub-tasks other than those in the focus set, system understanding will fail unless some focus relaxation strategy has been adopted. The more stereotypical the task structure is, the easier it is to define appropriate expectations provided that the user is *cooperative*. In the Danish Dialogue System information on sub-tasks in system focus is hardwired. This means that expectations are static, i.e. they are fixed at run-time. This approach will not work for mixed initiative dialogue because there the user has the opportunity to change (sub-)task by taking the initiative. When part of the initiative is left to the user, deviations from the default domain task structure may be expected to occur. In such situations, the system should be able to determine the focus set at run-time. Mixed initiative dialogue therefore either requires a dynamically determined focus set or an unlimited focus set.

2.4.2 Intentional Structure

We have chosen the term *intentional structure* (Grosz and Sidner, 1986) to subsume the elements that concern tasks and various forms of communication. These elements all concern intentions, or goals, and purposes. We distinguish between tasks, communication types and interaction level. The intentional structure serves to control the transactions of the system.

Intentions can be of many kinds, such as to obtain information, make somebody laugh or just chat, and are in general not tied to tasks. In today's interactive speech systems, however, spoken human–computer interaction is performed in order for a user to complete one or more tasks. From this task-oriented, shared-goal, viewpoint intentions coincide with task goals. According to Grosz and Sidner (1986), an intention I1 is said to *dominate* another intention I2 if the satisfaction of I2 contributes to and serves to satisfy I1. And intention I2 has *precedence* to I3 if it is necessary to satisfy I2 before it is meaningful or possible to satisfy I3. Similarly, a task T1 may include a sub-task T2, and T2 may have to precede T3. For example, to make a flight reservation one must determine, among other things, a route (origin and destination) and a time. Reservation thus includes the sub-tasks route and time. Moreover, as it is meaningless to determine the departure time until the route has been determined, route precedes time. Note that relevant intentions need not show up during interaction. For instance, one of the system's tasks in executing a reservation is to compute the price of the ticket. Although it might be *cooperative* to do so, a realistic application would not necessarily inform the user of the computed price but might simply store it in the reservation file.

A single interactive speech system may be able to accomplish several different superordinate tasks. These may all belong to a single domain, such as when the system both performs ticket reservation and provides information on a variety of travel conditions that are not directly related to ticket reservation; or the superordinate tasks may belong to unrelated domains, such as the provision of telephone access to e-mail, calendar, weather and stock exchange information (Martin *et al.*, 1996).

We distinguish between *well-structured* and *ill-structured* tasks. Well-structured tasks have a stereotypical structure that prescribes: (i) which pieces of information must be exchanged between the interlocutors to complete the task; and often also (ii) a natural order in which to exchange the information. If the stereotype is known,

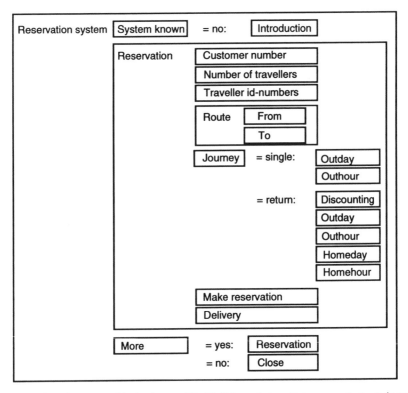

Figure 2.5: The task structure of the implemented Danish Dialogue System. Meta-communication tasks are not shown. A labelled box indicates a task. If box A contains another box, box B, then B is a sub-task relative to A. At some points during the dialogue the path to follow depends on the user's answer to the most recent system question. In such cases, an answer is indicated as "= (answer):" followed by the tasks to be performed in this case.

shared and followed by the interlocutors, the likelihood of successful completion of the task is significantly increased. Stereotypical tasks, even when comparatively large and complex, are well suited for the predominantly system-directed or user-directed interaction that is characteristic of today's interactive speech systems. An example is the ticket reservation task stereotype of the Danish Dialogue System shown in Figure 2.5. This structure conforms to the most common structure found in corresponding human–human reservation task dialogues recorded in a travel agency (Dybkjær and Dybkjær, 1993). Another example is MERIT (Stein and Maier, 1994) in which *strategies* captured by dialogue scripts suggest or prescribe certain sequences of dialogue acts. Strategies are global structures that combine speech acts into larger meaningful sequences. Strategies correspond to task templates and are domain-dependent and prescriptive.

Ill-structured or non-stereotypical tasks contain a large number of optional sub-tasks whose nature and order are difficult to predict. An example would be a comprehensive information system on travel conditions. This system would include many different kinds of information at many different levels of abstraction, such as fares, general discount rules, discounts for particular user groups or particular departures, departure times, free seats, rules on dangerous luggage, luggage fees, rules on accompanying persons, pets, etc. In specifying the Danish Dialogue System we found that a complex information task of this nature could not be modelled satisfactorily by being accomplished through system-directed interaction. The problem was that a user might want a single piece of information which could only be retrieved through a lengthy series of answers to the system's questions. This difficulty might be overcome through more sophisticated interaction models, such as the use of advanced mixed initiative dialogue (Section 9.2) combined with the use of larger active vocabularies than we had at our disposal.

Given a task-oriented approach to interaction theory, there is a relatively clear distinction between three types of interaction between user and system. The first is basic, task-oriented interaction or *domain communication*, which is what the dialogue is all about. We illustrate (Section 2.5.2) considerations pertinent to domain communication design through considering questions and feedback.

The second interaction type is *meta-communication* which has a crucial auxiliary role in spoken human–machine interaction. Meta-communication serves as a means of resolving misunderstandings and lack of understanding between the participants during task-oriented dialogue. In current interactive speech systems, meta-communication for interaction *repair* is essential because of the sub-optimal quality of the systems' recognition and linguistic processing of spontaneous spoken language. Similarly, meta-communication for interaction *clarification* is likely to be needed in all but the most simple advanced interactive speech systems. We shall have more to say later on this subject (Section 4.2).

Domain communication depends on the domain and the dialogue model. Models of meta-communication, on the other hand, might to some extent be shared by applications that are different in task and/or domain (Bilange, 1991). It should be remembered, however, that meta-communication is often domain-dependent, such as in "Did you say 7 o'clock in the morning?".

In addition to domain and meta-communication, most interactive speech systems need *other* forms of *communication* which do not belong to either of these two categories. Examples were mentioned in the walk-through of the dialogue in Figure 2.3 (Section 2.2), including the opening and closing of the dialogue and communication about the system. We will not go into a deeper analysis of these examples.

Finally, the *interaction level* expresses the constraints on user communication that are in operation at a certain stage during interaction. At least the five levels listed in Figure 2.6 may be distinguished. The interaction level may require hard constraints to be imposed on the user's vocabulary, grammar and style. In the extreme, the system may ask the user to spell the input (Level 1). At the other extreme, no constraints on user input exist beyond those of general user *cooperativity* (Level 5).

Level		Expected input
1	Spell.	The answer is spelled.
	How do you spell the name?	*'B' 'e' 'r' 'n' 's' 'e' 'n'*
2	Yes/no.	Yes or no.
	Do you want a return ticket?	*Yes.*
3	Multiple choice.	List of acceptable values.
	Do you want a one-way or return ticket?	*A return ticket, please.*
4	General but focused.	Any answer within current focus.
	Which day does the journey start?	*Monday next week.*
5	General and unfocused.	Any answer.
	How may I help you?	*Can I take a cat with me on the flight?*

Figure 2.6: Levels of interaction and their influence on expected user input.

The notion of interaction level has been employed in graceful degradation. Graceful degradation is a strategy for meta-communication according to which the system, in a stepwise fashion, adds constraints on user input to facilitate comprehension. In the Sundial Project (Section 1.3.1; Heisterkamp, 1993) graceful degradation was deployed in this way in case of system understanding failure. When interaction levels are used for this purpose, the level of expected input must be made clear to the user. There is *not* a one-to-one relation between system phrases and interaction level. For instance, the system's "Do you want more?" which literally is at the yes/no level is pragmatically being interpreted as belonging at the general and unfocused level.

2.4.3 Linguistic Structure

The linguistic structure of the interaction includes the elements: speech acts; references; and discourse segments.

The *speech act* is a basic unit of conversational theory (Searle, 1969). All speech acts have *propositional content*, i.e the state of affairs addressed by a particular speech act, such as "departure at 8 o'clock". Instances of different types of speech act may have the same propositional content. What distinguishes them, and hence what distinguishes different types of speech act, is what the speakers *do* with their speech. The departure at 8 o'clock, for instance, may be *questioned, promised, ordered*, etc. In the *request* in S9a in Figure 2.7 "On which date does the journey start?", the system tries to make the user respond with an *inform* statement whose

date	S9a	[request]	[..3] On which date does the journey start?
	U9a	[inform]	[.] [Ehm] A Friday.
	S10a	[confirm]	[..11] Friday the 13 of January.
hour	S10b	[request]	At which time?
meta	U10a	[request]	[..2] Change.
date	S11a	[inform]	[..3] The journey starts on Friday the 13 of January.
	S11b	[request]	Is this correct?
	U11a	[inform]	No.
	•••		

Figure 2.7: Segmentation of a dialogue between the Danish Dialogue System and subject number 2. The segmentation was done for the purpose of illustration only. "Date", "hour" and "meta" in the left-hand column indicate discourse segments. Following utterance identification (second column from the left), the speech act expressed in each utterance is shown in square brackets. [.] is a pause of less than 1 second, [..N] is a pause measured in seconds.

propositional content is a date, which follows in U9a. Speech acts are often called *dialogue acts* (Bunt, 1994; Stein and Maier, 1994) or *moves* (Carletta *et al.*, 1997a).

What types of speech acts are there? Searle (1969, 1979) identified the five generic speech act categories shown in Figure 2.8. Useful and even fundamental as these five types may be, they are not likely to be sufficient for interactive speech system development purposes. Although much work has been going on lately on this issue (Dybkjær and Heid, 1996), there still is no universally recognized taxonomy of speech acts available at a more detailed level. The speech acts types which have been added during annotation in Figure 2.7 thus cannot claim any particular status, neither theoretically nor in terms of standardization. Still, speech act identification not only constitutes a useful tool for increasing current understanding of spoken discourse, there is also good reason to believe that speech act identification by machine will be necessary in future advanced interactive speech applications. Clearly, it can make a huge difference to the system's understanding of, and action upon, user input whether the user expressed a commitment to book a certain ticket or merely asked a question.

Assertives	Commit the speaker to something being the case.
	E.g. "There is a departure at 8 o'clock."
Directives	Represent attempts by the speaker to get the hearer to do something.
	E.g. "Answer the questions briefly and one at a time."
Commissives	Commit the speaker to some future course of action.
	E.g. "I would like to reserve a ticket for Copenhagen."
Expressives	Express the psychological state with respect to a state of affairs specified in the propositional contents.
	E.g. "Sorry, ..."
Declaratives	Bring about some alteration in the status or condition of the referred object solely in virtue of the fact that the declaration has been successfully performed.
	E.g. "You have now booked one ticket for ..."

Figure 2.8: The five general categories of speech acts according to (Searle, 1979).

A particular problem is that speech acts can be indirect as well as direct. In a *direct* speech act, the surface language expresses the intended speech act. An *indirect* speech act is one in which the surface language used does not disclose the "real" act intended by the user. For instance, if someone asks if you have a match, it is likely that the question is not being asked merely in order to be able to record the fact. Rather than being a request for information, this act is a request for the act of providing fire for some purpose, such as lighting a candle. Indirect speech acts remain difficult to identify by machine. Several interactive speech research systems projects have been, or are, wrestling with this problem, such as Esprit PLUS (Grau *et al.*, 1994) and Verbmobil (Jekat *et al.*, 1995). We will return to this problem in Section 9.2.

A typical use of speech acts in interactive speech systems is to arrange them in a network to control the local exchange structure of the interaction. The *computational roles model* (COR) defines the local dialogue structure by sequencing it into dialogue acts (Figure 2.9). The COR model is symmetric with respect to user and system, and defines a hierarchical structure in which atomic dialogue acts are combined into moves. The COR model has been used in several systems, such as MERIT (Stein and Maier, 1994) and SPEAK! (Grote *et al.*, 1997).

The handling of *references* (or, strictly speaking, co-references) is a classical problem in linguistics. The problem is that many different words or phrases can refer to the same extra-linguistic entity or entities. Basically, language is not about itself, although it can be, but about something extra-linguistic. This means that expressions referring to extra-linguistic entities abound in written text and spoken discourse. Often, two or more expressions refer to the same extra-linguistic entity. Normally, the first occurrence of an expression will make its extra-linguistic reference quite clear. This is not always true but may perhaps be taken for granted in practical task-oriented written text and spoken discourse. However, given that the first expression has made clear its extra-linguistic reference, language offers many ways of economizing with the following, co-referring expressions, i.e. the expressions which have the same extra-linguistic reference as the first one. For instance, the system might say "Should the tickets be sent or will they be picked up at the airport?", to which the user might answer, using a pronoun instead of the original noun phrase (the

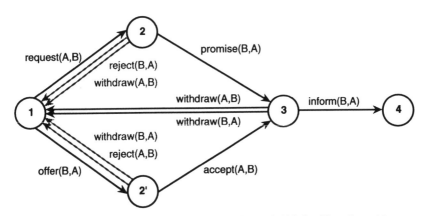

Figure 2.9: Basic dialogue act network of the COR model (Fischer.*et al.* 1994). A and B are the participants.

tickets): "They should be sent". Humans are very good at resolving co-references, such as the one in the systems utterance "... the tickets (i.e. the flight tickets around which the entire dialogue has been evolving) ...". So the system's human interlocutor is not the problem. However, current systems are far from experts in resolving co-references such as the one in the user's answer "They (i.e. the tickets) ...". So what do they do if they are "realistic" systems like the Danish Dialogue System and not specifically built to explore co-reference resolution algorithms?

Possibly the simplest answer to the question of the state of the art in co-reference handling in current realistic interactive speech systems, is that co-reference is not being handled at all but that the problem of co-reference constitutes one of the many reasons why many systems perform word spotting or "robust parsing" rather than full parsing of the users' input. The point is that co-reference resolution is hard – and not just for machines. Among other themes, the 6th Message Understanding Conference (MUC-6) in 1995 dealt with co-reference evaluation. It was found that human inter-annotator agreement on co-referring nouns and noun phrases (which is only a sub-set of co-referring expressions) was so low that the systems being evaluated could not improve much before they went up against the uncertainty about the applied metric itself (Hirschmann et al., 1997). However, with the increased sophistication required of the language processing component in interactive speech systems for complex large-vocabulary tasks, co-reference resolution is becoming an important practical research topic.

Discourse segments are supra-sentential structures in spoken or written discourse. They are the linguistic counterparts of task structure and, in the conversational theory of Grosz and Sidner (1986), intentions are restricted to those that are directly related to discourse segments. Each discourse segment is assigned one intention only, the *discourse segment purpose*. Furthermore, the intention as determined by the originator of a given discourse segment must be recognizable by the interlocutors in order to serve as a discourse segment purpose. Consider the example in Figure 2.7. In utterances S9a–S10a the purpose of the (date) discourse segment is to fix a date for the start of the journey. With the confirmation in S10a the system closes the segment and opens a new discourse segment, i.e. the hour segment, with the request in S10b. However, the user's utterance in U10a does not continue the hour segment. The system correctly interprets this utterance as a request for re-opening the date segment, and starts by stating its current information followed by re-negotiation of the departure date.

The example illustrates that the parts of a discourse segment have particular roles, just like words in a phrase (Grosz and Sidner, 1986). *The request–inform–confirm* structure, for instance, is very common in discourse segments. Other commonly described segment structures are *presentation–acceptance* (Clark and Schaefer, 1989) and *initiative–response* (Ahrenberg et al., 1995; Carletta et al., 1997a). LINLIN, a natural language dialogue system, employs dialogue grammars for such structures to control the dialogue (Jönsson, 1993). The dialogue grammars are extracted automatically from empirically annotated dialogues (Figure 2.10). Note how the grammar symbols combine dialogue acts and topics.

More elaborate relations between discourse segments than just the structural sequence of speech acts have been elaborated in *Rhetorical Structure Theory* (RST). RST was originally developed for written text segmentation (Mann and Thompson,

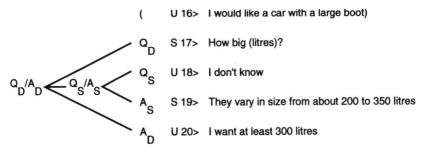

(U 16> I would like a car with a large boot)

Q_D S 17> How big (litres)?

Q_S U 18> I don't know

A_S S 19> They vary in size from about 200 to 350 litres

A_D U 20> I want at least 300 litres

Q_D/A_D — Q_S/A_S

Figure 2.10: Car selling example (Jönsson, 1993). The utterances are annotated with act–topic pairs. Acts are "Q" for query, "A" for answer. Topics are "D" for domain, "S" for system.

1987a) and later applied to dialogue systems (Fischer *et al.*, 1994; Stein and Maier, 1994). RST describes relations between discourse segments hierarchically. An example is shown in Figure 2.11. Asymmetrical relations occur between the *nucleus*, which contains highly relevant information, and *satellites*, which contain less significant information. A relation is described in terms of four fields, as exemplified by the following description of the *evaluation* relation in Figure 2.11.

- *Constraints on the nucleus*: the participants may possibly expect a given claim in the nucleus to be true.
- *Constraints on the satellite*: the participants either already believe the satellite or will find it credible.
- *Constraints on the combination of nucleus and satellite*: agreeing on the satellite will increase the participants' shared belief in the nucleus.
- *The effect*: The shared belief in the nucleus between the participants is increased.

Other relations are solutionhood, cause and reject. The extra information provided by the more elaborate segment relations may be used in the generation of more appropriate system utterances.

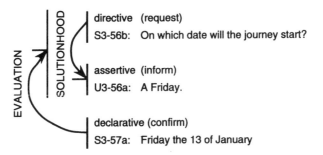

Figure 2.11: Rhetorical structures manually applied to a segment of a dialogue from the user test of the Danish Dialogue System. Utterances are tagged with speech act categories which constitute the atomic segments of RST. An arrow points from a satellite to a nucleus.

2.5 Language

Spoken language is very different to written language (Baggia *et al.*, 1994; Waibel, 1996). One of the differences is that people typically do not follow rigid syntactic and morphological constraints in their utterances (cf. Figure 2.1). This lack of written language formality in spontaneous spoken language makes linguistic analysis by machine both more difficult than, and different to, analysis of written language. However, Waibel (1996) reports that although cross-talk data have lower recognition accuracy (70%) than push-to-talk data (71% recognition accuracy), the transaction success in terms of speech-to-speech translation performance is much better for cross-talk dialogues (73%) than for push-to-talk dialogues (52%). One explanation is that although push-to-talk speech is closer to written language than cross-talk, cross-talk produces shorter turns that are easier to translate. As argued in Section 1.1, the corresponding added difficulties involved in the generation of spoken language are less pronounced, if only because human interlocutors are much more capable of decoding the machine's spoken messages.

The language layer includes two types of elements: user (input) utterances; and system (output) utterances. The term "utterance" is vague – some would say, fruitfully so – such as in the following definition: an utterance is a coherent, linguistically meaningful message that a person speaks during conversation (Nofsinger, 1991; Traum and Heeman, 1996). We will be using the terms "turn", "utterance" and "utterance unit" as follows: a *turn* is what is being said by an interlocutor from when this interlocutor starts speaking and until another interlocutor definitely takes over. A turn may consist of one or more *utterance units* (or sub-utterances, cf. Figure 2.3). Capitalizing on the vagueness of the term, an *utterance* is a turn or an utterance unit. Normally, turns are easily recognized by the machine. Yet problems remain with the classification of turns which include talk-over and, perhaps, turns which include very long pauses (Traum and Heeman, 1996). We will be treating talk-over as consisting of utterance units overlaid onto somebody else's turn. Utterance units are much more difficult to recognize by machine than turns, given the non-sentential characteristics of much of spoken language. It remains to be seen, however, whether this is a difficulty to be overcome by future progress in spoken language processing or whether the difficulty will just go away because systems do not need to recognize utterance units anyway.

The elements subsumed by user (input) utterances and system (output) utterances are: input lexicon; input grammar; input semantics; input style; output lexicon; output grammar; output semantics; and output style.

2.5.1 User Utterances

The *lexicon* is a list of words, a *vocabulary*, annotated with syntactic (including morphological) and semantic features. The fact that vocabularies of current interactive speech systems are still limited implies that some application domains cannot be addressed because the required vocabulary is too large. For those applications which may be addressed as far as their expected vocabulary size is concerned, the problem is to identify the vocabulary, and hence the lexicon, that the application needs.

Vocabulary identification is part of the larger enterprise of determining the *sub-language* for the application, including vocabulary as well as grammar. For the moment, sub-language identification has to be done empirically through simulation experiments, domain studies, human–human spoken interaction in the domain and/or field studies of user interaction with a system prototype.

Convergence is an important measure of success in sub-language vocabulary development. It means that iterated user–system interactions produce less and less new words that have to be included in the system's lexicon, thus converging on zero which is the situation in which the system has the vocabulary it needs for the application. Strictly speaking, convergence is a pragmatic notion. One can always find additional, more or less out-of-the-ordinary, words and phrases which may be used in accomplishing the task and which the system does not have in its lexicon. For instance, although the Roman Catholic Saints' calendar references were once known in Denmark, still survive in fragments and can be used in uniquely identifying travel dates, these references have not been included in the lexicon for the Danish Dialogue System.

Grammars describe how words may be combined into phrases and sentences. The input grammar for the application is specified empirically as part of the sub-language identification process. An important goal in input grammar specification is to include all intuitively natural grammatical constructs, possibly up to a certain level of complexity, in the system's input grammar. Users will have little patience with a system which does not accept perfectly ordinary and grammatically simple ways of saying things. User utterances usually consist of one or several lexical strings or graphs received from the recognizer. In some systems linguistic analysis of user utterances is done by parsers which use grammars derived from written language processing. This is the case in the Danish Dialogue System (Figure 2.12). The excessive formality of written prose compared to spoken language (cf. above) means that the system must apply "robust parsing" or "error" recovery procedures when the ordinary parsing fails (Music and Offersgaard, 1994; Povlsen, 1994). A promising approach to robust parsing is to focus the analysis on sub-sentences and phrases (Aust *et al.*, 1995).

Semantics are abstract representations of the meanings of words, phrases and sentences. We shall not go into issues such as the selection of semantic formalisms for interactive speech systems, or the advantages or disadvantages of carrying out syntactic and semantic analysis sequentially or in parallel. In the Danish Dialogue System syntactic and semantic analysis is done in parallel. Lexical entries are defined as *feature bundles* including lexical value, category (determiner, ordinal), semantic category (none, date), gender (common) and selectional features ("elvte" can be a month), cf. Figure 2.12. The grammar has several rules describing the construction of dates. Figure 2.12 shows the rule for forming a date from a determiner and an ordinal. The semantic mapping rules extract semantic values from syntactic sub-trees. The figure shows a rule for the extraction of a date from a sub-tree created from the Augmented Phrase Structure Grammar (APSG) rule example.

In general, *style* may be analysed in terms of the vocabulary used, which may be formal or informal, slang, etc., sentence length, use of adjectives, figures of speech, synonyms, analogies, ellipses, references, etc. (Jones and Carigliano, 1993). Style is generally described in terms such as terseness and politeness. In interactive speech

Input: Word String	"Den elvte" (*the eleventh*)

Lexicon	`den_1 = { lex=den, dalu=den, cat=det, scat=no,`
	`    defs=def, gend=comm, nb=sing }.`
	`elvte_1 = { lex=elvte, dalu=elvte, cat=ord,`
	`    scat=date, mth=yes, post_comb=no, int=11}.`

APSG: Augmented Phrase Structure Grammar	`date_p_1a =`
	`    {cat=date_p}`
	`        [{cat=det, scat=no, nb=sing, gend=comm},`
	`            {cat=ord_p, scat=date}`
	`    ].`

Semantic Mapping Rule	`date_p_map2a = { sem={day={ones={number=C}}}`
	`    {cat=date_p}}`
	`        [    {cat=det},`
	`            {cat=ord_p}`
	`            [ {cat=ord, scat=date, int=C}`
	`            ]`
	`    ].`

Output: Semantic Object	`day = {ones={number=11}}}`

Figure 2.12: Parsing and semantic representation of the user utterance "Den elvte" in the Danish Dialogue System (Music and Offersgaard, 1994).

systems, user *input style* may be considered an important dependent variable which must be influenced through instruction and example. The aim is to avoid users addressing the system in styles that involve lengthy, verbose or convoluted language, such as when users are excessively polite. A system introduction to that effect would appear useful in many cases (cf. Figure 2.3). Influencing user input style by example is done through the system's output (see below).

2.5.2 System Utterances

The design of system utterances is important to the user's perception and understanding of, and successful interaction with, the system as well as to how the user will address the system. It is somewhat difficult to distinguish between the effects of output lexicon, output grammar, output semantics and output style. It seems to be a well-established fact that the system's *style* of speaking influences the way the user addresses the system. If the system is overly polite, users will tend to address the system in a verbose fashion that does not sit well with the need for brief and to-the-point user utterances that can be handled by current speech and language processing (Zoltan-Ford, 1991). Style is a function of, among other things, *grammar* and *lexicon* (cf. above). It seems plausible, therefore, that output grammar and output lexicon do influence the grammar and lexicon to be found in the user's input. It follows: (i) that the output lexicon should not include words which the user may model but which are not in the input lexicon; and (ii) that output grammars should not inspire the user to use grammatical constructs which the system cannot understand.

The generation of system utterances is determined by elements in the control and context layers. For instance, the *interaction level* limits the form of user response expected and should be made clear in the system's utterances (Figure 2.6); the output vocabulary and language (formal or informal, etc.) is determined by the expected user group; the attentional state determines the narrowness of system questions (see below); and the interaction level, references, segment structure and speech acts may dynamically affect the kind and form of feedback from the system (see below).

System questions differ on a narrow to open scale, influenced by the attentional state. A *narrow* or *focused* question concerns a single topic, such as in "Where does the journey start?", whereas an *open* or *unfocused* question invites the user to address a range of different topics, as in "How can I help you?". The current version of the Danish Dialogue System ends the reservation task by asking the question on the left in Figure 2.13. However, although the intention was to elicit a yes/no answer from the user, many users would take the opportunity of the system's open request to raise any issue lingering on their minds from the preceding interaction. The system cannot handle such input and it is clear that the more specific and narrow question on the right is preferable. It does the job needed without inviting unpredictable user input. In other words, open questions are dangerous and should only be used in interactive speech systems when the task is constrained enough for the system to manage whatever the *cooperative* user may say.

S: Do you want more?	S: Would you like to make another reservation?

Figure 2.13: An unfocused and a focused system question.

It is useful to distinguish between explicit and implicit feedback (also called direct and indirect confirmation). In providing *explicit feedback* the system asks for explicit verification of the recognized input, whereas in providing *implicit feedback* the system merely includes the feedback information in its next turn and immediately carries on with the task. If the user accepts the feedback, no explicit response from the user is required. The example in Figure 2.14 is adapted from the Philips train timetable inquiry system (Aust *et al.*, 1995). The drawbacks of explicit feedback are an additional risk of system misunderstanding (the requested user answer may be misunderstood) and that explicit feedback demands additional turn-taking. By comparison, however, the implicit feedback (right) makes it easier for users to ignore the system's feedback, a problem also seen in the Danish Dialogue System. Niimi and Kobayashi (1995) show mathematically that explicit feedback may increase the probability that information in the user utterance is correctly conveyed, and that implicit feedback may reduce the average number of turns exchanged.

S: So you would like to go from Hamburg to Berlin?	S: When would you like to go from Hamburg to Berlin?

Figure 2.14: Explicit and implicit feedback.

S13-7b	Where does the journey start?
U13-7a	From Copenhagen.
S13-8a	From Copenhagen.
b	Where does the journey end?
U13-8a	Karup.
S13-9a	To Karup.
b	Do you want a return ticket?

S1	Where does the journey start?
U1	From Copenhagen.
S2	Where does the journey end?
U2	Karup.
S3a	From Copenhagen to Karup.
b	Do you want a return ticket?

Figure 2.15: Immediate and summarizing feedback.

A second distinction is between *immediate* feedback and *summarizing* feedback. The difference is shown in the examples in Figure 2.15. On the left, the system provides immediate feedback. On the right, the route information provided by the user is not confirmed until the end of the route sub-task (S3a). The two forms of feedback do not exclude each other (cf. S13b in Figure 2.3).

Concerning the effects of *output semantics,* in particular, as well as of part of what has been termed output style above, we will be much more specific later (Section 4.2). System *cooperativity* throughout the interaction is a function of its output semantics and, to a lesser extent, output style.

2.6   Speech

The speech layer concerns the relationship between the acoustic speech signal and a, possibly enriched, text (lexical string). The relationship is not simple. Speech includes a number of prosodic phenomena – such as stress, glottal stops and intonation – that are only reflected in text in a simplistic manner. Conversely, words, and their different spellings as we know them from text, do not have natural expressions in speech.

Speech recognition must cater for extra-linguistic noise and other phenomena, such as that the speech rate varies over time, the speech signal is mixed with environmental noise from other people speaking, traffic and slamming doors, the pronunciation varies with the speaker, and speech from different participants may overlap, for instance with the system's utterances (Baggia *et al.,* 1994; Waibel, 1996).

2.6.1   Speech Input

The input to the interactive speech system is an acoustic signal which typically, but not always, represents a spoken utterance. The transformation of the acoustic signal into some lexical representation, such as a word sequence or lattice, is called *speech recognition.* Basically, speech recognition is a mapping process in which the incoming acoustic signal is mapped onto the system's repertoire of *acoustic models,* yielding one or several best matches which are passed on to linguistic processing. The dominant speech recognition technology uses *hidden Markov models* combined with a dynamic programming technique (Bahl *et al.,* 1983; Kamp, 1992; Rabiner, 1988). The acoustic models may represent, for instance, triphones (context-dependent phonemes), phonemes, word forms or entire phrases. For historical reasons, acoustic models are sometimes called word models, but note that the number of acoustic models used may be very different from the *vocabulary size* which is the number of lexical entries that may occur in the output from the recognizer.

Current speech recognition techniques are typically limited to the extraction of lexical references, excluding information on pauses, stress, etc. The machine therefore has much more difficulty interpreting what the user said than humans have, because humans are also able to use *prosody* to decode input from their interlocutors (Buchberger, 1995). However, the Verbmobil system uses stress and pauses to support, for example, semantic disambiguation.

Typical measures of recognition quality are word accuracy and sentence accuracy. Word accuracy (or precision) is the proportion of correctly recognized words to the total number of words in an orthographic transcription of the input. Similarly, a sentence has been correctly recognized if every word it contains has been recognized correctly and no extra words have been inserted.

The recognition may assume *isolated words* (words spoken one at a time, clearly separated by pauses), *connected words* (words pronounced as isolated words, but with less stress and no, or little, separation) or *continuous speech* (standard naturally spoken language with contracted words and no separation of words) as input. Isolated and connected word recognition techniques are somewhat simpler than continuous speech recognition and yield better recognition results. However, these techniques require that the user speaks with a strained unnatural voice, which is unnatural and in the longer term may damage the vocal cords.

When accepting connected words and continuous speech, the recognizer has some simple *syntactic model* (or *grammar*) of utterances. Typical examples are *bigrams* (allowed word pairs) and *finite transition network grammars*. The amount of syntactic constraints to impose is a trade-off: syntactic constraints increase the likelihood that input conforming to the model is recognized correctly, but highly constraining syntactic models allow fewer user utterances to be recognized.

In general, it is desirable to have available a large number of acoustic models for spontaneous speech recognition. In practice, the number needed depends on the task and the user group. On the other hand, a large number of acoustic models increases the search space, with the result that more memory is required and a faster CPU is needed to maintain real-time performance, and the models tend to become more similar to one another, making it harder for the recognizer to find the right match. This trade-off is similar to that between the syntactic models mentioned above.

A frequently adopted approach to avoid these trade-off problems is to let the *active grammars* and the *active vocabulary* (and the acoustic models needed) be contextually constrained by the focus set. If the sub-languages related to different focus sets are sufficiently different in nature, and each is smaller than the language of the application, then contextual constraints may be employed whilst keeping low the risk of users not being able to conform to the constraints. Often, however, equally good results may be obtained by using a *phrase spotting* technique where the recognition concentrates on extracting keywords or key phrases from the input.

Recognition may run in *real-time* or *batch*. For interactive systems, real-time recognition is a necessity. Today's commercial recognizers run in real-time, perhaps with a slight delay for long utterances.

Recognition may be *speaker-dependent* or *speaker-independent*. Speaker-independent recognition is necessary in all public service systems. Speaker-dependent recognition has better performance and may be used in personal computers, for example.

Recognition may be *speaker adaptive*, i.e. the speech recognition may adapt to groups of users (sex, dialect, language) or may be individually trained. The latter is often the case with speaker-dependent systems. However, speaker-independent recognition may extend its vocabulary through on-line training (automatic or explicit), or it may recognize which language the user speaks from several different ones.

Two examples of current state-of-the-art recognizers are the IBM voice dictation system and the Philips continuous speech recognizer. IBM provides as part of the operating system ,Warp4, a recognizer which is intended for dictation and command purposes: it is real-time, speaker-independent with a 30K words vocabulary and 90% word accuracy, and is speaker adaptive with 95% word accuracy and adding up to another 40K words, it accepts isolated word dictation and continuous speech commands (IBM, 1996). Philips has produced German and Swiss public train timetable information systems which use speech recognition via the telephone: the recognizer is real-time, speaker-independent, recognizes continuous speech, has a word accuracy of about 75% and a fixed vocabulary of about 1800 words (Aust *et al.*, 1995). The accuracy of the two systems cannot be compared. The IBM measures concern the overall performance using a good microphone, whereas the Philips measure concerns only the recognizer and is measured over an ordinary telephone line.

2.6.2   Speech Output

Computer speech is produced by generating an acoustic speech signal from a digital representation.

Hansen *et al.* (1993) distinguish coded and parametric speech. *Coded speech* is pre-recorded words and phrases which are concatenated and replayed. Coded speech ensures a natural voice and is widely used in voice response systems. The drawbacks are that prosody is impossible to get completely right, and that maintenance of system phrases may be difficult and costly. New phrases to be added must be produced by the speaker who did the previous recording(s), and using the same voice quality, or all words and phrases must be re-recorded.

For *parametric speech* (or synthetic speech), a synthesizer generates an acoustic signal based on a model of human speech. Prosodic features, such as intonation, pauses and stress, may be included in the model and employed on the basis of prosody markers from the system utterance generation inserted on the basis of discourse information (Hirschberg *et al.*, 1995). Parametric speech makes it easy to generate new system phrases at any time. A drawback is that the parametric speech quality is still low for many languages.

2.7   Performance

Any advanced interactive speech system has many of the elements described in the previous sections but no current system has them all. Together, the elements determine the observable behaviour or *performance* of the system during interaction. The system's performance itself has a number of more or less complex properties that emerge from the nature of the elements presented above and which should be considered during development. We discuss these interdependent properties in terms of the performance elements *cooperativity*, initiative and the system's influence on user behaviour.

2.7.1 Cooperativity

Habitable user–system interaction requires that both user and system behaviour be *cooperative*. It is a well-established fact that today's interactive speech systems are based on the assumption of cooperative user dialogue behaviour (Eckert and McGlashan, 1993; Smith and Hipp, 1994). This fact does not, however, pose much of a problem for dialogue developers because the penalty for non-cooperativity is that users fail to get their task done. There is no point in designing the dialogue for non-cooperative users who do not care whether they succeed with their task or not. Indeed, this design goal is impossible to achieve in the foreseeable future. However, if the system fails to be cooperative, penalties can be severe, ranging from users having to repeatedly initiate clarification and repair meta-communication with the system through to failing to get the task done or abandoning interactive speech systems technologies altogether. We believe that system cooperativity is crucial to successful interaction model development: it contributes to smooth interaction and reduces the need for meta-communication. cooperativity and its use in the development of interactive speech systems will be treated in depth in Sections 4.2 and 8.3.

2.7.2 Initiative

The interlocutor who determines the current topic of the interaction is said to have the *initiative* or to control the course of the interaction. Initiative appears to be a function of the speech acts performed by the interlocutors. Depending on the speech act performed, a speaker who already has the initiative may offer it to the interlocutor as in the question (a): "How may I help you?"; or show a wish to keep the initiative as in the question (b): "Where does the journey start?". The interlocutor may leave the initiative with the speaker, for instance in responding to question (b): "The journey starts in Copenhagen"; take the offered initiative in responding to question (a): "I would like to book a ticket from Copenhagen to Aalborg"; or take the initiative without having been invited in responding to question (b): "I want to travel on Monday". The relationship between speech act and initiative is potentially useful to system developers. Whittaker and Stenton (1988) propose generalizations such as the following: the speaker has control in a request unless followed by a request or directive; in an assertion unless it is a response to a request; and in directives (commands); the listener has (gets) the control in a prompt because the speaker abdicates control. If valid, such rules may enable the system to derive who has the initiative once it has identified the speech act. The latter is difficult, however. For instance, both (a) and (b) above look like requests (for information) but (a) acts as a prompt that gives initiative away whereas (b) acts as a request that preserves initiative (cf. Section 2.4 above).

It is useful to distinguish between the following modes of interaction from the point of view of who has the initiative or who controls the course of the dialogue. An interactive speech system is called *system-directed* if the system has the initiative throughout the interaction; *user-directed* if the user has the initiative throughout; and *mixed initiative* if both (or all) interlocutors may take the initiative at some or all points during interaction. These modes of interaction may all be found in today's interactive speech systems except, perhaps, the "free" variety of mixed initiative interaction in which any interlocutor may take the initiative at any time. Several advanced interactive speech systems, such as the Danish Dialogue System and the Philips train timetable inquiry system (Sections 1.2 and 1.3.2), use *limited mixed initiative* interaction in which one of the interlocutors may take the initiative at some points during interaction. *Free mixed initiative* systems do not yet appear feasible for any but the simplest of tasks. In the Sundial Project (Section 1.3.1), experiments were made with free mixed initiative dialogue openings of the "Can I help you?" type. This opening turned out to strongly invite human–human style, lengthy and complex accounts from users which the system had no chance of understanding. As the modes of interaction have been defined above, most future advanced interactive speech systems may be expected to have limited mixed initiative. A further distinction among such systems is proposed by (Smith and Hipp, 1994).

2.7.3 Influencing User Behaviour

In contrast to the system and its behaviour, users are system-external factors that cannot be controlled directly. The fact is, however, that interactive speech systems are vastly inferior to ordinary humans as communication partners. If users do not realize this, they may have unnecessary difficulty in completing their interactive task with the system. Somehow, therefore, a reasonably adequate model of how to interact with the system must be communicated to users. Part of this user interaction model can be directly and explicitly conveyed. However, it would be counter-productive to try to explicitly communicate all the system's peculiarities and relative deficiencies as an interactor. Rather, at least the following sources may help users build a reasonable user interaction model.

- Explicit system instructions provided in the system's introduction (cf. S2a in Figure 2.3) or elsewhere during the interaction.
- Implicit system "instructions".
- Explicit developer instructions.

Implicit system "instructions" is the most interesting item on this list. What we call "implicit instructions" build on the fact that speakers adapt their behaviour to the observed properties of the listener. Some of these "instructions" are provided through the system's vocabulary, grammar and style as discussed above (Section 2.5). Moreover, it appears that people tend to use less sophisticated spoken language when they believe that they are communicating with a computer system rather than a human being (Amalberti *et al.*, 1993). This is useful, and whatever strategy may be found to induce users to treat the system as an *idiot savant* should be considered by developers. Finally, of course, the system's repair and clarification meta-communication will affect the user interaction model by making some of the system's recognition and understanding difficulties clear to users. However, developers should not interpret the latter point as a license to ignore the central goal of optimizing system cooperativity (Section 4.2). Strong system meta-communication facilities are not an acceptable alternative to smooth interaction which requires little or no meta-communication. Furthermore, strong meta-communication facilities do not yet exist in interactive speech systems.

Explicit designer instructions comprise all sorts of (system-) external information provided to users prior to use of the system. The provision of such information may make sense in, for example, controlled user tests. Similarly, speaker-dependent interactive speech systems may come with ample written instruction for their users. One of the crucial advantages of advanced interactive speech systems, however, is that speaker-independent spontaneous speech is a highly natural modality which is extremely well suited to walk-up-and-use applications; and for such systems it is often not possible to provide written instructional material.

2.8   Characterizing Systems

The presentation of speech interaction theory in the preceding sections provides few specific choices of means of representation or algorithms. Its primary aim is to offer a standard conceptual structure for speech interaction theories, models and systems. In later chapters, the theory will be used to guide discussion and structure presentations.

In this section, we illustrate the theory's potential for providing high-level system overviews. Literature on systems, parts of systems and system experiments tends to document only selected parts of the overall system, and the documentation does not have any standard conventions to follow. It is therefore often difficult or impossible to compare results, because of insufficient context, and systems, because of insufficient and incomparable information. One approach to reducing these very real problems is to use a standardized scheme which may provide the minimum information required for describing an interactive speech system in a way which contextualizes the results presented and allows comparison with other systems. Figure 2.16 presents one such scheme which, based on speech interaction theory, describes the Danish Dialogue System.

The interaction model of the Danish Dialogue System	
The Danish Dialogue System is a realistic research prototype of a telephone based interactive speech system for reservation of Danish domestic flight tickets.	
System performance	
Cooperativity	Conformance with the guidelines (Section 4.2).
Initiative	Overall system initiative; users may initiate meta-communication.
Influencing users	Explicit and implicit user instructions; walk-up-and-use system.
Speech input	Continuous; speaker-independent; Danish.
Acoustic models	Based on HMMs; whole word models; approximately 500 words; at most 100 words active at a time; word-accuracy (laboratory) 78%.
Grammar	Bigrams and finite state network mixture.
Prosody	-
Speech output	Normal human voice; Danish.
Coded/parametric	Coded speech.
Prosody	-
User utterances	
Lexicon	Approximately 500 words; lexical entries defined as feature bundles.
Grammar	APSG.
Semantics	Mapping rules extract semantic values from syntactic sub-trees.
Style	Terse.
System utterances	
Lexicon	Pre-defined words and phrases.
Grammar	Simple grammar for concatenating pre-defined words and phrases.
Semantics	-
Style	Terse.
Attentional state	
Focus	Current sub-task plus meta-communication tasks.
Expectations	Predictions sent to recogniser and parser; task dependent parsing.

Figure 2.16: High-level description of the Danish Dialogue System (cf. Figure 2.2) (*continued on next page*).

Figure 2.16 (*continued*)

Intentional structure	
Tasks	Danish domestic flight ticket reservation; well-structured task.
Communication	System-directed domain communication.
	Mixed initiative meta-communication; users may initiate meta-communication through keywords.
	System-directed other communication, such as the opening and closing of a dialogue.
Interaction level	Some questions are yes/no or multiple choice, most are general and focused.

Linguistic structure	
Speech acts	Primitive distinction between commands (meta-communication) and statements (answers) in user input; use of commands (questions), and statements for providing feedback, error messages and other information in output.
References	No anaphora resolution; ellipses are handled.
Segments	-

Interaction history	
Linguistic	Only semantic contents.
Topic	Order of exchanges.
Task	Information exchanged.
Performance	-

Domain model	
Data	Timetable, fares, flights, customers, reservations.
Rules	Completions and constraints.

User model	
Goals	Assumed to be flight ticket reservation.
Beliefs	Handled to a moderate extent at run-time.
Preferences	Determined at run-time; the scope is the current reservation task.
User group	System novice/expert distinction; the system's introduction and discount information is optional.
Cognition	Natural response packages addressed; cognitive overload problem.

3. *Developing Interactive Speech Systems*

3.1 Introduction

In the following chapters we describe the development and evaluation of interaction model and dialogue component aspects of advanced interactive speech systems in accordance with the idea of a rationalized development process presented in Section 1.2. Ideally, development and evaluation would be exhaustively presented on the basis of a consolidated and transparent version of a theory of spoken interaction such as the one presented in Chapter 2. For the time being, we can offer only a less comprehensive and more fragmented view. Advanced interactive speech system development has so far taken place mainly in research projects and a complete best practice methodology which can support, improve, make more efficient and help standardize the development and evaluation of advanced interactive speech systems is still far away. The methodology should specialize software engineering best practice to the particular purposes of advanced interactive speech system engineering by specifying in detail the methods (procedures, guidelines, heuristics), concepts and tools to be used in developing and evaluating advanced interactive speech systems as well as providing guidelines on when and how to use each method, set of concepts or tool.

This chapter sketches a development and evaluation life-cycle model for advanced interactive speech systems. The survey process is discussed in more detail including requirement specification, evaluation criteria and design specification. Iterative analysis, design and evaluation are only outlined (Section 3.2), as these aspects will be addressed in detail later. The following three sections each present a prototype tool or method in support of the specification of interactive speech systems. Section 3.3 presents a preliminary method in support of completeness and consistency in requirement specification. Section 3.4 presents a simple tool which supports the explicit representation of requirements, design decisions and design reasoning throughout the development process. A second tool helps decide whether speech is appropriate for the application to be developed given the evolving specification (Section 3.5).

3.2   The Development and Evaluation Process

A General Software Engineering Life-cycle Model

At a high level of abstraction, any standard software engineering life-cycle model, such as Sommerville (1992) and Yourdon (1982), applies to the development and evaluation of advanced interactive speech systems. However, as such models are aimed at describing software development processes in general, they do not specialize to the development and evaluation processes which are specific to particular classes of systems, such as advanced interactive speech systems. In addition, general software engineering life-cycle models do not include advise on the methods and tools to be used when developing such systems.

Figure 3.1 shows a general software engineering life-cycle model which has been slightly specialized to the development and evaluation of interactive speech systems. Obviously, the model only provides an overall framework. Based on the model, we review the development and evaluation process for advanced interactive speech systems. Figure 3.1 shows the development and evaluation phases which will be discussed in Chapters 3–8. Development and evaluation phases beyond the acceptance test stage, such as system maintenance and system re-engineering, will receive little discussion (Section 3.4). Development and evaluation processes sometimes differ depending on whether the system being developed is a research system or a commercial system. We shall mention some of the differences as we go along.

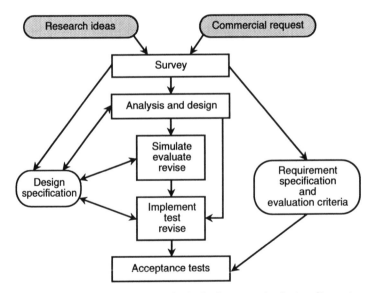

Figure 3.1: A software engineering life-cycle model for the development and evaluation of interactive speech systems. Rectangular boxes show process phases. The development and evaluation process is iterative within each phase and across phases. Arrows linking process phases indicate the overall course of the process. The requirement specification and evaluation criteria, and the design specification (rounded white boxes), are used throughout the development process. The rounded grey boxes indicate that the system to be developed may be either a research system or a commercial system.

Survey

System development projects begin with a *survey*. The aim of the survey is to provide a reasonable and reliable estimate of project feasibility. If the project is judged to be feasible, the survey should also produce a proper basis for the project in terms of well-defined goals and constraints. If, on the other hand, the project is considered not to be feasible, it should be stopped at once to minimize waste of resources.

In order to make a reliable estimate of project feasibility, strategic goals must be determined, system goals and constraints must be defined, and resource constraints identified. Possible *strategic goals* include, for example, cost savings, service improvements or technology exploration. In the case of interactive speech systems, *system goals and constraints* concern the elements of interactive speech theory discussed in Chapter 2, including, for instance, domain, interactive tasks, user group and type of spoken output. A central problem is that many of these elements may pose major development difficulties. Proper feasibility estimation, therefore, should involve close scrutiny of each element needed for the application in order to prevent unpleasant surprises later. Finally, *resource constraints* concern, for example, the manpower and time available for developing the system, the hardware and software to be used, as well as configuration requirements.

Sources of information that may provide useful input to the survey are identified and tapped. The sources include brainstorming meetings, literature, experience from the development of similar systems, input from domain experts and interviews with relevant stakeholders, such as the procurer and the future users. For instance, the idea of the Danish Dialogue System arose in a brainstorming meeting in 1991 which made it plausible that: (i) speaker-independent continuous speech recognition would become a commercial reality within the next 5 years; (ii) ordering tasks involving large service providers would be a target for such systems; and (iii) such tasks of medium complexity had not been addressed before.

Requirement Specification

Identified goals and constraints are represented in a *requirement specification document*. The purpose of this document is to list, eventually, all the agreed requirements which the envisaged system should meet, including strategic goals, system goals and constraints, and resource constraints. Figure 3.2 shows the initial requirement specification for the Danish Dialogue System. As the system should be accessed over the telephone, real-time performance was considered mandatory for a usable system. In the context of the chosen hardware, and given the expected limitations of the speech recognizer, the real-time requirement gave rise to additional constraints on active vocabulary size (at most 100 words at a time) and user utterance length (three or four words on average and at most 10 words). Because of limited project resources, the system vocabulary size was set to about 500 words. We knew that a vocabulary this size was likely to be insufficient given the chosen domain of application. In a commercial development context, an *infeasibility* constraint of this nature would, of course, be meaningless. In research projects, on the other hand, such constraints are taken as facts of life. What matters, instead, is to distribute the effects of the overall project resource constraints on issues which do not prevent the research from addressing the real scientific and technical problems it aims to solve. Vocabulary incompleteness is such an issue because complementing the vocabulary later does not normally pose any novel scientific or technical problems. In addition to real-time performance, the main usability requirements were: sufficient task domain coverage; robustness; natural forms of language and dialogue; and flexibility of interaction.

The Danish Dialogue System as an Example
Evaluation Criteria

Based on the requirement specification, a set of *evaluation criteria* is established for use in evaluating the final system. These criteria mainly refer to the system goals and constraints. The evaluation criteria state the parameters that should be measured and the measurement results that should be achieved for the final system to be acceptable. For instance, if the requirement specification includes a requirement of

---

Strategic goals:
- To build realistic prototypes of advanced interactive speech systems, focusing on the integration of speech technology, natural language processing, knowledge representation and human-machine interaction.
- To explore speech technology.
- To create and consolidate know-how.

System goals and constraints:

Overall performance:
- Real-time performance is required.
- The system must be robust and flexible.

Speech input:
- Continuous, speaker-independent.

User utterances:
- Danish.
- The vocabulary size should not exceed 500 words.
- At most 100 active words at a time.
- The average user utterance length should not exceed 3-4 words.
- The maximum user utterance length should not exceed 10 words.
- The system must allow the use of natural forms of language and dialogue.

Domain model:
- The system should cover the domains of reservation, change of reservation and information on departures, fares and travel conditions for Danish domestic flights.

User model:
- Walk-up-and-use system.

System utterances:
- Danish.

Resource constraints:
- Available resources are about 30 person years.
- The system is accessed via the telephone.
- The system must run on a PC.

Figure 3.2: Initial requirements for the Danish Dialogue System. The requirements are split into three groups: strategic goals; system goals and constraints; and resource constraints.

real-time performance then real-time performance should be included among the evaluation criteria, and run-time performance will be among the parameters measured during evaluation of the final system. A reconstruction of the evaluation criteria for the Danish Dialogue System is shown in Figure 3.3.

- Close-to-real-time performance is required.
- The recogniser can only be expected to perform in close-to-real-time and achieve acceptable recognition rates if the average user utterance length does not exceed 3-4 words and the maximum user utterance length does not exceed 10 words.
- The system's vocabulary will not exceed 500 words although this size may be insufficient. Out-of-vocabulary words will be counted.
- The system must sufficiently cover the task domain.
- The system must be robust, i.e. it must be able to cope in a reasonable way with input which is either not understood or non-cooperative.
- Restrictions on language and dialogue must be principled so that users can use restricted but intuitive and natural forms of language and dialogue.
- Flexibility must be optimised within the frames of the given constraints and criteria.

Figure 3.3: Evaluation criteria for the Danish Dialogue System. The list of criteria is a reconstruction and hence to some extent a rationalization. During the project, the criteria were never stated very explicitly. This is reflected in the figure. For instance, "acceptable recognition rates" are not explained in more detail, and "sufficient" domain coverage is a somewhat subjective measure.

Open Issues

Requirement specification and evaluation criteria should preferably be finalized in the survey phase. It is on the basis of the requirement specification that the question of project feasibility must be determined. Well-defined specific points of difficulty on which decisions cannot be made at this stage may, however, be left open for consideration later in the development process as long as these are not crucial to project feasibility. An example could be the question of whether it would be feasible to allow relatively free mixed initiative meta-communication. If an alternative, less advanced but still feasible and acceptable, solution is known to exist, the question may be left open for later decision.

Commercial Contracts

In commercial development projects, requirement specification and evaluation criteria are key elements of the contract which must be satisfied by the system provider. The contract must be precise and expressed in a language which the procurer understands. Whether the requirement specification should be expressed using some formal or semi-formal technique depends on the background and preferences of the procurer. If the requirement specification and evaluation criteria are not met by the final system, the procurer typically has the right to turn down the system or request that shortcomings be repaired or penalties paid.

Research Systems

Befitting their exploratory purpose, the framework for research system development is often loosely defined compared to that of commercial systems. The requirement specification and evaluation criteria do not serve contractual purposes. This means that they can be more easily modified later in the development process because there is no procurer who has to approve of the changes made. In the Danish Dialogue Project, for instance, it was decided, following a series of simulation experiments, to only implement those parts of the system which addressed the reservation task. The change of reservation task and the information task were eventually left out because they were not considered feasible under the specified goals and constraints. Moreover, aspects of key importance to commercial system development are sometimes de-emphasized in research projects. For instance, the evaluation criteria for the Danish Dialogue System as specified in Figure 3.3 would not be sufficient in a commercial context. They are too vague and do not include measurement to specified criteria of such factors as transaction success and user satisfaction, as is typically required in commercial projects.

Realistic Settings in Research Projects

As a final point on requirement specification, we want to mention a problem caused by the fact that many advanced interactive speech systems are being developed as research prototypes. Whilst commercial systems by default are based on real-life needs, research systems often have no procurer and no real users who can provide requirements to the system to be developed. This, of course, makes life easier in some respects as one can do with a sloppy requirement specification document without being severely punished by a procurer, and it is much easier to make changes later in the development process because the document does not have the role of a contractual commitment. On the other hand, if the research prototype is intended as a quasi-realistic exploration of future applications, it is highly desirable to be able to measure acceptability on the basis of firm requirement specification and evaluation criteria. The best way to overcome the problems of a missing procurer and real end-users is probably to involve organizations in the specification process which potentially could be real procurers or end-users. This creates a semi-realistic environment for establishing a requirement specification and evaluation criteria, and may later provide a testbed for the implemented system.

The requirement specification for the Danish Dialogue System was created in such a semi-realistic environment. As the objective was to develop a realistic, application-oriented research prototype rather than a real application, we did not have any actual procurer or users to talk to. However, contact was established with a travel agency during which we interviewed travel agents and made recordings of human–human reservation and information dialogues. The aim was to create a system which was realistic in the sense that it could meet, as far as possible, the needs and desiderata of potential customers and users. The system should offer an economic advantage to potential customers, and the choice of domain and technology should be reasonable in view of potential demands for interactive speech applications. One effect of these considerations of application realism was that the system should be able to run on a PC so that Danish travel agencies could easily afford the required hardware. Had we chosen more powerful hardware, the constraints on the system would have been somewhat less severe.

Design Specification

During the survey focus is on the requirement specification. However, other important ideas, decisions and constraints often make their appearance at this stage without properly belonging in the requirement specification document. This happens because of the survey's necessary role of "looking ahead" in order to ensure feasibility. Such ideas, decisions and constraints are included in the *design specification*. For instance, many issues concerning the operational aspects of system design considered in the survey phase do not belong to the requirement specification but are clearly needed in the design specification. Design specification therefore starts, typically at a low speed, in the survey phase, and comes into focus in the *design and analysis* phase following the survey (see Figure 3.1).

The purpose of the design specification is to describe and eventually make operational how to build a system which will satisfy the requirement specification and meet the evaluation criteria. The design specification, therefore, will be clearly related to, and may simply include, the requirement specification. The design specification must be sufficiently detailed to serve as a basis for implementation and, in contrast to the requirement specification, is often expressed in a formal or semi-formal language understood by the system developers and serving its operational purpose.

A number of sources provide input to the design specification. The sources include those used in the survey phase as well as available theory, concepts, tools, methods, guidelines and reusable software from other projects.

To serve its purpose the design specification must be constantly updated to include the most recent additions and revisions. If this is to be done systematically and coherently an explicit representation of the changing and accumulating design decisions is needed to keep track of the development process. This is good engineering practice but difficult to do. If it is not done, it becomes hard, or even impossible, to: (i) keep track of the design decisions that have been made and why they were made; (ii) explain to new developers joining the team what is going on; and (iii) carry out informed maintenance and re-engineering once the project has been completed. A prototool in support of good engineering practice in these regards is presented in Section 3.4.

Analysis, Design and Evaluation

Subsequent development phases will be discussed in more detail in later chapters. The phase following the survey is often called "analysis and design", although analysis and design also forms part of later phases during which analysis and design alternate with evaluation (see Figure 3.1). Revisions always require analysis and some form of re-design, and may be needed as late as in the acceptance test phase.

In the analysis and design phase the aim is to develop the design specification of the system to such a level of formal detail that it can serve as a basis for implementation, as will be discussed in Section 4.1. The system model may be implemented directly (Chapter 6), or it may be iterated, refined and adjusted through a *simulate–evaluate–revise* cycle prior to implementation. The latter approach is often used in advanced speech interaction model design (Chapter 5). The simulate–evaluate–

revise approach is structurally similar to the *implement–test–revise* approach because "simulate" includes "run the simulated system" and "test" includes "run and evaluate the implemented system". One difference among several is that software-related tests, such as the blackbox and glassbox tests (Chapter 6), are only performed on the implemented system, whereas most other evaluation measurements will be the same for both systems (Chapter 8). Transcription and analysis is needed both after simulation and after implementation (Chapter 7). When the implemented system is considered complete, a number of *acceptance tests* are performed before and/or after installation. These may include controlled user tests, field tests and a final acceptance test in which the installed system has to meet the requirement specification and the agreed evaluation criteria (Chapter 8).

3.3 Supporting Completeness and Consistency of Requirement Specification

No Available Method Ensures Completeness and Consistency

Unfortunately, there is no method available which may ensure complete and consistent requirement specifications for innovative systems, such as those developed in most advanced interactive speech system projects. When specifying such systems, many difficult issues have to be considered from early on and mistakes may have severe consequences, such as making the system unfeasible in the framework of the given constraints. Currently, the best way to create reasonable requirement specifications and evaluation criteria is to rely on the craft skills of experienced system developers. Even then, it remains possible that requirement specification and evaluation criteria will have to be modified later in the light of unexpected obstacles discovered during the development process.

Usually, overall system functionality requirements are specified quite early during the survey. These requirements concern, for example, domain and domain coverage, expected user groups(s), interactive tasks, type of speech recognition, such as speaker-independent and continuous speech recognition, and language, such as Danish. Resource constraints are typically defined from the very beginning of the survey, including maximum person power available, maximum budget and hardware to be used. However, nothing prevents the list of requirements from being incomplete or inconsistent. A method which could support the early creation of complete and consistent requirement specification, providing a solid background for an estimation of project feasibility, is therefore highly desirable.

Using the Elements in Chapter 2 as a Basis for a Method

The structured set of elements of speech interaction theory as presented in Chapter 2 might serve as a highly preliminary version of such a method. Jointly, the elements may support *completeness* of requirement specification by acting as a checklist of functional aspects to be considered for inclusion. *Consistency* may be supported, and inconsistencies detected, through information on relationships between the individual elements. In the following we describe and exemplify this manner of use of the speech interaction theory elements of Chapter 2.

Completeness

When used as a checklist, the set of elements may generate questions and statements such as the following, semi-formally expressed: (i) "Have you considered if you need element x and possibly what sub-type of element x?"; and (ii) "If you want element y, you must also have element z". This may be illustrated as follows.

(i) As can be seen from Figure 3.2, the initial requirement specification for the Danish Dialogue System did not mention any particular goals and constraints concerning speech output and system utterances, except that utterances should be in Danish. Had we used the method being described here we would have added decisions on the form of speech output to use, whether or not to address output prosody, and which restrictions to impose on lexicon, grammar, semantics and style of output utterances.

(ii) Owing to hardware constraints and given the expected limitations of the speech recognizer, the real-time requirement gave rise to rather severe constraints on active vocabulary size in the Danish system. To ensure sufficient domain coverage for the chosen task, the system would need a larger vocabulary than could be active at any one time. These points imply that the system would need expectations concerning the next user input to be communicated to the input speech and language module(s). Moreover, active vocabulary limitations require that ways are found to make the user remain within the active vocabulary at any one time. This may be done by having the system ask questions throughout, thus making domain communication system-directed. In other words, expectations and initiative serve to realize the system within the given vocabulary constraints.

In general, if the requirement specification omits reference to some element, and if this element is also not mentioned in the design specification, it should be checked to see whether the element was left out on purpose or just ignored.

Some of the elements in Chapter 2 may directly generate system goals and constraints, whereas others do so only indirectly. The former group of elements, such as the tasks to be handled, the type of output speech to use and the type of input speech to be accepted, should be considered not only as regards the goals and constraints which they themselves might impose on the system but also with the aim of detecting possible obstacles or additional constraints which they might impose on development. For instance, the constraints on active vocabulary size and user utterance length and style (terse) in the Danish Dialogue System were imposed by other system goals and constraints (real-time, hardware, speech recognizer, task and domain). Other elements, in particular those in the control and context layers, do not directly generate system goals and constraints for inclusion in the requirement specification. Rather, they support and influence the operationalization of certain system goals and constraints in ways which make it important to consider their implications. Among the latter might well be new or revised goals and constraints. For instance, both a linguistic history and a topic history may be needed to achieve the goal of handling user meta-communication as stated in the requirement specification. Although these histories are not goals in themselves, the need for them might mean that meta-communication will not be possible as specified.

Consistency

When used for consistency checking, the set of elements may help demonstrate that inclusion of a certain element would make the project unfeasible given the specified goals and constraints. The element would either have to be excluded or the goals and constraints revised or relaxed in some way. In this case, the set of elements may generate statements such as the following, semi-formally expressed: (iii) "If you want element x, you must have element y not element z"; and (iv) "You cannot have both element x and element y". Note, however, that the formal expressions (ii), (iii) and (iv) above assume that speech interaction theory includes relationships of *implication* among its elements. Such relationships are still rare in the theory presented in Chapter 2.

A simple, albeit somewhat non-specific, example of (iii) would be for most current advanced interactive speech system projects: don't start by simulating or implementing free mixed initiative dialogue because you will not succeed in building a workable system! An example of (iv) would be: suppose that, given the requirements in Figure 3.2, the developers were to allow the system to ask a completely open question to users at some point, such as "How may I help you?". This would be inconsistent with the limitations on active vocabulary. Note that, in this case as in many others, constraint relaxation might be achieved in several different ways. One solution could be to considerably relax the constraints on vocabulary size; another to reduce the domain. The former solution implies that real-time performance is no longer feasible unless yet more constraints are relaxed.

3.4   Representing Design Space and Design Reasoning

Difficulties in Performing Design Rationale

As already pointed out (Section 3.2), it is good engineering practice to constantly update the design specification to include the most recent additions and revisions, and perhaps the rationale for major design decisions as well. However, perhaps the term "ideal" engineering practice should be used instead because, in practice, few design teams do this in any systematic way. Certainly, they fail to do so at a price. The price is that it becomes more difficult to keep track of design decisions as they are made than it would otherwise have been, more difficult than necessary for newcomers joining the team to fully understand what is going on, and hard to maintain or re-engineer somebody else's, or even one's own, system later on should that be required.

The reason why so many software developers pay the price probably is that, so far, they have not found acceptable tools for keeping track of the development process and its rationale. The reason, certainly, is not that no such ways have been proposed in the literature nor have been tried in real life. On the contrary, since 1970, a number of approaches to what is commonly called *design rationale* have been proposed and trialled by software developers around the world. A good many of these are presented in Moran and Carroll (1996). Some of the real reasons why an appropriate tool for keeping track of the design process and important parts of designer reasoning is still missing, seem to be the following. First, design decision making is often remarkably *fast and implicit*. Secondly, it takes a good deal of thinking and *time* to explicitly reconstruct a productive design session. Is it really worthwhile to produce fully explicit representations of all the reasoning which took place and which led to design decisions? Is it possible? Is it worthwhile to explicitly represent the many details that have to be decided upon in, for instance, graphical interface design? Thirdly, *who* should do this job which is often quite thankless in the short term? Fourthly, if someone does it, the fellow developers will have to discuss the results at the next design meeting at which they will often *disagree* with them, which leads to "endless" meetings. Fifthly, who *can* do it in the first place, considering such facts as that many important design decisions are often made after hours in the car park or elsewhere? Sixthly, many of the existing approaches to design rationale are full of complex, semi-formal notation. Who wants to *learn* this notation to do such an apparently simple job as that of keeping track of design decision making? Moreover, even the most complex notations around are quite likely to be found *lacking in expressiveness* in practice.

3.4.1 DSD/DR

Still, it makes good sense to keep track of design decision making and reasoning throughout the development and evaluation process. We shall briefly present a tool which we have used ourselves in developing the interaction model for the Danish Dialogue System. Among the comparative virtues of this tool is that it is simple, adds some amount of systematicity, structure and explicitness to design processes, can be easily modified to suit the purposes of new users, does not involve complex notation, and seems capable of adequately capturing the important, early design process stages where completeness and consistency are vital for ensuring a feasible system concept. The tool is currently being developed as a shared hypertext application. It is called *Design Space Development and Design Rationale* (DSD/DR) because it is actually two tools in one (Bernsen, 1993a; Bernsen and Ramsay, 1994).

DSD

DSD, the first part of the tool, uses a simple frame structure to keep track of consensus building during development and evaluation. Requirements and the design decisions on which these are based are viewed as *constraints* on the interactive speech system (or artefacts more generally) to be developed. The design process is viewed as a process of increasingly constraining the design space around the system. As these constraints *interact,* they may conflict and their explicit representation provides an occasion to detect such inconsistencies early on (cf. Section 3.3). Constant updating is handled by representing the design process as a *series* of DSD frames representing the emerging constraints on the system. Each DSD frame thus represents, or provides a snapshot of, the design space structure and designer commitments at a given point during system design. Figure 3.4 shows DSD frame No. N which was constructed for the purpose of this book. Some of the actual DSDs constructed during the Wizard of Oz phase when developing the Danish Dialogue System can be found in Bernsen (1993b). DSD No. N includes the information in Figure 3.2 above, together with some additional information. As in actual DSD use, the information which has been added since the generation of the previous DSD representation (i.e. DSD N-1), is shown in italics. Part (A) of a DSD frame represents the most general requirements of the system to be developed. Part (B) specifies the general requirements in increasing detail. The fields "Collaborative aspects" and "Organizational aspects" are empty because the project did not involve any significant information of these kinds. The "Comments and actions" field is used for representing information on who-does-what, difficulties encountered, etc. The

Design Project: The Danish Dialogue Project			
DSD No. N	**Start date:** 28.1.97	**Rev. date:** 29.1.97	**Sign:** LD

A. General constraints and criteria

Overall design goal(s)

To build realistic prototypes of advanced interactive speech systems, focusing on the integration of speech technology, natural language processing, knowledge representation and human-machine interaction.

To explore speech technology.

To create and consolidate know-how.

General feasibility constraints

Available resources are about 30 person years.

Scientific and technological feasibility constraints

Limited capability of current speech and natural language processing.

Open research questions, e.g. insufficient research in dialogue theory.

Design process type

Research prototype development.

Designer/user preferences

Use of the Dialogue Description Language (DDL).

Realism criteria

The system must run on a PC (i.e. on machines which could be purchased by a travel agency).

Functionality criteria

The system must be robust and flexible.

Make sure that the artefact can do the tasks done by the human it replaces.

Usability criteria

Unless a naturalness criterion cannot be met for feasibility reasons, it should be incorporated into the system.

B. Constraints and criteria applied to artefact within design space

Collaborative aspects

Organisational aspects

System aspects

Continuous, speaker-independent speech input.

Real-time performance is required.

Input is in Danish.

The vocabulary size should not exceed 500 words.

At most 100 words active at a time.

Output is in Danish.

The system must allow the use of natural forms of language and dialogue.

Interface aspects

The system is accessed via the telephone.

Figure 3.4: DSD representation of some of the major requirements for the Danish Dialogue System (*continud next page*).

Figure 3.4 (*continued*)

Task aspects The system should cover the domains of reservation, change of reservation and information on departures, fares and travel conditions for Danish domestic flights.
User and user experience aspects The average user-utterance length should not exceed 3-4 words. The maximum user-utterance length should not exceed 10 words. Walk-up-and-use system.
C. Comments and actions
D. Documentation
E. DSD No. (n) indicates the number of the current DSD specification.

"Documentation" field is useful for referring to relevant additional documentation. The "semi-random" character of the information contained in DSD No. N is actually typical of early design. In the Danish Dialogue Project, as well as in other development projects that were investigated as case studies during the development of DSD/DR, we found that information gets inserted into the DSD frames in no particular, not to mention logical, order.

DR

The second part of the DSD/DR tool, the DR frames, are used for representing particularly important pieces of design reasoning. A DR frame represents the reasoning about a particular design problem encountered during design. It discusses the design options, constraint trade-offs and solutions considered, and argues why a particular solution was chosen. An important point is that design reasoning is highly contextual and reflects the design space at the time. If the context is not made explicit, it can be virtually impossible to decode the represented design reasoning. In fact, it becomes difficult to represent the design reasoning in the first place. In DSD/DR, the immediately preceding DSD frame explicitly represents the context of the design reasoning presented in a certain DR frame. In many cases, a DR frame will lead to additions to the following DSD frame. DR frames thus act as links between subsequent DSD frames. Typically, there will be several DR frames acting as links between two consecutive DSD frames. When combined with DR representations, DSD makes design space context and constraints explicit in support of reasoning, traceability and re-use.

Figure 3.5 shows one of the DR frames that were produced in response to the blackbox test of the Danish Dialogue System. The test revealed a series of design problems of different severity and demanding different amounts of time and resources for their repair. We used DR frames to explicitly represent our reasoning about each of these problems and, when it became clear that resource constraints would prevent us from solving them all, we used the generated series of DR frames as a basis for setting priorities on the problems. DR frame No. 6, shown in Figure 3.5, refers to DSD No. 8 as being the DSD frame that was prepared through DR frame No. 6. During early specification of the system, we produced seven consecutive DSD

Design Project: The Danish Dialogue Project			
Prepares DSD No. 8	**DR No. 6**	**Date:** 24.5.94	**Sign:** LD
Design problem: No price information Users cannot get the price of the tickets they have reserved.			**Discovered by:** LD

Commitments involved:	
1.	It should be possible for users to fully exploit the system's task domain knowledge when they need it.
2.	Avoid superfluous or redundant interactions with users (relative to their contextual needs).

Justification:

Only some users are interested in getting information on the price. Professional users loose time on an extra dialogue turn if they are asked whether they want it. On the other hand, for users wanting the price information this may be very important.

Options:	
1.	Provide full price breakdown information at the end of a reservation task.
2.	Ask users if they want to know the price of their reserved tickets.
3.	Always inform users about the total price of their reservation (but not its breakdown into the prices of individual tickets).

Resolution: Option 3

There is a clash between the two design commitments because of the existence of different needs in the user population. Option 3 was identified and selected as a compromise between the two relevant design commitments. Option 3 does not require extra turn taking but mentions the price briefly.

Comments:

P1 already computes the price. It will be easy also to output the price to the user.

It would be a possibility to allow the user to obtain additional price information (a breakdown into the prices of individual tickets) via the help function (see DR 12).

Links to other DRs: 12 (help).	
Documentation: Notes 24.5.94	**Insert in next DSD frame:** Option 3.

Time estimate: Less than 1 day.

Modules(s) involved: P1.ddl

Importance of change: Important, in order to avoid user questions.	**Action to be taken:** Do the implementation.

Date of change: 30.5.94	**Time spent:** 2 hours	**Sign:** HD

Modified files: P1.ddl, messages/*, BEKRÆFT1/ (new phrases)

Date of test of changes: 3.6.94	Sign: LD

Figure 3.5: A DR frame representing a problem detected during the blackbox test of the implemented interaction model.

frames. DSD frame No. 8 is the frame which was produced following the blackbox test to represent the additional design decisions (or commitments) made at that stage. The "Commitments" listed in DR frame No. 6 derive from DSD frame No. 7 which formed the context of the design decision making at the time. Among the many commitments in DSD frame No. 7, those particular commitments were judged as being contextually relevant to the problem addressed in DR frame No. 6. The "Justification" following the listed commitments is a justification *not* of the solution but of there being a problem in the first place. After the problem justification follows the design options considered and the chosen solution to the problem. The "Comments" part of the DR frame provides additional observations of the problem. Note that the selected option (3) will be inserted into DSD frame No. 8.

Experiences From Using DSD/DR

We have had a positive experience with DSD/DR during the design of the Danish Dialogue System. Some of the problems encountered were: (1) the design space structure represented by the entries in the DSD frames is not self-explanatory. Training is required for inserting new information in its "right" place. DR frames are easier to master. (2) As development progresses, and if the development project is a major one, DSD frames become quite lengthy and complex. Hypertext might alleviate this problem. (3) DSD has an "imperial" tendency to become *the* central design and development document. This in itself is not a problem but one should be aware of the fact. (4) Maintaining a series of DSD frames takes quite some effort, which is, of course, more acceptable the more central the maintained representation is as a vehicle of communication among the developers. Still, it is these joint investments of effort which have to be measured against the advantages gained through DSD use. We believe this trade-off to be positive but still lack evidence from use of DSD by others than the originators of the approach.

3.5   Speech Functionality

Speech Functionality: The Need For Systematic Guidance

It is a basic observation of this book that use of speech input to, and speech output from, computer systems is spreading at a growing pace. This means that an increasing number of developers of systems and interfaces are faced with the question of whether to use speech input and/or speech output for the applications they are about to build. This is the issue of *speech functionality,* i.e. of the circumstances under which speech is, or is not, as the case may be, appropriate for an application to be developed. The literature offers no systematic guidance on speech functionality, although there is consensus in the field that systematic guidance is highly desirable (Baber and Noyes, 1993). Rather, system developers address the functionality of speech based on common sense hypothesizing, trial and error or results from user testing of, or laboratory experimentation with, different but, hopefully, related systems. Systematic guidance, on the other hand, requires theory, but theory alone is not sufficient. Once developed, the theory must be transformed into practical useful methods or tools which can be applied by non-theoreticians.

We would like to be able to address the issue of speech functionality on a systematic basis during early design. Given early requirement specification, we could then decide whether speech should really be included in the application, in what form(s) and, possibly, under which specific conditions. It will often be the case, of course, that the requirement specification itself states that speech is to be used for the application. In such cases, general knowledge about speech functionality might sometimes indicate that the application is unfeasible given other constraints, such as development budget or time. These constraints would then have to be modified or the development project would have to be abandoned.

The Study, Types of Claim

The speech functionality problem was investigated in Bernsen (1998a). The aim was to examine a large number of claims that have been made about speech functionality to see whether it was possible to find theoretical means of evaluating those claims. If this turned out to be the case, the theoretical basis identified might: (a) enable evaluation of a potentially much larger number of claims about speech functionality; and (b) form the basis of a practical tool that might support reasoning about speech functionality during early applications design. Results were encouraging and will be presented below. The scope of the results reported go beyond interactive speech systems and address, in addition, speech systems which do not perform natural language understanding or generation (cf. Figure 1.1). In the study mentioned, 120 non-redundant data points, each consisting of a single claim about speech functionality, were systematically collected from Baber and Noyes (1993). The claims were found to be of the following types.

1. Combined speech input/output recommended.
2. Speech output recommended.
3. Speech output positively compared to other modalities.
4. Speech input recommended.
5. Speech input positively compared to other modalities.
6. Conditional claims on the use of speech.
7. Combined speech input/output negatively compared to other modalities.
8. Speech output not recommended.
9. Speech output negatively compared to other modalities.
10. Speech input not recommended.
11. Speech input negatively compared to other modalities.

Representativeness of Claims

Conditional claims on the use of speech are claims which state that if some speech modality is to be used, then it should be used subject to the condition that, for instance, headphones are used in public spaces to protect privacy. Claims of the following form were excluded from consideration: claims comparing speech/non-speech multimodal combinations with other speech/non-speech multimodal combinations. Of the 13 possible types of claim, given the distinctions underlying the typology above, two were not found among the data. They were: claims positively comparing combined speech input/output to other modalities; and recommendations against the use of combined speech input/output. This probably does not significantly reduce the representativeness of the data set. More generally speaking, it is our hypothesis that the claims set is representative of standard approaches to the speech functionality issue in a number of important respects. As an example, consider the following claim (C):

(C) Speech input is likely to be inadequate for complex spatial manipulation tasks. The respects are: (i) the *sources* of claims, such as experimental work, user testing, common sense hypothesizing or designer experience. For instance, (C) might have been suggested by a user test; (ii) the generic *variables* referred to in the claims, such as "speech modality", "generic task" or "cognitive property" (Figure 3.7). In (C) the instantiated variables are "speech modality" (instantiated as "speech input") and "generic task" (instantiated as "complex spatial manipulation tasks"); (iii) the *types* of claim, such as recommendation, negative comparison, or conditional recommendation. Claim (C) is a negative recommendation; (iv) the *epistemic modifiers* involved in claims, such as "may be preferable to", "use this modality for", "was perceived to be useful" or "is dubious compared to". The nature of the epistemic modifier determines the "strength of conviction" behind a certain claim and the consequent requirements on the justification for that claim. In (C), the epistemic modifier is "is likely to be"; (v) the (sometimes insufficient) *scoping and level of precision* of claims. Claim (C) appears to be adequately scoped. Examples of less precise or less adequately scoped claims will be provided below.

Modalities

The term "speech" or "spoken language" designates several different unimodal input or output modalities, such as "speech input notation", "spoken input labels/keywords" or "speech output discourse", that is, standard spoken language. A *modality* is simply a form (or mode) of representing information as output from, or input to, a computer system (Hovy and Arens, 1990). A *unimodal* modality is a modality which is not itself composed of other modalities and which may form a component of a multimodal interface (Bernsen, 1994). Some unimodal modalities, including the speech modalities, are perfectly capable of being used alone in exchanging information with computer systems.

Minimum Complexity of the Problem

It is rather trivial to point out that speech is not suited for every kind of human–computer information exchange. It is an equally trivial generalization that, in some cases, other modalities are preferable to speech if we want to optimize the human–computer interface from the point of view of information exchange. On the other hand, sometimes speech actually *is* suited to the system and interface design task at hand, and sometimes speech is preferable to other modalities as well. The hard question is: in which specific cases are these generalizations true? This question not only is a hard one to answer in a principled way; a principled answer might also bring important benefits to system and interface design practice by removing some of the uncertainties which presently characterize the choice of speech modalities for the design of particular artefacts. Figure 3.6 shows why the question of when to use, and when not to use, speech in interface design is a hard one. This is because of the underlying complexity of the question, which derives in part from the large number of domain variables that may be involved (in bold type in the figure). Figure 3.6 semi-formally expresses the complexity of the speech functionality problem as derived from the data.

Empirical Approach Impractical

It should be noted that, unless factors could be trivially constrained or eliminated, Figure 3.6 expresses the *minimum* complexity of the speech functionality problem. There may be more relevant domain variables involved than those found in the data. In addition, Figure 3.6 does not distinguish between different technologies so familiar to the speech [combined speech input/output, speech output, or speech input modalities M1 and/or M2 and/or M3 and/or M4 etc.] are

[useful or not useful] for

[**generic task** GT and/or **speech act type** SA and/or **user group** UG and/or **interaction mode** IM and/or **work environment** WE and/or **generic system** GS and/or **performance parameter** PP and/or **learning parameter** LP and/or **cognitive property** CP] and/or

[preferable or non-preferable] to [alternative modalities AM1, AM2, AM3, AM4 etc.] and/or

[useful on conditions] C1, C2, C3 and/or C4 etc.

Figure 3.6: The minimum complexity of the problem of accounting for the functionality of speech in system and interface design. Domain variables are in bold type.

community, such as isolated words input, connected speech input, continuous speech input, speaker-dependent speech input, speaker-independent speech input, parametric speech output and coded speech output. These distinctions were made so infrequently in the data that they have been omitted from the expression in Figure 3.6. Yet the complexity expressed in Figure 3.6 is huge. If, in order to solve the problem of speech functionality, we were to empirically investigate each and every possible combination of the domain variables in Figure 3.6, then we would never finish the task in time to be able to provide much needed support of modality choice in early system and interface design. At best, we would end up with a very large, albeit still incomplete, number of low-level generalizations based on having made all possible mistakes at least once. The generalizations in question would look more or less like the data points shown in Figure 3.7.

How to Read the Standardized Data Points

The original claims on which the study was based were often quite complex individually and jointly rather heterogeneous, which is why they were transformed into the common formas illustrated in Figure 3.7. Data point 11 in Figure 3.7 should be read as follows: speech output can be useful for providing instructions to users during their performance of procedural tasks requiring limb and visual activity. The original claim in Baber (1993a) says: "An increasingly popular use of speech output is in providing instructions for users of sophisticated technology, such as video cassette recorders

Data point 11. **Speech act** [instruction] + **generic task** [follow procedure, e.g. for using a video recorder or an ATM]: speech output can be useful.

Assumption: The procedures to be followed require limb and visual activity.

Data point 121. **Generic multimedia systems** [office] + **generic task** [speech input text editing + keyboard text entry]: speech input has no advantage in **performance parameters** [speed, accuracy, and ease of use].

Figure 3.7: Examples of low-level generalizations on speech functionality for system and interface design. Domain variables are in bold type.

or ATMs. It has proved a popular application in toys, and can provide information on how to use a product". Note that Claim 11 in Figure 3.7 is only valid provided that at least one unstated assumption is being added. Lacking a theoretical framework, the claims about speech functionality made in the literature cannot be expected to be fully explicit nor to incorporate all the assumptions necessary.

Data point 121 in Figure 3.7 should be read: speech input has no advantage in speed, accuracy and ease of use when used for text editing in keyboard-based office text-entry systems. The original claim in Noyes (1993) says: "One solution to overcome the limitations inherent in the recognizer technology has been the suggestion of a multimodal system for office applications. For example, all editing and formatting commands should be given verbally, while text is entered via the keyboard. ... but the benefits to the users are not immediately obvious. When considering the indices of speed, accuracy, ease of use, there appears to be little advantage in introducing speech to the system".

Modality Theory and the Basic Approach

If, as argued above, the speech functionality problem cannot be solved empirically, the question becomes: which theory might be able to evaluate 120 claims on speech functionality which are representative of the claims made in the literature? We have used an existing theory of output and input modalities, called Modality Theory, for the purpose (Bernsen, 1994, 1998b). The basic idea of the approach to speech functionality is the following. Suppose that the requirement specification or design specification for a specific system and interface design task SID(t1) include information to the effect that, for example, the user needs hands- and eyes-free operation. Suppose, in addition, that we already know that some modalities of information representation M1–Mn allow hands- and eyes-free operation. Together, these two pieces of information imply that the modalities M1–Mn can be suggested as potentially appropriate modalities for the system to be designed. The fact that, for instance, modality M1 allows hands- and eyes-free operation is called a *modality property* of M1. Knowledge of modality properties thus allows the system developer to carry out a *mapping* from known requirement specification or design specification information onto candidate modalities.

The Modality Properties and Their Use

From one perspective Modality Theory can be viewed as a large, hierarchically organized, set of modality properties. Some modality properties are properties of the unimodal speech modalities of which there are six: input spoken discourse; input spoken labels/keywords; input spoken notation; output spoken discourse; output spoken labels/keywords; and output spoken notation. Most of the modality properties, however, are properties of other unimodal modalities. Some of these other modalities are acoustic modalities just like speech; others are graphical modalities; and yet others are haptic (touch) modalities. In principle, any modality property may be relevant to the problem of speech functionality, given the fact that claims about speech functionality often involve comparison with non-speech modalities.

So the task of using the modality properties which form part of Modality Theory, for evaluating the 120 claims, consists of searching the theory for properties of modalities which might serve to justify the claims under investigation. The result of the search was 18 such properties, shown in Figure 3.8, each of which would serve

Modality	Modality property
MP1 Linguistic input/output	Linguistic input/output modalities have interpretational scope. They are therefore unsuited for specifying detailed information on spatial manipulation.
MP2 Linguistic input/output	Linguistic input/output modalities, being unsuited for specifying detailed information on spatial manipulation, lack an adequate vocabulary for describing the manipulations.
MP3 Arbitrary input/output	Arbitrary input/output modalities impose a learning overhead which increases with the number of arbitrary items to be learned.
MP4 Acoustic input/output	Acoustic input/output modalities are omnidirectional.
MP5 Acoustic input/output	Acoustic input/output modalities do not require limb (including haptic) or visual activity.
MP6 Acoustic output	Acoustic output modalities can be used to achieve saliency in low-acoustic environments.
MP7 Static graphics	Static graphic modalities allow the simultaneous representation of large amounts of information for free visual inspection.
MP8 Dynamic output	Dynamic output modalities, being temporal (serial and transient), do not offer the cognitive advantages (wrt. attention and memory) of freedom of perceptual inspection.
MP9 Dynamic acoustic output	Dynamic acoustic output modalities can be made interactively static.
MP10 Speech input/output	Speech input/output modalities, being temporal (serial and transient) and non-spatial, should be presented sequentially rather than in parallel.
MP11 Speech input/output	Speech input/output modalities in native or known languages have very high saliency.
MP12 Speech output	Speech output modalities may simplify graphic displays for ease of visual inspection.
MP13 Synthetic speech output	Synthetic speech output modalities, being less intelligible than natural speech output, increase cognitive processing load.
MP14 Non-spontaneous speech input	Non-spontaneous speech input modalities (isolated words, connected words) are unnatural and add cognitive processing load.
MP15 Discourse output	Discourse output modalities have strong rhetorical potential.
MP16 Discourse input/output	Discourse input/output modalities are situation-dependent.
MP17 Spontaneous spoken labels/keywords and discourse input/output	Spontaneous spoken labels/keywords and discourse input/output modalities are natural for humans in the sense that they are learnt from early on (by most people). (Note that spontaneous keywords must be distinguished from designer-designed keywords which are not necessarily natural to the actual users.)
MP18 Notational input/output	Notational input/output modalities impose a learning overhead which increases with the number of items to be learnt.

Figure 3.8: The 18 modality properties (MPs) used in justifying, supporting or correcting the claims.

to justify at least one claim, sometimes in conjunction with other modality properties. In some cases, although no modality property has been found which could fully justify a certain claim, that property could nevertheless *support* the claim to a greater or lesser extent. In other cases, neither justification nor support could be found in

Modality Theory for a certain claim which would therefore be marked as one for which *no justification* had been found. Not surprisingly, claims from any of those three categories might sometimes be in partial or full conflict with Modality Theory. In such cases, *correction* was introduced to the claim in question based on reference to a specific modality property. The notion of (full) *justification* used in the data analysis amounts to the claim that, given a set of modality properties and a specific claim on speech functionality, a designer is practically justified in making that claim on speech functionality based on that set of modality properties. In other words, armed with the modality properties, the designer would in principle be able to make the claim even without the benefit of the particular source of the claim.

Comments on the Modality Properties

Without going into unnecessary detail, a few words of explanation on Figure 3.8 follow. In MP1 "interpretational scope" refers to a basic limitation in the expressiveness of linguistic modalities compared to analogue modalities (Bernsen, 1995). For instance, one can *say* (linguistic modality) "she went down the stairs" without providing the listener with any further specification whatsoever of the stairs down which she went. The expression "the stairs", just like the expressions "she", "went" and "down", has interpretational scope and allows an infinite number of possible interpretations of the specifics of what the quoted words refer to. However, one cannot *draw* (analogue modality) the fact that she went down the stairs without providing a specific interpretation of the referents of the expressions "she", "went", "down" and "the stairs". Furthermore, if one tries to linguistically express the vast amount of specific information that is being represented in the drawing, one is faced with an almost impossible task. It is for this reason that linguistic modalities are badly suited to represent spatial detail.

In MP3 "arbitrary" modalities are representations whose meaning has been decided on ad hoc, such as the ad hoc introduction of particular sounds in acoustic alarms. In MP7 and MP8 "freedom of visual/perceptual inspection" means that the user has all the time desired to decode particular representations. This is true of, for instance, static graphic representations. However, as stated in MP9, even dynamic acoustic representations can be made interactively static by replaying them. In MP15 and MP16 "discourse" means the basic form of free speech exchange which is situation-dependent and rhetorical. From the point of view of the user, discourse output is preferable to "spoken labels/keywords" output in the sense that, being free-form and unconstrained in length, discourse can remove the ambiguities which we often encounter in labels or keywords, be they spoken, graphic or haptic. Similarly, discourse input is preferable to (designer-determined) spoken labels/keywords input in the sense that users do not have to remember the particular keywords they must use in order to make their speech application execute. Discourse is also preferable to spoken "notation" (MP18) in the sense that notation, being an add-on to natural language rather than a part of it, imposes an additional learning overhead which may not be appropriate in all applications. Spoken input through a fixed (or designer-determined) set of keywords imposes a learning overhead similar to that of spoken input notation.

It should be noted that the modality properties MP1–MP18 are simply those that were required to justify as many of the claims as possible. This set of modality properties does not have any form of theoretical closure, and Modality Theory could have provided more, or other, properties had the data been different. There is no doubt, therefore, that a full investigation of speech functionality would have to draw upon additional modality properties.

Illustrations of the Different Evaluations of Claims

In what follows we give illustrations of the four different kinds of evaluation of the claims: justification; support; no justification; and correction.

Figure 3.9 shows a "straight" justification from a single modality property, which does not need auxiliary assumptions (contrast Figure 3.7, data point 11). The claim addresses comparison between speech output and static text with respect to the domain variable "cognitive property". The cautious epistemic modifier "may be

Data point 100. Speech output may be preferable to static text for **cognitive property** [setting a mood]. Justified by MP15: "Discourse output modalities have strong rhetorical potential".

Figure 3.9: A straightforward justification of a comparative claim based on one modality property. Domain variables are in bold type.

preferable to" is quite common in the data.

Figure 3.10 shows a typical example of support for a claim which is complex in terms of the number of domain variables involved. The claim compares speech input with typed language input. The epistemic modifier "is likely to" is a rather strong one. MP17, therefore, cannot fully justify Claim 119. Even though the users are non-expert typists, data entry tasks differ widely along dimensions, such as size of the data set and source of the data to be entered. Similarly, non-expert typists have different typing skills. It is not evident that the fact that speech is natural (in some speech modalities) generalizes across all these differences to justify the claim that speech input will always be faster than typed language data entry. A general finding with respect to the cases for which Modality Theory "merely" provided support was that these cases dealt with rather complex relationships between the domain variables. It is simply difficult or impossible to produce full theoretical justifications of complex relationships. As long as the theories we use in justifying modality choice, whatever their nature, have limited complexity, there will always exist claims which are too complex to be justified by those theories. In such cases, empirical investigation is the only solution to a speech functionality problem.

Mostly, the cases of no justification are cases of unclear, questionable, possibly or probably false claims. For instance, the claim that "speech input is fast" cannot be evaluated because it is too general and non-specific. It would appear that speed of

Data point 119. **Generic task** [data-entry] + **user group** [non-experts]: speech input is likely to be **performance parameter** [faster] than haptic [keyboard] modality. Supported by MP17: "Spontaneous spoken labels/keywords and discourse input/output modalities are natural for humans in the sense that they are learnt from early on (by most people)."

Figure 3.10: A claim which is supported, but not justified, by Modality Theory. Domain variables are in bold type.

Data point 24. Many individual **speech acts** [warnings]: speech output is preferable to acoustic non-speech because of its expressiveness and **cognitive property** [human discrimination capacities].

Assumption: The acoustic non-speech referred to is the arbitrary acoustic modality.
Correction: Humans would appear able to discriminate between hundreds of sounds. Rather, S-O is preferable to acoustic non-speech if the latter is an arbitrary modality.

Corrected by MP3: "Arbitrary input/output modalities impose a learning overhead which increases with the number of arbitrary items to be learned."

Justified by MP17: Spontaneous spoken labels/keywords and discourse input/output modalities are natural for humans in the sense that they are learnt from early on (by most people).

Figure 3.11: A corrected claim about speech output. Domain variables are in bold type. S-O means speech out-

input modalities is an essentially comparative notion. In three cases it was found that Modality Theory should have been able to provide full justifications but could not because the theory still has not been fully developed for input modalities.

Perhaps the most interesting case of correction occurs with respect to Claim 24 (Figure 3.11). In this complex argument the assumption first states that "acoustic non-speech" can be positively characterized as arbitrary acoustics, i.e. acoustics which bear arbitrary relationships to their ad hoc assigned meanings. The correction then points out that the reason why arbitrary acoustic output is inferior to speech output is *not* that humans cannot discriminate between different types of arbitrary acoustic representations. Appreciation of music is probably dependent upon the ability to discriminate between large numbers of individually different sounds, each of which does not carry any particular meaning. Rather, the inferiority of arbitrary acoustics is due to the learning overhead which is needed for humans to learn the meaning of many different arbitrary acoustic representations (MP3). Finally, MP17 argues why Claim 24 is true after all. This is not because arbitrary acoustics cannot be made arbitrarily expressive of the meaning of different alarms but because speech output is "expressive for free" to humans. This example provides a good illustration of why we need a firmer and more articulate theoretical background on which to think and reason about the properties of speech and other modalities.

Overall Results

The overall results of the evaluation exercise were that out of the 120 data points, 91 were justified by reference to one or more of the modality properties listed in Figure 3.8; 15 data points were supported by modality properties; and no justification was found in 14 cases. Among the cases of no justification, 11 did not deserve justification. Corrections by reference to modality properties were made in nine cases. The fact that three in four claims on speech functionality could be justified, through reference to a small number of modality properties, suggests the following hypothesis: the making, during early design, of reliable claims about the suitability or unsuitability of one or more speech modalities for aspects of the system and interface design task at hand, can often be done based on an understanding of the information representation properties of a limited set of input/output modalities. In addition to understanding the relevant modality properties, designers should, of course, understand their design task, which includes understanding how the relevant domain variables are instantiated in the design space defined by the design task. If the present data are representative, three in four design recommendations concerning speech functionality do not require empirical experimentation, user testing, common sense hypothesizing or designer trial and error. If the above hypothesis is correct, Modality Theory helps address a problem for a solution for which no other viable approach is in sight.

Comments on the Results

In interpreting the results described above, it should be borne in mind that design recommendations on speech functionality, whether based on Modality Theory or on empirical methods and intuition, are not decisions to *actually use* speech in the design of a particular application. The latter decisions are "holistic" or highly contextual, i.e. they must take into account all the peculiarities of the design space as specified in the requirement and design specifications, and often have to trade them off against one another. It is hard to believe that these decisions and trade-offs can be made the subject of explicit generalizations which uniquely determine the selection of particular modalities in context. Rather, the design recommendations for which Modality Theory, on the one hand, and empirical methods and intuition, on the other, can and do provide justifications are recommendations to consider to use speech, or not to use speech, or to consider to use speech rather than some alternative modality, or not to do so, or to consider using speech on certain stated conditions – given certain properties of the design space under consideration as characterized by the requirement and design specifications. Such design recommendations are important in early design and development because they serve to constrain the design space with respect to the available candidate modalities for the design task. It follows that the recommendations may in principle be overridden by other design considerations, such as, to take a simple example, the absence of speech synthesizers in the machines to be used for an application for which synthetic speech would otherwise have been a good choice. In other words, predicting speech applicability, or predicting modality applicability in general, is always a "ceteris paribus" matter: if everything else equally favours the competing modalities, then use modality Mx because of its modality property MPy.

Conclusion

The conclusion is that Modality Theory represents a principled and stable approach whose justificatory power might well be made available to system and interface designers who have to make modality choices during the early design stage of speech-related systems and interfaces. Empirical studies will still be needed of important, high-complexity speech interaction problems. If this conclusion is true, the next question becomes that of how to actually use available knowledge of modality properties in practical system and interface design. System and interface designers are not likely to find the modality properties presented in Figure 3.8 sufficiently helpful for this purpose. What these properties lack, as they stand, to be of help in design practice, seems first and foremost to be concretization and illustration of their import with respect to practical design decision making. Underneath any generalization lies a wealth of concrete instances, or practical cases, which by way of illustration can help suggest how to understand and apply the generalization. To mention an extremely simple example, MP4 states that acoustic input/output modalities are omnidirectional. MP4 justifies Claim 9 that speech output can be displayed to several people simultaneously. A link between MP4 and Claim 9 might draw attention to the fact which might otherwise be overlooked, that the latter follows from the former.

The follow-up question becomes: how to provide sufficient, and easily accessible, concretization and illustration of the modality properties? One possible solution is to use hypertext links between modality properties, a case base, such as the 120 data points discussed above, the domain variables and their instantiations in the cases. For instance, to view the explanatory scope of a certain modality property one clicks on the property and obtains a series of cases which that property has justified, supported or corrected. Or to view a representative list of instantiations of a domain variable one clicks on the variable and obtains its instantiations in the case base. How to do this cannot be shown in a static graphic medium, such as the present book, but has been illustrated in Bernsen (1998a).

4. *Interaction Model Analysis and Design*

4.1 Introduction

Iterative Development of the Design Specification

Interaction model analysis and design is a core issue in the development of advanced interactive speech systems (cf. Section 5.4). It starts at a low speed in the survey phase, is the focal point in the analysis and design phase, and continues during subsequent phases alternating with evaluation (Figure 3.1). Revisions always require analysis, and some form of re-design may be needed as late as in the acceptance test phase. In the analysis and design phase the aim is to develop the interaction model to such a level of formal detail that it can serve as a basis for implementation. The design specification initiated during the survey (Section 3.2) serves as a basis for establishing an interaction model for the system to be developed. The design specification is iteratively extended in the analysis and design phase because many new questions typically arise during interaction model design. These questions must be addressed, new design decisions made and conflicts arising from design decision making resolved, often through trade-offs among conflicting constraints. Results in terms of new design goals, constraints and modifications are added to the design specification and the development of the interaction model is continued on this evolving basis.

Development of the First Interaction Model

As shown in Figure 3.1, interaction model development may proceed along two different routes. Given a first version of the interaction model, one may either proceed straight to implementation, following the implement–test–revise strategy, or one may choose to simulate the interaction model before implementation. We discuss simulation in Chapter 5 and implementation in Chapter 6. However, both of these strategies assume the existence of what might be called *a first interaction model*. It is tempting to think that the first interaction model must be much more specific and formal to serve the implement–test–revise strategy than it has to be if simulation is to precede implementation. This is true to the extent that the simulation strategy is often chosen when it is too difficult to build a sufficiently specific model straight away. Nevertheless, one may also save significant resources by designing an interaction model which is as detailed as possible prior to simulation.

The factors to consider in developing the first interaction model are all or most of the elements of interactive speech theory discussed in Chapter 2, no matter whether the purpose is simulation prior to implementation or straight implementation. Tools and methods in support of first interaction model development are almost non-existent. Today's first interaction model development for advanced interactive speech systems is based primarily on common sense, the individual designer's experience and intuition, and trial and error, rather than on established interaction development guidelines. If the designers are not very careful, in addition to being lucky, many problems of interaction may still remain, only discovered during simulation, implementation and later tests of the system. Best practice tools or methods for interaction model development are therefore needed. A sound and comprehensive set of interaction design guidelines might serve as an efficient and systematic development and evaluation tool during early analysis and design. This could significantly reduce development time by reducing the efforts needed for lengthy simulation experiments, modifications of implemented models, controlled user testing and field trial cycles, thereby reducing overall development cost. We shall present one such tool in this chapter.

cooperativity Guidelines

During the development of the Danish Dialogue System we developed a set of guidelines for the design of cooperative spoken human–machine interaction. An initial set of guidelines was produced on the basis of a corpus of simulated human–machine dialogues from the Wizard of Oz experiments to be described in Chapter 5. These guidelines were then compared to a body of maxims for cooperative human–human conversation, leading to refinement of the guidelines. The resulting set of guidelines was then tested as a tool for the diagnostic evaluation of spoken interaction in the controlled user test of the implemented Danish Dialogue System. We present the test and its results in Chapter 8. In this chapter, the guidelines are presented as a whole in Section 4.2. Individual guidelines are exemplified in Section 4.3. Their development is described in Section 4.4.

4.2   Guidelines for cooperative Interaction Design

The Call For Guidelines

The call for guidelines in support of interaction model design is not new. Baber (1993b) reviewed the need for interactive speech system design guidelines, considering examples such as Grice's well-established conversational maxims of human–human spoken conversation (Grice, 1975) and Schneidermann's "eight golden rules" for the general design of human–computer interaction (Schneidermann, 1987). Baber concluded that it is not obvious how to use the Gricean maxims for developing interactive speech system design guidelines and that general rules, such as those of Schneidermann, lack the clarity and specificity needed to support interactive speech system design.

cooperativity is a Key to Successful Interaction Design

Current interactive speech system design is subject to many constraints on the interaction between user and system. These constraints partly derive from the technology, partly from engineering skill limitations reflecting the immaturity of the field and partly from insufficient theoretical foundations. As argued in Chapter 2, interaction design is complex and not fully understood. Yet it is clearly possible to design fully usable or habitable advanced interactive speech systems for certain classes of task.

A key to successful interaction design, we claim, is to ensure *adequate co-operativity on the part of the system during interaction.* Habitable user–system interaction requires that not only the user but also the *system's* interaction behaviour be cooperative. This is a crucial interaction design goal in order to facilitate smooth interaction in domain communication, meta-communication and other types of communication. Miscommunication always leads to additional user–system exchanges and causes bumpy interaction. cooperative communication facilitates smooth interaction and prevents unnecessary user-initiated clarification and repair meta-communication, as well as other kinds of unexpected user behaviour with which the system cannot cope. This is important because, with current technologies, the possibilities of on-line handling of clarification and repair meta-communication are seriously limited. It is sometimes assumed that, as long as the system has powerful meta-communication abilities, it matters less how it behaves during domain communication. This is already false because the generation of bumpy interaction is always inefficient and induces user dissatisfaction. What is worse, however, is that really powerful meta-communication abilities are not feasible today. User needs for clarification meta-communication that arise from the way the system addresses the domain can easily surpass its meta-communication skills. For instance, if the system uses a patently ambiguous term it is unlikely that it will be able to respond sensibly to the user who asks what the system means by that term; and, if the user unknowingly selects a non-intended meaning of an ambiguous term, the interaction may be well underway towards failure without the system being able to do much about it.

Meta-communication and Levels of Communication as Aspects of cooperativity

What we would like to argue, therefore, is that high-quality, on-line repair and clarification meta-communication skills only constitute one aspect of what it means to have a cooperative system. Such skills are, of course, needed and important. In particular the speech recognition capabilities of interactive speech systems are still fragile. Meta-communication functionality is needed to overcome the effects of system misrecognitions. Users will also sometimes need to have the system's latest utterance repeated, for instance because they did not pay enough attention to what the system just said. Beyond these two unavoidable types of user-initiated repair meta-communication, however, the *system* should not cause the need for other kinds of clarification and repair meta-communication. As we shall see, it is particularly important to avoid all or most forms of user-initiated clarification meta-communication. *Users* are likely to cause the need for additional meta-communication functionality, but that is a different matter which may sometimes pose hard problems to interaction model developers, as we shall see in Chapter 8. The *levels of interaction* concept (Chapter 2) is another aspect of system cooperativity. It is useful for preventing transaction failure when user input is particularly difficult to recognize or understand. However, system cooperativity requires more than meta-communication and graceful degradation.

The Guidelines as an Operationalization of cooperativity

Speaking generally, the system should always behave in a way which optimizes the likelihood that the cooperative user gets the task done. At any stage during interaction the cooperative user should know what to do and how to do it, without having been misled or left without guidance by a non-cooperative system. cooperative interaction design addresses all forms of system communication, and it might well be asked whether there is anything else to good interaction design apart from the design of a cooperative system. Perhaps there is, and politeness design might be a case in point but we shall not address this issue in what follows. The practical problem therefore becomes: how to design cooperative system behaviour? To our knowledge, this question has not been addressed in any systematic way. Answering the question appears to generate a potentially useful set of guidelines for cooperative spoken interaction design. The guidelines are shown in Figure 4.1.

The guidelines in Figure 4.1 represent a first approximation to an operational definition of system cooperativity in task-oriented, shared-goal interaction. Their purpose is that of achieving the shared goal as directly and smoothly as possible. It is exactly when a guideline is violated that miscommunication is likely to occur, which again may seriously damage the user's task performance.

Interaction Aspects, Generic and Specific Guidelines

The guidelines cover seven different *aspects* of interaction as shown in Figure 4.1. The distinction between guideline and aspect is important because an aspect serves to highlight the property of interaction addressed by a particular guideline, thus identifying dimensions of cooperativity over and above the level of the cooperative guidelines themselves.

We distinguish between generic and specific guidelines. A *generic guideline* is general and typically states: "Do (make, be, avoid, provide, etc.) X". A generic guideline may subsume one or more *specific guidelines* related to the generic guideline in a *kind-of* relationship. Specific guidelines specialize the generic guideline to certain classes of phenomena. Although subsumed by generic guidelines, the specific guidelines are important in interaction design because they serve to elaborate what the interaction model developer should be looking for when designing cooperative system behaviour.

Guidelines May Overlap and Conflict

It should be noted that guidelines may support one another as well as conflict when applied during actual interaction design. When guidelines conflict, the designers have to trade-off different design options against one another, with each option having a different weighting of the guidelines. When designing a system introduction, for instance, developers may find that GG2 (don't say too much) conflicts with GG1 (say enough), SG4 (tell what the system can and cannot do) and SG5 (instruct on how to interact with the system). If the introduction is long and complex, and even if all the points made are valid and important, users tend to get bored and inattentive. On the other hand, if the introduction is brief, or even non-existent, important

Interaction Aspect	G/S G no.	Generic or Specific Guideline
Aspect 1: **Informa tiveness**	GG1	*Make your contribution as informative as is required (for the current purposes of the exchange).
	SG1	Be fully explicit in communicating to users the commitments they have made.
	SG2	Provide feedback on each piece of information provided by the user.
	GG2	*Do not make your contribution more informative than is required.
Aspect 2: **Truth and evidence**	GG3	*Do not say what you believe to be false.
	GG4	*Do not say that for which you lack adequate evidence.
Aspect 3: **Relevance**	GG5	*Be relevant, i.e. be appropriate to the immediate needs at each stage of the transaction.
Aspect 4: **Manner**	GG6	*Avoid obscurity of expression.
	GG7	*Avoid ambiguity.
	SG3	Provide same formulation of the same question (or address) to users everywhere in the system's interaction turns.
	GG8	*Be brief (avoid unnecessary prolixity).
	GG9	*Be orderly.
Aspect 5: **Partner asymmetry**	GG10	Inform the users of important non-normal characteristics which they should take into account in order to behave cooperatively in spoken interaction. Ensure the feasibility of what is required of them.
	SG4	Provide clear and comprehensible communication of what the system can and cannot do.
	SG5	Provide clear and sufficient instructions to users on how to interact with the system.
Aspect 6: **Background knowledge**	GG11	Take partners' relevant background knowledge into account.
	SG6	Take into account possible (and possibly erroneous) user inferences by analogy from related task domains.
	SG7	Separate whenever possible between the needs of novice and expert users (user-adaptive interaction).
	GG12	Take into account legitimate partner expectations as to your own background knowledge.
	SG8	Provide sufficient task domain knowledge and inference.
Aspect 7: **Repair and clarification**	GG13	Enable repair or clarification meta-communication in case of communication failure.
	SG9	Initiate repair meta-communication if system understanding has failed.
	SG10	Initiate clarification meta-communication in case of inconsistent user input.
	SG11	Initiate clarification meta-communication in case of ambiguous user input.

Figure 4.1: Guidelines for co-operative system interaction. GG means generic guideline, SG means specific guideline. Generic guidelines are expressed at the level of the Gricean maxims (marked *), and are grouped into their aspect of interaction. Each specific guideline is subsumed by a generic guideline.

information may have been left out increasing the likelihood of miscommunication during task performance.

4.3   Guidelines Illustrated and Explained

In this section we look at each guideline in turn, providing a justification of the guideline followed by commented examples of its application. The presentation is ordered by aspect of interaction, generic guidelines expressing that aspect and specific guidelines subsumed by each generic guideline. Each guideline is expressed in abbreviated command form followed by its "canonical" expression in Figure 4.1. Based on observation of the effects of guideline violation, justifications refer to the nature of the damage that may be done to user–system interaction if a guideline is violated. The examples consist of fragments of user–system interaction and are shown in the left-hand columns of the figures below. Comments are provided in the right-hand columns. Comments on guideline violations include suggestions for repair of the problem illustrated by the violations. In the examples, S means system and U means user. ••• indicates that part of the transcribed interaction has been omitted. Text in square brackets in the left-hand column provides context for the interaction fragment. After each comment in the right-hand column a reference in square brackets refers to the dialogue from which the example commented on was drawn. All examples derive from user dialogues with the Danish Dialogue System during various stages of its development, from Wizard of Oz (WOZ) simulations (indicated by WOZxSyDz, i.e. WOZ iteration x, subject y, dialogue z) to the user test of the implemented system (indicated by user test, followed by a unique dialogue identifier).

Interaction Aspect 1: Informativeness

The first group of two generic and two specific guidelines address the amount of information that should be provided in an interaction turn.

GG1: *Say enough*
   Make your contribution as informative as is required (for the current purposes of the exchange).
   If the system's contribution is not sufficiently informative, this will typically lead to misunderstanding which may only be detected much later during interaction or, at best, lead to an immediate request for clarification by the user. Requests for clarification tend to be difficult for the system to handle. GG1 is illustrated in Figure 4.2.
   The two specific guidelines subsumed by GG1 elaborate on how to say enough in an interaction turn, given the context.

SG1 (GG1): *State commitments explicitly*
   Be fully explicit in communicating to users the commitments they have made.
   In spoken human–machine interaction design, as well as in spoken human–human conversation, it is good practice to summarize the commitments made during the dialogue to make sure that the key information exchanged has been correctly understood. This is sometimes called "summarizing feedback". "Commitment" means that the user has made a commitment to do, buy, etc., something. Examples

are ticket reservation, hotel room booking, and agreeing on a meeting date and hour. In information tasks, as distinct from ordering (or reservation) tasks, there are no such user commitments and hence no possibility of applying SG1. In the absence of summarizing feedback, the user does not get a final opportunity to detect misunderstandings that occurred earlier in the interaction. When the flight ticket for the wrong day arrives, it may be too late to do anything about it. SG1 is illustrated in Figure 4.3.

S: Are you particularly interested in discount? U: Yes. ••• S: At which time? U: It must be on Saturday at 7:20. S: There is no departure at 7:20. The closest other red departure is at 10:50.	**Violation:** The system withholds important (non-requested) information. The user is not being told that there is a *blue* departure at 7:20. The system should have said that there is no red departure but that there is a blue departure at the chosen hour. [User test, T32a]
S: There is no departure at 21:00. The closest other red departures are at 19:45 and 22:40. Do you want one of these departures? U: Yes. S: Which? U: Repeat. S: There is no departure at 21:00. Which one?	**Violation:** The system withholds requested information. It only repeats part of its previous response excluding the list of possible departures. The easiest solution is to let the system repeat its entire previous utterance since it is impossible to know in advance which part a user will be most interested in having repeated. [User test, G33a]
S: Do you want more? U: Yes, I have two people who are going to Aalborg on Monday January 23 in the morning.	**Violation:** The system question is too open and non-specific. It invites the user to take the initiative and say all sorts of things. The question should be rephrased into: 'Do you want to make another reservation?', since this is essentially what was intended and what the system can handle. [User test, T31a1]
S: At which time? U: Afternoon. S: In the afternoon on Sunday January 29 there is a departure from Sønderborg to Copenhagen at 17:00. Do you want this departure?	**Full departure information as requested:** The system provides a full list of existing departures (in this case only one) within the time interval indicated by the user. [User test, G13b]

Figure 4.2: Examples of GG1: say enough.

SG2 (GG1): *Provide immediate feedback*
  Provide feedback on each piece of information provided by the user.
  In interactive speech system design it is good practice to provide some kind of immediate feedback on each of those pieces of information provided by the user which are intended to contribute to the achievement of the goal of the dialogue, such as making a flight ticket reservation. Among other things, speech recognizers are still fragile and this is one reason why it is more likely that misunderstandings will occur in human–machine interaction than in human–human interaction. The sooner misunderstandings can be corrected, the better. Immediate feedback provides users with an opportunity to detect misunderstandings immediately. A problem with immediate feedback is that it tends to make the interaction somewhat "heavier" than corresponding human–human exchanges. This is why various forms of "lightweight" feedback have been introduced as shown in the examples below, preserving full explicit feedback for the more difficult cases in which something has already gone wrong or there is a high risk of understanding failure. Full, immediate explicit feedback is an example of graceful degradation. SG2 is illustrated in Figure 4.4.

[The user has made a change to a ticket which was booked earlier. Another person is going to travel instead.] S: Do you want to make other changes to this reservation? U: No I don't. S: Do you want more? U: Ah no ... I mean is it okay then? S: The reservation with reference number 420 has been changed into a ticket for Aksel Hansen with id-number 23. U: Yes that's fine. S: Do you want more?	**Violation:** The interaction had been designed such that no summarizing feedback was provided on the commitments made by the user. A summary of the commitments made during the interaction allows the user to easily detect if everything has been correctly understood. In the example, the wizard improvises a confirmation when directly asked for it. [WOZ6, S12D2]
S: You have now booked one ticket for id-number 2 Jens Kristiansen from Aalborg to Copenhagen on Monday January 16th at 7:20 returning on Monday January 16th at 17:45. Your reference number is 52. The total price is 1410 kroner.	**Commitment to buy a ticket:** When, towards the end of a reservation dialogue, the system has all the information needed to book a flight ticket, it communicates explicitly to the user the commitments s/he has made. [User test, G14a]

Figure 4.3: Examples of SG1: state commitments explicitly.

GG2: *Don't say too much*
Do not make your contribution more informative than is required.

The user may become inattentive or try to take the initiative if too much information is being provided in a single system turn. Also, the user may become confused about the actual interaction focus and the point of relevance, initiating, for instance, clarification meta-communication as a result. However, guideline GG2

S:	Do you want a return ticket?	**Violation:** Boldface shows overlapping user speech. There is no immediate system feedback on the user's answer to the question whether s/he wants a return ticket. This makes it difficult to detect misunderstandings at once unless one knows the system and/or the domain well. Discount is not offered on one-way tickets. However, if the user does not know this (which in the current case s/he apparently does not), the misunderstanding will only show later in the interaction when the system asks for a return date. To solve the problem, the system should provide immediate feedback. [User test, T21a]
U:	No, we will book that one later. [Pause] **It's okay. They are not going back.**	
S:	Red discount may be obtained on certain weekday departures and green discount may be obtained in weekends. In case of red discount the home journey may only start after two days at the earliest. Are you particularly interested in discount?	
S:	Where does the journey start?	**Echo feedback:** The system echoes the key contents of the user's input. This allows the user to detect a misunderstanding immediately. No extra turns are needed if the input was correctly understood because the system does not ask the user for explicit confirmation. [User test, T32a]
U:	The journey starts in Aalborg.	
S:	From Aalborg. Where does the journey end?	
U:	In Copenhagen.	
S:	In Copenhagen. Do you want a return ticket?	
S:	At which time?	**Implicit feedback:** The system provides implicit feedback by including in its answer which date and time of the day it is talking about. [User test, G13b]
U:	Afternoon.	
S:	In the afternoon on Sunday January 29th there is a departure from Sønderborg to Copenhagen at 17:00. Do you want this departure?	
S:	One person. Please state the id-number of this person.	**Explicit feedback:** The system provides explicit feedback by asking the user to confirm whether the information it has is correct. [User test, G11b]
U:	Change.	
S:	One person. Is that correct?	

Figure 4.4: Examples of SG2: provide immediate feedback.

must be fairly heavily violated to produce an interaction problem that may endanger the success of the interaction. In most cases GG2 problems will be revealed through users' subsequent comments and opinions on the system. GG2 is illustrated in Figure 4.5.

U: I want information on discount for children. **S:** Accompanied children between 2 and 11 years of age may obtain discount on return journeys: red discount at 323 kroner or green discount at 400 kroner. Children between 12 and 19 years of age may obtain green discount at 550 kroner. Red and green discount can only be obtained on certain departures. Children less than two years old do not need a separate ticket if accompanied by an adult. Do you want information on other discount possibilities? **U:** Hmm .. I want to know more on children. What about children travelling alone?	**Violation:** A user in WOZ5 complained that the system talked far too much, that she got bored during interaction and that she had forgotten what she wanted when she was finally allowed to speak. This complaint probably does not refer to any particular point in the quoted system turn but rather to its overall design. In particular, the system talked too much when providing information on travel conditions. The quoted system answer perhaps is not exceptionally long in itself. However, if most system turns are this long and if the user does not really get the information s/he wants because navigation in system directed information tasks tends to be cumbersome, then users may easily feel that the system talks far too much. In such cases, the entire dialogue structure should be examined to remove superfluous material. [WOZ5, S3D5]

Figure 4.5: An example of GG2: don't say too much.

Interaction Aspect 2: Truth and Evidence

The aspect of truth and evidence is addressed by two generic guidelines which state that if one believes something to be false, or if one does not have sufficient evidence that something is in fact true, then one should not make others believe that it is true. These guidelines are evidently quite fundamental to cooperative task-oriented spoken interaction where the whole point of using the system is that it acts as a complete domain expert within its stated domain of competence. Guidelines GG3 and GG4 differ from the rest of the guidelines in that they refer to mental states, such as those of believing something or having evidence for something. All other guidelines appear to be more behavioural in nature, stating what the system should do or avoid doing. Some might question whether present-day computers have anything akin to mental states. Whatever the answer to this philosophical question, however, it is crucial to design the system's interaction, and the system more generally, such that it does not produce false beliefs in its users.

GG3: *Don't lie*

Do not say what you believe to be false.

It is obviously important that the user can trust what the system says. Users have good reason to become annoyed if the system provides them with false information on, for example, departure times, prices or meeting venues. Still, this may happen despite all effort to the contrary by the developers, for instance because of bugs in the database or wizard errors, as the examples demonstrate. GG3 is illustrated in Figure 4.6.

GG4: *Check what you say*

Do not say that for which you lack adequate evidence.

It is not sufficient to believe that something probably is right. For the system this means that it must make sure before giving the information to the user. Otherwise, the implication may be very much the same as for GG3, namely, discontented users. GG4 is illustrated in Figure 4.7.

S: At which time? **U:** Morning. **S:** The green morning departures are fully booked.	**Violation:** According to the flight file the first departure on this particular day is 9:15. This hour is not defined as 'morning' but as 'before noon' by the database (the term 'morgen' in the Danish denoting a more restricted time interval than the English 'morning'). The corresponding flight is not fully booked. Therefore, the system's message should have been that there are no morning departures. Apparently there is a bug in the database which should be found and corrected. [User test, G13b]
S: Id-number 89, Carl Frederiksen has two reservations. One on Friday September 11 from Aalborg to Copenhagen and one on Saturday September 10 from Aalborg to Copenhagen. Is it one of these? **U:** Ahm ...something is wrong because Saturday September 10 must be a Thursday if September 11 is a Friday. Hmm ... Friday September 11 at 7:20.	**Violation:** The system's information on dates clearly cannot be true as pointed out by the user. The error was made by a wizard. Careful domain model design is needed to avoid such problems. [WOZ6, S6D4]

Figure 4.6: Examples of GG3: don't lie.

> **Violation:** We did not observe any violations of GG4 during WOZ and in the user test. An example could have been the following. A user asks for two tickets. The system checks and finds that there are just two free seats left on the desired flight. It then confirms that everything is OK and that the reservation has been made. However, if confirmation is given to the customer before the database has actually made and confirmed the reservations, another customer calling the system at approximately the same time might have managed to book the same two seats. Contrary to the system's confirmation, the former customer gets no tickets. In fact, the travel agency in which we made our corpus recordings had had this problem because they did not have on-line access to the database.

Figure 4.7: An example of GG4: check what you say.

Interaction Aspect 3: Relevance

Irrelevant system utterances are such which do not address the current topic of the interaction. Just as system developers are likely to be vigilant in ensuring database correctness (cf. GG3 and GG4), interaction designers can be expected to generally avoid designing irrelevant system utterances. When relevance problems occur, they are often produced by factors other than the interaction design itself.

GG5: *Be relevant*
    Be relevant, i.e. be appropriate to the immediate needs at each stage of the transaction.
    Lack of relevance in the system's utterances will typically lead to clarification dialogue. The user will want to ask what the interaction is about at all or what the system meant by what it just said. System irrelevance may be caused by misrecognition.

S: At which date will the journey start? **U:** The journey starts on January 23. **S:** Today is not the 23rd of January.	**Violation:** A system misrecognition (grammar failure) triggers an error message which is rather irrelevant to the user, who did not mention today. In the present case the system clearly should be able to correctly parse what was said. So the grammar needs modification. Recognition failure is more difficult. Threshold values (score values) for evaluating the probability of correct recognition might be helpful. These would allow the system to initiate repair if the score is too low rather than producing a response which in all likelihood is based on misunderstanding. [User test, G22a]

Figure 4.8: An example of GG5: be relevant.

In such cases it may be hard to avoid violation of the guideline. The system's reply may be perfectly relevant given its interpretation of the user's utterance but totally irrelevant given what the user actually said. GG5 is illustrated in Figure 4.8.

Interaction Aspect 4: Manner

The aspect of manner concerns the way in which intended meaning is being expressed. Whereas it is rather unlikely for developers to forget to design databases and interaction according to the guidelines of truth, evidence and relevance discussed above, it is much easier to design infelicitous expressions which violate the guidelines of manner. However, the misleading effects on users, if this happens, can be disastrous.

GG6: *Avoid obscurity*
Avoid obscurity of expression.
Obscurity naturally leads to doubt and need for clarification in the user. As emphasized above, the system is unlikely to be able to understand and respond appropriately to most clarification sub-dialogues initiated by the user. GG6 is illustrated in Figure 4.9.

S: At which time? **U:** He wants to depart at 10:45. **S:** There is no departure at 10:45, the closest other departure is at 17:00. Do you want this departure?	**Violation:** The system provides misleading information since the departure at 17:00 is the only departure that day. The user is left in doubt as to whether there might be an earlier departure. S/he therefore proposes an earlier departure no less than three times during the subsequent interaction (not shown) but is still only offered the departure at 17:00 hrs. The system should have said that the departure at 17:00 is the only departure on that day. [User test, T53a]
S: At which time? **U:** Before noon. **S:** In the morning on Friday January 27th there is a departure from Copenhagen to Karup at 9:10 and 11:50 sold out. Do you want this departure?	**Violation:** The system's answer is difficult to understand because of its incorrect grammar. The intended meaning is that only the 9:10 departure has free seats whereas the departure at 11:50 is already fully booked. The output phrase should be rewritten in a grammatically correct and non-obscure form. [User test, G11b]

Figure 4.9: Examples of GG6: avoid obscurity.

GG7: *Avoid ambiguity*
Avoid ambiguity.

Ambiguity creates a need for clarification *if* detected by the user. If undetected, as often happens, the effects of ambiguity can be even worse. If the user unknowingly selects a non-intended meaning of a word or phrase uttered by the system, all sorts of things can go wrong leading to repair meta-communication or even transaction failure. GG7 is illustrated in Figure 4.10.

The specific guideline subsumed by GG7 expresses a strategy for avoiding ambiguity in a relatively limited class of situations.

S: Hello, this is the DanLuft reservation service for flights between Copenhagen and Aalborg. Please answer the following questions briefly and one at a time. You may answer "interrupt" whenever you want. Do you want to have information, make a reservation or change a reservation? ••• **S:** Do you want more? **U:** No thanks. I interrupt.	**Violation:** The keyword "interrupt" was intended to act as a command which would suspend domain communication and allow meta-communication to start. However, the intended meaning of the keyword was never explained to users. Users interpreted the keyword as shown in the example, i.e. as a signal that one wants to break off the interaction. To break off is probably the most frequent meaning of the word "interrupt" in Danish. The keyword "interrupt" should either be explained or, preferably, replaced by a contextually non-ambiguous command. [WOZ6, S11D2]
S: Where does the journey start? **U:** It starts in Hellerup.	**Violation:** Hellerup is not the name of an airport. It is a suburb of Copenhagen and is not in the system's vocabulary. The user rightly considers that the journey starts at home, that is in Hellerup, rather than at the airport. A more precise and unambiguous system question would be to explicitly ask for the departure airport. [User test, T52a]

Figure 4.10: Examples of GG7: avoid ambiguity.

SG3 (GG7): *Ensure uniformity*
Provide the same formulation of the same question (or address) to users everywhere in the system's interaction turns.

Given similar contexts, different formulations of, for instance, the same question will not necessarily be interpreted in the same way by users. Even a uniform formulation of, for example, the same question may be interpreted differently if there are no domain restrictions. However, in limited domains, such as those of interactive speech systems, use of uniform formulations in similar contexts tends to remove all ambiguity. An added advantage is that the use of uniform formulations helps reduce users' vocabulary because users tend to model the phrases used by the system. Note that SG3 is most emphatically *not* appropriate during graceful degradation. If the user does not understand what the system says or the user's response is not understood by the system, the last thing the system should do is to mechanically repeat itself. SG3 is illustrated in Figure 4.11.

GG8:   *Be brief*
    Be brief (avoid unnecessary prolixity).
    The user may become bored and inattentive or may try to take over the initiative if the system talks too much. This guideline must be fairly heavily violated to cause a real interaction problem. Rather, the problem will be revealed through users' comments and opinions on the system. GG8 is illustrated in Figure 4.12.

S: At which time does the flight you want leave? **U:** I don't know. **S:** At which time? **U:** On Friday evening.	**Violation:** In the early WOZ iterations there were many examples of different formulations of the same system question or answer. In this example, the first question may be interpreted as a request for a precise hour of departure which the user apparently does not know. The second question, however, is interpreted more broadly and gives the user the opportunity to provide a time interval. [WOZ3, S0D4]
S: At which time?	**Same formulation wrt. hour of departure:** The system uses the same formulation when it asks for the hour of departure no matter whether the topic is the out journey or the return journey. [User test, T24a]

Figure 4.11: Examples of SG3: ensure uniformity.

S: Which time of the day are we talking about? **U:** We are talking about 17:45.	**Violation:** The lengthy formulation of the question is unnecessary. Moreover, the user is being made to model the superfluous part of the question. This results in an unnecessarily long user answer. Compare the following example. [WOZ5, S2D2]
S: At which time? **U:** 7:20.	**Brief question on hour of departure:** The system question is stated very briefly and so is the user's answer. [User test, G14a]

Figure 4.12: Examples of GG8: be brief.

GG9: *Be orderly*

Be orderly.

The system should address the task-relevant topics of interaction in an order which is as close as possible to the order expected by the user. If the user expects some topic to come up early during interaction, that topic's non-occurrence at its expected "place" may cause a user-initiated clarification sub-dialogue which the system cannot cope with. Studying the structure of human–human conversation in the domain for which the system is being designed may provide useful clues to orderly interaction design. GG9 is illustrated in Figure 4.13.

S: On which date will the return journey start? **U:** Preferably Sunday. **S:** At which time do you want a departure? **U:** I would like a departure late in the afternoon. Is there ah ... any kind of discount possibility?	**Violation:** In the WOZ3 iteration we found several problems of the kind illustrated in the example. Having expected the topic of discount to come up for some time, users began to inquire about discount when approaching the end of the interaction. From WOZ6 onwards, users were asked early on whether they are interested in discount fares, thus blocking impatient questions about discount possibilities. [WOZ3, S0D6]
See the dialogue in Figure 2.3.	**Orderly dialogue structure:** The interaction structure for flight reservation was carefully designed to be as naturally ordered as possible. Among other things, this was done by studying the structure of human-human conversation concerning the same task.

Figure 4.13: Examples of GG9: be orderly.

Interaction Aspect 5: Partner Asymmetry

Interaction partner asymmetry means that important differences exist between the interlocutors which are likely to influence the course and eventual success of the interaction. When learning to speak we implicitly learn what is a "normal" or "standard" partner in spoken interaction. Unless otherwise told, we assume that our partner(s) in an interaction is "normal" or "standard". If it turns out that this is not the case, we are trained to adjust our manner of speaking to the partner's abilities, such as when speaking to children, the poor of hearing or interlocutors who find themselves in noisy environments. The computer is, in many respects, a non-standard partner in spoken interaction and strongly needs to make its users aware of this fact on the penalty of generating all sorts of miscommunication which it cannot possibly handle.

GG10: *Highlight asymmetries*

Inform interaction partners of important non-normal characteristics which they should take into account in order to behave cooperatively during interaction. Ensure the feasibility of what is required of them.

GG10 is an important and slightly complex guideline. In addition to guidelines stating how the *system itself* should behave to act cooperatively during interaction, such as the ones discussed above, guidelines are needed according to which the system should *transfer* part of the responsibility for cooperation to the user. Failure to do so will demonstrate that the system is not a cooperative speech partner. The guideline is that the non-normal interaction partner should inform its partners of the particular non-normal characteristics which they should take into account in order to act cooperatively. Consider an example from human–human conversation. To be cooperative, the human interlocutor who is in a noisy environment should inform the partners in conversation that this is the case. Having done that, it will be up to the partners to demonstrate their cooperativity by suitable modifications of their conversational behaviour. In human–human conversation this is normally accomplished without significant difficulty. Designers of spoken human–machine interaction can rely on the same flexibility in their intended human users, provided that the system actually does inform its users about its important non-normal characteristics, as stated in the first part of GG10. However, the interaction designers may easily ignore the crucial precondition stated in the second part of GG10. It is that what they demand of the system's users should actually be feasible for them to do. In other words, it is *not* sufficient for co-operative interaction design that the system tells the users that, to be understood by the system, they have to do X. The reason is that doing X may not be *cognitively* feasible for the users. Owing to problems of cognitive overload or other factors, they may simply be unable to do what the system requires them to do during inter-action; and if they are thus unable, then it will be difficult for the users to get their task done through interaction with the system. Therefore, the user coopera-tivity asked for by the system should be feasible for its users. If it is not, difficult or impossible cases of miscommunication may proliferate. GG10 is illustrated in Figure 4.14.

The specific guidelines subsumed by GG10 concern communication of what the system can and cannot do, and instructions on how to interact with the system.

SG4 (GG10): *State your capabilities*

Provide clear and comprehensible communication of what the system can and cannot do.

It should be made clear to users what the system knows about, what it does not know about and what its limitations are as a partner in spoken interaction. Users should not waste time on interaction which eventually will show that the system does not possess the knowledge they look for. Nor should they be misled into attributing to the system more advanced comprehension skills than it actually possesses. As discussed in Section 2.7, making these things sufficiently clear to users can be dif-ficult indeed. SG4 is of particular importance in walk-up-and-use systems where users cannot be expected to have access to independent, e.g. written, information about the system. SG4 is illustrated in Figure 4.15.

U:	Yes, please. I would like to have 9:40.	**Violation:** In its introduction, the system has asked its users to use the keyword 'change' if they want to take the initiative in order to make a correction to the system's understanding of some previous utterance of theirs. During the actual interaction, however, the user is too preoccupied with the ticket reservation problem at hand to remember to use the designer-designed keyword 'change'. It is simply unnatural for the user to use a specific keyword in situations such as the one illustrated. More natural mixed-initiative meta-communication should be allowed. [User test, T22a]
S:	22:40. At which date will the return journey start?	
U:	No, 9:40.	
S:	At which time?	**Violation:** In its introduction, the system has asked its users to answer its questions briefly and one at a time. In this example, the user is in fact being brief and only answers the question asked by the system. However, instead of providing a straight answer, the user provides an indirect answer. In human-human conversation, indirect answers such as the one illustrated are perfectly correct answers. An indirect response simply indicates that the interlocutor does not possess the information necessary to provide a direct answer. In response to the indirect user answer shown, a human travel agent would list the relevant departures. An interactive speech system, however, having limited inferential capabilities, will be unable to cope with most indirect responses. It is the task of the interaction model designer to either prevent indirect responses, such as the one illustrated, from happening, or enable the system to understand indirect responses of this type. [User test, T34a]
U:	They must arrive at 9:30 at the latest.	
S:	At which time?	**Violation:** In its introduction, the system has asked its users to answer its questions and only take the initiative by using one of the two keywords 'change' and 'repeat'. Nevertheless, the user in this example asks a question and thus takes the initiative. What the example shows is that reservation dialogue, in its very nature, so to speak, is *informed reservation* dialogue. It is natural for users who are going to make a reservation or, more generally, order something, that they do not always possess the full information needed to decide what to do. In such cases, they ask for the information. Since the system poses as a perfect domain expert, this is legitimate. What users overlook, however, and despite what was said in the system's introduction, is that the system does not have the skills to process their questions. Again, the interaction designers
U:	Which possibilities are there?	

Figure 4.14: Examples of GG10: highlight asymmetries (*continued next page*).

Figure 4.14 (*continued*)

		have failed to take into account that users should only be asked to do what is feasible for them. [User test, T12a]
S:	On which date will the journey start?	**Violation:** In its introduction, the system has asked users to answer its questions briefly and one at a time. However, in the shown example the user answers two questions at a time. What this suggests is that users sometimes naturally store information in "packages" consisting of several pieces of information. In such cases, they are unlikely to consistently split these packages into single pieces of information despite having been told to do so by the system. This must be taken into account when designing the system's input understanding capabilities. [User test, T31a1]
U:	The journey starts on Friday January 20 at 8:15.	

S:	Customer number 2. Is that correct?	**Violation:** Boldface shows overlapping user speech. The user tries to make a change. However, the system does not listen during its own turns. Users were not informed on this as they should have been. [User test, T31a2]
U:	No id-numbers 1 and 4.	
S:	Customer number 4.	
U:	**Wrong, the customer number is 2.**	
S:	How many people will travel?	
S:	At 19:50.	**Violation:** Boldface shows overlapping user speech. The example shows a phatic expression which overlaps with the system's turn. This is a common way for humans to express that the conversation is being followed with interest during the interlocutor's turn. Pauses, in particular, may be filled this way. In such cases it does not matter that the system does not listen during its own turns. However, users were not informed on this as they should have been. [User test, T41a]
U:	**Yes.**	
S:	You have now booked ...	
S:	Hello, this is the DanLuft reservation service for domestic flights. Do you know how to use this system?	**Communication of what the system can do:** The system informs the user from the very beginning on which task it can solve. [User test, T11a]
U:	No.	
S:	The system can reserve tickets for Danish domestic flights.	

Figure 4.15: Examples of SG4: state your capabilities.

SG5 (GG10): *State how to interact*

Provide clear and sufficient instructions to users on how to interact with the system.

Like SG4, SG5 addresses both the system's task capabilities and its communication capabilities. If the system is unable to handle some task in a standard way or is only able to handle the task in one of several standard ways, this should be communicated to users to prevent interaction failure. If the system needs particularly reduced forms of user input, this should also be stated or otherwise clearly communicated. SG5 is of particular importance in walk-up-and-use systems where users cannot be expected to have access to independent, e.g. written, information about the system. SG5 is illustrated in Figure 4.16.

Interaction Aspect 6: Background Knowledge

This aspect addresses the fact that the system and its developers need to recognize relevant differences among users and user groups in terms of background knowledge.

S:	At which time?	**Violation:** The user is supposed to book a round-trip ticket and, as is common, perceives the task as one of booking a return ticket. Round-trip tickets, however, can only be handled by the system as two separate single reservations. When asked about the home departure hour for the second time, the user tries and fails to input a departure airport for the home journey that is different from the arrival airport for the out journey. The system does not provide information on how to handle round-trips as it should have done. [User test, G54a1-2]
U:	At 18:10.	
S:	There is no departure at 18:10. The closest other departures are at 18:00 and 22:00. Do you want one of these departures?	
U:	No.	
S:	At which time?	
U:	15:45 from Esbjerg.	
S:	The system can reserve tickets for Danish domestic flights. You use it by answering the system's questions. In addition you may use the two special commands 'repeat' and 'change' to have the most recent information repeated or changed. The system will only understand you when you answer its questions briefly and one at a time.	**Instructions on how to interact:** In its introduction, the system informs its users on how to interact with it. However, it turned out that what was required of users was often not feasible for them (cf. the examples under GG10). The use of keywords for repair and clarification meta-communication is not natural. Moreover, information is often naturally packaged, such as date and time together, which means that it may be difficult to answer the system's questions one at a time. [User test, T11a]

Figure 4.16: Examples of SG5: state how to interact.

S:	Red discount may be obtained on certain weekday departures and green discount may be obtained in weekends. In case of red discount the home journey may only start after two days at the earliest.	**Information on discount types:** In particular novice users cannot be expected to have any background knowledge on discount types. The system therefore provides information on these to users who have said earlier that they do not know the system. [User test, G12b]

Figure 4.17: An example of GG11: be aware of users' background knowledge.

These differences not only concern the novice–expert distinction among users but also other types of background knowledge differences, and may even include recognition of widespread *erroneous* background assumptions among users. The system must also take into account the expectations users may have with respect to *the system's* background knowledge. Based on this recognition, the system either has built prior to interaction, or adaptively builds during interaction, a model of the user which serves to guide system cooperativity.

GG11: *Be aware of users' background knowledge*
Take users' relevant background knowledge into account.
The system needs to adjust to users' background knowledge and inferences based thereon. Otherwise, the users may fail to understand the system and initiate clarification meta-communication. GG11 is illustrated in Figure 4.17. We do not currently have any example of a violation of GG11 that is not also a violation of one of its subsumed specific guidelines.

The specific guidelines subsumed by GG11 concern inferences by analogy and the distinction between novices and experts.

SG6 (GG11): *Be aware of user inferences*
Take into account possible (and possibly erroneous) user inferences by analogy from related task domains.
If the system does not take into account possible user inferences by analogy, this may invite users to ask clarification questions or leave them, probably discontentedly so, with unanswered questions. SG6 is illustrated in Figure 4.18.

S:	Do you want more?	**Violation:** The user wants discount and does not know that this is unavailable on one-way tickets. The system should take into account users' background knowledge by mentioning that, if the user has chosen one-way tickets, discount cannot be obtained. [User test, T13a]
U:	Did I get a discount?	

Figure 4.18: An example of SG6: be aware of user inferences.

SG7 (GG11): *Adapt to novices and experts*
Separate whenever possible between the needs of novice and expert users (user-adaptive interaction).

There are major differences between the needs of novice and expert users of the system, one such difference being that the expert users already possess the information needed to understand system functionality. If the system favours expert users, it is likely to fail as a walk-up-and-use system. If it favours novice users, it is likely to be perceived as cumbersome and redundant by expert users. SG7 is illustrated in Figure 4.19.

S: Hello, this is the DanLuft reservation service for domestic flights. Do you know this system? **U:** No. **S:** The system can reserve tickets for Danish domestic flights. You use it by answering the system's questions. In addition you may use the two special commands 'repeat' and 'change' to have the most recent information repeated or changed. The system will only understand you when you answer its questions briefly and one at a time. **S:** Please state your customer number.	**Optional system introduction:** The example shows the system introduction which users will get if they answer 'no' to the first system question. If they answer 'yes' the system will immediately ask for a customer number. [User test, T11a]

Figure 4.19: An example of SG7: adapt to novices and experts.

S: At which time? **U:** 20:10. **S:** The departure at 20:10 is fully booked. The closest other departures are at 19:00 and at 22:05. Do you want one of these departures?	**Violation:** At first sight nothing is wrong here. However, when you call a travel agency and the flight you want is fully booked, you are usually offered to be put on a waiting list. The user pointed this out in a telephone interview after her interaction with the system. She rightly missed this option during interaction and might as well have started asking questions about it during her interaction with the system. The waiting list functionality should be included among the system's capabilities. [WOZ7, S16D3]

Figure 4.20: An example of GG12: be aware of user expectations.

GG12: *Be aware of user expectations*

Take into account legitimate user expectations as to your own background knowledge.

When the system can be assumed to be a perfect expert within its declared domain of expertise, it must possess the amount and types of background knowledge which a user legitimately may expect it to have. If this is not the case, users may become confused or annoyed with what they rightly regard as a deficient system. GG12 is illustrated in Figure 4.20. This illustration might also have been used for SG8.

The specific guideline subsumed by GG12 concerns the system's task domain knowledge and inference capabilities.

SG8 (GG12): *Cover the domain*

Provide sufficient task domain knowledge and inference.

An interactive speech system is often if not always supposed to be a perfect expert within its declared domain of expertise. This includes task domain coverage and relevant inferences. The system must be able to provide the appropriate domain information when and as required by its users. The system must also be able to make appropriate inferences to avoid lengthy and inefficient turn taking which only serves to clarify something which the system could have inferred on its own. SG8 is illustrated in Figure 4.21.

Interaction Aspect 7: Repair and Clarification

This aspect addresses the need for meta-communication design. Meta-communication is typically initiated for purposes of clarification and repair. We do that in human–human spoken conversation when we say, for example, "Please repeat – I didn't hear what you just said" (repair); "Sorry, I said 'recognize speech', not 'wreck a nice beach'" (repair), "Is 'speech recognition' the same as 'speech understanding'?" (clarification) or "What do you mean by 'red departure'?" (clarification). Meta-communication is likely to be needed in all interactive speech systems but should be reduced to a minimum to optimize interaction efficiency.

GG13: *Enable meta-communication*

Enable repair or clarification meta-communication in case of communication failure.

Users as well as systems need to initiate clarification or repair meta-communication from time to time. The need may have many different causes, such as system violation of a cooperativity guideline, user inattention or system misunderstanding. GG13 covers user-initiated repair and clarification meta-communication, as well as system-initiated meta-communication. As said before, user-initiated clarification meta-communication is generally very difficult to handle and should be prevented as far as possible. This is probably true not only for system-directed interaction as in the Danish Dialogue System. GG13 is illustrated in Figure 4.22.

The specific guidelines subsumed by GG13 address system-initiated repair and clarification meta-communication in cases of missing understanding, inconsistent input and ambiguous input.

S:	At which time [out journey]?	**Violation:** The problem concerns the hour of departure for the home journey. The system checks the temporal relationship with the out journey. The home departure time 'a quarter to six' is being understood as AM by default. However, it is not ambiguous in the present context and should have been understood as 17:45. The system should provide a general solution to the class of problems exemplified by: if out and home journey are on the same day and the home departure time is 'a quarter to six' then understand the answer as '17:45'. [User test, T14a]
U:	A quarter past seven. ...	
S:	At which time [home journey, same day]?	
U:	A quarter to six.	
S:	The home journey must not be earlier than the out journey.	
S:	The tickets will be mailed in a couple of days.	**Violation:** There are only two possibilities concerning ticket delivery: tickets may either be mailed or picked up at the airport. Although the user has stated that the tickets should not be mailed, the system does not make the obvious inference but asks again whether tickets should be sent or will be picked up at the airport. The system should not ask superfluous questions but deduce what the user wants when this is obvious. If only two user answers are possible, then understand rejection of one of them as confirmation of the other. [User test, G44a]
U:	Change.	
S:	The tickets should be sent; is this correct?	
U:	No.	
S:	Should the tickets be sent or will they be picked up at the airport?	
S:	On which date will the return journey start?	**Date inference:** The user has asked for a journey starting on January 26. The system correctly infers that when the user then answers 'same day' to the question of return journey, this means January 26. [User test, G34a]
U:	Same day.	
S:	Thursday January 26	
S:	At which time?	**Departure information:** The system provides appropriate information on departures in the given context (the user has asked for discount and a departure time before noon). [User test, G12b]
U:	Before noon.	
S:	Before noon on Wednesday February 1 there is a red departure from Aalborg to Copenhagen at 10:50. Do you want this departure?	

Figure 4.21: Examples of SG8: cover the domain.

S:	id-number 1, Jens Hansen. Where does the journey start?	**User initiated repair:** The system has misunderstood the user's input as regards the id-number of the traveller. The user correctly initiates repair to change the misunderstood information. [User test, T11b]
U:	Change.	
S:	id-number 1, Jens Hansen. Is that correct?	
U:	No, id-number 4.	
S:	There is no departure at 21:00, the closest other red departures are at 19:45 and 22:40. Do you want one of these departures?	**User initiated repair:** The user probably forgot which departure times were mentioned and asks the system to repeat them. [User test, G33a]
U:	Yes.	
S:	Which?	
U:	Repeat.	
S:	Friday evening from Copenhagen to Aalborg there are the following departures: at 17:45, at 19:30 and at 22:15.	**User initiated clarification:** The user wants a discount ticket. Since the system does not provide any information on discount along with the listed departure hours, the user asks for clarification. [WOZ3, S1D2]
U:	Are any of them green departures?	

Figure 4.22: Examples of GG13: enable meta-communication.

SG9 (GG13): *Enable system repair*
Initiate repair meta-communication if system understanding has failed.
If user input cannot be interpreted as meaningful in context, the system needs the ability to ask for repetition or to otherwise indicate that it did not understand what was said. SG9 is illustrated in Figure 4.23.

S:	At which time?	**System-initiated repair:** The word 'cheap' is not in the system's vocabulary and neither of the two user utterances in the example are recognised as meaningful in the context. The system therefore correctly initiates repair, informing the user that the input was not understood. [User test, T13a]
U:	It must be as cheap as possible.	
S:	Sorry. At which time?	
U:	Cheap.	
S:	Sorry, I did not understand.	

Figure 4.23: An example of SG9: enable system repair.

SG10 (GG13): *Enable inconsistency clarification*

Initiate clarification meta-communication in case of inconsistent user input.

If the user's input is inconsistent, clarification becomes necessary. The system should not try to second-guess the user's priorities because if the guess is wrong, the user will have to initiate meta-communication instead, possibly in the form of clarification. SG10 is illustrated in Figure 4.24.

SG11 (GG13): *Enable ambiguity clarification*

Initiate clarification meta-communication in case of ambiguous user input.

If the user's input is ambiguous, clarification becomes necessary. The system should not try to second-guess what the user actually means because if the guess is wrong, the user will have to initiate meta-communication instead, possibly in the form of clarification. SG11 is illustrated in Figure 4.25.

S: Are you particularly interested in discount? **U:** Yes. **S:** On which date will the journey start? **U:** Monday. **S:** Monday January 16. At which time? **U:** At 7:20. **S:** There is no departure at 7:20. The closest other red departure is at 10:50.	**Violation:** The user inconsistently wants both the 7:20 departure and discount. There is, in fact, a departure at 7:20 but it does not offer discount. The system implicitly assigns priority to discount over departure time without sufficient reason. Instead, the system should ask for the user's priorities, saying, for instance: "7:20 is not a discount departure. Red discount can be obtained on the departures at x, y and z. Which departure do you want?" [User test, G14a]

Figure 4.24: An example of SG10: enable inconsistency clarification.

U: Around 7 o'clock. **S:** 19 o'clock. At which date will the return journey start? **U:** Change.	**Violation:** All departure times which may be understood as being before noon (AM), such as 7 o'clock, are automatically understood as such. If there is no flight at the time, the dialogue manager automatically adds 12 hours to the departure time. If there is a flight at this time, input will be interpreted as being PM yielding, in the example, 19 o'clock. This rule does not work in practice. Instead, the system should ask the user for clarification in case of ambiguous temporal input which cannot be resolved by context. [User test, G32a]

Figure 4.25: An example of SG11: enable ambiguity clarification.

Concluding Remarks

In order to discover interaction problems at an early stage, developers need to know what to look for in the emerging interaction model. The guidelines for cooperative spoken interaction design are used by manually evaluating whether each system utterance in isolation, as well as in context, violates any of the generic or specific guidelines. If it does, it is a potential source for communication failure which should be removed. Using the guidelines as design guidelines thus means to apply them to analytical "walk-throughs" through the emerging interaction model for the interactive speech system that is being designed. This requires training and skill. An interactive speech system designer who simply receives the guidelines as represented in Figure 4.1, may not quite know what to do with them in practice. We believe that a representation of the guidelines which includes their justification as well as an extensive set of example violations, as illustrated above, might be of help.

4.4   Development and Justification of the Guidelines

The guidelines for cooperative spoken human–machine interaction have been validated in three ways. First, they were developed on the basis of the dialogue corpus produced by the Wizard of Oz (WOZ) experiments described in Chapter 5. Secondly, the guidelines were compared with Grice's maxims of cooperative human–human conversation (Grice, 1975). Thirdly, the guidelines were tested against the dialogue corpus from the user test of the implemented Danish Dialogue System. This section describes the development and validation process which resulted in the consolidated set of guidelines presented above.

4.4.1   Establishing the Guidelines

Development of the First 14 Guidelines

The interaction model for our flight ticket reservation system was developed by the WOZ experimental prototyping method. This produced a corpus of 125 transcribed dialogues. A major concern during WOZ was to detect problems of user–system interaction in the transcribed dialogues. Towards the end of the WOZ process the actual and potential problems of interaction identified in the WOZ corpus were analysed, classified and represented as violations, made by the system, of guidelines for cooperative interaction. Each problem was considered a case in which the system in addressing the user had violated a guideline for cooperative interaction. The guidelines were made explicit based on the problems analysis. To illustrate the WOZ corpus analysis we present an example of an identified problem type (a) and the cooperative guideline (in DSD terms: "design commitment", cf. Section 3.4) which has been violated (b). A justification of the guideline is provided (c), followed by examples of how it was found to be violated (d). Under (d) we note whether a particular example was discovered empirically (i.e. from actual problems of interaction) or analytically (i.e. through design analysis revealing a potential problem). Finally, a solution to each problem is proposed and sometimes discussed (e). The template (a)–(e) was applied to each problem that had been identified in the WOZ corpus (Bernsen, 1993b).

(a) *Problem*: Non-separation between novice users, who need introductory information about what the system can and cannot do, and intermediate and expert users, who do not need such information and for whom listening to it would only delay task performance.

(b) *Violation* of design commitment: Separate, whenever possible, between the needs of novice and expert users (user-adaptive interaction).

(c) *Justification*: There are major differences between the needs of novice and expert users, one such difference being that expert users already possess the information needed to understand system functionality.

(d) *Examples*: Introduction (WOZ7): A new question was added: "Do you know this system?" First-time users may obtain additional information about the functionality of the system and about how to communicate with it. Other users may proceed directly with their task. This problem was discovered from user problems. Users complained that the system talked too much. Consideration of this complaint led to the described design improvement.

(e) *Solution*: In WOZ7 it was made optional for users to listen to the introduction to the system.

Note that in this case the solution was reasonably straightforward. In many other cases solutions were only found through more or less difficult reasoning of the kind amenable to DR representation (see Section 3.4). One example is the question of when the system should raise the issue of discount. In WOZ6 the wizard would say: "Are you *particularly* (stressed by the wizard) interested in making use of special fares?". The word "particularly" was introduced in order to avoid those users who did not want to make use of special fares answering "yes". Experience with user responses during earlier iterations had shown that this might otherwise happen. The change caused an improvement, but the problem did not go away. In the discussion we came across the possibility that users would interpret the system's question (with or without "*particularly*") as asking whether they had an interest in travelling as cheaply as possible, which perhaps most people have. Several alternative design options were discussed, including:

Option a: Special fares are offered only after all the information relevant to the reservation has been entered into the system's database. This will not do, however, as users who are interested in special fares may have to go through most of the reservation dialogue once again.

Option b: At an early stage in the dialogue the system asks whether the user's choice of time of travel depends on the possibility of obtaining special fares.

This problem was discovered from user problems.

Solution: Option b was preferred.

The described procedure led to the identification of 14 guidelines for cooperative human–machine interaction based on analysis of 120 examples of user–system interaction problems (Figure 4.26). The guidelines were at this point called "principles", which is why they are numbered P1–P14 in the figure. Figure 4.26 includes a justification of each guideline, which serves the additional purpose of clarifying its meaning and scope. Although not explicitly stated in each justification, we took it to be straightforward that violations of any of the guidelines may lead users to initiate meta-communication, or other non-desirable interaction behaviour, because this is the strategy naturally adopted in human–human conversation in such cases. To facilitate

Guidelines	Justification
P1. Provide clear and comprehensible communication of what the system can and cannot do.	Risk of communication failure in case of lacking knowledge about what the system can and cannot do. Violation of this principle leads users to have exaggerated expectations about the system's abilities, which again may lead to frustration during use of the system.
P2. Provide sufficient task domain knowledge and inference.	Risk of communication failure in case of lacking task domain information. Full task domain knowledge and inference within specified limits is necessary in order to satisfy all relevant user needs in context. Otherwise, users will become frustrated when using the system.
P3. Provide same formulation of the same question (or address) to users everywhere in the system's interaction turns.	Need for unambiguous system response (consistency in system task performance). The principle is meant to reduce the possibility of communication error caused by users' understanding a new formulation of a question as constituting a different question from one encountered earlier.
P4. Take users' relevant background knowledge into account.	Need for adjustment of system responses to users' relevant background knowledge and inferences based thereupon. This is to prevent that the user does not understand the system's utterances or makes unpredicted remarks, such as questions of clarification, which the system cannot understand or answer.
P5. Avoid 'semantical noise' in addressing users.	Need for unambiguous system response. This design commitment is meant to reduce the possibilities of evoking wrong associations in users, which in their turn may cause the users to adopt wrong courses of action or ask questions which the system cannot understand.
P6. It should be possible for users to fully exploit the system's task domain knowledge when they need it.	Risk of communication failure in case of inaccessible (or not easily accessible) task domain information. In such cases, users may pose questions which the system is unable to understand or answer.
P7. Take into account possible (and possibly erroneous) user inferences by analogy from related task domains.	Need for adjustment to users' background knowledge and inferences by analogy based thereupon. Users may otherwise fail to understand the system.

Figure 4.26: The early co-operative spoken interaction design guidelines (left-hand column) and their justifications (right-hand column) (*continued next page*).

Figure 4.26 (*continued*)

P8. Provide clear and sufficient instructions to users on how to interact with the system.	Risk of communication failure in case of unclear or insufficient instructions to users on how to interact with the system. Users may become confused about the functionality of the system.
P9. Separate whenever possible between the needs of novice and expert users (user-adaptive interaction).	There are major differences between the needs of novice and expert users, one such difference being that expert users already possess the information needed to understand system functionality.
P10. Avoid superfluous or redundant interactions with users (relative to their contextual needs).	Users tend to get irritated and inattentive from unnecessary system turns.
P11. Be fully explicit in communicating to users the commitments they have made.	Users need feedback from the system on the commitments made in order to ensure correctness.
P12. Reduce system talk as much as possible during individual interaction turns.	Users get bored and inattentive from too much uninterrupted system talk.
P13. Provide feedback on each piece of information provided by the user.	Immediate feedback on user commitments serves to remove users' uncertainty as to what the system has understood and done in response to their utterances.
P14. Provide ability to initiate repair if system understanding has failed.	When system understanding fails, the system should initiate repair meta-communication and not leave the initiative with the user.

comparison with maxims of cooperative human–human conversation (Section 4.4.2), each occurrence of the term "system" in the stated guidelines may be replaced by "speaker", and each occurrence of the term "user" may be replaced by "interlocutor" or any other favoured term, such as "dialogue partner" or "recipient".

4.4.2 Comparison With Grice's Maxims

Having developed the guidelines shown in Figure 4.26, we became aware of the link between our work and Grice's cooperative Principle and maxims. Grice's cooperative Principle (CP) is a general principle which says that to act cooperatively in conversation, one should make one's "conversational contribution such as is required, at the stage at which it occurs, by the accepted purpose or direction of the talk exchange in which one is engaged" (Grice, 1975). Grice proposes that the CP can be explicated in terms of four groups of simple maxims which are not claimed to be jointly exhaustive. The maxims are marked with an asterisk in Figure 4.1. All the maxims are generic guidelines.

Relevance of the Comparison

There is little point in discussing the relationship between our early guidelines of cooperative spoken interaction design and Grice's maxims of cooperative human–human conversation, unless it can be demonstrated that Grice's maxims *actually serve* a purpose which is more or less identical to that served by the guidelines. If this is the case it does not matter whether the maxims might have been designed with other purposes in mind. In fact, this may be why Grice did not identify all the aspects of cooperative interaction to be discussed below. We shall speak interchangeably about "conversation" and "interaction" as these terms denote the same phenomenon for present purposes.

Our guidelines were developed to avoid or prevent miscommunication and user needs for initiating clarification and repair meta-communication through, for example, asking questions of the system during task-oriented spoken interaction. Grice assumes that any particular conversation serves, to some extent, a common purpose or set of purposes which may be more or less definite and either fixed from the start or have evolved during the conversation. In such conversations, he claims, adherence to the maxims is rational because it ensures that the interlocutors pursue the shared goal(s) most efficiently. Spoken task-oriented interaction, such as that served by the Danish Dialogue System, is a prototypical case of shared-goal conversation: throughout the interaction, user and system share *one common* and *specific* goal, namely that of completing the flight ticket reservation task. Correspondingly, the aim of interaction design is to maximize efficiency of information exchange. Thus, Grice's CP clearly purports to be relevant to the design of task-oriented interaction.

Grice, however, did not develop the maxims for the purpose of preventing communication failure in shared-goal interaction. Rather, his interest was in the inferences which interlocutor B is able to make when interlocutor A *deliberately* violates one of the maxims, assuming that B is aware that the violation was indeed deliberate. So, for instance, if A says something irrelevant in context, intending that B recognizes *that* it was irrelevant *and* said on purpose, then B might be able to infer some interesting conclusions, such as that A wishes to avoid a certain subject. Humans do such things quite often in conversation. Grice calls such deliberate interlocutor's messages "conversational implicatures" (Grice, 1975, 1978). Both the notion and the theoretical issues associated with conversational implicature were absent in our work, and appear to be absent from all other efforts in spoken interaction design that we are familiar with. Rather, spoken interaction design focuses on making the machine state, as literally as possible, and hence without invoking conversational implicature, what needs to be stated in context. Grice was not interested in the miscommunication and needs for meta-communication that may arise the moment an interlocutor *non-deliberately* fails to adhere to the CP and the maxims. However, the fact that miscommunication may arise at this point would seem perfectly compatible with Grice's theory: in such cases, one interlocutor (the user) fails to grasp any conversational implicature because there isn't any, and fails to understand the other interlocutor's communicative intention more or less. The CP *cum* maxims, he says, imply that at each stage of conversation some possible conversational moves would be excluded as conversationally unsuitable. If such moves are nevertheless made non-deliberately, miscommunication is likely to arise. If and when discovered, meta-communication is the natural cooperative mechanism which serves to bring the dialogue back on track. For a more detailed account of Grice's CP and its discussion in linguistics and cognitive science see Bernsen *et al.* (1996).

We conclude that the CP and the maxims, as a necessary side-effect of improving understanding and enhancing communication and thereby ensuring as smooth an interaction as possible, serve the purpose of preventing unwanted spoken interaction behaviour as well as the need for clarification and repair meta-communication. Conversely, one way of reducing miscommunication and the need for its clarification and repair is to rely on guidelines that enhance communication. Our guidelines are of this type.

Thus, the main difference between Grice's work and ours is that the maxims were developed to account for cooperativity in human–human conversation, whereas our guidelines were developed to account for cooperativity in spoken human–machine interaction. Given this commonality of purpose, it is of interest to compare guidelines and maxims.

Maxims and Guidelines Compared

In the following we show that the guidelines include the maxims as a sub-set and thus provide a corpus-based confirmation of the validity of the maxims for spoken human–machine interaction. Moreover, the guidelines manifest aspects of cooperative task-oriented interaction which were not addressed by Grice. The maxims concerned are GG1, GG2 and GG5–GG9 in Figure 4.1. The guidelines are P1–P14 in Figure 4.26.

We first demonstrate that a sub-set of the guidelines are roughly equivalent to the maxims. The following guidelines have counterparts among the maxims.

P5: *Avoid "semantical noise" in addressing users*

P5 is a generalized version of GG6 (non-obscurity) and GG7 (non-ambiguity). Its infelicitous expression was due to the fact that we wanted to cover observed ambiguity and related phenomena in one guideline but failed to find an appropriate technical term for the purpose. P5 may, without any consequence other than improved clarity, be replaced by GG6 and GG7. For examples see Figures 4.9 and 4.10.

P6: *It should be possible for users to fully exploit the system's task domain knowledge when they need it*

P6 has a formulation which lacks any direct correspondence among the maxims. P6 can be considered an application of GG1 (informativeness) and GG9 (orderliness), as follows. If the system adheres to GG1 and GG9, there is a maximum likelihood that users obtain the task domain knowledge they need from the system when they need it. The system should say enough and address the task-relevant topics of interaction in an order which is as close as possible to the order expected by users. Eventually saying enough is not sufficient for cooperativity. If the user expects some topic to come up early in the interaction, that topic's non-occurrence at its expected "place" may cause a clarification sub-dialogue which the system cannot understand. For examples see Figures 4.2 and 4.13. P6 may be replaced by GG1 and GG9 without significant loss. This assumes that GG9, when applied to the ticket reservation task, would yield the implication that orderliness is defined by the user's expectations.

P10: *Avoid superfluous or redundant interactions with users (relative to their contextual needs)*

P10 is virtually equivalent to GG2 (do not overdo informativeness) and GG5 (relevance). Grice observed the overlap between GG2 and GG5 (Grice, 1975). P10 may, without any consequence other than improved clarity, be replaced by GG2 and GG5. For examples, see Figures 4.5 and 4.8.

P12: *Reduce system talk as much as possible during individual dialogue turns*

P12 is near-equivalent to GG8 (brevity). For examples, see Figure 4.12.

Summarizing, the generic guidelines P5, P6, P10 and P12 may be replaced by maxims GG1, GG2 and GG5–GG9. These maxims are capable of performing the same task in guiding interaction design. In fact, as argued, the maxims are able to do a better job because they, i.e. GG6 and GG7, and GG1 and GG9, respectively, spell out the intended contents of two of the guidelines. This provides corpus-based confirmation of maxims GG1, GG2 and GG5–GG9, i.e. of them stating basic guidelines of cooperative, task-oriented spoken human–machine interaction. However, for interaction design purposes, the maxims may be supplemented with task-specific or domain-specific guidelines. The specific guidelines have no counterparts among the maxims. Yet these guidelines appear useful to interactive speech systems design. What we need, in order to discover interaction problems at an early stage, is to know what to look for in the emerging interaction model. The specific guidelines extend the generic guidelines by further specifying their import.

P3 (now SG3): *Provide same formulation of the same question (or address) to users everywhere in the system's dialogue turns*

P3 represents an additional precaution against the occurrence of ambiguity in machine speech. It can be seen as a special-purpose application of GG7 (non-ambiguity), which is not needed in human–human conversation. For examples see Figure 4.11.

P11 (now SG1): *Be fully explicit in communicating to users the commitments they have made*

P13 (now SG2): *Provide feedback on each piece of information provided by the user*

These two guidelines are closely related. The novel cooperativity issue they introduce is that of requiring the cooperative system to produce a specific contribution to the interaction, which explicitly expresses an interpretation of the user's previous contribution(s). P11 requires the system to do this provided that the user has made a contribution of a certain type, such as a commitment to book a flight. Feedback (P13), on the other hand, should be provided in response to each individual piece of user information. Corresponding to the use of feedback in our system, one standard use of explicit feedback in human–human conversation is when one interlocutor makes important commitments *vis-à-vis* another interlocutor, such as an important concession during formal negotiation. However, it is far from clear under which conditions it may be maintained that, in human–human conversation, the cooperative interlocutor is expected to provide explicit feedback on information provided by other interlocutors. We propose that these guidelines be subsumed by GG1 (informativeness). For examples see Figures 4.3 and 4.4.

Grice's maxims of truth and evidence (GG3 and GG4) have no counterparts among our guidelines but may simply be included among these. The reason is that one does not design an interactive speech system which provides false or unfounded information to customers. In other words, the maxims of truth and evidence are so self-evidently important to the design of interactive speech systems that they are unlikely to emerge in scale during interaction design problem solving. This notwithstanding, one of the worst breakdowns during the WOZ experiments actually occurred when the wizard accidentally came up with an inconsistent day of the week-date pair (see Figure 4.6). During system implementation, one constantly worries about truth and evidence. It cannot be allowed, for instance, that the system confirms information which has not been checked with the database and which might be false or impossible. Still, errors happen as shown in Figure 4.6. Grice (1975) observed the fundamental nature of the maxims of truth and evidence in general, and GG3 in particular. Similarly, Searle (1992) pointed out that the requirement of truthfulness is an internal constitutive rule of the notion of a statement. It therefore seems to have a different status to the rest of the maxims. GG4 is illustrated in Figure 4.7.

4.4.3 Non-Gricean Guidelines

Section 4.4.2 looked at those among the original guidelines in Figure 4.26 which could be either reduced to, replaced by or subsumed by the Gricean maxims. The guidelines discussed in this section appear irreducible to maxims and thus serve to augment the scope of a theory of cooperativity in spoken interaction.

Interaction Partner Asymmetry

The responsibility for cooperative human–machine interaction does not only lie with the system. The system may also impose cooperativity on the user and it is the task of the interaction designers to make sure that this happens when necessary. Interaction partner asymmetry occurs, roughly, when one or more of the partners is not in a normal condition or situation. For instance, a partner may have a hearing deficiency or be located in a particularly noisy environment. In such cases, cooperativity depends on taking into account that participant's special characteristics. As these examples show, interaction partner asymmetry needs not have anything to do with differences in background knowledge (see below). For obvious reasons interaction partner asymmetry is important in interactive speech system design. The machine is not a normal partner in interaction and users have to be aware of this if communication failure is to be avoided. The following two guidelines address interaction partner asymmetry:

P1 (now SG4): *Provide clear and comprehensible communication of what the system can and cannot do*

P8 (now SG5): *Provide clear and sufficient instructions to users on how to interact with the system*

Being limited in its task capabilities and intended for walk-up-and-use application, our interactive speech system needs to protect itself from unmanageable user contributions by providing users with an up-front mental model of what it can and cannot do (cf. Figure 4.15). If this mental model is too complex, users will not acquire it; and if the model is too simplistic, its remaining details must be provided elsewhere during interaction. For instance, the Danish Dialogue System will explain its inability to handle special discounts for groups of more than 10 people only if the user states a number of travellers that exceeds 10. Whereas an equally massive asymmetry never occurs in human–human conversation, related asymmetries do occur when there are marked differences in task capabilities among human partners in conversation. P1 adds an important element to the analysis of cooperativity in spoken interaction by aiming at improvements in user cooperativity. This shows that, at least in human–machine interaction, cooperativity is a formally more complex phenomenon than anticipated by Grice. In addition to guidelines stating how a system should behave, guidelines are needed whereby the system should consider transferring part of the responsibility for cooperation to the user. More specifically, the non-normal partner in spoken interaction should inform the partners of these particular non-normal characteristics, which they should take into account in order to act cooperatively. P8 has a role similar to that of P1 (cf. Figure 4.16).

The guidelines examined in this section introduce a new aspect of cooperativity into spoken interaction, namely partner asymmetry and the system's consequent obligation to inform the user(s) of its relevant non-normal characteristics as a partner in spoken interaction. Owing to the latter element, the guidelines cannot be subsumed by any other guideline or maxim. We propose that P1 and P8 are both *specific* guidelines subsumed by a new *generic* guideline:

GG10: *Inform the dialogue partners of important non-normal characteristics which they should take into account in order to behave cooperatively in interaction*

The term "non-normal characteristics" refers to communication deficiencies in the system and aspects of the environment which impede the system's ability to communicate. The feasibility condition on GG10 (see Figure 4.1) was added as a result of testing the guidelines on the user test corpus from the Danish Dialogue System. The feasibility condition will be discussed in Section 4.4.4. For examples see Figure 4.14.

Background Knowledge

P4 (now GG11): *Take users' relevant background knowledge into account*

P4 appears to be a genuine addition to Gricean cooperativity theory, at least as far as human–machine interaction is concerned. It is expressed at the level of generality of Grice's theory. The guideline explicitly introduces two notions central to a system's cooperativity in interaction. The first notion is that of the interlocutors' background knowledge, including skill-based knowledge of the natural language in which the dialogue is being conducted, domain knowledge, etc. The second is the notion of possible differences in background knowledge between different user groups and individual users. P4 appears to be *presupposed* by maxims GG1, GG2 and GG5–GG9 in the sense that it is not possible to adhere to any of these maxims without adhering to P4. Moreover, in order to adhere to P4, it is necessary for the system to recognize relevant differences among users and user groups in terms of background knowledge.

P4 cannot be reduced to GG1 (informativeness) because, first, GG1 does not refer to the notions of background knowledge and differences in background knowledge among users. Second, a system may adhere perfectly to "exchange purpose" (cf. GG1) while ignoring important issues to do with the user's background knowledge (cf. Figure 4.17). Design analysis showed that such cases may arise when, for instance, a user happens to know about a departure which was not offered by the system because the flight was already fully booked, or when a user wants a discount on a certain departure but is not offered that departure because it does not allow discount. Third, as argued above, P4 is presupposed by maxims GG1, GG2 and GG5–GG9. Grice, however, does not claim that GG1 is presupposed by those maxims whereas he does argue that GG3 (truth) and GG4 (evidence) are presupposed by them (Grice, 1975). For similar reasons GG5 (relevance) (Sperber and Wilson, 1987) cannot replace P4. Informativeness and relevance, therefore, are not only functions of the purpose(s) of the exchange of information but also of the knowledge of the user.

P7 (now SG6): *Take into account possible (and possibly erroneous) user inferences by analogy from related task domains*
P7 is a *specific* guideline subsumed by GG11 (user background knowledge). It was developed from examples of user misunderstandings of the system due to reasoning by analogy. For instance, the fact that it is possible to make reservations of stand-by tickets on international flights may lead users to conclude (erroneously) that this is also possible on domestic flights (see also Figure 4.18).

P9 (now SG7): *Separate whenever possible between the needs of novice and expert users (user-adaptive interaction)*
P9 is another *specific* guideline subsumed by GG11. Users may belong to different populations or groups with correspondingly different needs of information in cooperative interaction. For instance, a user who has successfully used the interactive speech system on several occasions no longer needs to be introduced to the system but is capable of launching into the ticket reservation task right away. A novice user, however, will need to listen to the system's introduction (cf. Figure 4.19).

P2 (now SG8): *Provide sufficient task domain knowledge and inference*
P2 may appear trivial in support of the design of usable information service systems. However, designers of such system are continuously confronted with questions about what the system should know and what is just within, or barely outside, the system's intended or expected domain of expertise. The system should behave as a perfect expert *vis-à-vis* its users within its declared domain of expertise, otherwise it is at fault (cf. Figure 4.21). Because P2 deals with the system's knowledge it cannot be subsumed by P4. We therefore propose to introduce a new *generic* guideline which mirrors P4:

GG12: *Take into account legitimate partner expectations as to your own background knowledge*
P2, then, is a *specific* guideline subsumed by GG12. GG12 is illustrated in Figure 4.20.

Meta-communication

Even if an interactive speech system is able to conduct a perfectly cooperative inter-action, it will need to initiate *repair and clarification meta-communication* whenever it has failed to understand the user, for instance because of speech recognition or language understanding failure:

P14 (now SG9): *Provide ability to initiate repair if system understanding has failed*

P14 states what the cooperative system should do in case of failure to understand utterances made by the user. Our system adheres to P14 in that it communicates its failure to understand what the user just said (cf. Figure 4.23). The system currently lacks the ability to express, or otherwise act on, the degree of certainty it has that it correctly understood the user. P14 cannot be subsumed by GG1 (informativeness) which ignores communication failure. P14 is a specific guideline of human–machine interaction which may be subsumed by:

GG13: *Enable repair or clarification meta-communication in case of communication failure*

GG13 covers the enabling of user-initiated meta-communication as well as system-initiated meta-communication. GG13 is illustrated in Figure 4.22.

SG10 and SG11 were not included in the initial set of guidelines in Figure 4.26. They were discovered as a result of testing the guidelines on the user test corpus from the Danish Dialogue System. They are discussed in Section 4.4.4. For examples see Figures 4.24 and 4.25.

Summary and Comparison With Human–Human Conversation

Comparison between our guidelines and Grice's maxims has shown that there are more generic guidelines of cooperativity in human–machine interaction than those identified by Grice. Three groups of guidelines reveal aspects of cooperative inter-action left unaddressed by the maxims. This produces a total of seven interaction aspects, each of which is addressed by one or more generic guidelines (see Figure 4.1). It may be asked why Grice was not aware of the three generic aspects of inter-action: partner asymmetry; background knowledge; and meta-communication. It seems obvious that it cannot be because these aspects are absent from human–human conversation. More plausibly, interaction partner asymmetry is absent from prototypical cases of human–human conversation; background knowledge is so pervasive as to be easily ignored; and Grice explicitly was not concerned with inter-action failure pure and simple.

The Gricean maxims are broadly recognized as applying to shared-goal spoken human–human conversation, and in this section have been empirically validated for task-oriented spoken human–machine interaction. Similarly, the generic and specific guidelines have been empirically validated for task-oriented, system-directed, spoken human–machine interaction. As to the specific guidelines, it does not appear warranted to claim their applicability beyond human–machine conversation. The question to be briefly addressed below concerns the scope of the non-Gricean *generic* guidelines. Is their scope similar to that of Grice's maxims?

We have as yet no empirical basis for claiming that the generic guidelines GG10, GG11, GG12 and GG13 share the scope of the maxims. Theoretically, however, it may be argued that they do. GG10 (asymmetry) appears equally valid for human–human conversation. If a partner in shared-goal spoken interaction has important non-normal characteristics of which the interlocutor may be unaware, and the non-observation of which is detrimental to the achievement of the goal, then the interlocutor must be informed about them. Otherwise interaction cooperativity will be decreased until the interlocutor discovers these characteristics. GG10 is irrelevant to symmetrical human–human conversation. However, when an asymmetry is present, the guideline assumes a fundamental role. Suppose, for instance, that ambient noise prevents you from clearly following your interlocutor's spoken contributions. If you deliberately omit to inform the interlocutor that this is the case, the implication (or conversational implicature) is that you do not really care to accomplish the goal of the conversation.

Ignoring a user's relevant background knowledge (GG11) clearly detracts from the system's cooperativity in interaction. The same is true when a system ignores legitimate user expectations as to the system's background knowledge (GG12). In both cases, the implication is that something other than the shared goal is at stake. Furthermore, as argued earlier, GG11 is presupposed by the Gricean maxims. This implies that GG11 shares the scope of the maxims. GG13 (repair and clarification) appears also to share this scope.

In conclusion, when performing shared-goal conversation, people, just like machines, should communicate their communication deficiencies, take background knowledge into account, and initiate repair and clarification meta-communication when needed. Failure to do so detracts, sometimes seriously, from the rationality of the shared-goal conversation.

On one condition the maxims and generic guidelines are in fact *symmetrically* applicable to interactive speech systems and their human users. This condition is that users should assign priority to what the machine says according to GG10 (asymmetry) and otherwise make their spoken contributions conform to the maxims and generic guidelines. As applied to our interactive speech system, GG10 essentially informs users that the system is severely constrained in its language-understanding capabilities, background knowledge, inferential abilities and acceptance of user initiative. If these limitations are respected, the system will enable otherwise cooperative users to complete their task.

4.4.4   Testing the Guidelines
Additions Needed to the Guidelines

Having consolidated the guidelines of cooperative system interaction through comparison with Gricean theory, we were keen to analyse how the guidelines worked in the user test of the implemented Danish Dialogue System (see also Chapter 8). It should be noted that the guidelines had not been systematically used as guidelines in *designing* the implemented system. The user test thus cannot be considered a test of the guidelines in the crucial sense of indicating to what extent successful design of cooperative system behaviour may result from using the guidelines for design. Rather, the user test acted as a test of the *scope* of the guidelines. It provided an indication of whether the present set of guidelines converge on a complete set. If analysis of user–system interaction in the user test produces a significant number of novel guidelines, then the present set of guidelines are still far from complete. On the other hand, if the analysis fails to produce more guidelines, then this would at least suggest that convergence on completeness is well under way.

The user test corpus, consisting of 57 transcribed dialogues, was analysed to identify dialogue interaction problems. It turned out that almost all of the 119 individual interaction design problems identified could be ascribed to violations of the cooperative guidelines established during WOZ and refined through comparison with Grice's maxims. The user test thus confirmed the broad coverage of the guidelines with respect to cooperative spoken user–system interaction.

Only three additions had to be made to the guidelines. Two specific guidelines of meta-communication were added, i.e. SG10 and SG11 in Figure 4.1. As meta-communication had not been simulated during WOZ, the fact that the WOZ corpus contained few examples of meta-communication therefore came as no surprise.

More interestingly, we had to add a modification to GG10, namely that it *should be feasible* for users to do what they are asked to do. For instance, the Danish Dialogue System asks users to use the keywords "change" and "repeat" for meta-communication purposes and to answer the system's questions briefly and one at a time. A significant number of violations of the system's instructions nevertheless occurred in the user test. These violations (cf. Figure 4.14) were initially categorized as user errors. However, upon closer analysis they were re-categorized as interaction design errors. Although the system had clearly stated that it had non-normal characteristics and users should therefore modify their natural interaction behaviour, this is not cognitively possible for many users. In an extreme example: had we asked users to always use exactly four contextually relevant words in their responses to the system's questions, this would clearly have been a cognitively impossible demand on users. Similarly, what the system's introduction asked users to do turned out to be unrealistic given the interaction behaviour that is natural to most people.

4.4.5   Status of the Guidelines

Credibility of the Guidelines

We believe that the comparison between our original guidelines (Figure 4.26) and Gricean theory has strengthened the credibility of the current guidelines set (Figure 4.1). Additional support came from the user test because only two new specific guidelines had to be included, guidelines which, moreover, addressed issues that were not prominent in the original WOZ corpus. The user test also led to an addition to a generic guideline. Jointly these results suggest that the guidelines of a cooperative system interaction represent a step towards a more or less complete and practically applicable set of design guidelines for cooperative spoken interaction.

However, it cannot be excluded at this stage that the guidelines are somehow tied to the task domain and complexity of interaction characterizing our particular interactive speech system. Analysis of interaction design problems in systems, whether simulated or implemented, that address different task domains or have lower or higher complexity of interaction than our system may reveal additional specific, or even generic, guidelines.

We are currently investigating the generality and transferability of the guidelines. *Generality* is being tested by applying them to: (i) *systems that are different* to the

Danish Dialogue System; and which (ii) cover *different task domains*. Moreover, (iii) the guidelines are being applied as a *design guide* prior to implementation rather than to the diagnostic evaluation of an implemented system. Finally, (iv) they are being applied in *less controlled circumstances* compared to those that are obtained in a controlled user test. *Transferability* is being tested by investigating: (a) what it takes for a novice interactive speech system developer to learn to master the guidelines; and (b) how the required learning steps may be supported and "packaged" for transfer to other developers so that they can easily learn how to use the guidelines. Preliminary results are presented in Bernsen *et al.* (1997). Although the work is not yet finished, it has been demonstrated that the guidelines can be used as a design guide during early design in much the same way as it is used for diagnostic evaluation of implemented systems. We therefore believe that the guidelines, even in their present form, can be used to support the design of a first interaction model no matter whether this model is intended for simulation prior to implementation or straight implementation.

5. *Wizard of Oz Simulation*

5.1 Introduction

WOZ in the Design Process

When the first interaction model has been designed (cf. Section 4.1) interactive speech system development may either go through a phase of Wizard of Oz (WOZ) simulations as will be described in this chapter, or go straight to implementation (Chapter 6) following the implement–test–revise approach (Figure 3.1). Today's research on interaction model design for advanced interactive speech systems often includes the WOZ experimental prototyping method. In WOZ a human (the wizard) simulates whole or part of the interaction model of the system to be developed, carrying out spoken interactions with users who are made to believe that they are interacting with a real system. WOZ is a relatively costly development method because: (1) the wizard needs a significant amount of training and support; (2) involving experimental subjects, WOZ experiments require careful planning and preparation and take time to run; and (3) experimental results have to be transcribed and analysed, which takes time and requires skill to benefit further system development. On the other hand, by producing data on the interaction between a (fully or partially) simulated system and its users, WOZ provides the basis for early tests of the system and its feasibility, as well as of the coverage and adequacy of requirements prior to implementation. The use of WOZ has so far been justified through the comparatively higher cost of having to revise an already implemented interactive speech system whose interaction model turned out to be seriously flawed, or of having to discard a system which users will not use. As recognition and parsing techniques continue to improve and the body of standard software grows, implement–test–revise methods are likely to gain ground in the design of advanced interactive speech systems.

For simple dialogues and in most industrial settings, WOZ is normally replaced by the implement–test–revise approach based on emerging development platforms. Whether or not WOZ is preferable to implement–test–revise depends on several factors, such as the novelty of the development objectives relative to the skills, methods and tools available to the developers, the complexity of the interaction model to be designed, the task domain, and the risk and cost of implementation failure. Low complexity speaks in favour of directly implementing the interaction model without interposing a simulation phase, especially if the developers have built similar systems before. High complexity, on the other hand, may advocate iterative simulations.

Uses of WOZ

Over the years WOZ has been used for many purposes other than interaction model design and development. However, one goal seems to be shared by all WOZ simulations. This is the goal of studying the behaviour of humans when communicating with a computer. Many WOZ experiments include a comparative aspect, such as comparison between human–human and human–computer interaction. WOZ has been used to investigate whether people's communication with computers differs from their communication with fellow humans. Hauptmann and Rudnicky (1988) compared users' behaviour during interaction with an e-mail system. Some users typed into the system, others had a speech interface to a simulated system, and yet others spoke to a human operator. Amalberti *et al.* (1993), Morel (1989) and Richards and Underwood (1984) made WOZ experiments in the domain of travel information and compared users' behaviour when talking to a simulated system and to a person. There is evidence that people's communication with computers differs to their communication with humans. It appears that as long as the computer demonstrates appropriate functionality, people are prepared to simplify their input behaviour and accept simplified system output. Research on this issue is discussed and reviewed in Amalberti *et al.* (1993). Lexical variability in spontaneous dialogue (Brennan, 1996) and the influence of system politeness on user responses (Richards and Underwood, 1984; Zoltan-Ford, 1991) have been investigated, providing suggestions for how systems should speak to users in order to influence their language in ways which may improve system recognition and understanding. Comparative studies of the influence of scenario design, user backgrounds and voice distortion will be discussed in Section 5.6.2.

WOZ experiments for interactive speech system development aim at collecting information on user behaviour in order to evaluate the system's interaction model and the feasibility of developing an acceptable system. Examples of use of WOZ for the development of interactive speech systems are found in Basson *et al.* (1996) (user satisfaction with speech systems for handling telephone services that have not been automated before, and with speech systems replacing touch-tone systems), Boyce and Gorin (1996) (confirmation and re-prompt strategies in a telephone service system), Guyomard and Siroux (1988) (yellow pages) and Ponamalé *et al.* (1990) (airline ticket booking). WOZ has also proved useful in exploratory design of multimodal systems. Examples are Bertenstam *et al.* (1995) (speech and text data collection for a multimodal system providing information on boat traffic in the Stockholm archipelago), Hauptmann (1989) (manipulation of graphic images on a video screen), Life *et al.* (1996) (interface design and language collection for a multimodal service kiosk for train travel information and reservation), Maulsby *et al.* (1993) (instructible intelligent agent) and Vossen (1991) (conversion of CAD drawings into a form suitable for CNC machines).

This Chapter

In this chapter, we examine WOZ primarily as a practical technique for interactive speech system development. In addition, we illustrate how WOZ may be simultaneously used to empirically investigate particular phenomena of interest. WOZ is presented in more detail in Section 5.2. Section 5.3 describes how to plan and set up a

WOZ simulation. WOZ-related issues in the development of a first interaction model are discussed in Section 5.4. Section 5.5 describes the use of WOZ in iterative interaction model development. Finally, Section 5.6 presents three cases in which WOZ was used to investigate phenomena of interest to interactive speech system developers.

5.2   Wizard of Oz for Interaction Model Development

What is WOZ Suited For

WOZ is well-suited for the iterative development and evaluation of interactive interfaces when the input modality (or modalities) can be only partially decoded by computers but is easily understood by humans, and/or when the output modality (or modalities) can be easily produced by humans but is only produced with difficulty by the computer. In such cases, human performance is superior to that of the computer and a human is able to simulate the computer's intended behaviour with some degree of accuracy. Moreover, these are exactly the cases which need investigation if we want to make the computer emulate a partner in natural human–human face-to-face communication. Spoken language input and output belong to this category. Design goals and constraints can be iteratively adjusted through a series of WOZ simulations until acceptable trade-offs have been found, if possible.

WOZ Compared to Other Prototyping Techniques

WOZ differs from other prototyping techniques in that it does not rely on reductions of the system and/or the task domain into presumed "essential" or "representative" features whose identification is often questionable. This means that, *ideally,* the end result of the WOZ simulate–evaluate–revise cycle will be a design which can be implemented on the assumption that the cycle has helped the designers to identify nearly all potential problems with the future system. However, as indicated above, WOZ is not equally suited to support all interactive speech system design processes. Current WOZ techniques are not sufficient to produce an interaction model that is sufficiently formalized for straightforward implementation. Moreover, WOZ is less than ideal in other respects, as we shall see. We propose to more specifically delimit the design process types for which WOZ should be considered.

Which Design Processes is WOZ Good For

First, the interactive system behaviour to be simulated should be behaviour which humans are good at performing. Otherwise, humans cannot appropriately perform the required simulation. There exists a broad class of cognitively demanding tasks which humans are naturally good at, such as natural language understanding and generation, gesture recognition or visual scene understanding.

Secondly, current computer systems should be clearly inferior to humans in the tasks. Otherwise, WOZ is not needed.

Thirdly, as systems with close to human interactive skills are still difficult to build, it is necessary to focus on the design of systems having relatively narrow and well-defined application domains as far as their cognitively demanding task aspects are concerned. Otherwise, even a WOZ supported development project will fail.

Fourthly, as WOZ is no "quick and dirty" prototyping method but somewhat demanding in resources, the system to be built should be high risk in the sense that the cost multiplied by the risk of having to re-build the artefact more or less from scratch after prototype failure is sufficiently high. Otherwise, WOZ does not warrant the investment in a more costly but strongly risk-minimizing prototyping technique. For less high risk interactive tasks there are likely to exist rapid prototyping methods which are preferable to WOZ in cost-benefit terms.

Finally, cognitively demanding interaction often, if not always, relies on natural and spontaneous skill-based user input behaviour such as gesture or spoken discourse. The technology will normally enforce restrictions on the system's capacity for understanding spontaneous user input. In such cases, realistic system development should be undertaken only if there is some way of ensuring that the user input which the system can understand is not restricted in unnatural or unprincipled ways. If such restrictions on "correct" user input are imposed, input production will be practically impossible for the users who are unable to modify their skill-based behaviour at will according to the system's instructions (cf. Section 4.4.4). For instance, whereas users may quickly learn to practice short input sentences, unnaturally restricted grammar can make a system practically useless. WOZ offers mechanisms which support the detection of unnatural or unprincipled restrictions on user input.

Despite the comparative virtues of WOZ listed above, the downside to the fact that the human simulating the future system is massively superior to the system as a communication partner, is that the human will have difficulty simulating important aspects of the performance of the future system. For instance, it is difficult or impossible for the wizard to precisely simulate the limited speech recognition of the future system as well as its limited vocabulary, grammar, semantics and discourse processing. Although it is possible to some extent to support the wizard in behaving less skilled than s/he actually is, this means that WOZ does not allow exact predictions on how spoken interaction with the implemented system will work.

5.3   Planning Wizard of Oz Simulations

This section describes how to set up a WOZ experiment in general. It discusses in detail the system side and the user side of the set-up, and how to make data collection of the communication on both sides.

5.3.1   General Set-up of a WOZ Experiment

WOZ Set-up and Minimum Requirements

Figure 5.1 shows the elements that are potentially included in a WOZ set-up. Some of these elements are mandatory whilst others are optional. The mandatory elements are: a person (the wizard) simulating the interaction model of the system, a subject acting as user and a subject–wizard interface which conceals the fact that the subject is interacting with a human rather than with a real system. Usually, a simulation support tool representing the interaction model to be simulated, and one or more data collection tools are also considered mandatory. If these are absent, the wizard will have to know the interaction model by heart and data collection can be done by observation only so that no track record will be left after the experiment. All other elements in Figure 5.1 are optional but may provide useful support during simulation. Elements are discussed in detail in Sections 5.3.2 and 5.3.3.

In practice, details of the set-up of a WOZ experiment may vary considerably. The elements used in the WOZ set-up for the Danish Dialogue System are shown in Figure 5.3. Other examples are presented in Francony *et al.* (1992) and Hauptmann (1989).

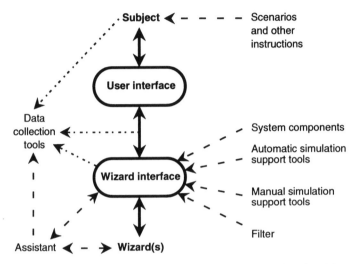

Figure 5.1: General set-up of a WOZ simulation. The main communication line is along the solid arrows. Dotted arrows indicate logging. The dashed arrows on the right-hand side of the figure mean "used by". On the left-hand side dashed arrows show the assistant operating the data collection tools and communicating with the wizard and the wizard interface.

The Experimenter

An important element which has not been mentioned yet is the experimenter. The experimenter is not part of the simulation as such but is nevertheless involved in all simulations. It is the experimenter's job to take care of all practical matters related to the simulation experiments, including all contacts with the subjects. The experimenter and the assistant may be one and the same person. However, the experimenter and the wizard should be different people. Otherwise, users may recognize the wizard's voice during simulation if no voice distortion is being used.

5.3.2 The System (Wizard) Side of WOZ

Introduction

During simulation, the system side consists of wizard(s) and wizard support. We shall in the remainder of this chapter use the singular in referring to the wizard, with the implicit understanding that several wizards might be involved, each simulating a particular part of the system. The wizard simulates the interaction model of the system or those parts of it which have not yet been implemented. In a full simulation of the interaction model of an interactive speech system, simulation covers input understanding and output planning and generation, including appropriate response times which are important in the evaluation of the usability of such systems.

The Wizard

The Wizard's Task and Problems

The wizard's task is hard primarily because of the high demands on working memory that result from the number and difficulty of the activities which the wizard has to simultaneously perform during interaction. Counter-measures include careful training of the wizard and ample support. Response time measurements are useful for judging whether the wizard needs more training or support. Wizard training starts before the simulations begin, continues during simulation and pertains to application domain knowledge, the intended system's skills and how to use the support tools. The wizard must be able to operate these components quickly and reliably.

The wizard's main problems typically are of two kinds. One main problem is that the wizard has superior knowledge and skills compared to the intended system (cf. Section 5.2). The wizard must, for instance, consistently simulate limited language comprehension skills in terms of vocabulary, semantics, grammatical complexity, or flawed or non-standard user input, and/or limited language generation skills in terms of rhythm and intonation. The wizard must simulate misrecognition or no recognition if the user input exceeds the envisioned capabilities of the system. This is very difficult to do. Reduced skills are much harder to simulate in close to real-time than is reduced knowledge, partly because skills are automated and partly because efficient external support is more difficult, or even impossible, to provide. Skill superiority tends to make the wizard understand input which the final system cannot understand, as well as generate responses beyond the capacity of the final system. Reduced knowledge is easier to simulate. Much can be achieved through practice and through explicit external representation of what the system is intended to know.

Another main problem is due to the fact that, in some areas, the wizard has inferior knowledge and skills compared to the intended system. Humans are inferior to computers with respect to computation and database look-ups. Implemented system components that can do these parts of the work would strongly support the wizard. Other ways of supporting the wizard include, for instance, pre-computed values to be used during a session with users. This can be done if the user scenarios are fairly precise and known to the wizard. Finally, an assistant can do part of the work which would otherwise have to be done by the wizard, as described below.

Supporting the Wizard

The system end of the interface (the *wizard interface)* includes at least an interface device that is connected to a user interface device, typically a computer or a telephone, which conceals the fact that the system is being simulated.

The interaction model to be simulated must, of course, also exist in some form. As a minimum the interaction model must exist in the head of the wizard, but usually it is explicitly represented to facilitate the wizard's job and support an adequate and consistent simulation in accordance with the design requirements. In the latter case it is considered part of the simulation support. Because the interaction model is the focal point in WOZ experiments, the question of how to establish such a model will be discussed in a separate section (Section 5.4). Other simulation support is discussed in the following.

Filters are hardware/software tools inserted in the communication channel connecting wizard and subject to enable manipulation of input and/or output quality during simulation. The aim is to help the wizard perform to the system's expected level of performance. Examples of filters are vocoders for distorting spoken output or input, speech synthesizers, filtering of typed input according to whether it belongs to the system's lexicon or not, and, in the case of typed output, response facilities which conceal the wizard's typing rate and correct misspelled words.

The purpose of system output filters is typically to support the subjects' belief in communicating with a real system (Fraser and Gilbert, 1991a, 1991b). Several authors have emphasized the importance of using voice distortion during simulation in order to maintain the subjects' illusion of communicating with a computer (Amalberti *et al.*, 1993; Fraser and Gilbert, 1991a, 1991b; Guyomard and Siroux, 1988; Luzzati and Néel, 1989; Richards and Underwood, 1984). In particular, owing to the influence of science fiction films, users in the recent past may have expected a "machine-like" voice from the computer. In these films computers are usually equipped with a somewhat metallic and monotonous voice which is markedly different to a human voice. As voice response systems are gaining ground, however, people are getting used to computers which use a human voice. In Denmark, for instance, voice response systems equipped with pre-recorded human speech are now common. When users expect human voice quality or when the wizard succeeds in using a monotonous voice and controlled intonation, additional voice distortion during simulation would appear to have little effect (Section 5.6.2). If the final system is to include a synthesizer, it may be useful to include it in the WOZ experiments. The synthesizer will help in emphasizing that it is a computer that speaks, at the same time providing data on how well users understand the synthesized voice.

Input quality affects recognition and may vary widely. The omnipresent and time-variant noise on the telephone line, for instance, affects the quality of the speech that the system must recognize. To support simulation of the final system's expected input misrecognition rates, input may be distorted (Guyomard and Siroux, 1988) or, better still, a real input recognizer may be included as a system component (see below). To support the wizard at the skill-based level, principled decisions should be made, to the extent possible, on how to handle, for instance, non-standard accents, dialects, indistinct voices, pauses, input/output overlaps and interruptions, turn-taking cues, etc. Simulation of the corresponding error-recovery mechanisms should be trained.

System components are completed and implemented system modules. An increasing number of such components, such as databases, speech recognizers or speech synthesizers, may be incorporated over time during system development. The components act as support tools because they allow the wizard to concentrate on a smaller part of the interaction model. In addition, they may help reduce response times. However, they also require the wizard to act as intermediary and sometimes as operator. For instance, if a database and a speech synthesis component are present, the wizard will have to listen to the user's input and decide whether the database must be consulted. If this is the case, the wizard must create a query to the database in an appropriate language, incorporate the database output in the answer to the user and express the answer in the format required for input to the speech synthesizer. Several cooperating wizards may be needed if several system components are involved (Salber and Coutaz, 1993a, 1993b). A simulation which includes one or more implemented system modules is sometimes called a *bionic* wizard system.

Simulation support tools may be manual or automatic and may be defined negatively as wizard support which is non-human and does not fall into the categories of filters and system components. An example of a support tool which automates part of the simulation are pre-recorded phrases which can be easily selected and replayed on the wizard's command. This supports reduced language generation skills and consistent output generation. An example of manual simulation support is a hand-written record of the information exchanged so far during the interaction. Other support tools are, for instance, tools which show the dialogue structure on paper or on the computer screen, or which actively support navigation in the interaction model. When automatic simulation support tools are involved, the wizard usually has a screen with a set of windows, one for each functionality, such as one window showing information provided by the user and another showing the wizard's dialogue decisions so far. Several such tools were briefly reviewed in Section 1.3.3. The precise nature and extent of the simulation support tools that will be useful in an experiment depends on the missing system components. In particular, in later development phases, implemented system components may partially replace simulation and allow the use of more automatic simulation tools which are interfaced to the existing components. For instance, in the controlled user test of the Danish Dialogue System only the recognizer was simulated, all other system interaction was performed by implemented components. The simulation environment included three automatic tools: one tool was used to expand the wizard's abbreviations of, for example, airport names; a second tool corrected the wizard's typos; and a third tool was a simulated recognizer, which would take as input the utterance keyed in by the wizard and produce a string which could have been recognized by the real recognizer; that is, out-of-vocabulary words and grammar would either not be recognized or would be misrecognized. For more details on the user test see Chapter 8.

An *assistant* is a person who assists the wizard on the system simulation side and does not communicate with the subjects. It is strongly recommended to off-load the wizard in this way. The assistant may share part of the simulation support tools with the wizard. For instance, the assistant may take notes during the wizard's interaction with subjects. These notes are passed to the wizard for use during later stages of the interaction (Section 5.6.1). The assistant may also act as the wizard's interface to system components (Francony *et al.*, 1992), and help operate other parts of the equipment including the data collection tools (see below). To minimize response times and reduce error, the assistant needs to be trained.

5.3.3   The User Side
Controlled and Uncontrolled WOZ

The user side consists of subjects who may be selected according to certain criteria and who are usually instructed on their roles in various ways. When subjects are selected and instructed, the WOZ experiment corresponds to a controlled user test of the simulated system. In some cases WOZ experiments correspond, rather, to field tests of an as yet not fully existing system. In a field test subjects are real users acting in their proper task environments and performing the tasks when they need to do them. In such cases, subjects are neither selected nor instructed by the system developers. Field tests conducted as WOZ experiments are reported in Basson *et al.* (1996) (test of various telephone service systems for banking and otherwise) and Francony *et al.* (1992) (test of a tool for corpus collection). In the following, we focus on the approach corresponding to a controlled user test.

The Subjects

Because users tend to act differently depending on whether they communicate with humans or with machines, it is important that they believe that the simulated system is a real system. To conceal the fact that the system is being simulated, the user end interface device (typically a telephone or a computer) should be the same as the one to be used in the final system. In addition, subjects should preferably act in their habitual or intended environments in order to make the setting as realistic as possible and remove the stress factor imposed by a laboratory environment.

The number of subjects to be used in a WOZ simulation is subject to debate and depends on the purpose of the simulation. Simulations that are mainly aimed at training the wizard may involve relatively few subjects. However, to collect a reliable set of data on user–system behaviour, several subjects are needed. In fact, the more subjects, the more reliable the data will be, but, typically, resources tend to impose strong limitations on the number of subjects to involve and the number of dialogues to be collected because the process of running the experiments and handling and evaluating the corpus is time consuming. Nielsen (1993) estimates that the use of 13 subjects will yield a 90% chance that the true values, i.e. those which will be measured in the final system, will be no more than 15% different from the mean values measured in the experiment. From a cost–benefit perspective Nielsen (1993) suggests using 15 subjects, whether or not several iterations are needed. Several smaller tests may be preferable to a single larger test. Fraser and Gilbert (1991b) point out that "in principle, the cycle of simulation and specification should be repeated many times, but in practice, two or three phases are likely to be sufficient". Reducing the need for WOZ iterations to this minimum requires careful: (i) planning of experiments; (ii) analysis of the collected data; and (iii) re-design of the interaction model.

Early WOZ experiments serve the purpose of training the wizard and delimiting the domain. These experiments are often rather informal, involving, for instance, colleagues or students rather than intended end-users, and taking place in ad hoc settings rather than in realistic work environments. In the later experiments which are aimed at producing reliable data on the system being developed, subjects should be selected such that their backgrounds and skills correspond to those of the expected end-users, in order that their behaviour during simulation will approximate that of end-users. Background and skills are not only a question of being novice or expert in the domain. Subjects' educational and professional background also seems to influence the way in which they communicate with the system (see Nielsen (1993) and Section 5.6.2).

If the main objective of the WOZ simulations is the investigation of specific phenomena, such as language use or users' reactions to certain kinds of system prompts, more subjects and a broad representation of backgrounds and skills may be desirable.

Instructing the Subjects

As it is desirable that subjects believe that they are interacting with a real system, they should not be told the truth in advance. Neither should they be told a direct lie for ethical reasons (Nielsen, 1993, Section 6.4). Instead, they should be given vague information which may be interpreted as if the system is a real one. Unless the experiments are of a kind where no instructions are provided and subjects do not know that they are acting as such, care should be taken to ensure that subjects know exactly what they are expected to do and are able to perform their tasks in as natural a way as possible. This can be done through a variety of means. Users may be informed orally, for instance on the telephone, and/or they may receive written instructions. The written instructions may include, for instance, information on the experiment and the subject's role and tasks, general information on the system's capabilities and how to communicate with it, information on how to use the system through an example of an actual dialogue with the system, and scenarios which subjects are expected to perform.

A scenario represents a task which the subject has to perform through interaction with the system. Scenarios are important tools in interactive speech system development and evaluation. Nevertheless, the literature on interactive speech systems has little to say about scenario design and on the many problems to be aware of. The purpose of using scenarios is to develop and test the interaction model in realistic situations of use of the system under construction, while at the same time being able to control more precisely what is being tested (see below), and to introduce some amount of systematicity into the testing process. There is, however, no known method for designing scenarios which are representative of all possible situations of use of the artefact which is being designed (Klausen and Bernsen, 1993). So a basic problem in scenario design is to capture, in a limited set of scenarios, as many probable situations of use as possible.

It is useful to distinguish between development scenarios and evaluation and test scenarios (Campbell, 1992). *Development scenarios* are intended to more or less systematically cover the intended system functionality, and are normally designed by the system designers. User-designed scenarios will typically not be appropriate for the purpose of system development. They will fail to address all aspects of system functionality and it may be difficult or impossible to figure out what it is that the user attempts to achieve. However, the risk in using only designer-designed scenarios is that designers may ignore important task aspects and other constraints, ending up with an implemented system which works well only in a fictitious world. *Evaluation and test scenarios* often cover only selected aspects of system functionality because a user test aims at covering typical cases rather than all possible cases. For instance, possible but unlikely cases of communication failure will often be left out, but it must be carefully considered precisely what to test and why. It is recommended that scenarios for evaluation and testing of the system be developed jointly by designers and end-users to ensure sufficient realism.

A central problem in scenario design is that users tend to model the scenarios whenever possible, treating the scenario as a text which has to be reproduced in detail when interacting with the system. This is a problem because a vocabulary defined on the basis of interactions in which users model the phrases used in the scenarios may not be sufficiently representative of realistic language use. On the other hand, it is not always a solution to provide open scenarios in which subjects have to define most of the details themselves and are thus forced to use their own phrases. The reason is that a controlled test cannot be carried out when it is not known precisely what is being tested. Thus, scenarios clearly have to describe, to some necessary extent, the tasks to be performed by the subjects while at the same time avoiding the subjects directly modelling the phrases used in the scenarios. A possible solution to this problem will be further discussed and illustrated in Section 5.6.2.

5.3.4   Data Collection

WOZ produces a wealth of important data on interaction including information on the system's task domain coverage, users' sub-language vocabulary, utterance length, grammatical complexity of input, input utterance (un)grammaticality, number of turns per scenario, users' task ordering preferences and problem-solving strategies, dialogue act types, system output/user input correspondences with respect to vocabulary, grammar and style, scenario design problems, interaction design problems, user errors, non-linguistic user behaviour, etc.

To capture these data, interaction at the user interface and activity at the wizard interface is normally logged and recorded for later analysis. Results of the analyses are used to improve the simulated system as a basis for subsequent iterations or implementation. The input/output modalities involved in user–system interaction guide and constrain the choice of hardware for data logging. If spoken language is the only input/output modality involved, a tape recorder will often be sufficient for logging the interaction. Depending on the purpose of the experiment, it may be useful or even necessary to use a camera to record the subject's physical behaviour during spoken interaction, including facial expression, gesture and movement. If system components and/or automatic support tools are being used in an experiment, a log of system internal communication will be needed as well to generate a complete trace of the interaction flow.

In general, as WOZ simulations tend to generate large amounts of data, there is a strong need for improved facilities for data filtering, indexing, transcription, viewing and analysis. We shall return to this issue in Chapter 7.

5.3.5   Post-experimental Contacts

When subjects have interacted with the system, contact with them is not necessarily over. Important input on system functionality and user satisfaction may be obtained through questionnaires and interviews.

Questionnaires may be distributed along with other material given to subjects, such as scenarios. When designing questionnaires, care should be taken to phrase and present the questions in a neutral way in order not to guide subjects in one direction or another. A section on "any other comments or observations" should be included in the questionnaire. The filling-in of a questionnaire should not require too much effort because subjects may then either not do it or do it superficially. On the other hand, it must be ensured that, if answered properly, the questions will provide useful input for subsequent work on the interaction model. This is not necessarily easy to do, and questionnaires can be hard to interpret (see Section 8.5). Questionnaires have become a scientific subject in themselves. Useful references are Anastasi (1988) and Miller (1984).

Face-to-face or telephone interviews should be carried out immediately after subjects' interaction with the system. It should be decided in advance which questions to ask as a minimum. Asking the same questions in all interviews enables comparison of the subjects' responses. Compared to questionnaires, interviews often provide additional information on user–system interaction. Subjects may be willing to orally tell about experiences with the system which are either too lengthy to write down or which they simply do not want to put in print. They may also tell things which just come to mind in a non-committal interview but which they were prevented from thinking of in the more formal questionnaire context. The interview tends to capture subjects' immediate impression of the system whereas the questionnaire tends to capture their reflections upon having used the system. A useful reference on interviewing is Ericsson and Simon (1985).

5.4   Developing the First Interaction Model

Before the first WOZ experiment can start, a first interaction model must be established and represented in a way which makes it easy to interpret for the wizard. It is useful during its design to consider all the elements of interactive speech theory from Chapter 2. It may be helpful as well to make use of the guidelines for cooperative spoken human–machine interaction discussed in Chapter 4. The aim in what follows is to highlight the wizard's problems and discuss solutions to these. Many issues that arise during WOZ cannot be planned in advance. Still, much can be done to prepare a detailed and realistic interaction model for the first WOZ iteration, thereby accelerating system development. To structure the presentation, each element of interactive speech theory is discussed with regard to its relevance for the design of a WOZ interaction model with no implemented components. If implemented components are used in the WOZ set-up, the elements handled by these components can be disregarded and an interface for the wizard to the components should be considered instead. The implemented components still form part of the interaction model and must fit the simulated elements.

The design of the first interaction model focuses on what we have called system performance including cooperativity, initiative and influence on user behaviour. Each element to be included in the model should support system performance and help optimize system functionality within the constraints imposed by the requirement specification.

Speech Input

Recognition including acoustics, grammar and prosody comes for free in simulated interaction because humans are excellent speech recognizers, superior in most respects to the system being designed. This means that detailed decisions are needed on which input the system will be able to recognize, followed by training of the wizard. It is difficult to remember when to reject something as not being recognized when one actually did recognize it perfectly well. Moreover, it is impossible to simulate precisely the errors which the implemented system will commit. Still, misrecognition should be simulated at some stage during WOZ in order to learn about users' reactions when this happens and collect generally reliable data on user-system interaction. The restrictions imposed on the wizard's recognition should be few and simple in order to be manageable. Examples of simple rules are: "do not recognize more than the first 10 words in a user utterance, more or less; if the utterance is longer than that then skip the rest"; "do not understand any person names" and "do not understand negations". The wizard may to some extent acquire the skill of failing to understand words that are clearly outside the system's intended vocabulary. Many and/or complex rules dictating limitations to the wizard's recognition of input grammar or prosody would appear unmanageable. The precise rules to follow often cannot be planned in advance but must be determined or adjusted on the basis of the simulations themselves. Input filtering may be used to provoke wizard misrecognitions. If this is properly done, the wizard may avoid having to follow explicit rules.

User Utterances

The wizard's understanding of user utterances, including lexicon, grammar, semantics and style, also comes for free in most cases during simulation and is tightly interwoven with recognition. Precautions similar to those mentioned for speech input should be taken.

Attentional State

Focus belongs to the attentional state. The focus set determines which sub-tasks the system is able to communicate about at a given time. If the system's focus set is to be limited relative to its entire capacity for domain communication, the wizard should try to simulate the current focus limitations (corresponding to the system's expectations), possibly helped by the assistant.

Intentional Structure

Restrictions on the wizard's input understanding may be imposed by the intentional structure. If the user's domain communication addresses other tasks than those known to the system, then such user utterances should not be understood. The structure of each planned system task, i.e. the sub-tasks of which it consists and their order, if any, must be considered prior to simulation. This will enable the wizard to know which information is required to perform a certain task. In the case of system-directed interaction the task structure will be fixed. If the user tries to address a sub-task other than those which are in focus, the wizard should not understand the user. The user and the system may communicate in terms of domain communication, meta-communication and other types of communication. Provided that the wizard follows rules of limited understanding, such as those exemplified above, the WOZ experiments are guaranteed to produce a certain amount of knowledge about user–system meta-communication. It must also be decided which forms of user-initiated meta-communication the wizard should understand, such as asking for correction or repetition. The wizard's meta-communication behaviour must be carefully planned and revised in the light of experience. It must be determined to what extent other types of system communication are needed, such as the opening and closing of the interaction. The interaction level strategy, which defines the constraints on user communication that are in operation at a certain stage during interaction, may be used for graceful degradation of the interaction. In that case, it must be considered to what extent the strategy will be feasible and how it should be simulated by the wizard.

Linguistic Structure

Restrictions on the wizard's understanding and generation of linguistic structure elements may contribute to a more system-like behaviour. If, for example, the system will be using system-directed dialogue then user questions, or other possible speech acts in which the user takes the initiative in the interaction, should not be accepted. A problem with this strategy, however, is that as long as the system itself is not being able to identify speech acts, it is difficult to judge the relevance of the strategy. Or, if it is known that the final system cannot accept more than one or two pieces of information at a time, then the wizard should reject part of user turns containing more than one or two pieces of information. Depending on their type, references may be difficult to handle in an implementation because of missing techniques. It should be considered which kinds of references the wizard should be able to understand. For instance, it may be decided that references to parts of the interaction other than the immediately preceding utterance should not be understood by the wizard. Discourse segmentation is unlikely to be simulated in a WOZ experiment.

Interaction History

To some extent, most systems need to keep track of the history of the interaction. Linguistic history, topic history and performance history mostly come for free in a simulation because they form part of the wizard's natural capabilities. However, consideration of their implemented versions might impose restrictions on the wizard's performance. For instance, it may be decided that the user's performance should not lead to modification of the wizard's interaction behaviour. Most interactive speech systems will need a task record. Wizards, like other humans, are prone to forget precisely what information has been exchanged during the interaction so far. The task record therefore should be maintained during simulation, for instance by the assistant who writes down the information provided by the user.

Domain Model

The domain model of the system includes data and rules. The data comprise the domain facts needed by the system. Domain facts might, for instance, be a list of names and addresses, a table of departure times or a list of fares. One should be aware that database look-up may be slow when performed manually. The wizard must therefore have easy access to the domain facts and must have a notion of the extent to which the planned system will be able to do inferencing. The wizard must be able to check or retrieve facts when needed, for instance by checking whether a certain name is in the database or inferring a date from a relative time expression. The wizard may or may not know something about the domain in advance. Knowing too much may be a problem because the wizard will then have to simulate less knowledge than is actually present. Knowing little or nothing may also be a problem because the domain then has to be learnt. In both cases training is needed. The exact amount of domain inferencing needed for the application will probably have to be determined through WOZ and cannot easily be planned in advance.

User Model

One of the key functions of WOZ is to provide solid information on how people actually behave when interacting with an interactive speech system that is constrained in multiple ways. So in many respects the user model relevant to the system under design, including the actual user goals, beliefs, expectations, preferences and cognitive processing problems, will only emerge from the simulations themselves. Still, the developers are potential users themselves and they are advised to put considerable effort into acting as real users when building the first interaction model. Moreover, it is useful to consider from the start the extent to which the simulation should provide a different treatment of different user groups. If differential treatment will possibly be provided, the wizard should simulate ways of doing that.

System Utterances

System utterances including lexicon, grammar, semantics and style, are much easier to generate for a human than for machine. It is therefore important to consider from early on which output the system should be able to generate, taking into account what the system will be able to understand, as users will often model the system's language. An interactive speech system is typically programmed to express itself rather uniformly in contexts which are identical to one another. Humans, on the other hand, tend to constantly vary their language, even in identical contexts. Again, the wizard must be prepared to modify his or her natural behaviour in spoken interaction. Fortunately, the wizard's output behaviour can be supported by external means, such as sets of pre-defined phrases for consistent use in similar situations whenever they occur during interaction. The wizard's style of expression is another important factor which can be decided upon in advance. A terse style is recommended.

Speech Output

Given the regimentation of the wizard's utterances just described, speech output comes partially for free in a simulation. Text-to-speech or replaying techniques may be very helpful. If these are not being used, the wizard must be able to exert voice control, avoiding phenomena such as stumbling over words, false starts, non-speech sounds, undue hesitations, etc. This requires training. It must also be decided how the wizard's voice should sound, i.e. whether it should sound human or more or less "synthetic". If the latter is chosen, this again requires training of the wizard or use of voice distortion equipment. Wizards can become quite good at speaking evenly and monotonously.

Interaction Model Representation

Two major issues in interaction model representation are the following. First, as already mentioned, the model should be easy for the wizard to interpret and should allow fast navigation. Graphs are useful for these purposes. Figure 5.2 shows part of

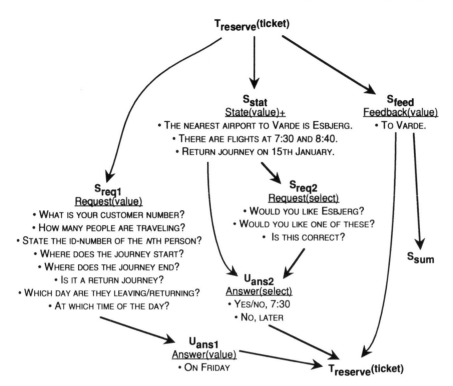

Figure 5.2: Simple interaction model of domain communication. The central path is repeated via S_{req1}, U_{ans1} and S_{feed}, until all items of the reservation task have been determined. In S_{req1} the system phrases for all items are indicated in order to support the wizard. Most other system nodes and all user nodes include examples only. The examples of phrases in S_{stat} and S_{req2} correspond so that the first two phrase pairs are used after a vague U_{ans1} or after S_{error} (not shown), whereas the last phrase pair is used after U_{change} (not shown). Note how the split of S_{stat} and S_{req2} together with the arrows to U_{ans2} allows the user to either respond immediately when the values have been stated or after the system's request.

an interaction model represented as a graph. The representation provides structure to the interaction and allows a fair amount of flexibility of navigation at the same time. Moreover, the model is of manageable size (compare Figure 5.9). Secondly, system development can proceed more rapidly if the WOZ interaction model is represented in a form which is amenable to implementation. If an automatic WOZ simulation environment is available, it may be possible to represent the interaction model using the graph part of a graphical programming language.

5.5   Iterating the Interaction Model

When the WOZ set-up has been completed and tested to make sure that it works, and a first interaction model designed, the first experiments can start. The wizard and the assistant (if any) must have made themselves familiar with the set-up and the equipment used. The wizard interface and the simulation environment should be adjusted if they turn out to cause problems. Typically, the first iteration is carried out with internal subjects, i.e. the designers themselves and perhaps a few colleagues. Although the data resulting from the first iteration will hardly be sufficiently reliable to serve as a basis for implementation, the first series of experiments will provide rough estimates of system and user performance, help train the wizard, and allow new constraints to be added to the specification and unforeseen problems to be solved.

Each WOZ iteration is costly. This is particularly true of the "core" iterations which involve external subjects and which typically involve more subjects than the training iteration(s). The number of core iterations should therefore be reduced as much as possible through careful planning and analysis. It cannot be decided in advance how many iterations are needed to obtain a satisfactory specification of user–system interaction. Fraser and Gilbert (1991b) recommend three or four iterations.

As each iteration produces large amounts of data, it is necessary to selectively focus on data parameters which will be subjected to closer analysis. When used for interactive speech system development, WOZ typically serves as a basis for collecting a sub-language from data on users' vocabulary and use of grammar. Other relevant data parameters follow from the requirement specification, evaluation criteria and design specification. After parameter selection, the actual data are obtained through transcribing the simulated interactions, annotating the transcriptions, and collecting the results for analysis and quantification. Analysis and quantification serve to measure the extent to which design goals have been achieved and constraints satisfied, and the extent to which the evolving system performs according to specifications. Anyone who has been through this process in practice will have realized the need for time-saving, special-purpose automatic annotation and analysis tools (see Chapter 7).

Part of the data available in a WOZ corpus are *quantifiable data*, such as information on subjects' vocabulary in the task domain (full word types, word stem types, non-words); utterance length (average per turn, maximum); (word) type/token ratio; number of turns per task scenario (average, maximum); percentages of questions and statements; grammatical complexity (number and type of grammatical constructs); ungrammatical phenomena (number and type); hesitations and false starts; and number and type of discourse phenomena (anaphora, ellipsis, etc.). Data on wizard performance may be important as well, for instance when measuring against training target levels, such as number of deliberate recognition errors or number and types of errors due to "over-skilled" performance. A central purpose in collecting quantified data is to discover *developmental patterns* in the data across a series of iterations. For one thing, such patterns will show the extent to which specified feasibility constraints on the system are gradually being met across several WOZ iterations. Secondly, developmental patterns can be used to quantify the effects of interaction design changes, from major changes in task domain coverage to subtle changes in the semantics of system utterances, showing whether a certain change actually removed some discovered problem or not. In the design of systems undertaking cognitively demanding tasks, such as interactive speech systems, quantitative development patterns are particularly important because the system must be able to interpret natural and spontaneous user behaviour. In many cases, such as anaphora resolution, we still lack part of the theoretical understanding that may make this possible in the general case, and in a larger number of cases we lack the tools and algorithms necessary to implementation. This means that the capabilities to manipulate developing patterns in user behaviour and to accurately measure the effects of interaction design manipulations are essential to successful design.

WOZ also produces *qualitative* data, for instance from the user questionnaires. The questionnaires are analysed to identify particular problems, general complaints, subjects' overall impression of the system, subjects' qualitative evaluation of selected aspects of the system, etc. Qualitative data will also be produced by the user interviews recommended above. Having been provided orally, these data will have to pass through the interviewer's interpretation before they are put on paper. The qualitative system aspects addressed in questionnaires, such as system naturalness or flexibility, can be operationally quantified by having subjects score these aspects on some arbitrary scale. When this has been done, subjects' scorings from several subsequent WOZ iterations can be compared to identify developmental patterns, as discussed above.

In addition to quantitative and qualitative information there is often a need for extracting and analysing *structural information*, such as variations in the expression of identical messages, users' task or sub-task ordering preferences and stereotypes, or their problem-solving strategies. This information may be used to improve, for instance, the system's task model, its input vocabulary and grammar or its output utterances.

Detection of the problems users have in interacting with the system constitutes an important goal of data analysis. Each problem may suggest that one or more of the cooperativity guidelines presented in Chapter 4 has been violated and that there is a need to change the interaction design. Such problems may be revealed from analysis of the transcribed corpus and from other sources as well, such as the questionnaires. A practical method for quantifying interaction problems is described in Chapter 8.

The process of data analysis and evaluation forms the basis for decisions on whether and how to change the simulated system, or revise the system specification, and for estimating whether another WOZ iteration is needed or not. The decision to end the WOZ simulation phase must be based on evaluation of how well the system performs and meets the goals and constraints specified in the requirement specification, evaluation criteria and design specification. All feasibility constraints should be satisfied at this point. For instance, the sub-language should be more or less known and known to be processable by the system; the transaction success rate should be comparable to what is specified in the evaluation criteria; other important development patterns in the data should converge on satisfying the evaluation criteria for the implemented system, and all the major problems of system cooperativity that were discovered during WOZ should have been removed.

5.6   Uses of WOZ

As mentioned in Section 5.1, a WOZ simulation may be used for two different purposes: as an interactive speech system development technique; and as an experimental method for investigating particular phenomena of general interest to interactive speech system development. This section illustrates the different uses of WOZ by considering the development of the Danish Dialogue System.

5.6.1   Use of WOZ For Development: The Danish Dialogue System

The interaction model for the Danish Dialogue System was developed during seven iterations of WOZ simulations. The first five iterations produced only a few dialogues each, whereas the two last iterations each produced a corpus of 47 dialogues. From the seven iterations a total of 125 dialogues were transcribed, amounting to about 7 hours of spoken language dialogue. Twenty-five early dialogues were never transcribed.

The purposes of the experiments were: (i) to optimize the usability aspects of the system while still satisfying the resource and technological constraints (cf. Section 3.2); and (ii) to collect a sub-language which could serve as a basis for specifying the input vocabulary and input grammars of the system. The task domain was Danish domestic flight ticket reservation, change of reservation, and information on departures, fares and travel conditions.

The WOZ Set-up

Figure 5.3 shows the WOZ set-up. Subject and wizard are connected via a telephone. At the wizard's end, an assistant follows the spoken interaction between the subject and the simulated system. All components will be explained below.

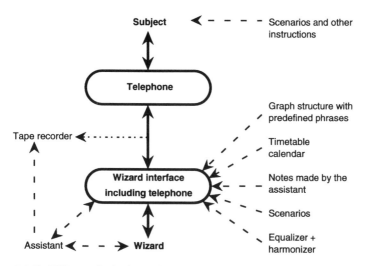

Figure 5.3: The WOZ set-up for developing the Danish Dialogue System. The main communication line follows the solid arrows. The dotted arrow indicates logging. The dashed arrows on the right-hand side of the figure mean "used by". On the left-hand side, dashed arrows show the assistant operating the tape recorder and communicating with the wizard and the wizard interface.

The Experimenter

In the first four iterations there was no need for an experimenter as only system developers were involved as subjects and wizard. The need for an experimenter arose from WOZ5 onwards. In WOZ5 colleagues acted as subjects, and in WOZ6 and WOZ7 most subjects were external. The experimenter contacted subjects and asked if they were willing to participate. When subjects agreed to participate, the experimenter would take care of distributing all relevant material to them. The experimenter acted as contact person before, during and after the simulations. Having interacted with the system in WOZ6 and WOZ7, subjects were debriefed by the experimenter through interviews.

The System (Wizard) Side

The system simulation side consisted of a wizard and wizard support, including, in some iterations, an assistant. All seven iterations were full simulations, i.e. no implemented system modules were included. Simulation thus covered input understanding and output planning and generation, including appropriate response times.

The Wizard

The wizard was one of the system developers. Initially, two system developers took turns acting as wizard but it was soon realized that, because of the amount of wizard training needed, only one person should act as wizard. We used five WOZ iterations for wizard training and for adjusting the interaction model. This was too many even if the individual iterations were small. WOZ1–WOZ4 only included between two and six dialogues each and WOZ5 included 13 dialogues. We started our WOZ work more or less from scratch and without sufficient operational guidance from the literature. We now believe that, given careful planning of the series of iterations and awareness of the problems, the results we obtained from seven iterations could have been achieved in three or four iterations. This agrees with the recommendations of Fraser and Gilbert (1991b).

Supporting the Wizard

The interface device used in all experiments was a telephone. The only kind of *filter* we used on output was a combination of an equalizer and a harmonizer which served to distort the wizard's voice. The hardware gave the wizard's voice a slightly metallic sound with a distant echo-effect. The filter was only used in WOZ7. See Section 5.6.2 for details on the effect of output filtering. No input filters were used.

None of the *simulation environment tools* used in the seven WOZ iterations were automatic. A number of manual tools were used, however. The most important tool was the interaction model. In the first two iterations, the interaction model was represented as a collection of loosely organized output phrases on paper. From WOZ3 onwards, a graph representation with system phrases in the nodes and key contents of user input along the edges was used instead (Figures 5.7 and 5.8). A flight timetable, a list of prices and a calendar were used to represent the domain model part of the interaction model.

In order to keep track of the information provided by the subject, a note sheet was filled in by the assistant (Figure 5.4). At the beginning this was done during the session with the user. We then realized that we could speed up those wizard answers which required "database" look-ups if the look-ups were made prior to the interaction with subjects and the values inserted in the note sheet. This became fairly easy to do when, from WOZ5 onwards, the scenarios became quite detailed. The wizard and the assistant also had copies of the scenarios used by the subjects. In the later WOZ iterations, pre-computed ticket prices were inserted in the wizard's version of the scenarios. This was done to speed up the wizard's response times in cases where subjects asked for a ticket price. The wizard had access to the note sheet and the scenarios whenever needed during the interaction. Moreover, the note sheet was

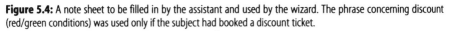

TRAVEL INFORMATION   (tape/side/counter: /   /   )   date:
Assistant: Wizard: User:
You have now booked   ticket(s)
from   to
for (name(s))
on (day, date)   at (time)   ,
returning on (day, date)   at (time)   .
The tickets are on (red/green)   conditions.
Your reference number is   .
Are the tickets to be mailed or will the traveller pick them up at the airport.

Figure 5.4: A note sheet to be filled in by the assistant and used by the wizard. The phrase concerning discount (red/green conditions) was used only if the subject had booked a discount ticket.

organized so that the wizard could read it aloud as summarizing feedback by the end of a reservation dialogue.

From WOZ5 onwards an *assistant* helped off-load the wizard. The assistant was also the experimenter. The assistant operated the *tape recorder*, took *notes* on the information provided by subjects and provided other practical support, such as guidance to the wizard if he lost his way in the graph representation of the interaction model.

The User Side

The user side involved a total of 24 subjects in the seven iterations. During simulation, all interaction with subjects was carried out via the telephone to make the situation as realistic as possible and to allow subjects to communicate in their normal environments.

The Subjects

Only the three system developers participated as subjects in the first four iterations. One system developer and two colleagues participated in WOZ5. WOZ6 and WOZ7 were the "core" iterations that would eventually form the basis for the implemented interaction model including the sub-language. Each of these two iterations involved 12 subjects. The majority of the subjects were external end-user representatives, the rest were colleagues. Apart from three colleagues, none of the subjects in WOZ6 and WOZ7 had tried the system before. Almost all subjects in WOZ6 and WOZ7 had backgrounds as office secretaries, linguists or computer scientists. See Section 5.6.2 for more details on subjects' backgrounds.

Instructing the Subjects

Subjects were contacted by the experimenter. Having agreed to participate, each subject in the fifth, sixth and seventh iterations received instructions in terms of: (i) a letter which briefly introduced the system and gave information on the experiment; (ii) four scenarios; and (iii) a questionnaire to be filled in and returned immediately after interaction with the system. Before an experiment the experimenter would call the subject at work and ask the subject to call the system. Subjects were not told in advance that the system was simulated. The introductory letter was phrased in a way which made people believe that they were about to interact with a real system.

> You study at the Academy of Music in Aalborg. You are going to visit your parents in Copenhagen for Christmas. They have promised to pay your ticket.

Figure 5.5: An early WOZ scenario.

> Book two return tickets from Copenhagen to Aalborg for Tuesday 27th October for Jens Høst and Anton Sigurdsen (id-numbers 27 and 28). They want to travel at 7:00 or 7:30. For the home journey they want the departure at 17:25. The customer number is 110.

Figure 5.6: A late WOZ scenario.

The letter gave information on the background and use of the system, comparing the system to voice response systems which most subjects would have already tried.

Throughout the simulations, interaction with the system was based on scenarios. The first four WOZ iterations were based on a set of 10 loosely defined scenarios describing cases that the system should be able to handle (Figure 5.5). The scenarios had not been designed to systematically represent as many situations of use as possible but were primarily intended for domain and task exploration and for training of the wizard. Subjects often revised a scenario and sometimes invented a new scenario on the spur of the moment which was never written down. In the last three WOZ iterations a new set of scenarios was used. This second scenario set included a total of 28 scenarios. Only some of these were used in WOZ5, whereas all were used in WOZ6 and WOZ7. The scenarios were designed on the basis of the dialogue structure that had emerged from WOZ4. By then the scenarios could be more systematically designed as most of the domain and task structure had been uncovered. The scenarios in the second set contained more detail than those in the first set, and left few or no decisions to the subject (Figure 5.6). This would facilitate the wizard's job because, as mentioned, s/he would be able to anticipate more or less exactly what a user would answer at a certain point during interaction. However, the detailed scenarios turned out to have the negative effect that users began to model the details of the scenarios' phrases. See Section 5.6.2 for more details on the design and use of scenarios.

Whereas the domain coverage of the second set of scenarios was reasonable, the scenarios had not been designed to enable simulation of meta-communication. The scenarios did not provide incorrect information to subjects, and the subjects were not otherwise asked to cause miscommunication. This proved to be a drawback during implementation as we had no information to work on from on users' meta-communicative reactions.

Data Collection

All interactions were recorded on tape. No videotaping was used and, as no computer was involved, no electronic log files were produced. Apart from the recorded interactions, all documentation from the experiments was in paper form.

Post-experimental Contacts

The questionnaire that was distributed to the subjects contained three types of question. First, subjects were asked about their background with respect to the domain and their use of computers. Secondly, they were asked a series of multiple-choice questions that had been designed to elicit their opinion of the system. Each question was to be answered by choosing a point on a five-point scale from positive to negative. Finally, three questions were asked, inviting subjects to state: (1) what they would like to have changed in the way they had to address the system; (2) what they liked about the system; and (3) what they did not like about it. Nearly all subjects answered and returned the questionnaire. Results from the questionnaire are shown in Figure 8.31.

Following their interaction with the system, subjects received a debriefing telephone interview. Unfortunately, the interviews were not pre-structured as advised in Section 5.3 above, and hence their results are difficult to compare. In the WOZ7 debriefing subjects were asked whether they believed that they had interacted with a real system. The majority of external subjects believed that the system was real whereas, of course, our colleagues knew that it was simulated.

Development of the Interaction Model

The first interaction model for the Danish Dialogue System was not developed systematically on the basis of the elements of interactive speech theory presented in Chapter 2. We did not have the theory at the time, nor did we have the cooperativity guidelines for interaction model design (Chapter 4). It is probably correct to say that the first interaction model was built ad hoc. As discussed in Chapter 3, it had been decided that the system should be able to handle Danish domestic flight reservation, change of reservation, and information on departures, fares and travel conditions. All three system developers had some basic knowledge in the domain. Moreover, publicly available flight timetables and interviews with travel agents provided input for interaction model development.

In the first interaction model, system output was represented as a loosely ordered set of pre-defined, task-relevant phrases. There were no constraints on which phrases could be used in which circumstances nor on who could take the initiative and when. The choice of system output was left fully to the wizard who, as a result, had great problems in consistently using the same phrase in similar situations as well as in simply finding the appropriate phrase among those listed. In addition, the domain coverage was not yet adequate with the result that a needed output phrase was sometimes absent from the interaction model.

Following each iteration, except the very first ones, all recorded interactions were transcribed, annotated, analysed and evaluated in order to assess the extent to which the system goals and constraints had been satisfied. These processes will be described in detail in Chapters 7 and 8.

Evaluation results were used to improve the interaction model before the next WOZ iteration. Obviously, the WOZ1 interactions were far from complying with the requirement specification and, as mentioned, the wizard had severe problems simulating the system in the first place. Although more phrases were added to the interaction model after the first iteration, the second iteration continued to create problems of information management for the wizard. Clearly, a more powerful representation was needed to effectively support the wizard and facilitate his work, as well as to obtain a consistent interaction model which might eventually satisfy the requirement specification. From WOZ3 onwards, a graph structure (a state transition network) having pre-defined system phrases in the nodes and expected

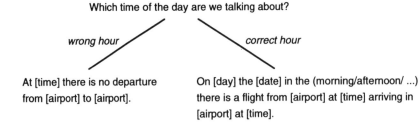

Figure 5.7: Part of the TIME sub-graph from WOZ3 (translated from Danish).

contents of user input along the edges was used for interaction model representation (Figure 5.7). This representation provided much more structure to the tasks that the system should be able to handle. For instance, the graph helped in making explicit the information which the system would need from its user in order to book a ticket. The graph also partially fixed the order in which sub-tasks could be carried out. For each node in the graph there would typically be between one and three possible edges to follow, as illustrated in Figure 5.7. The wizard's task was to decide which edge to follow given the user's input. The number of edges from a single node were to grow later on (Figures 5.8 and 5.9).

Over the following two iterations (WOZ3 and WOZ4), the domain coverage gradually became more well circumscribed and complete. Once the first graph structure was in place, analytical task walk-throughs, as well as scenario-based user interactions, helped reveal missing system phrases and missing graph edges which would force the wizard to improvise during interaction. Figure 5.8 shows a far more elaborate version of the part of the interaction model which deals with hour of departure (compare Figure 5.7).

From WOZ5 onwards, when the task domain structure had become reasonably well defined, development focus shifted towards attempts at satisfying the specification's constraints on system vocabulary, user utterance length and user topic predictability (cf. Chapter 3). Subjects had been explicitly asked to be brief from WOZ4 onwards.

Work on the vocabulary constraint led to elaboration of the language used in the pre-defined system phrases. The idea was that this might contribute to decreasing the size of the vocabulary used by subjects as they would often re-use the system's expressions. Care was taken that the same expressions and phrases were used in similar contexts by the system. It was particularly clear that subjects modelled the system's phrases when offered a choice between several possibilities, but similar behaviour could be observed in other situations as well, such as re-use from system questions. For instance, if the system asked "Where does the journey start?", many subjects would reply "The journey starts in …".

Work on the user utterance length and user topic predictability constraints led us to take away the initiative from subjects to elicit more predictable answers. Interaction thus became increasingly system-directed, partly through the transformation of user questions into system questions. Users' answers are typically shorter than their questions. After each iteration, we looked for system phrases or utterances which caused too lengthy or unpredictable answers, or which confused

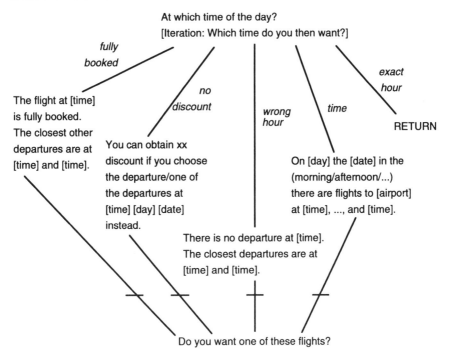

Figure 5.8: Part of the TIME sub-graph from WOZ6 (translated from Danish).

subjects into asking questions. Such phrases or utterances were revised and often made more specific. Sometimes intonation was used to make the meaning of the system's output clearer. Finally, the wizard had been training from early on to use a monotonous, machine-like voice. This was meant to support users in believing that they communicated with a real system, which again might influence their use of language, making it simpler and briefer.

Between the fifth and sixth WOZ iteration we recorded a corpus of 25 Danish domestic flight reservation dialogues in a travel agency, corresponding to about 1 hour of spoken human–human conversation. The original intention had been to make these recordings early in the design process and prior to the development of the first interaction model, but this had proved impossible because of practical problems. Based on the recordings, the WOZ6 interaction model was adjusted in the light of typical task order structures identified in the human–human flight reservation conversations.

In WOZ6 and WOZ7 restrictions were imposed on what the wizard would be able to understand. This was not done on the basis of explicit rules as recommended in Section 5.4. It was left to the wizard to judge when user input was too far from what the final system would be able to manage. When this happened, the wizard would ask again for the information.

In WOZ7 most constraints were satisfied. Those which were not, or whose satisfaction remained unknown, were essentially the following three. First, although the vocabulary size in each individual iteration was well within the 500 word limit, no convergence was found. The prediction therefore was that 500 words would be insufficient for the application. Secondly, meta-communication had been virtually ignored

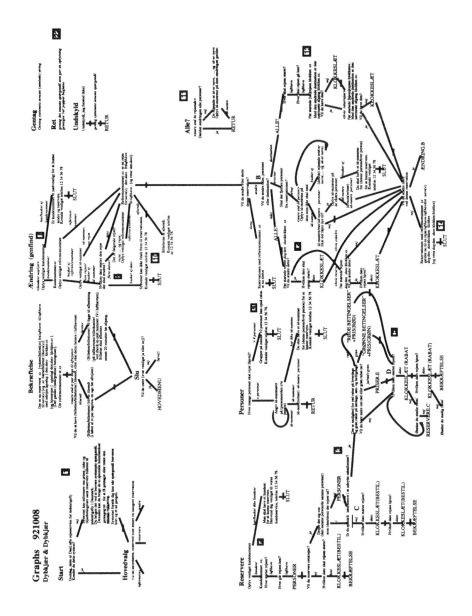

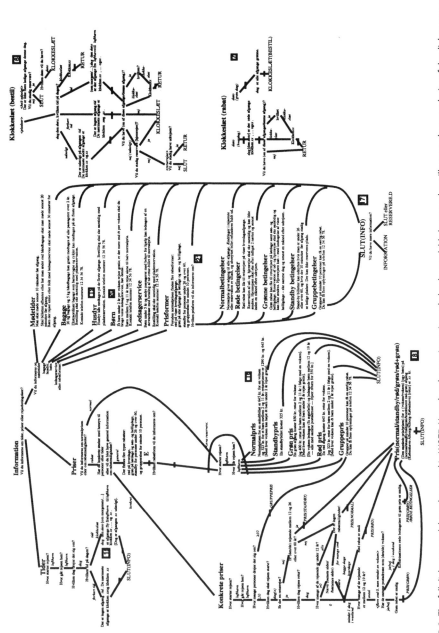

Figure 5.9: The full dialogue model graph as used in WOZ2. Note that the text is not intended to be readable but merely to illustrate the complexity of the dialogue model.

during simulation. Thirdly, the need for system-directed interaction meant that two of the three tasks originally planned for the application, i.e. the information and change of reservation tasks, could be handled only in a very unnatural, menu-like way which we did not consider acceptable to users. Under the given constraints those two tasks were considered unfeasible.

5.6.2   Uses of WOZ For Experimentation

We used the WOZ simulations for studying or experimenting with some parameters of potential importance in the use of WOZ for interactive speech system development. Three studies are presented below. The first experiment addresses the influence of voice distortion. The second study addresses the effects of users' backgrounds. The third experiment investigates users' modelling of scenarios. The latter study was performed during the user test of the Danish Dialogue System. However, as scenario design is basic to WOZ, the investigation will be presented in this chapter.

Voice Distortion

In half of the WOZ7 interactions system output was filtered to distort the wizard's voice. We wanted to test the influence of output filtering on subjects' behaviour and beliefs about the system. In contrast to much of the literature, such as Amalberti *et al.* (1993) and Fraser and Gilbert (1991a, 1991b), we found that system output filtering had no significant effect on user performance or on subjects' beliefs about the system. When parameters, such as number of turns, word types, word tokens and word tokens per turn, were compared there was a small difference between interactions in which system output was filtered and those in which no filter was used. However, this difference was not significant. Furthermore, the subjects who heard the distorted voice on average used more turns, word types, word tokens and word tokens per turn than the subjects who heard the wizard's undistorted voice. Our hypothesis is that, in our case, the potential effects of output filtering had already been achieved by a combination of strongly system-directed dialogue and the wizard's (mostly successful) use of monotonous voice and controlled intonation (Dybkjær and Dybkjær, 1993).

Subjects' Backgrounds

In WOZ6 and WOZ7 most subjects were either professional secretaries, academic linguists or academic computer scientists. We looked at how the users' backgrounds affected their interaction with the system. The secretaries had considerable domain knowledge. The computer scientists had considerable general system knowledge but were not domain experts. The linguists neither had considerable general system knowledge nor were they domain experts.

The results obtained during WOZ6 and WOZ7 provide confirmation that subjects' professional backgrounds affect their interaction with the system. Figure 5.10 shows that the linguists tended to use many word tokens and many different word types. They experimented with the system to figure out which words and grammatical constructs it would understand. The secretaries were much more cooperative, trying to reach the goal of the interaction as easily and quickly as possible. One group of computer scientists were cooperative, focusing on the goal of the interaction and apparently took care to express themselves briefly as they had been asked to do. The second

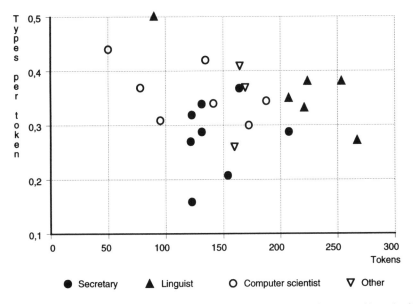

Figure 5.10: Average number of word types per word token in relation to number of tokens used by each subject in WOZ6 and WOZ7.

group of computer scientists experimented with the system, but not, like the linguists, with grammatical constructs but, rather, with the system's semantics (Dybkjær and Dybkjær, 1993).

Although hardly based on statistically significant numbers of subjects, Figure 5.10 illustrates a simple point. This is the importance of choosing the right user groups for WOZ experimentation. Because subjects' backgrounds appear to affect their interaction with the system, it is important to choose subjects with a background corresponding to that of the users of the final system. Ignoring this precaution runs the risk of obtaining data which are less reliable than they might have been. Just as an untrained human wizard cannot fully simulate an interactive speech system, it seems probable that having a certain type of background, experience and training cannot be simulated. It is therefore not sufficient just to ask any person, such as a student, to behave in the WOZ experiment as s/he believes that, for instance, a professional secretary would behave. The parameters which were in focus in the WOZ development of the Danish Dialogue System, such as vocabulary and utterance length, cannot be simulated straightaway. What is a natural way of communication in context for a professional secretary is not necessarily quite as natural for an academic linguist.

Priming Effects of Scenarios

Analysing the Problem

In parallel with the user test of the Danish Dialogue System, we investigated to what extent subjects were primed by scenarios. The reliability of the collected data on users' sub-language depends on the fact that subjects' use of spoken language during interaction with the system is not overly influenced by the written language used in the scenarios. When interacting with the implemented system users will use spontaneous speech rather than read-aloud speech. It is crucial that the system's sub-language is developed on the basis of spontaneous speech similar to that used by the eventual user population. During the final WOZ experiments we discovered that subjects tended to repeat the date and hour of departure expressions used in the scenarios. We therefore decided to test the extent of these priming effects and how they might be avoided.

First, a set of scenarios were systematically generated as follows. Because the flight ticket reservation task is a well-structured task in which a prescribed amount of information must be exchanged between user and system, it was possible to extract from the dialogue structure a set of sub-task components, such as number of travellers, age of traveller and discount or normal fare, any combination of which should be handled by the system. The scenarios were generated through systematically combining these components. This process generated a set of 20 scenarios described in written text much like those from the late WOZ experiments (see Figure 5.6).

We then considered how to prevent users from modelling the scenario language in order to avoid the risk that the language understood by the final system would be that of the designers rather than that of the end-users. For each sub-task in the dialogue structure, the type of question posed by the system was categorized. There were four types of question. One type invited a yes/no answer. A second type invited an answer containing an item from an explicit list of alternatives, i.e. a multiple-choice question. The third type invited the user to state a proper name or something similar to a proper name, such as an airport name or the user's own customer number. The fourth type were open questions about a specific topic, such as the date of departure. In the first three cases, the key information to be provided by the user can be cooperatively expressed only in one of several closely related ways, which means that it does not matter whether users model the expressions of the scenario representation. For instance, there are only two different names for the airport in Copenhagen ("Copenhagen" and "Kastrup") and both must be included in the system's vocabulary no matter which name is being used in the scenarios. It is only in the fourth case that cooperative user answers may express the key information in many different ways. It is exactly in these cases that it is desirable to know how users would spontaneously express themselves and, hence, mandatory to prevent them from modelling the scenario expressions. Questions of this type all concerned date and hour of departure. We therefore decided to focus on masking the scenario expressions of date and hour of departure.

In general, dates are either expressed in relative terms as being relative to, for instance, today, or in absolute terms as calendar dates. Hours are either expressed in quantitative terms, such as "10:15 AM" or "between 10 and 12", or in qualitative terms, such as "in the morning" or "before the rush hour". The masked scenario representations never included re-usable expressions referring to dates or hours of departure. *Relative dates* were expressed through presenting a list of days from today onwards. *Absolute dates* were expressed as calendar indices such as might be used by a customer when booking a flight. *Quantitative hours* were expressed using the face of a clock. *Qualitative hours* were expressed using (travel) goal state temporal expressions rather than departure state temporal expressions, such as in "they want to arrive early in the evening". This means that the user had to: (i) make an inference from the hour indicated in the scenario representation in order to determine when it would be desirable to depart; and (ii) spontaneously articulate the result of that inference. This would exclude the possibility of priming.

Rikke Hansen (customer number 4, ID-number 2) from Copenhagen is going to travel to Rønne in Bornholm on January 23 at 10:15. Rikke is 10 years old.

Figure 5.11: Scenario T21 described in written text only.

Rikke Hansen (customer number 4, ID-number 2) from Copenhagen is going to travel to Rønne in Bornholm as shown in the calendar and on the clock. Rikke is 10 years old.

JANUARY 1995								FEBRUARY 1995							
M	T	W	T	F	S	S	WEEK	M	T	W	T	F	S	S	WEEK
						1	52			1	2	3	4	5	5
2	3	4	5	6	7	8	1	6	7	8	9	10	11	12	6
9	10	11	12	13	14	15	2	13	14	15	16	17	18	19	7
16	17	18	19	20	21	22	3	20	21	22	23	24	25	26	8
23	24	25	26	27	28	29	**4**	27	28						9
30	31						5								

Figure 5.12: The same scenario as in Figure 5.11 but represented through a combination of text and analogue graphics (G21). The journey start date and week are in bold type, i.e. Monday (M) 23 January 1995 in Week 4.

To test the effects upon users' language of masking all temporal expressions in the scenario representations, subjects were divided into two groups, one serving as the control group. Each test scenario was represented in two different ways (Figures 5.11 and 5.12). The masked version (Figure 5.12) combines language and analogue graphics, whereas the control group version (Figure 5.11) uses standard written text. The test involved a total of 12 subjects. Six subjects received text scenarios and another six received analogue graphic scenarios. Each subject interacted with the system on the basis of four different scenarios. Subjects sometimes repeated a scenario if they did not succeed the first time. In this way, 32 dialogues based on text scenarios and 25 dialogues based on graphic scenarios were recorded. For more details on the user test see Chapter 8.

Our hypotheses as regards date and time were that: (1) there would be a massive priming effect from the text scenarios and none from the graphic scenarios; and (2) the dialogues based on graphic scenarios would contain a richer vocabulary than those based on text scenarios in terms of (i) total number of different words and (ii) out-of-vocabulary words. The reason for the first hypothesis was explained above. The reason for the second hypothesis was that the richness of the spontaneous spoken language of the users would exceed that of the designers. The first hypothesis was confirmed but the second was not. In addition, we found an unexpected result which could provide a strong argument in favour of using analogue graphic scenarios in (sub-language) interaction model development.

Priming Effects

As expected, there was a massive priming effect from the text scenarios and virtually none from the graphic scenarios. The first row of Figure 5.13 shows the "cleaned" number of user turns for which priming from the scenarios was possible. "Cleaned" means that we have counted only the first occurrence of a user answer containing a date or a time in response to each of the four system questions concerning the dates and times of out and home journey departures. In these cases, there is no immediate priming from the expressions used by the system itself and figures are not influenced by repeated or changed user answers.

	WOZ7	Text	Graphic
First date and time answers	74	106	84
Primed answers	59	59	1
Primed out date	91%	45%	-
Primed home date	83%	23%	-
Primed out hour	68%	78%	-
Primed home hour	73%	71%	-

Figure 5.13: Priming effects in WOZ7 and in text scenario-based and graphic scenario-based interactions, respectively (see text).

Each date or time expression in the users' answers was compared to the scenario text. Complete matches and matches where *optional* parts of the date or time expression had been left out or added were counted as primed cases. If *non-optional* parts of the date or time expression had been changed, the case was considered as non-primed. For example, if the scenario said "Friday the second of January", then "the second of January" and "Friday the second" would count as primed but not "the second of the first" which is a common Danish calendar expression. All annotation and counting concerning priming was done independently by two of the system developers, and compared and discussed in case of disagreement.

In the text scenario-based interactions, priming was not equally distributed across date and time. This may have the following explanation. The time expressions used in the scenarios were similar to the feedback expressions used by the system and chosen from among the most common expressions of time in Danish. A broader variety of date expressions was used in the text scenarios, although most frequently of the form "the second of January". Furthermore, there are several frequently used date expression formats in Danish. The system's feedback was of the form "the second of the first". The decrease from 45% (out date) to 23% (home date) partly seems to be due to the fact that users went from modelling the scenario text to modelling the system's feedback when answering the question about home date, and partly due to the use of relative dates such as "the same day".

Throughout the WOZ scenarios the date format "Friday the second of January" was used, which was in accordance with the system's feedback. This, and the general frequency of this expression, may explain the high date priming percentage in WOZ7.

It was controlled that the observed priming from the text scenarios was not simply an effect of using standard expressions which subjects would have used anyway. The date and time expressions used in the interactions based on graphic scenarios were compared to the corresponding expressions used in the text scenarios. As the graphic scenarios often contained no precise hour, time expressions were also compared by form. The result is shown in Figure 5.14. A full match means that if the expression had been found in the corresponding interaction based on the text scenario, it would have been considered primed. In a form match only, the form of the expression is the same as in the text scenario but not its exact value. Figure 5.14 clearly shows that the observed effect in Figure 5.13 cannot be ascribed merely to the use of standard Danish date and time expressions in the text scenarios.

	Full matches	Form matches	Total no. of expressions	Full + form matches
Primed answers	17	10	86	31%
Primed out date	8	-	25	32%
Primed home date	3	-	18	17%
Primed out hour	3	7	25	40%
Primed home hour	3	3	18	33%

Figure 5.14: Priming effects in the graphic scenario-based dialogues when the text scenario priming criteria are

Vocabulary Effects

The use of graphic scenarios did not result in a significantly richer spontaneous vocabulary containing more word types than did the use of text scenarios, nor did the use of graphic scenarios elicit more out-of-vocabulary words. On the contrary, interactions based on graphic scenarios contained *less* different words (Figure 5.15). The scenario sets generated no out-of-vocabulary date terms and only nine new time terms.

Graphic scenario users massively replaced relative dates with absolute dates. This may be because people generally tend to do so in reservation tasks, or because people tend to do so in interaction with machines which they know are inferior with respect to language understanding. Whichever explanation is true, the effect is that subjects tended to standardize their date vocabulary by using exact dates rather than using their relative dates vocabulary.

Similarly, graphic scenario users tended to replace qualitative time with quantitative time, although less strongly so than in replacing relative dates by absolute dates. Again, the tendency is towards exactitude at the expense of using the language of qualitative time. The effect is another limitation on the vocabulary used.

	Text scenarios	Graphic scenarios
no. of subjects	6	6
no. of different scenarios	20	20
no. of dialogues	32	25
no. of user turns	547	451
no. of user turns*	181	178
no. of user word tokens	1606	862
no. of user word tokens*	705	451
no. of user word types	151	94
no. of user word types*	85	63
average user utterance length	2.94	1.91
average user utterance length*	3.90	2.53
longest turn	23	11
number of turns > 10 word tokens	16	1

Figure 5.15: Comparative data on interactions based on two different scenario types. * indicates that the figures presented only concern the parts of the interactions dealing with date and time.

We see three implications of these findings:

(i)   The introduction of graphic scenarios into interactive speech system develop-
      ment is not a means of doing away with good task scenario designs which may
      efficiently explore the task domain, users' language and user task performance.
      Good scenario design, however represented in the scenarios, is still essential to
      good interaction design.

(ii) Given the fact that neither text nor graphic scenarios are able to elicit the full
      diversity of potential user language *vis-à-vis* the system, field trials of interac-
      tive speech systems are still essential to the design of workable real-life systems.

(iii) The good news is that, in the graphic scenarios, subjects demonstrated a clear
      tendency towards expressing themselves in exact terms as regards dates and
      times.

More information on priming and vocabulary effects, including the statistics
involved, can be found in Dybkjær *et al.* (1996, Chapter 15).

An Unexpected Result

We found a significant difference in word tokens per turn, i.e. average user utterance length, between interactions based on text (2.94) and graphic scenarios (1.91),
respectively (Figure 5.15). Apart from the scenario representations, all subjects
received identical information. They were asked the same questions and they all
believed that they were communicating with a machine. Task contents were identical in the two sets of scenarios. There were no significant differences between the
two user populations. The most plausible explanation, therefore, seems to be that
the observed difference is produced by the different scenario representations themselves. In the text-based interactions, subjects *read aloud* from their scenario representation. What they produced was, in effect, not spontaneous spoken discourse
but read-aloud text.

In the graphic-based interactions, subjects could not read aloud from their scenario
representation because it does not contain textual expressions for date and time. To
communicate the task contents of the graphic scenarios, therefore, subjects had to
produce spontaneous spoken language.

When developing realistic interactive speech applications, we need to copy or
imitate realistic situations of use to the extent possible. Use of read-aloud text in
communicating with the system is hardly close to realistic situations of use of most
interactive speech systems. This would imply that textual development scenarios
which afford read-aloud solutions for communicating with the system, are unsuited
for interactive speech system development. Other solutions should be found in order
to ensure that subjects actually do produce spontaneous speech in communicating
with the system. One solution is to use analogue graphic representations of scenario
sub-tasks when necessary. We believe to have shown that this is, in fact, possible to
do for the representation of temporal scenario information.

6. *Implementational Issues*

The implementational issues of interactive speech systems, neither in principle nor in practice, differ much from those of any other software system. Nevertheless, this chapter illustrates some important implementational issues raised in particular by the nature of the dialogue control layer.

In Section 6.1 the overall structure of the Danish Dialogue System is described from an implementational viewpoint, emphasizing the physical architecture and the overall flow of control and data. Section 6.2 describes in more detail the dialogue control layer. Finally, Section 6.3 discusses the problem of debugging. As such, debugging is a rather well-developed area of software engineering. It is included in this book because the emphasis on human–machine dialogue highlights problems that have received little treatment in the standard literature, although similar problems have begun to appear in papers concerning the testing of graphical user interfaces.

6.1   The Overall Dialogue System

Current, limited interactive speech systems have a rather uniform architecture (cf. Figures 1.2 and 2.2). Moreover, the basic functionalities are obligatory. Thus, a combined development and production platform, tailored to interactive speech systems, is useful for the cost-efficient development of such systems. Examples of platforms are GDS (generic dialogue system) (Bækgaard, 1996), and SpeechActs (Martin *et al.*, 1996). Figure 6.1 shows the GDS architecture that was used in the Danish Dialogue System.

Figure 6.2 shows how the structure relates to speech interaction theory. Being hardware, the telephone and telephone line interface actually do not belong to the theory of Chapter 2, but are shown here to indicate the relationship to Figure 6.1. The figure is somewhat simplified, e.g. the bigram is derived from the input grammar, and the semantic output from the parser is post-processed in the dialogue manager (denoted *User input* in Figure 6.3) before it is handed over to the item handler which manages the attentional state and intentional and linguistic structures of the control layer. The term *task item* or just *item* refers to a piece of information that is part of the dialogue task, and will also be used to refer to the *task item object*, i.e. the system representation of the value and status of an item. This will be treated in more detail in Section 6.2.

Figures 6.1 and 6.2 also illustrate that speech interaction theory (Figure 2.2) is a generic conceptual construct that may have different physical expressions. For instance, language generation, dialogue control and most of the dialogue context have been aggregated into one module, whereas the domain context is split into a system-internal domain handler and a system-external database.

The dynamic flow of data is illustrated in Figure 6.3 (cf. the description accompanying Figure 2.3). The illustration shows a dialogue on the route task of a reservation, corresponding to a single exchange of one user utterance followed by the system's feedback. The user has already specified that the journey starts in Copenhagen (code CPH). The user produces a speech signal which, using the recognizer, is converted to the string of lexical references "rejsen går til Aalborg" (*the journey goes to Aalborg*). The parser determines the semantics of the string to be a destination (designated *to* as opposed to *from*) with the value *Aalborg*. This is represented as a *semantic object* "{to=Aalborg}". The item handler then instantiates the task item object TO to the value ALB representing *Aalborg* and some control fields checking and status (cf. Section 6.2). Using the simple query language which forms part of the communication manager protocol, the domain handler then sends a request "eve icm app MOD_DBROUTE (CHP ALB)" to the database to check that the destination pair (CPH ALB) forms a valid route. The request means "an 'event' from the 'ICM' (which is interpreting the dialogue control structure that the domain handler is part of) to the 'application' (alias the database), with the 'modifier' 'database route' and data part 'from Copenhagen to *Aalborg*'". The database in this case responds positively with an OK,

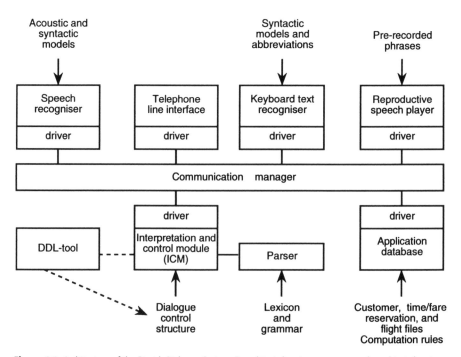

Figure 6.1: Architecture of the Danish Dialogue System. Boxed text denotes a program, unboxed text denotes a resource. Connections represent data flow, with arrowheads indicating single direction only. The dotted lines indicate that the DDL-tool offline generates the dialogue control structure and provides on-line control of the interpretation and control module (ICM), which is an interpreter of the event-driven dialogue description language (DDL). Programs equipped with a driver may run on different machines, communicating via the TCP/IP-based communication manager.

the item is updated with system status `yes`, and the user can be `informed`. Finally, the generation makes a list of the phrase names for the echo feedback "til *Aalborg*" (*to Aalborg*) which is used by the player as names of sound files to be replayed concatenatively.

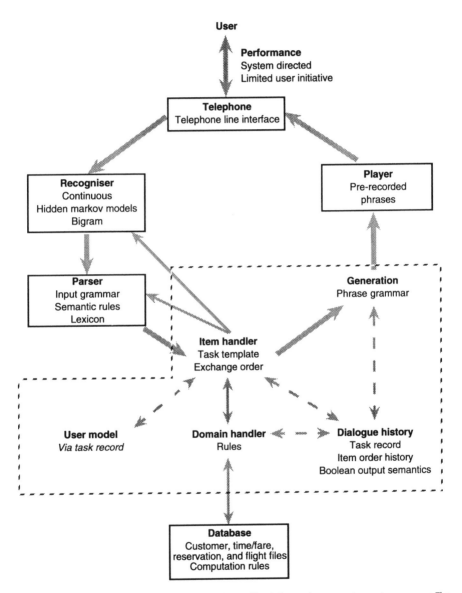

Figure 6.2: Interaction model of the Danish Dialogue System. The six boxes show separate running processes. The dashed box is the dialogue manager, i.e. the ICM plus the dialogue control structure of Figure 6.1. The arrows denote information flow between processes. Dashed arrows are merely reading or updating data structures. The performance is not a process but the behavioural sum-total of the system's processes.

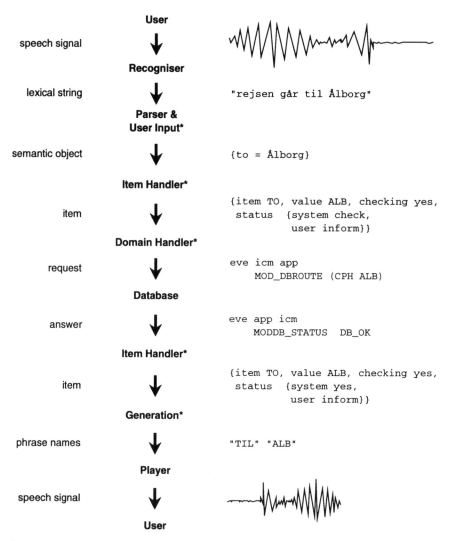

Figure 6.3: Typical data flow from user input to system output in the Danish Dialogue System. *Pre-context:* The FROM task has been completed, establishing that the travel starts in (is from) Copenhagen. Now the task TO is initiated, the item preconditions have been checked, and the item record is {item TO, value _, checking yes, status {system bottom, user bottom}}. *Post-context:* The item record is completed with a value {item TO, value ALB, checking yes, status {system yes, user yes}}. The item post-conditions are checked, i.e., if the change affects any other items that should be re-established, then the corresponding tasks are invoked. Finally, checking is set to false, and control transferred to the next task and item, typically "do you want a return ticket?".

6.2 Dialogue Control

The dialogue control of the Danish Dialogue System separates two issues in a two-level structure: that of the *tasks* to be executed; and that of the *exchanges* to be made for each task. The two levels are linked via *task items*, which are objects describing the domain

System status		
Value	**Reading**	**Meaning**
DB	bottom	No information from the domain representation is recorded about the item.
DN	reject	The value is erroneous according to the domain representation.
DC	check	The value must be checked with the domain representation.
DP	partial	The domain representation has returned a list of possible values.
DA	accept	The value is in accordance with the domain representation.

User status		
Value	**Reading**	**Meaning**
UB	bottom	No information from the user is recorded about the item.
UN	reject	The user has rejected the value (e.g., said "no").
UC	check	The value must be checked with the user.
UP	partial	The user has mentioned an imprecise (partial) value (e.g., "morning" for hour).
UI	inform	The user must be informed about the value.
UA	accept	The user has accepted the value.

Figure 6.4: Possible status values of items in the control structure of the Danish Dialogue System. Note how the values (bottom, reject, partial, accept) describe the system's model of the user's opinion of the value whereas the values (check, inform) describe a need for certain system actions towards the user concerning the current value. The values (check, inform, accept) express different levels of system belief about user agreement.

value and control status of sub-tasks. Below we describe the Danish Dialogue System using these three concepts. The section finishes with more general considerations on dialogue patterns, dialogue formalisms and representations of dialogue models.

Items

The information and reservation types of dialogue tasks, of which flight reservation is an example, may be viewed as information slot filling processes. In the Danish Dialogue System these information slots are modelled by task items. The set of items used is shown in the task template in Figure 2.5. Each item has the three dynamic fields:

- checking: register if this item is currently being checked;
- status: the status that the system assigns to the current value with respect to the domain and the user. The status expresses which action to perform next;
- value: the value of the item, if any.

The possible status values are listed in Figure 6.4. The potential 30 combinations of system and user status are reduced via a table to the seven possibilities: OK; ask for new/choice/confirm; check item; feedback; and error (Figure 6.5). In every case priority is given to the system status, thereby assigning top weighting to the guidelines of truth and evidence (Chapter 4).

For each item a set of statically defined methods or operations is specified. The methods are (cf. also Figure 6.5 below).

- Check pre-required items. For instance, date and route must be established before the departure hour item can be handled.
- Check affected items. After finishing an item it is checked whether other items have potentially been affected. For instance, changing a date is almost certain to affect the departure hour.
- Ask the user for a value, and await an answer. For instance, "What is the destination?".
- Check value. Before inserting a value into an item it must be checked that the value has a valid format and is consistent with the current context.
- Feedback. Tell the user the current item value. For instance, "To Copenhagen".
- Provide error message. Tell the user that a value is wrong. For instance, "There is no route between Aalborg and Århus".

The Task Level

The task level defines the overall structure of the dialogue. It is controlled via a *task template* (cf. Figure 2.5) that describes a static default order for the sub-tasks, and a *dependency table* that describes the dynamic communicational relationships of the tasks. The task template is defined on the basis of the domain (for instance, a route consists of an origin and a destination) and on the basis of naturalness (for instance, field studies of conversation between customers and a travel agent show that traveller identities should preferably be defined before route and time). It is mainly the guidelines of orderliness and background knowledge that must be satisfied in these cases (Chapter 4). An important issue in the specification of items and task template is that of granularity. For instance, we decided to treat *date* as one atomic item and to allow a restricted range of standard linguistic expressions such as "on Friday" and "14 March", combined with semantic rules for completing or expanding these into fully qualified date expressions such as "Friday 14 March 1997", finding the year 1997 from the general dialogue context. The low-level alternative would be to ask separately for day of month and month. The more sophisticated alternative would be to start by asking for the whole date (as happens now), but then ask separately for missing sub-items such as day and month if only some of these are missing (and not directly inferable) in the user input (as recognized by the system). This approach is taken with respect to the route in the Danish Dialogue System.

A task dependency table describes which items must be specified before which other items, and how changes in some items may affect the values of other items. These dependencies are derived from the domain descriptions of the items and are not affected by the dialogue design guidelines of Chapter 4, other than perhaps truth and evidence. The whole dialogue might in principle be driven by the task dependency table just by starting with the reservation item. By applying the dependencies recursively, the dialogue control will eventually wind up asking for all the necessary sub-items. This accentuates that the role of the task template primarily is conversational, to obtain a higher degree of naturalness: from the task domain dependencies taken by themselves, one might very well start by asking, for example for the point of departure, and purely conversational questions such as "Do you know this system?" would never be asked.

The Exchange Level

The atomic tasks are described by the exchange structure, also called the dialogue pattern, and each of them is in a one-to-one correspondence with an item. The dialogue pattern is specified in terms of item operations – the double boxes of Figure 6.5 – and two additional user events. The pattern has four main parts. First, when entering the item handling it is checked that all pre-required items are present. Second, when finishing an atomic task it is checked whether other task items have been affected. Third, there is a means of user-initiated meta-communication via the keywords "repeat" and "change". Not included in Figure 6.5 is the possibility of the system to react with time-out in the case of excessively long pauses. Fourth, there is the central status loop defining the possible structure of exchanges between the user and the system concerning the actual item.

Dialogue Patterns

The item exchange structure, described above, is an example of a dialogue pattern. A *dialogue pattern* is a control structure controlling the low-level structure of

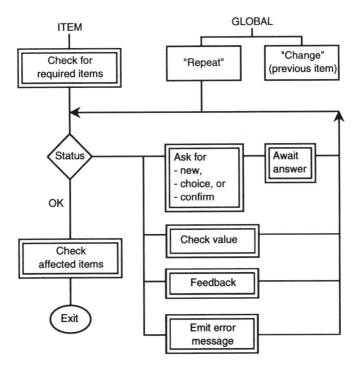

Figure 6.5: Item exchange structure in the Danish Dialogue System. Works co-routinely with task structure (cf. Figure 2.5). All double boxes are parameterized by the item.

exchanges. In the Danish Dialogue System only one single pattern was used. Having a uniform pattern across all items allows the use of few, but well-defined, dialogue acts that are easy to grasp by the user and easy to maintain and grasp by the dialogue designer. Moreover, item-specialized exchange structures work as re-usable dialogue patterns. For instance, in the Danish Dialogue System similar items such as origin/destination and out-hour/home-hour are defined in terms of generic airport and hour items.

The general formulation of dialogue patterns as programming constructs is non-trivial. Novick and Sutton (1996) have experimented with similar dialogue patterns in the CSLUrp generic system. However, the CSLUrp patterns do not solve many of the complex problems encountered when using the common exchange pattern in the Danish Dialogue System. These problems relate to the discussions of object-oriented programming, programming patterns and reusability in general that flourish in computer engineering research. As a concrete example from the Danish Dialogue System, consider the case of dates. The out date and the return date have a quite similar structure which is closely related to that of the generic date. Most grammar, semantics and domain rules may thus be reused. There are differences, however. The *generated phrases* must be different: the system clearly indicates whether it asks for out journey or for home journey. This is handled by the generation module (Figure 6.2). *Semantics* are different: out date is completed relative to today whilst return date is relative to out date – if today is Monday and the user wants to travel on Sunday and return on Tuesday, then (assuming correct recognition) the *Tuesday* is not tomorrow but Tuesday of next week. This is handled in the domain handler module (Figure 6.2). Other differences may turn up, but this example already shows that dialogue patterns, although representing an obvious idea, must be parametrizable in quite advanced ways and cannot be fully separated from the domain and the task.

Dialogue Formalisms

Figure 6.6 shows the item exchange structure of Figure 6.5 as implemented in the Danish Dialogue System using the dialogue description language DDL. Other dialogue description languages are CSLUrp which as a visual programming language is similar to DDL, Philips' HDDL which is a textual formalism, and GADL/IPSIM of Smith and Hipp (1994). Common to all these languages is that they are event-based and have a range of primitive operations that support the speech and language layers of interactive speech theory (Figure 2.2). DDL does not support control above very short and simple touch-tone communication, although it does provide handling of abstract semantic events. The item exchange structure described above, something which is absolutely necessary in any but the simplest dialogues, was programmed in DDL using DDL as an ordinary programming language at the level of Basic or C. For instance, the language does not support inheritance from a common item exchange class; instead, specializations are explicitly implemented by the programmer using 20-way case switches on task item names. HDDL provides some support of operations, such as those shown in Figure 6.6. Only GADL/IPSIM seems to provide strong support of the context layer.

It remains, however, an open question to what extent primitives of any of the languages just mentioned scale up beyond relatively simple, well-structured tasks. Some of the language primitives necessary seem to be:

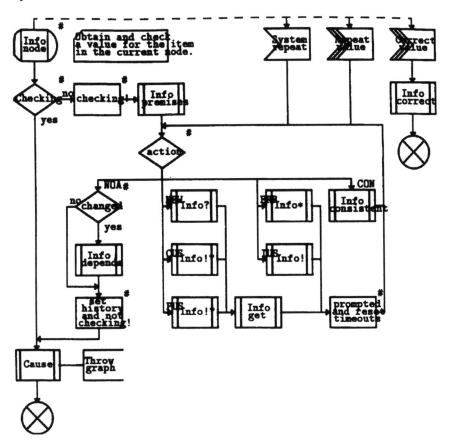

Figure 6.6: The DDL representation of the item exchange structure (cf. Figure 6.5).

- Events, both primitive and more abstract ones, programmer customizable in various ways. Most current dialogue description languages support this to varying degrees.
- Means such as classes, objects and libraries for programming generally, as will be necessary when task complexity grows based on increased dialogue design experience and more robust, large vocabulary recognizers. None of the current dialogue description languages supports this.
- Primitives specialized to the elements of interactive speech theory, such as the specification and generation of system phrases. None of the current dialogue description languages supports all elements, mainly because interactive speech theory is not yet sufficiently well developed. However, those languages do not either support designer extensions with new primitives. See also the following points.
- Support of the speech and language layers. As mentioned, this seems to be the best developed part of current dialogue description languages.
- Support of the control layer (basic item structures, exchange structures, degradation mechanisms, etc.). Given the discussion of dialogue patterns above, some means of constructing objects or components should be available.

• Support of the context layer in terms of standardized database queries, domain constraints and user model. Only GADL/IPSIM is relatively strong here, but lacks support of standard database queries.

Dialogue Model Representations Compared

It may be of interest to compare the three different representations of quite similar models presented in this book, following the chronological order of our work with spoken dialogue models.

The direct representation (Figures 5.7–5.9). The tasks and the exchanges are represented in one single graph, with tasks determining the overall structure. Every detail is hardwired. The aim is to provide a rather detailed and complete, yet easy to survey view of the model for the wizard's use in simulations.

The graph representation which showed the model on one board supported the wizard nicely. However, the model became difficult to survey at a glance, and yet it did not include, by far, all of the relevant structure. A rough calculation showed that should all the tasks be represented in as much detail as the (still incomplete) "hour" sub-graph, then the total graph would have to grow by a factor of 10.

The implementational representation (Figures 2.5, 6.5 and 6.6). The tasks and the exchanges are separated into two independent structures, interacting as co-routines and via guarded (user) events. The common structures are represented in a single dialogue pattern, delegating all specific details to a parametric structure. The aim is to have a complete, yet maintainable and uniform, operational specification that runs as a computer program.

The task template, the pre- and post-conditions, and the parametric item exchange structure together yielded a very flexible structure which, due to its uniformity, strongly supported the final specification of all the system phrases. However, apart from the overall item exchange structure, the representation is difficult to read for the wizard.

The dialogue act representation (Figure 5.2). The tasks and the exchanges are represented in one single structure, with exchanges determining the overall structure. Tasks are determined implicitly via the allowed transitions between system and user dialogue acts. The common structures are represented in a set of dialogue patterns, delegating all specific details to a parametric structure (specified by example). The aim is to present a maintainable, uniform, easy to survey, operational specification for the wizard's use during simulations, a representation which, moreover, facilitates the transition to a computer program.

The dialogue act representation may be viewed as turning the direct representation inside-out. The dialogue act representation takes all the common exchange structures out of the tasks to form the overall structure, letting tasks be defined implicitly inside the node phrases and preconditions. The idea was inspired by the implementational representation described above, as well as by the idea of felicity conditions for speech acts. The representation is very operational and presumably comes close to a computational system. Its graphic, "all on one board" representation is easy to follow during interaction with a user, the more so because of its compactness: the dialogue act representation presents more or less the same information on four A4 pages as the direct model does on 16 A4 pages.

6.3   Debugging

Program testing or debugging is an important part of system development and evaluation. It is the process of making the system behave as intended. Debugging serves
to detect errors in the implemented program and requires a diagnosis to be made
of what is wrong in each case so that errors can be corrected. Basically, there are two
strategies for testing an implemented system: it may be tested bottom-up or top-
down. In *bottom-up* testing, each system module is tested separately by embedding
it in artificial test surroundings and providing it with input of the form requested
by the module in question. By contrast, *top-down* testing is a test of the system as a
whole. Missing parts are replaced by dummies simulating the effect of the absent
parts. System input in a top-down test corresponds to input to the final system.

The advantage of bottom-up testing is that system components developed at
different sites and/or not finished at the same time can be tested separately and independently of the existence of other components. The drawbacks of bottom-up testing are that artificial test surroundings must be built, which may be costly, and that
disagreements on formats in the communication exchange between the modules are
not necessarily revealed.

Top-down testing requires an (almost) final system and the construction of
dummies if there are unfinished parts. This form of testing will reveal disagreements
on formats and is necessary to make sure that all the modules behave together as
intended.

The typical tests carried out during debugging are glassbox tests and blackbox
tests. These tests may be followed by a controlled user test and/or a field test, and
an adequacy test, all of which are kinds of user test (Figure 6.7).

There is no general agreement on the definitions of glassbox and blackbox tests.
By a *glassbox test* we understand a test in which the internal system representation
can be inspected. The test should ensure that reasonable test suites, i.e. data sets,
can be constructed that will activate all loops and conditions of the program being
tested so that nothing is superfluous. The relevant test suites are constructed by the

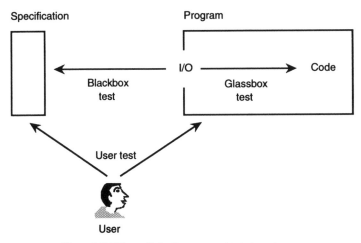

Figure 6.7: Different kinds of test are used to test a system.

system programmer(s) along with an indication of which program parts the test suites are supposed to activate. Via test print-outs in all loops and conditions, it is possible to check which ones were actually activated.

In a *blackbox test* only input to and output from the program are available to the evaluator. How the program works internally is made invisible. Test suites are constructed on the basis of the requirement specification and along with an indication of expected output. Expected and actual output are compared when the test is performed and deviations must be explained. Either there is a bug in the program or the expected output was incorrect. Bugs must be corrected and the test run again. The test suites should include fully acceptable as well as borderline cases to test whether the program reacts reasonably and does not break down in cases of errors in the input. Ideally, and in contrast to the *glassbox* test suites, the *blackbox* test suites should not be constructed by the system programmer who implemented the system as s/he may have difficulties in viewing the program as a *blackbox*.

User tests are discussed in detail throughout Chapter 8.

Blackbox testing and bottom-up and top-down test strategies have been used for the implemented Danish Dialogue System. Bottom-up testing was mainly used in the beginning. Glassbox testing was not really used during the debugging of the dialogue control structure (Figure 6.1). A more detailed presentation of the debugging of the dialogue control structure of the Danish Dialogue System is provided below.

6.3.1   Debugging of the Dialogue Component of the Danish Dialogue System

The dialogue control structure was not subjected to a *glassbox* test in the proper sense of the term. DDL, which is the programming language used for the dialogue control structure, contains a (textual-level) print-out function meant for debugging. However, the contents of the test output is only to some degree automatically generated and must in many cases be written by the programmer. Furthermore, because of the rapidly changing code it would have been almost impossible to maintain data for a complete *glassbox* test. It would have been much too time consuming in relation to what we would gain and to the resources available. Only for final commercial programs may a complete *glassbox* test be required, but it is rare even in these cases. So it was decided to concentrate on the *blackbox* test in the debugging phase.

For the *blackbox* test the implemented dialogue control structure was embedded in the entire system at the earliest possible stage, except for the speech recognizer which was disabled to allow reconstruction of errors. Internal communication between system modules was logged in on log files. We created a number of test suites all containing user input for one or more reservations of one-way tickets and return tickets with or without discount.

A test suite always had to include an entire reservation involving several interdependent system and user turns. In a query-answering system a task will often only involve one user turn and one system turn. Hence one may ask a question and simply determine from the system's answer whether the system functions correctly for the test case. In a task, such as ticket reservation which involves several turns, the system's reactions to the entire sequence of turns must be correct. An apparently correct system reaction, as judged from the system's immediate reaction, may turn out to have been partly wrong when the sequence of interdependent system reactions are inspected. Hence, to test our dialogue model it was not sufficient to test, for example, isolated transactions concerning customer numbers, possible destinations or a selection of dates. Also the combinations of the transactions had to be considered. Moreover, whereas in principle there may be several legal sequences of input transactions, this is in reality not the case for system-directed dialogues. This meant that knowledge about the requirement specification was not enough. Also the task structure had to be known to the person who constructed test suites which included their expected results. Furthermore, because each test reservation can only test a limited number of cases we had to create a long series of test reservations.

The main issues to be tested as regards the dialogue control structure were:

- Does it behave as intended with respect to domain communication and is the behaviour reasonable?
- Does it handle meta-communication as intended and in a reasonable way?
- Does it permit reservations as intended and in an acceptable way?

The dialogue control structure was implemented and tested through a kind of prototyping. This is reflected in the division of the debugging into three phases.

The First Debugging Phase

Before a real blackbox test could start, the programmer debugged the program until it functioned reasonably for basic input. In the beginning, a bottom-up strategy was used. As soon as possible, however, all system modules were integrated and run together as an entire system, and the bottom-up test was stopped and replaced by a top-down test. The top-down test allowed the functionality of each module to be tested in its real surroundings and the specification of input to the dialogue control structure was facilitated. The speech recognizer was left out in the top-down test of the dialogue control structure because it is important that errors can be reconstructed. The speech recognizer is very sensitive to noise and to the way in which an utterance is spoken (voice quality and intonation), which means that one cannot ensure reproduction of input in such a way that it will be recognized as the same input each time. Therefore, messages from the recognizer were simulated through direct textual input to the parser via the Dialogue Communication Manager. Leaving out the speech recognizer means that all misrecognitions which would have been caused by this module are eliminated and that the same input will always create the same output.

The input to and the output from each module were sent as output to the screen by the Communication Manager (Figure 6.1), and could be logged in a script file. The typed input had a format corresponding to that which the speech recognizer would produce, i.e. it contained a prefix, the user utterance and a post-fix, and it was sent directly to the parser. To facilitate input specification a program was constructed which would allow specification of input as ordinary typed utterances. The program would then expand each piece of input to the format expected by the ICM (Figure 6.1), which would produce input to the dialogue control structure via the parser.

Three test files were constructed for the first debugging phase. The first one included the minimum input needed for reservation of a single ticket. The second one was a basic reservation of a return ticket. The third file was a reservation of a return ticket in which each user utterance providing information was followed by user utterances asking for repetition and for correction of the input.

The Second Debugging Phase

When the dialogue control structure allowed the basic reservations specified in the three test files of the first test phase to be made without system break-downs, a *blackbox* test was performed. Test data for this test were constructed by the system developer who had been least involved in programming the dialogue control structure.

Basically, three types of reservation had to be tested: single tickets; return tickets; and discount return tickets. A thorough test of each of these types includes test cases with legal input, borderline cases which may be either legal or illegal, and clearly illegal input. In many cases it was possible to make an exhaustive test of legal key information, i.e. information which should be accepted and not cause error messages. By key information we mean the information asked for by the system, such as the name of a destination airport or a customer number. The key information may be embedded in many different formulations of which only a selection was tested along with the dialogue control structure. Different grammatical formulations were not in focus in the dialogue control structure test. A thorough test of formulations, i.e. which linguistic formulations lead to complete and relevant semantic objects, belongs to the parser module test, which is not discussed here (Music and Offersgaard, 1994).

The task structure formed the basis for a specification of what to test, cf. Figure 2.5 which shows the final task structure. The task structure has changed somewhat over time but this does not influence the basic idea of how it can be used for constructing test cases.

Because domain communication is system-directed, the system will ask a number of questions which the user is expected to answer. The types of question asked by the system may be divided into four categories, as described in Section 5.6.2, i.e. questions inviting yes/no answers, multiple-choice questions, questions inviting a proper name or something similar to a proper name, and questions about a specific topic.

Legal key information in answers to questions belonging to the first three categories can be tested exhaustively. Legal answers to yes/no questions and to multiple-choice questions are obviously limited in amount. There is also a limited amount of existing customer numbers, traveller id-numbers, and airport names stored in the database. Only for questions belonging to the fourth group can the key information be expressed in many different ways. These questions concern date and time of departure. For this group we selected a number of different date and time values. Also borderline cases and illegal cases have been tested. Borderline answers are only possible in the last two categories of questions. Examples of cases which have been tested for the four categories of question immediately above are:

1. Legal: yes; no
   Illegal: I don't know
2. Legal: please send it; he will pick it up in the airport
   Illegal: I want the ticket on Monday

3. Legal: all existing customer numbers including the smallest and largest ones
   Illegal: smallest existing customer number −1; largest existing customer number +1; 1000 (which does not exist as a customer number in the database)
4. Legal: August 31; 31.12 (December 31); today; on Monday
   Illegal: February 29 1994; August 32; 1.13; yesterday; St. Hans' Day.

The three basic reservation types overlap (cf. Figure 2.5). For instance, customer number and route are needed in all cases whereas a date for the home journey is only applicable to the reservation of return tickets, including discount tickets.

User meta-communication was tested, i.e. the keywords *change* and *repeat* were used in every possible position.

All parts of the running system, apart from the speech recognizer, were to a certain extent tested in connection with the blackbox test of the dialogue component. Errors found were reported to the site at which the component containing the error had been developed. When the bug had been fixed, the test was repeated to see how the dialogue behaved.

However, focus was on the dialogue control structure and the blackbox test was not exhaustive due to lack of resources. Nevertheless, the test did reveal a number of problems. Ordinary bugs and minor problems were corrected immediately as they appeared, including disagreement on formats between the individual system modules. In addition larger inconveniences were discovered which could not be repaired on the spot.

Design rationale (DR) frames (Section 3.4) were used as a tool for representing such major problems and their analysis (cf. Figure 3.5). DR frames represent larger problems encountered during the development process, violated design commitments and reasoning about how to solve the problems and why one solution may be preferred to others. Twenty major problems were discovered during the blackbox test in the second test phase and represented in DR frames.

Resources were not available for implementing solutions to all the problems discovered. It was therefore considered, for each problem, how time consuming the implementation of a solution would be and how important it was. The hard problems were in several cases due to the fact that system-directed dialogue is not entirely sufficient to handle the sub-tasks which caused the problems. Solutions to such problems were not implemented because these solutions would probably be sub-optimal anyway as long as the system-directed dialogue paradigm is maintained. Examples are round-trip tickets and reservations concerning, for example, one passenger travelling out alone but returning together with another person. Both examples deviate from the standard reservation task and in the present system they have to be carried out as two separate reservation tasks. A round-trip ticket must be booked as two one-way tickets and the second example would have to be resolved by booking one return ticket and one one-way ticket.

On the basis of these considerations, solutions or partial solutions to about half of the discovered problems were implemented. While implementing the chosen solutions, the programmer discovered and solved other problems caused by the changes. Also a few new problems were revealed.

The Third Debugging Phase

In the third phase, a blackbox test using the same input as in the second phase was run on the improved dialogue control structure and identified bugs were corrected. Some of the test suites had been slightly revised because of changes influencing the task structure, such as removing system questions due to functionality problems.

During the third test phase a number of bugs were corrected but no new and previously unknown larger problems were discovered. However, it became increasingly clear that the use of system-directed dialogue could be a problem in cases where the information expected from the user may depend on information s/he will get from the system later in the dialogue, and vice versa. For example, users may prefer to have information on departure times before they decide on the date of departure and also on whether they want discount tickets. Moreover, it was clear that a number of problems remained for the repair of which resources were not available. Problems of these kinds therefore also appear in the controlled user test of the system (cf. Section 8.3.3).

7. *Corpus Handling*

7.1 Introduction

A corpus is a collection or body of linguistic data, organized in a manner that will facilitate investigation of, and reference to, the data. By today's standards, corpora are in machine-readable form. Dictionary publishers maintain corpora of citations and word uses, and researchers collect huge (millions of words) corpora of texts of all kinds for many different purposes. Corpus linguistics is both a well-established discipline and an active research area (McEnery and Wilson, 1996). A growing sub-discipline focuses on spoken language (Leech *et al.*, 1995). *Spoken corpora* are collections of usually transcribed spoken language such as monologues, interviews, conversations or task-oriented dialogues. This chapter focuses on the transcription, markup and coding of spoken dialogue corpora, emphasizing the representations, procedures and tools that are relevant to the design of interactive speech systems.

Spoken dialogue corpora are used for analytical purposes (including evaluation of systems and components) and are often created with one particular analysis in mind. Once in existence, however, a corpus is very often later used for analytical purposes other than those originally intended. Typical uses of spoken dialogue corpora address the following layers of speech interaction theory (Chapter 2):

- Context: who are the participants, what goals do they try to achieve, which domain data and rules are necessary?
- Control: analysis of speech acts, references and discourse segmentation; tasks and meta-communicative phenomena; focus.
- Language: extraction and evaluation of vocabulary, grammar, semantics and style.
- Speech: model training for speech recognition; prosody, dialectal variation, evaluation of speech recognition.
- Performance: analysis of initiative, user and system cooperativity.

A spoken dialogue corpus may be analysed across the layers of speech interaction theory, for instance with respect to the relation between prosody, on the one hand, and discourse structure and semantics on the other (Hirschberg *et al.*, 1995; Kompe *et al.*, 1997). Moreover, a corpus of spoken human–computer dialogues may be used together with log data in the system development process for testing, for example, the behaviour and quality of system components, or the users' language (see Chapter 8).

Use of a spoken dialogue corpus, both for planned purposes and purposes which were not originally intended, requires that the corpus and the analysed phenomena are represented in a computer tractable, transformable and generally well-described fashion. A spoken dialogue corpus is represented in some textual (usually computer readable) form, a *transcription*. The transcription is obtained by *transcribing* the speech together with other recorded material, as will be discussed in Section 7.2. The transcription is usually extended with *markup* (or tags or codes), i.e. formal annotation that delimits, marks and documents identified features and phenomena in the corpus, as discussed in Section 7.3. The process of inserting *markup* is called *coding* (or tagging or annotation) of the corpus. A *coding scheme* specifies how and when to code, i.e. defines the *markup*, procedures for inserting it and how to ensure the coding quality, as discussed in Section 7.4. *Tools* for handling corpora are discussed in Section 7.5. The corpus from the user test of the Danish Dialogue System will be used for illustration below. This corpus has been subjected to statistical analysis, as well as to more qualitative analysis of user problems (see Chapters 5 and 8). The formal structure of the corpus has been essential to the automation of the statistics and transformations applied.

7.2   Transcription

The raw data that researchers and developers of interactive speech systems work upon are voice recordings of human conversation and human–machine spoken interaction, log files of system modules (if any) and additional material relevant to the conversation or interaction, such as scenario descriptions and descriptions of the set-up for data capture. The first task facing the corpus user is to transform the raw data into a convenient, machine readable and consistent form. One should, of course, be careful to conserve the original material.

The initial transcription is important because features such as overlaps, pronunciation, ahs and ehms, prosody and pauses can be marked only on the basis of the original recordings. A fundamental recommendation is that a digitized version of the entire speech recordings is included as part of the corpus.

A first basic choice in the transcription process concerns what should go into the transcription. Having considered several transcription schemes, Llisterri (1996) proposes that the transcription of words conform to one of three levels:

- S1: orthographic transcription of the text (Figures 7.1 and 7.2).
- S2: phonemic representation of words in citation form, i.e. the form in which words are pronounced in isolation. An example is /gUd mO:nIN/ for "good morning" (Roach and Arnfield, 1995).
- S3: phonetic transcription reflecting a discrete symbolic representation of the perceived actual realization of the utterance. An example is "'ælsgͨkɑɑn'asda'bo'" for "elsker Karen Asta Bo", literally "loves Karen Asta Bo". Only the absence of stress ("'") on "Karen" shows that the question means "does Karen Asta love Bo", and not "does Karen love Asta Bo" ("Bo" is both a male first name and a family name) (Brink *et al.*, 1991).

Most transcriptions are in orthographic form. Often standard variations reflecting pronunciation are used, such as "ik" for "ikke", and usually extra-linguistic features such as pauses, ahs and ehms, and other acoustic events are added (Figure 7.2).

Phonemic and phonetic-level transcriptions use the same special symbols, such as the International Phonetic Alphabet (IPA) (Llisterri, 1996). In particular, the phonetic-level transcriptions require trained phoneticians for their production.

S3-29	Please state the customer number.
U3-29	Number four.
S3-30	Customer number four. How many people will travel?
U3-30	Two adults and two children.
S3-31	Two people. Please state the id-number of the first person.
U3-31	Change.
S3-32	Two people. Is this correct?
U3-32	No.
S3-33	How many people will travel?
U3-33	Four.
S3-34	Four people.

Figure 7.1: Orthographic, turn-based transcription of recorded speech from the user test of the Danish Dialogue System. The dialogue has been divided into numbered turns (29–34). S3 and U3 indicate the system and the user, respectively, during a session with user number 3. By including the user number and consecutively numbering the turns in the series of dialogues conducted in a session, turn numbers become unique throughout the entire user test corpus. Translated from Danish.

```
A>
1>
2>jaT  og  mor  og  far  var  så  heldige  at  forsvaret  betalte  mit
   yesT and mum and dad  were so  lucky  that the defence  paid  my
```

```
A>    (griner)                                    jo
      (laughs)                                    yes
1>    ja   nå ja (uf                       )      han fik et
      ya   oh ya (uf                       )      he  got a
2>(griner) men så fik jeg såT   en del af orglet ik'
   (laughs) but so I got thenT a part of the organ eh'
```

```
A>
1>halvt orgel som mor kaldte det ik' PP så kom det ja da jeg blev
  half organ  as  mum called it  eh' PP so it came ya when I got
2>                          ja
                           yes
```

Figure 7.2: Orthographic parallel line transcription from Gregersen and Pedersen (1991). The transcription is an excerpt from an unstructured interview with people from Nyboder, Copenhagen, for use in socio-linguistic investigation. A is the interviewer, 1 and 2 are the informants. T is a hesitation, PP is long pause and uf is something unintelligible. The English translation has been added.

On top of these transcription levels – typically, the orthographic one – prosodic coding may be added, symbolically representing the linguistically relevant variations that occur in the domains of time, frequency and intensity in the sound wave corresponding to a speaker's utterance (Llisterri, 1996).

A second basic choice is whether to structure the transcription into turns (Figure 7.1) or into parallel lines of speakers, as in representing the different voices of a musical score (Figure 7.2). The turn structure tends to be used in conversational analysis, whereas the score structure is useful for analysing the temporal acoustic event structure. In turn transcriptions, the turntaking may be marked as latching or overlapping, or more precise temporal information on overlaps may be inserted using explicit anchor points and references.

Transcribing the User Test Corpus

The process of producing a transcription depends on the available data sources and editing tools. The large variability in recording conditions and the lack of standardized tools imply that transcription is usually approached in a pragmatic or ad hoc manner. We present main points from the process of transcribing the user test corpus from the Danish Dialogue Project. In this test in which only the speech recognizer was simulated, each subject had a single session with the system, interacting on the basis of four task scenarios in one or more telephone calls (see Section 8.2.2). The user–system interaction was recorded on tape. In addition, a log file was created during the session, containing:

- What the wizard keyed in as constituting the users' utterances;
- All communication between the ICM (interpretation and control module) and the devices, i.e. the simulated recognizer (textrec), the player and the database (cf. Figure 1.5).
- The parse tree and the resulting, filled semantic slots.
- The full text of the system's utterances.

The communication between the ICM and the devices was time-stamped, although no direct link to the discourse structure can be inferred as the internal clock signals are not synchronized. The other data (keyed-in utterances, parsing data and system utterances) would appear in roughly chronological order, with the keyed-in phrases usually appearing delayed in the log.

For each session, the log file and the tape recording were converted and merged into a single TEI conformant transcription (see Section 7.3). The conversion was semi-automated, using emacs-lisp functions in several iterative phases and using visual inspection of the transcriptions to check correctness and completeness. The following steps were followed:

- Extract general information for the TEI header, such as identification of the version of each system module.
- Sort the rest of the log file output chronologically.
- Throw away everything not directly related to the user–system database communication. For instance, start/stop commands sent to the (simulated) recognizer were deleted.
- Put system phrases together to form the system's turns.
- Use the keyed-in phrases as a first approximation to the actual user utterances.

- Transform everything into TEI format.
- Transcribe the corpus by using the tape recordings for correcting the keyed-in user utterances and the system's phrases as represented in the log files. Insert pauses and other non-vocal events.
- Expand the database codes into mnemonics and transform the database query/ answer parameters into a reader-friendly form.

A two-utterance fragment from the user test transcription is shown in Figure 7.3. Using the keyed-in utterances as a first approximation to the actual user utterances saved a lot of time in the transcription process because the person transcribing could concentrate on correcting the relatively few errors in what the wizard had keyed in. A similar approach can be used for the output from a sufficiently robust recognizer.

7.3 Markup

Although the base transcription in Figure 7.1 is well suited to a human reader, it is inadequate for computer processing and when more features need to be distinguished. What is needed is explicit *markup*, i.e. formal notation that unambiguously denotes the features of interest. Its precise form is less important as long as the markup is consistent, unambiguous and well described.

A proposal for a standard markup format already exists. The Association for Computers and the Humanities, the Association for Computational Linguistics, and the Association for Literary and Linguistic Computing have initiated the *Text Encoding Initiative* which in 1994 produced a markup format and a set of guidelines for its use in the markup of text corpora of any kind (Burnard and Sperberg-McQueen, 1995; Ide and Véronis, 1995). The format and the guidelines are often referred to as TEI-P3 or just TEI, and the TEI Guidelines or just the Guidelines, respectively.

TEI defines an SGML document type definition (dtd), thereby providing a formal, machine processable structure for text markup. SGML (Standardized Generalized markup Language) itself is not a markup language but a definition language. Via the SGML dtds, the Guidelines aim to provide specialized packages of markup elements that can be combined according to the type of text, such as drama or verse, and the purpose of analysis of the corpus. Furthermore, the Guidelines aim at supporting the exchange of electronic texts, and prescribe how to extend the TEI format with new markup elements.

One of the TEI packages is aimed at the markup of transcribed speech (Burnard and Sperberg-McQueen, 1995, Chapter 11; Johansson, 1995). The main markup elements provided by TEI for the basic markup of speech are (Johansson, 1995):

- `<text>`: a transcription of speech treated for some purpose as a unit.
- `<div>`: a sub-division of a spoken text comprising one or more utterances treated as a unit for analytic purposes.
- `<u>`: an utterance, i.e. a stretch of speech usually preceded and followed by silence or change of speaker.
- `<s>`: a sub-division of an utterance according to prosodic or syntactic criteria.
- `<pause>`: a pause either between or within utterances.
- `<vocal>`: any vocalized but non-lexical phenomenon.

- `<kinesic>`: any non-vocalized but communicative phenomenon, such as a gesture.
- `<event>`: any non-vocalized, non-communicative phenomenon, such as a slamming door.

Please note that in markup terminology the term "element" denotes a formal construct and does not refer to the elements of speech interaction theory (Chapter 2).

Figure 7.3 shows how the first two utterances in Figure 7.1 were encoded in TEI. Note how utterance identification is represented as an attribute of the element `<u>`. Elements may have several attributes holding values that are usually not part of the running transcription.

```
<u id="S3-29a"> Oplys venligst kundenummer! </u>
<u id="U3-29a"> Nummer fire. </u>
```

Figure 7.3: Utterances in the Danish encoded in TEI. See Figure 7.1 for an English translation.

There are several advantages of using TEI. First, it provides a formal markup scheme suited for computer processing. Secondly, as TEI is based on SGML, tools are available for manipulating and editing the text and the markup. Thirdly, being an international standard, TEI facilitates the exchange of corpora. Fourthly, TEI represents the investment of a considerable amount of effort put into uncovering problems of markup.

There are also disadvantages of TEI. It provides a basic standard for event and utterance markup, but most users of TEI are likely to need more features, such as part of speech, syntactic trees or speech acts. TEI tries to avoid precluding any particular style of coding by enabling many different encodings of the same feature, but for more focused areas, such as spoken human–machine interaction, there is no reason to have a plethora of possibilities. These may act, instead, as an extra source of confusion. Within the Eagles Project, CES, the Corpus Encoding Standard (Ide, 1996), is an attempt to identify a minimal encoding level for standardized corpora for computational linguistics, providing a descriptive structural and linguistic representation, and a general architecture for using texts as databases. However, CES provides no recommendations on the encoding of spoken corpora apart from what is already in TEI, and does not embark on dialogue annotation. The problem with dialogue annotation is that little agreement exists on which are the necessary or right phenomena to encode, and on how these phenomena should be encoded. Standardization of spoken dialogue encoding is a current research theme. Finally, there are unsolved problems with respect to how to represent orthogonal, overlapping hierarchies of markup, such as providing different parse trees of the same utterances.

markup of the User Test Corpus

The transcriptions from the user test of the Danish Dialogue System include not only the spoken interaction itself but also the main communication of the system modules, as well as several additional features, such as word category, utterance topic and interaction phase (see below). TEI was used with the following elements added:

- `<keyed>`: what was typed by the wizard, after expansion of typing abbreviations.
- `<recognized>`: what was recognized, i.e. the result of applying a text recognizer

to the keyed-in text. The text recognizer simulated the real recognizer but with character-based textual word models instead of Markov models.

- <parse>: the semantic parsing result as transferred to the dialogue manager.
- <database>: the communication with the database is shown including all domain, type and status arguments.
- <t>: record of the type of certain tokens (words). For all other tokens the type is simply the literal expression of the token.

These elements are documented in more detail in Dybkjær *et al.* (1996). In Figure 7.4, the documentation of the <t> element is shown as an example.

With a few exceptions to be explained, care was taken to ensure that the described extensions conformed with TEI and to represent the transcriptions in TEI interchange format (Burnard and Sperberg-McQueen, 1995, Chapter 28). An example of the resulting markup is shown in Figure 7.5 which presents a single exchange from the user test with associated system module communication.

At the lower levels of transcription, some formal tags were used without defining a TEI conforming element, such as the use of "!" to denote a declarative system phrase, and the internal structure of <semantics> and <database>. The choice of these *microtags* is somewhat arbitrary and solely relates to the convenient readability of the transcriptions and the structure of the log files. The phenomena affected were

---

Types and tokens (<t>)
Record the type of certain tokens (words). For all other tokens the type is the literal expression of the token.
Example: `<t type=month value="FEB">February</t>`
All month tokens JAN...DEC count as one type. The seven types used are listed in the dtd.
dtd:

```
<!ENTITY %  t 'INCLUDE' >
<![ %t; [
<!ELEMENT %n.t;        - -   (#PCDATA)                    >
<!ATTLIST %n.t;             %a.global;
               type         (airport  | month    | week-day  |
                             name     | cardinal | ordinal   |
                             false-start)       #IMPLIED
               value        CDATA                %INHERITED
               TEIform      CDATA                't'
>
]]>
```

Comments: In the transcriptions one word is one token. Since the vocabulary is important in studies of human-computer spoken interaction, the domain specific tokens with a known range and a frequency known to be skewed are marked as an abstract token <t>. For example, all of the months January through December should be in the vocabulary even though only January and February occur in the corpus. All other tokens are implicitly taken to be their own type. For instance, 'rabat' is interpreted as if marked `<t type=rabat>rabat</t>`.

Figure 7.4: The <t> element in the user test mark-up (Dybkjær *et al.,* 1996, Section 6.3.9).

not in our analytical focus. Even then, given more advanced extraction and viewing tools, it might certainly have been preferable to encode these phenomena in conformance with TEI. Microtags have been used more formally in the markup of the Map Task corpus (Carletta *et al.*, 1996), both for improved readability and to preserve in textual form what TEI represents as attribute values. For instance, "hmm" is represented in the Map Task corpus as {fp:hmm} whereas TEI prescribes <vocal desc="hmm"> (Thompson, 1992).

```
<u id="S3-29a" who="S" topic=customer> Oplys venligst kundenummer! </u>
<u id="U3-29a" who="C-3" topic=customer> Nummer <t type=cardinal
        value="4">fire</t>. </u>
<keyed which="U3-29a">nummerfire</keyed>
<recognised which="U3-29a" grammar="Number" score=0.000000>nummer
        fire</recognised>
<parse which="U3-29a">
        | Current parsecontext: grammarset:  Command
        |              Command Command Yesno Number
        | semantic objects:
        | actionso(action ActionSO) [action --NULL--]
        | yesnoso(choice BooleanSO) [choice --NULL--]
        | customerso(number IntSO) [number [ones ••• ] ]
        | Resulting Parse Tree # 0
        | Subgrammar[ 5 ]: Number
        | L:[s_9,sem={number={ones={number=4}}}]:
        |                      {cat=s,stype=ellipse}.[
        |    L:[nummer_1]: {cat=n,nb=sing,semtype=id,
        |                      defs=indef, [ ••• ]
        | ]
        | set Slot number "4"
</parse>
<database type="query" modifier="CUSTOMER">
        | customer: 4  </database>
<database type="answer" modifier="STATUS">
        | status: DB_OK  </database>
<u id="S3-30a" who="S" topic=customer>kundenummer <t type=cardinal
        value="4">4</t></u>
```

Figure 7.5: A marked-up corpus fragment from the user test. Three utterances are shown: the system's question S3–29a "Please state the customer number", the user response U3–29a "Number four", and the system feedback S3–30a "customer number four" (cf. Figure 7.1). In addition, the figure shows the following system module actions: what was typed by the wizard; what was recognized; what was parsed; what the database was asked about; and what it responded. The "•••" denotes material omitted from the figure.

7.4 Coding

The insertion of markup or codes for particular features present in a transcribed corpus is called *coding*. Because the markup is being inserted for later use, the coding must be done with care. The extent of, and the efforts put into, the coding depend on the complexity of the features to be encoded, the resources available and the purpose(s) of the coding. In general, coding requires that the following points be taken into account:

(a) Defining precisely the feature to be encoded: which criteria are distinctive for the different cases of the feature.
(b) Defining the markup of the feature: how should it be represented, should it be fitted into an existing markup.
(c) Defining the coding procedure: what instructions and training should the coders have in how to actually do the coding.
(d) Defining a suitable level of coding reliability: how is the correctness and consistency of the coding ensured; are there any formal measurements.
(e) Actually coding the corpus.
(f) Checking the quality of the resulting markup.

A *coding scheme* comprises at least (a) and preferably all of (a)–(d). The actual coding comprises at least (e), is preferably based on a coding scheme and should include (f). Some coding schemes from solitary projects are Carletta *et al.* (1995), Gross *et al.* (1993) and Jönsson (1993, Sections 7.2 and 9.3). Defining a coding scheme that is generally valid across several types of corpora and purposes is much more difficult. In a series of workshops of the Discourse Resource Initiative (DRI), a group of researchers interested in discourse level annotation are trying to create a general discourse level coding scheme (Carletta *et al.*, 1997b). Currently, the scheme comprises information level (task, communication, or other), forward-looking speech acts (inform, directive, commissive, …), backward-looking speech acts (answer, accept, reject, …) and segmentation (identifying the units for dialogue annotation). The scheme only addresses (a), but is, of course, developed with a keen eye on reliability (item (d)).

In some cases, the coding process can be more or less automated. An example is the coding of a feature such as word class, also called *part-of-speech tagging*. For instance, in the context "I am a coder", "am" is the first person, singular, present tense of the verb "be". Part-of-speech taggers based on statistical training are now efficient and precise. Brill (1995) reports a tagging accuracy of 82.2% on unknown words and 96.6% overall. Automation ensures a consistent coding quality and enables expensive human effort to focus on those analyses that are not, or cannot be, automated. However, the feature to be encoded can rarely be defined through *criteria* that are precise enough for the application of computational algorithms. Usually, therefore, humans must be used as coders – and this is why annotated corpora are so precious.

Coding quality (items (d) and (f)) constitutes a research area of its own (Carletta, 1996; Carletta *et al.*, 1997a). The coding scheme may be tested by comparing different corpus samples coded by means of *coverability*; by comparing the results produced by different coders to assess *intercoder reliability*; and by comparing the results produced by the same coder on the same corpus sample at different times, for instance with a 1 week delay, to assess *consistency*. The coding quality may be assessed qualitatively through discussion of the coders' choices when they differ, or quantitatively through scoring measures. An important measure is *kappa* (κ), which describes how well (groups of) coders agree with each other:

$$\kappa = \frac{P(A) - P(E)}{1 - P(E)}$$

where $P(A)$ is the proportion of times that the coders agree and $P(E)$ is the proportion of times that they are expected to agree by chance. As a rule of thumb, *kappa* values between 0.67 and 0.8 tentatively show a certain agreement, and values above 0.8 show a certain agreement, although the values should be interpreted with care. A kappa value of 1 means perfect agreement ($P(A)$ is 1). Consider the segmentation example in Figure 7.6, which was annotated by two different coders. There are 70 words (inclusive of "ah") after which a segment may end, and after nine of the words a segmentation mark has been inserted by one or both of the coders. Using this to estimate the chance agreement, we get

$$P(E) = \Sigma p_i^2 \; (i = 1, 2) = (9/70)^2 + (61/70)^2 \approx 0.7759$$

where p_i is the probability of the ith case. The coders disagree in three cases, so the pairwise agreement is $P(A)=67/70 \approx 0.9571$. Using these figures we get $\kappa \approx 0.81$, which shows a certain agreement.

Two other measures, precision and recall, may be used if there is an "authoritative source" against which a coder may be compared. *Precision* expresses the proportion of the occurrences found that have been correctly coded:

$$\text{precision} = \frac{\text{found} - \text{incorrect}}{\text{found}}$$

where *found* represents everything that was marked by the coder, and *incorrect* represents the incorrect markups by the coder, as determined by the authority. *Recall* expresses the proportion of occurrences that have been found:

$$\text{recall} = \frac{\text{all} - \text{missing}}{\text{all}}$$

where *all* represents all occurrences present in the corpus, as determined by the authority, and *missing* represents those occurrences that were not identified by the coder.

Although the idea of an authoritative source – usually taken to be a human expert – often may be dubious, precision and recall together may form a simple and useful expression of quality when the assessed coder is a software program. Assume, for instance, that in Figure 7.6 coder 1 is an authoritative expert. Coder 2 has found eight segments two of which are incorrect, which yields the precision 75%. Coder 1 has provided seven segments in all, one of which was missed by coder 2, so the recall is 86%. These results indicate that the quality could be better, although subjectively the assessment will depend on how complex the task is judged to be.

The Coding Scheme For Scenario Priming

As described in Section 5.6.2, one of the simulation experiments in the Danish Dialogue Project involved two groups of subjects, one using text-only scenario

JBT000:	maybe we should get together to talk further about this @1@2 <"ah> how 'bout some time in the next couple of weeks @1@2
SRH001:	okay @2 well @1 I will be on vacation for the next two weeks @1@2<"ah> how about Friday the twenty-first @1@2
JBT002:	Friday the twenty-first is scheduled from early morning to late afternoon @1@2 could you perhaps choose another day @2 a morning on a Wednesday or an early afternoon on a Tuesday @1@2

Figure 7.6: Dialogue fragment from the Verbmobil corpus that was used for a segmentation exercise at the dialogue coding workshop at Dagstuhl, Germany, 1997. The exercise was to insert an @ after each segment that could be assigned a single dialogue act. The segmentations produced by two coders are shown as @1 and @2, respec-

descriptions, and one using an equivalent set of scenarios in which temporal information such as dates and hours of departure were represented by means of analogue graphics and tables. The purpose was to study the priming effects of the words used in scenario task descriptions.

The coding scheme for the priming effects is shown in Figure 7.7. Step (1) restricts investigation to the first occurrences of user utterances addressing the temporal topics in each interaction. The justification for doing so is to avoid confusing scenario prim-

Step 1) Select the first user utterance after the first system question for each of the topics outday, outhour, homeday and homehour within each interaction.

Step 2) Extract all user time expressions in these utterances. Time expressions are understood in a broad sense so as to include, e.g., "an early flight" or "the cheapest", but not "yes" or "no".

Step 3) Mark user time expressions as primed or not primed using the following examples of expected high-frequency time expressions as templates:

In scenario:	Primed if user says one of the forms:
Friday February 5th	Friday or
	February 5th or
	Friday February 5th
February 5th	February 5th
23 of February	23rd of February
Tomorrow	Tomorrow
10:50	10:50
10 o'clock	10 o'clock

Two rules supplementary to the table are:

• To be considered primed, a user time expression must contain nothing but parts from the priming scenario expression. For instance, the user expression "tomorrow February 5th" should not be marked as primed by "February 5th".

• Repetition of low-frequent (time) expressions from the scenario is priming.

Step 4) Code by two independent coders. Disagreements are resolved via discussion leading to consensus.

Figure 7.7: The scenario priming coding scheme.

ing effects with other phenomena, such as priming through the system's utterances. Step (2) further restricts the focus to expressions of time. Step (3) lists the actual priming criteria. The purpose of these criteria is to ensure consistency of categorization, both for each coder and between coders. The set of priming criteria was chosen restrictively, such that the cases defined as primed all clearly appear to have been primed by the scenarios. Moreover, excluding borderline cases leaves fewer cases to appeal to in support of the hypothesis under investigation, which reduces the risk of producing false positive evidence for the hypothesis. Step (4) ensures consistency of coding and is also likely to reveal weak points in the priming criteria. The coding quality is thus only being assessed qualitatively, but very few cases turned out to require discussion. An alternative to the applied consensus principle could be to throw away the cases of disagreement, which in this case would have been statistically sound (as fewer cases would work against the hypothesis of a priming effect), albeit less correct.

7.5   Corpus Tools

A number of tools are needed in the coding process. In most cases, today's interactive speech system projects waste large amounts of precious time because they manage with ad hoc tools. There is a clear need for more investment from public funding agencies in this area. More general tools are slowly appearing, most of which are still bound to particular project formats, however. The most important tool functionalities are:

- *Data collection*: The data need to be recorded, preferably in some convenient way. For instance, it is convenient if speakers are digitally recorded from the outset, and considerable effort can be saved if the speakers and their turns can be separated automatically at recording time.

   Examples of data collection tools are: the TecFaMoo tool collects logs of internet-based, multimodal interactions between humans and the computer (Schneider *et al.*, 1996; Traum and Dillenbourg, 1996). The Chiba tools support the creation of a corpus with temporal information (Tutiya, 1996).
- *Annotation*: It is useful to have an editor for easy insertion and change of markup and for presenting the corpus text with its markup in a way that is easy to read. This type of editors has much in common with structural editors for object-oriented programmes and systems.

   Examples of annotation tools are: DAT, the Dialogue Annotation Tool of Rochester (Allen and Core, 1997), is being developed in the framework of the TRAINS Project. It provides a simple means of annotating segmented dialogues with speech act markup (see Section 7.4), and has on-line access to the voice recordings of the segments. Currently, the system is tailored towards annotation of the scheme developed by the Discourse Resource Initiative (DRI). For the time being, there is no possibility of customizing the tool on-line for annotation of different schemes. Such an option is integrated in the Alembic Workbench (Day, 1996) (see below). Nb (Nota bene) (Flammia and Zue, 1995), developed by Flammia at MIT, has been used initially in the framework of the DRI. Although developed for the annotation of (hierarchical) discourse structures, it has also been applied to the coding of dialogue acts. The tool can be flexibly tailored to the annotation of any labelling system that exposes a flat or hierarchical structure. Based on these ideas, the annotation tool Nba has been developed at the University of Linköping. It can be used to annotate dialogues with discourse information as used in the LINLIN Project (Dahlbäck and Jönsson, 1992).

- *Presentation*: It is useful to be able to present the corpus with a focus on particular features and in a nicely readable form.

An example of a presentation tool is: TecFaMoo can present the multimodal information available to a human participant at any time during the recorded dialogue.

- *Extraction*: It is useful to be able to extract part of the corpus or its markup.

Examples of extraction tools are: the Nba (see above) extracts speech act structures from annotated dialogues. The CQP/XKWIC corpus query tools developed at the University of Stuttgart allow the extraction of text according to: (i) linguistic criteria (annotated); (ii) regular expressions over characters and/or word forms; and (iii) non-overlapping structural sub-divisions, such as sentences, paragraphs, sections, etc. The Alembic Workbench (see below) also allows the extraction of all corpus material that has been labelled with a specific category (Day, 1996).

- *Analysis*: A number of statistical functions are generally useful, such as the counting of frequencies and the computing of averages, *kappa* values, etc. Moreover, support of qualitative analysis is useful, such as the comparative presentation of structures of annotation.

An examples of an analysis tool is: the Nba (see above) can graphically present the speech act structures from two codings simultaneously, and it can convert a speech act structure into a dialogue grammar.

- *Conversion*: It is an advantage if a tool can read and write markup formats that are usable by other tools (of other project groups). This is a precondition of tool generality. Among the most prominent tools that can automatically translate an annotated corpus into a corpus labelled with categories of another scheme is latex2html. It converts LaTeX-code into code including HTML markup. Usually, such tools are only able to translate from one scheme to another, without any possibility of abstraction. Normally, a loss of information is inevitable when corpora are being translated. So far, none of the available tools inform the user about the information loss incurred.

- *Integrated platforms*: There are few platforms for integrating corpus tools. One example is the Alembic Workbench (Day, 1996) which has been developed recently by the MITRE corporation. This tool can be individually adapted to new coding schemes. The system also allows the annotation of non-hierarchical structures, as is necessary for the coding of referring expressions. The tool supports the representation of annotations in SGML. It also includes various methods for the visualization of annotations. Another example is LT NSL which is a development environment for SGML-based corpus and document processing, with support for multiple versions and multiple levels of annotation (http://www.ltg.ed.ac.uk/software/nsl/). It consists of methods for accessing and manipulating SGML documents and an integrated set of SGML tools.

Many of the tools presented above provide means for visualizing annotations: Nb, for example, provides a graphical representation which emphasizes the hierarchical nesting of discourse structures. Alembic allows the contrasting of two annotated corpora through pointing out stretches of discourse where the labelling of the two data sets disagree, highlighting corresponding labels by the use of the same colour.

A specific tool may have one or several of the functionalities listed above. It is important that tools can be easily adapted to changing needs if they are to be used outside a small group working on a particular project. Adaptation should preferably be possible without having to hack into the code of the tools, as is necessary with respect to virtually every available tool today.

Corpus Tools in the User Test

As described in Section 7.2, the raw data collected in the user test of the Danish Dialogue System consisted of a simple system log file and speech recorded on audio tape. These data were turned into a transcription by means of editing commands and tailored functions in the emacs editor. Later, the audio tapes were converted into digital format and segmented into utterances using the AudioTool on the Sun Solaris platform. The turn segmentation of the recordings took about 10 hours of labour for each hour recorded.

A mode (specialized editing environment) for the emacs editor was programmed, providing functions for easy insertion of markup, viewing parts of the markup and for computing simple statistics on the annotated corpus, such as frequencies.

A C++ program was written for the extraction of parts of the corpus into an HTML pretty-print format as shown in Figure 7.8. This made it possible to choose at will which part of the coded dialogue to present, as well as the markup elements to be presented.

customer	S3-29a	Please state the customer number!
customer	U3-29a	Number 4.

> keyed: numberfour
> recognised [Number/0.000000]: number four
> semantics: number "4"
> database [query/CUSTOMER]
> database [answer/STATUS] DB_OK

customer	S3-30a	Customer number 4
persons	S3-30b	How many people will travel?
persons	U3-30a	2 adults and 2 children.

> keyed: Twoadultsandtwochildren
> recognised [Persons/-76.000000]:
> okay nine and two children
> semantics: number "2" choice "1"

persons	S3-31a	2 people

Figure 7.8: Pretty-printed corpus extracts are used in the qualitative analysis discussed in Chapter 8. Key system module information has been included but its presentation does not obstruct the reading of the transcribed spoken interaction. The extracts have been generated by a program that converts TEI codes into HTML codes, removing large parts of the information in the process. The extract shown was adapted for this figure and translated from Danish. Turns S3–29 and U3–29 correspond to Figure 7.3.

8. *Evaluation*

8.1 Introduction

System evaluation is a highly important discipline which is tightly interwoven with system development. Evaluation is constantly needed throughout development to measure progress towards the goals that the system has to meet. Interactive speech system evaluation today is as much of an art and craft as it is an exact science with established standards and procedures of good engineering practice. In particular, little is still known about interaction model evaluation, including evaluation of dialogue components and integrated interactive speech systems. There is not even consensus on terminology. Following Hirschmann and Thompson (1996) (see also Gibbon *et al.,* 1997) we will distinguish between three types of evaluation which, although they are clearly not orthogonal, seem to cover the relevant aspects of evaluation, and subsume the scopes of other commonly used terms and distinctions. Each of these three types of evaluation may be used at any stage of system development:

- *performance evaluation,* i.e. measurements of the performance of the system and its components in terms of a set of quantitative parameters;
- *diagnostic evaluation,* i.e. detection and diagnosis of design and implementation errors;
- *adequacy evaluation,* i.e., how well do the system and its components fit their purpose and meet actual user needs and expectations.

Other common terms are "blackbox" and "glassbox" tests and "progress evaluation". *Blackbox and glassbox tests* may be considered as kinds of diagnostic evaluation, but these tests are carried out only on implemented components or systems. Blackbox and glassbox tests were discussed in more detail in Section 6.3. *Progress evaluation* compares two iterations of the same system during development, and is a kind of performance evaluation (see Section 8.2).

Performance, diagnostic and adequacy evaluation should be performed as integral parts of the development process to measure progress towards satisfaction of the requirement specification, evaluation criteria and design specification. *Performance evaluation* is made throughout the development process with more or less the same emphasis from one iteration to another. Some parameters are only measured while the system is being simulated, whereas the measurement of others only make sense when the system has been implemented (Section 8.2). *Diagnostic evaluation* is of central importance in the early development process but should require less effort in the final phase by which time most errors should have been removed. *Adequacy evaluation* typically includes a few central performance measurements as well as measurement of user satisfaction. Adequacy evaluation is used mostly in the later phases of development. This is because a number of adequacy aspects cannot be tested in a sensible way until an implemented and debugged system is available for the purpose. For instance, it does not make sense to measure real-time performance on a simulated system.

Another useful distinction is the distinction between objective evaluation and subjective evaluation. *Objective evaluation* addresses objectively measurable parameters of system or component performance. *Subjective evaluation* addresses the opinions which users have formed of the system. Performance evaluation and diagnostic evaluation are forms of objective evaluation, whereas adequacy evaluation includes both objective and subjective evaluation.

Many evaluation measurements can be made independently of whether the system has been implemented or not. However, as suggested above, there are cases where the state of the system being developed makes a difference to a given test. We will highlight such cases when encountering them below.

In addition to distinctions between different types of evaluation, such as the above, distinction may be made between different types of tests. Test types refer to aspects of the context of the evaluation, such as the users involved, whether scenarios are being used or not, or whether the system being tested is implemented or simulated. The tests mentioned below are controlled tests, field tests and acceptance tests. Roughly speaking, controlled tests are performed during simulation and often also after implementation; field tests are performed after implementation and towards the end of system development; and the acceptance test is the final test of a system. This notwithstanding, a test may be carried out as a controlled test or as a field test no matter whether the system is being simulated or not. Each test typically includes all of the three evaluation types mentioned above.

In a *controlled test,* the users need not be those who will actually use the final system. However, it is recommended that the test subjects are selected from the target user group to ensure that they have a relevant background (Section 5.6.2). In the controlled test, the tasks to be carried out (the scenarios) are not selected by the participants. To ensure reasonable representativity of scenarios with respect to system functionality and task domain coverage, and to bring the controlled test as close to benchmarking as possible, scenario selection should ideally be done by an independent panel according to guidelines on, for example, who should select the scenarios, their coverage of system functionality and task domain, the number of scenarios per user and the number of users. The panel should include end-users as well as system developers. A *field distribution problem* attaches to all results of controlled tests. The frequency of different tasks across the domain of application may be different in real life to that imposed in the controlled test. This may significantly affect the frequency of the interaction problems encountered in the test.

In a *field test,* the system is being tested by real end-users in their appropriate environments. This means that the tasks carried out will be real-life tasks which, however, may not necessarily be representative of the full range of system functionality unless the duration of the field test is very long. The field test option will not always be available for research systems due to the missing customer. It may be preferable to carry out a controlled test before undertaking a field test because the controlled test will allow an evaluation to be made which is close to benchmarking.

The *acceptance test* is the final test of the system before it is accepted for operational use (Sommerville, 1992). The test aims to demonstrate that the requirements in the contract (the requirement specification) have been satisfied and the evaluation criteria met. Often the system is tested with data supplied by the procurer or in a set-up specified by the procurer. Detected errors must be corrected immediately. In case of larger disagreements with, or omissions in, the requirement specification, developer and procurer must discuss what to do. In the worst case the procurer may turn down the system if the developer did not meet the requirements agreed upon (cf. Section 3.2). However, it is not always solely the system developer's fault that the system does not exhibit the performance and functionality anticipated by the procurer. In such cases, procurer and developer must negotiate what to do in order to reach an agreement.

This chapter presents a partial scheme for the evaluation of data produced in controlled tests from recorded, transcribed and annotated corpora of spoken interactions. Section 8.2 discusses performance evaluation. Section 8.3 addresses diagnostic evaluation. A systematic method for the detection of interaction problems is presented and a prototool provided for the classification and diagnosis of interaction problems. Section 8.4 discusses user errors as detected by the method presented in Section 8.3. Section 8.5 discusses adequacy evaluation.

8.2 Performance Evaluation

Together with the requirement specification, evaluation criteria, including performance parameters, should be established for the system to be developed (cf. Section 3.2 and Figure 3.3). The performance parameters are used during WOZ and/or in later tests of the system. As noted already, the measurement of certain performance parameters may not make sense during WOZ because only the wizard's and not the system's capabilities can be measured at this stage. Other performance parameters can only be sensibly used during WOZ. They are therefore not part of the evaluation criteria aimed at the final system but are nevertheless important for assessing WOZ progress. Such parameters include measurement of the completeness of the interaction model, i.e. the extent to which the wizard has to improvise as yet unspecified parts of the interaction model, and measurement of how well the wizard performs. Progress evaluation, i.e. comparison between iterations, is frequently used during WOZ. The performance parameters defined in the evaluation criteria may be numerous and differ from system to system. We illustrate performance evaluation through describing how it was carried out during the WOZ experiments for, and the user test of, the Danish Dialogue System.

8.2.1 Performance Evaluation During WOZ

Performance evaluation in our WOZ experiments measured the performance parameters in the list of evaluation criteria in Figure 3.3 (except for real-time performance), i.e. average and maximum user utterance lengths (Figures 8.1 and 8.2), and vocabulary size and convergence (Figures 8.4 and 8.5). In addition, we considered that it would be relevant to measure the longest turn per iteration (Figure 8.3), initiative (Figure 8.6), number of turns (Figure 8.7), interaction model complexity (Figure 8.8) and wizard performance in terms of ad hoc generated phrases and jumps (Figures 8.9 and 8.10). Information concerning utterance lengths, vocabulary size and turns was extracted automatically from the annotated corpus. The other parameters were measured manually. Performance results were compared to requirements to ascertain how close they were to meeting the design goals. Results were also compared to the results of earlier WOZ iterations in order to measure progress. Figures 8.1–8.10 allow comparison of all the performance parameters measured in the seven WOZ iterations.

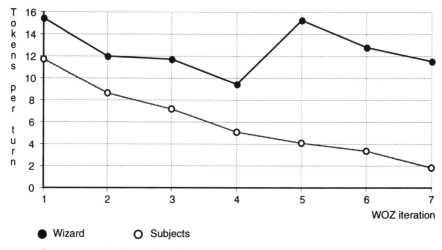

Figure 8.1: Average length of wizard and subject utterances in terms of tokens (words) per turn.

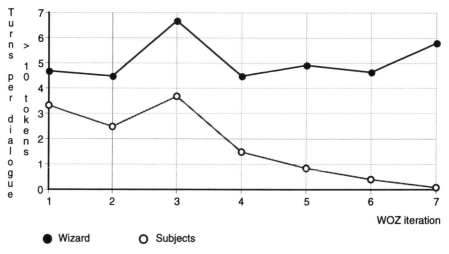

Figure 8.2: Average number of turns per dialogue exceeding 10 tokens (words).

Average and Maximum Utterance Lengths

The specification required an average user utterance length of three or four words and a maximum length of 10 words. These requirements were eventually satisfied. Figures 8.1 and 8.2 show average utterance length and average number of turns per dialogue exceeding 10 words, respectively. We also measured the longest turn in each iteration (Figure 8.3). In WOZ7 the longest utterance contained 12 words, and in total only three utterances exceeded 10 words. This was found acceptable. A main factor in reducing user utterance length was the transfer of initiative to the system. Answers are often briefer than questions and tend to use elliptical constructions.

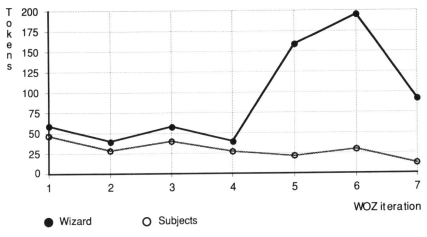

Figure 8.3: Longest user turn and system turn for each iteration.

Vocabulary Size and Convergence

For each iteration, the total number of words (tokens) and the number of different words (types) were measured. Figure 8.4 shows the average number of types and tokens per dialogue. As each iteration included a different number of dialogues, the total numbers of types and tokens could not be immediately compared. As an illustration, the subjects in WOZ1 used 608 tokens and 138 types in six dialogues; in WOZ6 subjects used 2171 tokens and 250 types in 47 dialogues; and in WOZ7 subjects used 1633 tokens and 165 types in 47 dialogues. Thus, the total number of types in each iteration was far from the upper limit of 500. However, each successive iteration generated relatively many new types. Therefore, although sufficiently small within each iteration, i.e. less than 500 word types, the deliberately artificial maximum of 500 words could easily turn out to be insufficient for the final system. Vocabulary convergence was measured in WOZ7 in terms of subjects' cumulative word type/token ratio (Figure 8.5). Convergence towards zero of the cumulative word type/token ratio is desirable because it indicates that the vocabulary size is sufficiently large for the application, i.e. it is not likely that a new user will introduce new word types. However, as shown in Figure 8.5, users' vocabulary in WOZ7 did not converge. This finding supported the assumption that 500 words may be too few for the application.

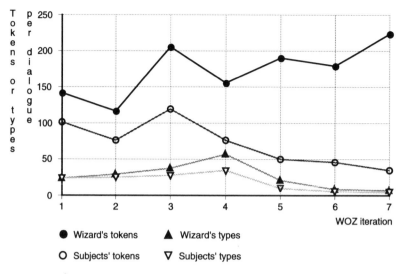

Figure 8.4: Average number of word types and word tokens per dialogue.

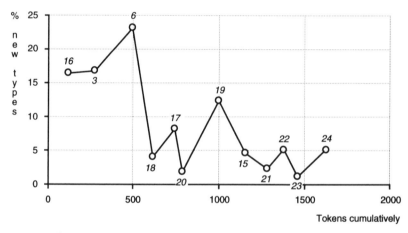

Figure 8.5: Cumulative type/token ratio for the subjects in WOZ7. The word types counted do not include numbers, week days, months, destinations, names and false starts. Subject numbers are indicated in the data points.

Initiative

To allow real-time performance, the active vocabulary could be at most 100 words at a time (Section 3.2). This strongly restricts the possibilities of user initiative during interaction. The early WOZ iterations allowed free mixed initiative interaction which was soon realized to be far from realistic in terms of the active vocabulary required. We therefore gradually transferred initiative to the system by letting the system ask questions of the user, thereby reducing average user utterance length and active vocabulary size. Initiative was roughly measured in terms of number of user questions and system questions, respectively (Figure 8.6). Much effort went into achieving an interaction structure which corresponded to the one that users would expect based on their experiences from human–human reservation dialogues. This

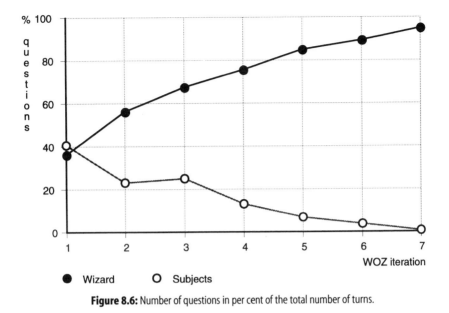

Figure 8.6: Number of questions in per cent of the total number of turns.

helped prevent the occurrence of user initiative. Domain interaction was eventually made completely system-directed, as this turned out to be necessary in order to meet the constraint on active vocabulary size.

Average Number of Turns Per Dialogue

This parameter was measured during WOZ in order to gain a rough idea of whether the interaction model appeared reasonable in this respect (Figure 8.7). If, for

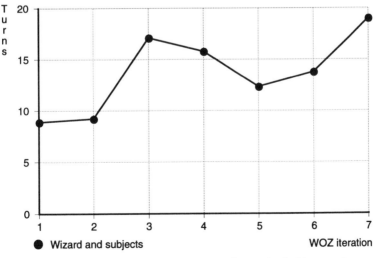

Figure 8.7: Average number of turns per dialogue for wizard and subjects together.

instance, completing the reservation task required, on average, two or three times the number of turns required in human–human interaction, user acceptance of the system might be in jeopardy. The average number of turns in the human–human dialogues which we recorded in a travel agency was 20 (Section 5.6.1). This average was never exceeded in the WOZ corpus, nor did we find any other indication that the number of turns was unreasonable.

In addition to the above performance parameters which were relevant throughout the development process, we measured the following performance parameters which were merely of interest during WOZ.

Complexity of the Interaction Model

The complexity of the interaction model represented as a transition network was measured in terms of the total number of nodes, the number of nodes containing system phrases (including questions) and the number of nodes containing system questions (Figure 8.8). The purpose was to assess the wizard's work load. The number of nodes increased throughout WOZ as the interaction model became more and more well defined. Similarly, the difference increased between the total number of nodes and the number of nodes containing pre-defined phrases. This difference indicates the increase in the number of nodes which only contained jumps to other parts of the network. Each jump is a sort of interruption where the wizard has to search for where to continue. The larger the mentioned difference is, the more difficult it is for the wizard to simulate the system appropriately and to do so in close to real-time.

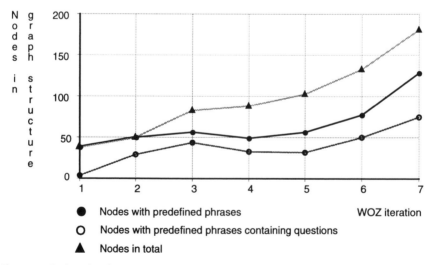

Figure 8.8: Total number of nodes in the graph representing the interaction model, number of pre-defined phrases and number of pre-defined phrases containing questions.

Number of ad hoc Generated Phrases

The number of ad hoc generated phrases (Figure 8.9) provides an estimate of how well the pre-defined phrases in the current interaction model cover the task domain.

To a certain degree, this measure is also an expression of how well trained the wizard is. In particular in the early iterations, the wizard often failed to find the relevant phrase even if it was present in the interaction model. The introduction of a graph structure for interaction model representation from WOZ3 onwards was of great help to the wizard in finding the relevant phrases.

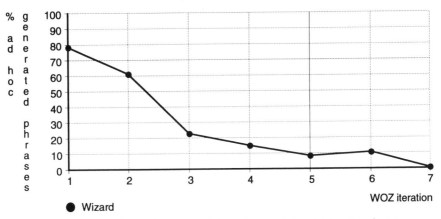

Figure 8.9: Number of ad hoc generated phrases in per cent of the total number of turns.

Number of ad hoc Generated Jumps

From WOZ3 onwards, the interaction model was represented as a state transition network consisting of a number of sub-graphs each of which included an indication of relevant jumps to other sub-graphs. The number of ad hoc jumps (Figure 8.10) includes error jumps as well as jumps missing in the interaction model graphs. Both kinds of ad hoc jumps occurred, particularly in the early WOZ experiments while the wizard was relatively untrained and the interaction model structure was not yet adequate.

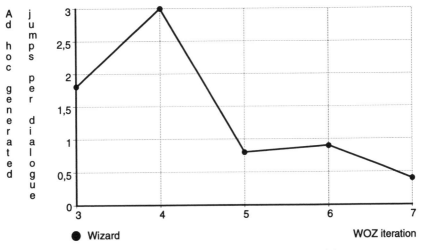

Figure 8.10: Average number of ad hoc generated jumps per dialogue.

After WOZ7, measurement of the various parameters described above had demonstrated levels of performance sufficient for proceeding to system implementation.

8.2.2 Performance Evaluation During the User Test

When the Danish Dialogue System had been implemented and debugged, a controlled user test was carried out with a simulated speech recognizer. A wizard keyed in the users' answers into the simulated recognizer. The simulation ensured that typos were automatically corrected and that input to the parser corresponded to an input string which could have been recognized by the real recognizer. In this set-up, recognition accuracy would be 100% as long as users expressed themselves in accordance with the vocabulary and grammar known to the system. Otherwise, the simulated recognizer would turn the user input into a string which only contained words and grammatical constructs from the recognizer's vocabulary and rules of grammar.

The user test was based on 20 different scenarios which had been systematically designed by the developers, as described in Section 5.6.2. Each scenario was represented in two different versions: a masked version combining language and analogue graphics; and a standard text version (see Figures 5.11 and 5.12).

Twelve external subjects who had never interacted with the system and who represented the target group, i.e. (mostly) professional secretaries, participated in the user test. The percentage of secretaries approximately corresponded to the percentage of secretaries among the customers who called the travel agency where we recorded our human–human dialogue corpus (Section 5.6.1). Subjects conducted the dialogues over the telephone in their normal work environments. Before interacting with the system, each subject received an introductory letter, a leaflet briefly describing the system, four scenarios and a questionnaire. After the experiment they received a telephone interview and filled in the questionnaire.

The subjects were given a total of 50 tasks based on 48 individual scenarios, two of which contained two tasks. A *task* consisted of ordering one or more tickets for one route. A *route* is a full trip, i.e. either a one-way trip, a two-way trip or a round-trip. The number of recorded dialogues was 57, of which 32 were based on text scenarios and 25 were based on graphic scenarios. Subjects sometimes reiterated a failed dialogue and eventually succeeded with the task. A *dialogue* is one path, whether completed or not, through the dialogue structure. If, at the end of the dialogue, the user selects to do a second reservation without hanging up, the user opens a new dialogue. As in the WOZ experiments, all dialogues were recorded, transcribed and annotated. In addition, all transactions between the individual system modules were logged.

In the user test we measured many of the same parameters as found in the WOZ experiments, including average and maximum utterance lengths, vocabulary size, longest turn, user initiative and average number of turns. Real-time could still not be reliably measured because a wizard was involved. Vocabulary convergence was not measured as the measurement of vocabulary size made it clear that 500 words were insufficient. Interaction model complexity and wizard performance in terms of ad hoc generated phrases and jumps were irrelevant to the user test. As in the WOZ experiments, as much information as possible was extracted automatically from the

	WOZ7		User test	
Subjects (total)	12		12	
Dialogues (total)	47		57	
	User	System	User	System
Turns (total)	881	905	998	998
Tokens (total)	1633	10495	2468	12185
Types (total)	165	350	188	189
Longest turn	12	92	23	87
Turns > 10 tokens (total)	3	272	17	253
Tokens per turn (average)	1.85	11.59	2.47	12.20
Types per turn (average)	0.19	0.39	0.19	0.19
Turns per dialogue (average)	18.74	19.26	17.51	17.51
Turns > 10 tokens per dialogue (average)	0.06	5.79	0.30	4.44
Tokens per dialogue (average)	34.74	223.30	43.30	213.77
Types per dialogue (average)	3.51	7.45	3.30	3.32
User questions (total)	4	—	4	—
User questions (% of turns in total)	0.45	—	0.40	—
Types per token (average)	0.10	0.03	0.08	0.02

Figure 8.11: Comparison of results from WOZ7 and the user test. All system turns except for the closing phrase contained a question. Cardinals, ordinals, destinations, names, months, days of week and false start items were counted as one group each, thus adding only seven word types to the total number of types.

annotated corpus. Figure 8.11 presents the results from the user test and allows comparison with the corresponding WOZ7 results. The user test results are discussed in the following.

Average and Maximum Utterance Lengths

The average user utterance length (average number of tokens per turn) was still well within the required limits. However, the prescribed maximum user utterance length (10 tokens) was exceeded in 17 cases, and the longest user utterance contained 23 words. Ten of the long utterances were produced by the same subject. Particularly in the first dialogue, this subject tended to repeat an utterance if the system did not answer immediately. The majority of long utterances, both for this subject and in general, was caused by user-initiated corrections which did not make use of the keyword "change" but were expressed free-style by users. Two long utterances were produced by subjects who took over the initiative when asked "Do you want more?". This question was clearly too open. Finally, subjects sometimes provided more information than had been asked for. All long utterances, therefore, were produced when subjects took over the initiative against the principles on which system-directed interaction is based. Still, the fact that only 1.7% user utterances exceeded the prescribed maximum appears acceptable.

Vocabulary Size

As predicted, the system's vocabulary was insufficient. This was no surprise because related ATIS results from other languages suggest a domain vocabulary of 1000–1200 words (Peckham, 1993). The test corpus showed 51 out-of-vocabulary word types. Excluding numbers, as well as names of months, days of the week, airports, names and false start items, this meant that 28.2%, or more than one quarter, of the user word types were out-of-vocabulary. In particular, the system's sub-language vocabulary regarding quantitative time expressions was insufficient.

Initiative

As in WOZ7, very few questions were asked by the users. In WOZ7, four of 881 user utterances were questions. In the user test, four of 998 user utterances were questions. One of these four questions was asked because the subject had misread the scenario text. The three other questions all concerned available departure times. This is not surprising because departure times constitute a type of information which users often do not have in advance but expect to be able to obtain from the system. When users lack information, the reservation task tends to become an *informed* reservation task and, hence, an ill-structured task (see Section 9.2.1).

Average Number of Turns Per Dialogue

The average number of turns per dialogue was actually a bit lower in the user test than in WOZ7, and still well below the average of 20 found in the human–human corpus from the travel agency. This was considered satisfactory.

There was reasonable correspondence between the final WOZ performance results and the performance results obtained during the user test. Nearly all parameters remained within acceptable limits in the user test, showing only limited deviations from the WOZ7 measurements. Only the vocabulary turned out to be clearly insufficient.

8.3   Diagnostic Evaluation

The process of diagnostic evaluation focuses on the detection, classification, diagnostic analysis and repair of recognition problems, linguistic problems, dialogue interaction problems and any other kind of problem which may affect user–system interaction. When problems have been properly repaired they are prevented from occurring in future user interactions with the system.

Apart from causing problems of user–system interaction, which may be fatal to the success of the transaction being made through spoken interaction, interaction problems tend to make user task performance unnecessarily bumpy and generate user dissatisfaction with interactive speech system technologies. It is the system developer's task to detect and diagnose such errors so that they can be repaired in order to prevent human–machine miscommunication from seriously damaging the user's task performance. Some forms of miscommunication cannot be prevented from occurring and must be handled on-line through meta-communication. User-initiated repair meta-communication functionality is needed to overcome the effects of system misrecognitions. In addition, users will inevitably provide input which, although recognized and understood by the system, requires system-initiated clarification meta-communication. Most user-initiated clarification meta-communication is difficult or impossible to handle on-line by current systems. Furthermore, miscommunication, even when successfully resolved, always leads to additional user–system exchanges which delay task performance. It follows that diagnostic evaluation with the purpose of reducing the amount of miscommunication that can occur is highly important to successful interaction design. Reduced meta-communication is a source of interactive speech system robustness and of increased interaction quality, smoothness and efficiency.

In spite of its clear importance, there is an evident lack of a rigorous methodology in support of systematic and exhaustive diagnostic evaluation. In the following, we present two approaches to the systematic detection of problems of user–system interaction. The first approach is used either to identify problems in an interaction model prior to using it with subjects, for instance prior to running a WOZ experiment, or to identify problems in an actual corpus of dialogues. The method mainly detects structural problems revealed through deviations from the interaction model. The second approach not only serves to identify deviations from the dialogue structure but addresses details of formulation as well. This in-depth approach has two parts. The first part helps system developers detect any kind of user–system interaction problem. The second part supports the classification, diagnosis and repair of dialogue interaction problems.

8.3.1 The Walk-through and Plotting Approaches

The walk-through or plotting approach can be used whenever the developers have some representation of the interaction model and examples of actual situations of use of the system, such as scenarios, available and mainly helps detect structural problems and missing parts of the interaction model. The approach may be used before as well as after a WOZ iteration. When the approach is used before a WOZ iteration, a *walk-through* is made of the current interaction model representation based on the scenarios to be used in the upcoming WOZ experiments. If a deviation from the interaction model representation occurs during the matching process, this indicates a potential interaction problem which should be analysed and removed, if possible.

When the approach is used after a WOZ iteration, we term it the *plotting* approach. The idea is to plot the transcribed dialogues onto the current interaction model representation in order to systematically detect interaction problems. As in the walk-through approach, deviations indicate interaction design problems. Deviations must be marked and their causes analysed whereupon the interaction model is revised, if necessary.

Both the walk-through version and the plotting version of the described approach were used during the WOZ experiments for the Danish Dialogue System. The WOZ interaction model was represented as a complex state transition network that had system output in the nodes and expected contents of user utterances along the edges (cf. Figures 5.7 and 5.8). For each scenario to be used we made a walk-through of the state transition network. Significantly, many problems were discovered analytically through these scenario-based designer walk-throughs of the interaction model. This seems to be typical of interaction model development and illustrates the need for a tool, such as a set of design guidelines (cf. Section 4.2), which could help designers prevent such problems from occurring. After each WOZ iteration we plotted the transcribed dialogues onto the state transition network representing the interaction model. This process also revealed many interaction problems.

Figure 8.12 shows a sub-network from WOZ6 onto which the corresponding part of a dialogue has been plotted. The annotation shows that the subject expected confirmation from the system. When it became clear that the system was not going to provide confirmation, the subject asked for it. The dialogue fragment in Figure 8.13 provides the background for the subject's deviation from the WOZ6 interaction model. The subject made a change to a flight reservation. After the user had stated the desired change, the dialogue continued as shown in Figure 8.13.

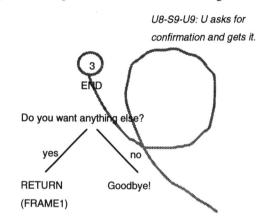

U8-S9-U9: U asks for
confirmation and gets it.

Figure 8.12: A plotted END of dialogue sub-graph from WOZ6. The encircled number 3 refers to the CHANGE of reservation sub-graph, cf. S7–U7 in the transcribed dialogue in Figure 8.13. The user is expected to say, in U8, either "yes" or "no" to the simulated system's question (S8) "Do you want anything else?" If "yes", the system will initiate a fresh dialogue by returning to the sub-graph FRAME1. If "no", the system will end the dialogue by saying "good-bye". What actually happens is that in S8 the user initiates the clarification sub-dialogue conducted through U8–S9–U9. The grey loop marks this deviation from the graph path which may reveal a dialogue design problem. The loop is annotated with numbered reference (in italics) to U8–S9–U9 and a description of the deviation. S refers to system and U to user.

S7:	Do you want to make other changes to this reservation?
U7:	No, I don't.
S8:	Do you want anything else?
U8:	Ah no ...I mean is it okay then?
S9:	[Produces an improvised confirmation of the change made.]
U9:	Yes, that's fine.
S10:	Do you want anything else?

Figure 8.13: The subject has made a change to a flight reservation. After the user has stated the change, the dialogue continues as shown. S is the simulated system, U is the user.

From this point onwards the dialogue finishes as expected. Analysis convinced us that the interaction model had to be revised in order to prevent the occurrence of the user-initiated clarification meta-communication observed in U8, which the implemented system would be incapable of understanding. In fact, the WOZ6 interaction model can be seen to have violated the following cooperativity guideline: *Be fully explicit in communicating to users the commitments they have made* (cf. Figure 4.1). As a result, system confirmation of reservation changes was added to the WOZ7 sub-graph on change of reservation.

It may be asked how the walk-through or plotting approach can be applied if there is no graph representation of the interaction model. Figure 8.15 shows an example of a walk-through of the scenario in Figure 8.14. The representation used is independent of the interaction model representation and, thus, more general than the

Marie Hansen from Copenhagen is going to Aalborg tomorrow together with her daughter Rikke Hansen who is 10 ten years old. The calendar below starts with today in boldface and shows the day of departure as the next day in boldface. Their id-numbers are 4 and 2 and their customer number is 4. They would prefer to arrive around noon. The flight and transportation from the airport takes about five quarters in total.

JANUARY 1996

T F S S M T W T F S S M T W T F S S

Figure 8.14: Scenario G11.

S	greet	(know)		S	feed	(one-way)
U	ans	(yes/no)		S	req	(date)
S	req	(customer no.)		U	ans	(Friday)
U	ans	(4)		S	feed	(Friday, January 19)
S	feed	(4)		S	req	(hour)
S	req	(no. of travellers)		U	ans	(before noon)
U	ans	(2)		S	feed	(before noon, date)
S	feed	(2)		S	stat	(9:40, 11:10)
S	req	(ID-no.)		S	req	(select)
U	ans	(4)		U	ans	(11:10)
S	feed	(4, MH)		S	feed	(11:10)
S	req	(ID-no.)		S	sum	(2 tickets
U	ans	(2)				for id-4, MH, and id-2, RH,
S	feed	(2, RH)				from Copenhagen to Aalborg
S	req	(from)				on Friday January 19 at 11:10.
U	ans	(Copenhagen)				price: 1060 DKK
S	feed	(Copenhagen)				deliver at airport
S	req	(to)				reservation no. B75)
U	ans	(Aalborg)		S	cont	(another reservation)
S	feed	(Aalborg)		U	ans	(no)
S	req	(return)		S	final	(bye)
U	ans	(no)				

Figure 8.15: Scenario-based walk-through of an interaction model. The scenario is shown in Figure 8.14. The interaction structure is one from the implemented Danish Dialogue System. S means system, U means user, req means request, ans means answer, feed means feedback, sum means summary, and cont means continue. Semantic key contents of expected system and user utterances are shown in parentheses.

one used in Figure 8.12. Figure 8.15 is based on the implemented interaction model of the Danish Dialogue System.

8.3.2   The In-depth Approach

For problem detection in the user test corpus, we used the methodology described below which enables the detection of any kind of interaction problem including recognition problems, linguistic problems, such as lacks in grammar and vocabulary, problems of dialogue interaction, and other problems, such as database errors and cases of system breakdown. In the following figures only dialogue interaction problems have been indicated as only these will be discussed in any detail.

Detection of interaction problems was carried out by comparing expected and actual user–system exchanges. (Designer) *expectations* were based on the task structure and on the scenarios given to users. *Actual exchanges* were taken from the recorded and transcribed user–system interactions. Potentially, an interaction problem has been detected if there is a deviation between the expected and actual user–system exchanges. Each such *deviation*, or *problem symptom*, is marked-up by inserting a brief and temporary description of what the problem appears to be. Following the markup process, a *diagnostic analysis* of the marked-up deviations is carried out. This analysis consists of: (i) *verification of the symptom* observed, including a check of the scenario interpretation underlying the presumed deviation; (ii) *problem diagnosis* through use of interaction transcriptions and system logs as necessary; (iii) identification of one or several system or interaction re-design *cures, or of measures* to prevent the occurrence of user errors, including evaluation of their feasibility; and (iv) *final classification* of the problem. The diagnostic analysis may show that a marked-up utterance contains more, or other, problems of interaction than temporarily indicated initially. Similarly, what was initially believed to be a user error (cf. Section 8.4), may be shown through analysis to be a dialogue interaction design problem, and what was initially believed to be a dialogue interaction design problem may turn out to be something else instead, such as a linguistic problem.

Symptom verification consists of checking, for each marked-up deviation between the expected and actual user–system exchanges, whether the expectation was correct. In particular the scenario interpretation should be checked. We found that a scenario sometimes may have legitimate interpretations other than the one envisioned by the system developers and reflected in the expected user input. If this is the case, the definition of the expected user–system exchange is modified. If, on the other hand, the expectation was correct or if the modified expectation still leaves a deviation, an actual problem of user–system interaction has been detected, and steps (ii), (iii) and (iv) above should be performed. How to do this is discussed in Section 8.3.3 and in Section 8.4. In the remainder of the present section, we illustrate the methodology up to and including step (i).

Figure 8.17 shows problem detection and final markup of dialogue interaction problems in a dialogue from the user test. Based on the ticket reservation task structure, Column 1 shows the system's questions in the order in which they would be asked. For system-directed interaction, an ordered list of system questions can

Anders Bækgaard (id-number 6), Paul Dalsgaard (id-number 3) and Børge Lindberg (ID-number 4) work in a department in Aalborg that has customer number 3. They are all going to Copenhagen on the first weekend in February. They want to depart by the earliest flight on Saturday at 7:20 and return by the latest flight on Sunday at 22:40.

Figure 8.16: Scenario T32.

be constructed because sub-tasks are addressed in a fixed order. For mixed initiative interaction and user-directed interaction, the order in which sub-tasks are addressed may depend on the scenario and on user preferences. A diagnostic evaluation template for such dialogues may therefore be less general and may have to be adapted to each concrete scenario and dialogue. Column 2 in Figure 8.17 shows the key contents of the expected user input, or normative user answers, which were filled into the template prior to the user test. In Figure 8.17, the normative user answers reflect Scenario T32 which is shown in Figure 8.16.

After the user test, the key contents of each actual user and system utterance were entered into Column 3 of the template. Note that "key contents" means the semantics of the core message rather than the surface language of an utterance. As can be seen from Figure 8.17, system feedback is only indicated in the case of misunderstandings or other problems. In all other cases, it appears superfluous to include system feedback because this will merely repeat what the user just said. Pointers from Column 3 to the transcribed corpus in terms of unique turn identifiers allow access to the complete surface language of the user–system exchanges and to a log of internal system module communication whenever needed during diagnostic analysis.

Finally, Column 4 in the template in Figure 8.17 serves the markup of interaction problems that have been detected through comparison between normative and actual user–system exchanges. Column 4 shows the *detection* of where in the dialogue a dialogue interaction problem occurred, and a *final classification* of that problem which indicates what went wrong. The previous, temporary markup is not shown. As an example, consider the temporary markup of U6-39 in Figure 8.18 which shows the part of Dialogue T32a in which miscommunication occurs. In S6-39 the system has misunderstood the user's indication of a date. The diagnostic analysis had shown that this misunderstanding was due to a lack in grammar and vocabulary, and it is therefore not marked in Figure 8.17. However, the subsequent answer by the user manifests several dialogue interaction problems. So in Figure 8.17 we wrote "the user only tries to correct part of the misunderstood date and s/he does not use the keyword 'change' to do this". It was only later that we became aware of the additional problem that, in U6-39, the user provides answers to two system questions in a single utterance.

Although not explicitly indicated in the diagnostic evaluation template, illustrated in Figure 8.17, it is assumed that meta-communication may occur at any time during interaction. Actual meta-communication *may* indicate an interaction problem, such as a lack in the system's vocabulary, although this need not be the case. Meta-communication is a natural phenomenon which will not go away completely however perfect the interaction design becomes.

0 Designing Interactive Speech Systems

Scenario: T32a User: 6 Date: 16 January 1995			
1. System questions	**2. Normative user answers**	**3. Actual system-user exchanges**	**4. Problems**
System already known	no / yes / -	-	
Customer number	3	S6-28: Is it customer number 4? U6-28: No, 3. S6-29: Number 10 does not exist. Which number? U6-29: 3.	
Number of travellers	3	S6-30: Number of travellers? U6-30: 3.	
ID-numbers	6, 3, 4	S6-31-33: ID-numbers? U6-31-33: 6, 3, 4.	
Departure airport	Aalborg	S6-34: From which airport? U6-34: Aalborg.	
Arrival airport	Copenhagen	S6-35: To which airport? U6-35: Copenhagen.	
Return journey	yes	S6-36: Return journey? U6-36: Yes.	
Interested in discount	no / yes	S6-37: Interested in discount? U6-37: Yes.	
Date of departure (out)	February 4	S6-38: Date of departure? U6-38: First weekend in February S6-39: Friday February 10.	
Hour of departure (out)	7:20	At which time? U6-39: Saturday at 7:20. S6-40: No departure at 7:20. Closest other red departure at 10:50. Do you want this? U6-40: No. S6-41: At which time? U6-41: Saturday at 7:20. S6-42: No departure at 7:20. Closest other red departure at 10:50. Do you want this? U6-42: Yes.	E2, GP10x2 GP1, SP10 GP10x2 GP1, SP10

Figure 8.17: The system's questions, key contents of the expected (normative) user answers, and actual user–system exchanges in Dialogue T32a. The notation in the fourth column refers to detected and classified dialogue interaction problems. E means user error, GP means generic dialogue design error and SP means specific dialogue design error. Note that the system's erroneous understanding of "first weekend in February" has not been marked because this problem is caused by a lack in vocabulary and grammar, and hence is a linguistic problem (*continued next page*).

Figure 8.17 (*continued*)

Date of departure (home)	February 5	S6-43: Date of return? U6-43: Sunday February 5. S6-44: Sunday February 12.	
Hour of departure (home)	22:40	At which time? U6-44: 22:40.	E2
Delivery	airport / mail	S6-45: Confirms the reservation. Should tickets be mailed or picked up at the airport? U6-45: Mailed.	E2
More	yes / no	S6-46: Do you want more? U6-46: Yes.	

S6-37:	Are you particularly interested in discount?
U6-37:	Yes.
S6-38:	On which date will the journey start?
U6-38:	The first weekend in February.
S6-39:	Friday February 10th. At which time?
U6-39:	It must be on Saturday at 7:20. **E2, GP10, GP10**
S6-40:	There is no departure at 7:20. The closest other red departure is at 10:50. Do you want this departure? **GP1, SP10**
U6-40:	No.
S6-41:	At which time?
U6-41:	Saturday at 7:20. **GP10, GP10**
S6-42:	There is no departure at 7:20. The closest other red departure is at 10:50. Do you want this departure? **GP1, SP10**
U6-42:	Yes.
S6-43:	On which date will the return journey start?
U6-43:	On Sunday February 5th.
S6-44:	Sunday February 12th. At which time?
U6-44:	22:40. **E2**
S6-45:	22:40. You have now booked 3 tickets for Anders Bækgaard, Paul Dalsgaard and Børge Lindberg from Aalborg to Copenhagen on Friday February 10th at 10:50 returning on Sunday February 12th at 22:40. The tickets are on green conditions. Your reference number is 51. The total price is 2820 kroner. Are the tickets to be mailed or will the travellers pick them up at the airport?
U6-45:	They should be mailed. **E2**

Figure 8.18: Excerpt from dialogue T32a from the user test of the Danish Dialogue System (translated from Danish). The dialogue is based on Scenario T32 (Figure 8.16). S means system, U means user. GPs and SPs are dialogue interaction problems, Es are user errors. The dialogue was a transaction failure.

COOPERATIVITY PROBLEM	
Aspect	**Generic or specific problem**
Group 1: **Informativeness**	GP1: System provides less information than required.
	SP1: System is not fully explicit in communicating to users the commitments they have made.
	SP2: Missing system feedback on user information.
	GP2: System provides more information than required.
Group 2: **Truth and evidence**	GP3: System provides false information.
	GP4: System provides information for which it lacks evidence.
Group 3: **Relevance**	GP5: System provides irrelevant information.
Group 4: **Manner**	GP6: Obscure system utterance.
	GP7: Ambiguous system utterance.
	SP3: System does not provide same formulation of the same question to users everywhere in its dialogue turns.
	GP8: Too lengthy expressions provided by system.
	GP9: System provides disorderly discourse.
Group 5: **Partner asymmetry**	GP10: System does not inform users of important non-normal characteristics which they should, and are able to, take into account to behave cooperatively in dialogue.
	SP4: Missing or unclear information on what the system can and cannot do.
	SP5: Missing or unclear instructions on how to interact with the system.
Group 6: **Background knowledge**	GP11: System does not take users' relevant background knowledge into account.
	SP6: Lacking anticipation of domain misunderstanding by analogy.
	SP7: System does not separate when possible between the needs of novice and expert users.
	GP12: System does not consider legitimate user expectations as to its own background knowledge.
	SP8: Missing system domain knowledge and inference.
Group 7: **Repair and clarification**	GP13: System does not initiate repair or clarification meta-communication in case of communication failure.
	SP9: System does not initiate repair if it has failed to understand the user.
	SP10: Missing clarification of inconsistent user input.
	SP11: Missing clarification of ambiguous user input.

Figure 8.19: A typology of dialogue co-operativity problems. GP means generic problem. SP means specific problem. GPs subsume SPs.

8.3.3 Dialogue Design Errors

In order to classify and diagnose dialogue design errors and provide clues to their repair, we used a typology of non-cooperative system interaction behaviour (Figure 8.19) developed on the basis of the design guidelines presented in Chapter 4. The underlying assumption is that *any dialogue design error*, apart, perhaps, from problems of system impoliteness, *can be viewed as a problem of non-cooperative system behaviour*. The typology of (system) cooperativity problems presented in Figure 8.19 distinguishes the same seven aspects of interaction as do the guidelines in Figure 4.1 and has a corresponding distinction between generic and specific problems.

In the template shown in Figure 8.17 several dialogue interaction problems are indicated, some of which represent dialogue design errors. In the following we exemplify the diagnosis, classification and repair of each type of dialogue design error given in Figure 8.17, i.e. GP1, SP10 and GP10. We then review the dialogue design errors found in the user test data more generally. Finally, we discuss why some of the error types in the typology were not found among the user test data.

In the diagnostic analysis of the user test data, each identified dialogue design error was: (a) characterized with respect to its *symptom*; (b) a *diagnosis* was made; and (c) one or several *cures* were proposed. The "cure" part of the diagnostic analysis may suggest several ways in which to improve system dialogue behaviour in order to prevent detected problems from occurring in the future. For an interaction problem to count as a dialogue design error, at least one of the proposed cures should specify revised dialogue design. Otherwise, the detected problem is not a dialogue design error. This is why problem classification, although used from initial problem detection onwards, can be completed only when possible cures for the problem have been identified. Furthermore, the "cure" part of the diagnostic analysis may show that a new *type* of dialogue design error should be added to the typology in Figure 8.19. What we found was that virtually all dialogue design errors in the user test could be classified according to this typology. Only two new underlying specific principles, and hence two new problem types (SP10 and SP11), were added. These had to do with the fact that system-initiated meta-communication had not been simulated during WOZ (cf. Sections 4.4.4 and 5.6.1).

A single utterance may represent several dialogue design problems as illustrated in Figures 8.20 and 8.21. In such cases each individual problem must be analysed separately. We shall sometimes refer to such co-existing problems in an exchange without providing a full symptom–diagnosis–cure treatment of them. In the figures to follow, S means system and U means user.

Figures 8.20 and 8.21 show the analysis of two problems from Figure 8.17. The analysis led to the error classifications indicated in the legends to the figures, i.e. GP1 and SP10, respectively. The classifications are inserted in the template, as shown in Figure 8.17, replacing the temporary markup of unclassified problems. In addition to problem classification, the typology also provides cues to problem repair, for instance by pointing to the fact that the system does not provide sufficient information. The "cure" part of the analysis provides a more detailed proposal for how to repair the problem. S6-42 in Figure 8.18 contains two dialogue design errors which are similar to those analysed in Figures 8.20 and 8.21.

> **Symptom:** S6-37: Are you particularly interested in discount? U6-37: Yes.
> S6-38: On which date will the journey start? U6-38: The first weekend in February.
> S6-39: Friday February 10th. At which time? U6-39: It must be on Saturday at
> 7:20. S6-40: There is no departure at 7:20. The closest other red departure is at
> 10:50. Do you want this departure?
>
> **Diagnosis:** The system provides insufficient information. It does not inform the
> user that there is a blue departure at 7:20 on Fridays.
>
> **Cure:** The system should provide sufficient information, for instance by informing
> the user that there is no red departure but that there is a blue departure at the chosen
> hour. The system should also mention that it still assumes the date to be Friday.

Figure 8.20: A dialogue design error from Dialogue T32a. The problem is of type GP1: the system provides less information than required. It may be debated whether the first part of S14 manifests a problem of type GP1 or of type GP3 (false information). Viewed in isolation, the information provided by the system is false but viewed together, with the rest of U14, the information rather appears insufficient.

> **Symptom:** S6-37: Are you particularly interested in discount? U6-37: Yes.
> S6-38: On which date will the journey start? U6-38: The first weekend in February.
> S6-39: Friday February 10th. At which time? U6-39: It must be on Saturday at
> 7:20. S6-40: There is no departure at 7:20. The closest other red departure is at
> 10:50. Do you want this departure?
>
> **Diagnosis:** There is, in fact, a departure at 7:20 but it does not offer discount. The
> system implicitly assigns priority to discount over departure time without sufficient
> reason.
>
> **Cure:** S should ask U about priority saying, for instance: "7:20 is not a discount
> departure. Red discount can be obtained on the departures at x, y and z. Which
> departure do you want?"

Figure 8.21: A dialogue design error from Dialogue T32a. The problem is of type SP10: missing clarification of inconsistent user input.

Figures 8.22 and 8.23 present analyses of a third dialogue design error from Figure 8.17. A single utterance turns out to exhibit two errors of the same type. In its introduction, the system asks users to use the keywords "change" and "repeat" for metacommunication purposes and to answer the system's questions briefly and one at a time. Despite the introduction, a significant number of violations of these instructions occurred in the user test. Figure 8.22 analyses the problem of a user attempting to make a change through a full-sentence expression rather than by saying "change". Figure 8.23 analyses the problem of a user answering several questions at a time. Although the system has clearly stated that it has some non-normal characteristics and users should thus modify their natural dialogue behaviour, this is not cognitively possible for many users. Therefore, the problems should be considered errors of dialogue design rather than user errors. These problems will be further discussed in Section 8.4. U6-41 in Figure 8.18 contains two dialogue design errors which are similar to those analysed in Figures 8.22 and 8.23.

Symptom: S6-39: Friday February 10th. At which time? U6-39: It must be Saturday at 7:20.

Diagnosis: The user is too occupied with the problem to remember to use the keyword 'change' when trying to change Friday into Saturday.

Cure: 'Change' is not natural. Prefer more natural mixed-initiative meta-communication.

Figure 8.22: A dialogue design error from Dialogue T32a. The problem is of type GP10: the system does not inform users of important non-normal characteristics which they should, and are able to, take into account to behave co-operatively in dialogue.

Symptom: S6-39: Friday February 10th. At which time? U6-39: It must be Saturday at 7:20.

Diagnosis: Natural user response package.

Cure: Allow naturally related information, such as date and time, to be provided in the same user answer.

Figure 8.23: A dialogue design error from Dialogue T32a. The problem is of type GP10: the system does not inform users of important non-normal characteristics which they should, and are able to, take into account to behave co-operatively in dialogue.

Figure 8.24 presents an overview of the types of dialogue design error that were identified in the user test. For each identified GP and SP, the actually observed dialogue design errors are briefly characterized with global indications of their causes and repair. The figure contains 13 GPs and SPs. Although the generic problems GP11, GP12 and GP13 were not directly observed in the user test data, these problems are still regarded as having occurred because cases of one or more of the specific problems subsumed by each of them were found in the data. The violation of GP3 was not, in fact, caused by a dialogue design error but by our database design.

Section 4.3 has shown other representative examples of dialogue design errors identified in the user test. Examples of errors of types GP1, SP10 and GP10 have already been shown above. All identified errors of type SP10 were very similar whereas the GP1 type errors were of three different kinds, as illustrated in Figure 4.2.

Errors of type GP10 were of four different kinds: users asked questions; provided indirect answers, such as answering "cheap" to the question of hour of departure; answered several questions at a time, often through providing two temporal expressions in the same utterance; and attempted to make changes through full-sentence expressions rather than by saying "change" (cf. Figure 4.14). The most frequent cases were changes through comments and answering several questions at a time. Almost all of these cases led to misunderstanding or non-understanding.

It is significant that the large majority of dialogue design errors could be straightforwardly classified. It is only to be expected, however, that some errors are borderline cases which may receive alternative classifications. One such case was mentioned in Figure 8.20. Figure 4.9 (first example) shows an example which was

COOPERATIVITY PROBLEM	No.	TF	CAUSE/REPAIR
GP1: System provides less information than required (final question too open; withholding important information, requested or not).	19		System question design (4). System response design (15).
SP2: Missing system feedback on user information (system misunderstandings only show up later in the dialogue).	2	1	System response feedback design.
GP3: System provides false information (on departures).	2		Database design.
GP5: System provides irrelevant information (irrelevant error message produced by grammar failure).	2	1	Grammar design *or* speech recognition design coupled with improved repair design.
GP6: Obscure system utterance (grammatically incorrect response; obscure departure information).	7		System response grammar design (1). System response design (6).
GP7: Ambiguous system utterance (question on point of departure).	2		System question design.
GP10: System does not inform users of important non-normal characteristics which they should, and are able to, take into account to behave co-operatively in dialogue (indirect response, change through comments, asking questions, answering several questions at a time).	33		Unreasonable system demands on users. Improve the system to handle the violations.
SP4: Missing or unclear information on what the system can and cannot do (system does not listen during its own dialogue turns).	33	1	Speech prompt design.
SP5: Missing or unclear instructions on how to interact with the system (under-supported user navigation: use of 'change'; round-trip reservations).	2	1	User instruction design.
SP6: Lacking anticipation of domain misunderstanding by analogy (user is unaware that discount is only possible on return fares).	3		User information design.

Figure 8.24: Typology of the 119 dialogue design errors (including two database errors) identified in the user test. The number (No.) of occurrences of each problem is shown, as is the responsibility for transaction failure (TF) per problem type. The extreme-right column shows the global cause(s) of the problems and, hence, what needs to be repaired to prevent them from re-occurring.

Figure 8.24 (*continued*)

SP8: Missing system domain knowledge and inference (temporal inference; inference from negated binary option).	4	System inference design.
SP10: Missing clarification of inconsistent user input (system jumps to wrong conclusion).	5	System clarification question design.
SP11: Missing clarification of ambiguous user input (system jumps to wrong conclusion).	5	2	System clarification question design.

categorized as a problem of type GP6 (obscure system utterance). Arguably, this example may instead be considered a problem of type GP3 (system provides false information). Obscurity and falsehood can be difficult to distinguish from one another.

Eight of the 24 problem types in the typology were not observed in the user test. Figure 8.25 explores why. Most of the problems in question are either easy to avoid during dialogue design once it has been decided to do so (SP1, SP3 and SP9); or it is difficult to tell from observed cooperativity problems whether or not concrete cases occur because these types of design error must be massively present for a concrete cooperativity problem to be observed (GP2, GP8 and SP7). If less

COOPERATIVITY PROBLEM	COMMENTS
SP1: System is not fully explicit in communicating to users the commitments they have made.	Easy to ensure once this has been decided.
GP2: System provides more information than required.	Difficult to test through identified co-operativity problems.
GP4: System provides information for which it lacks evidence.	The system cannot directly commit this error. Problems SP10 and SP11 indirectly raise issues of this kind.
SP3: System does not provide same formulation of the same question to users everywhere in its dialogue turns.	Easy to ensure once this has been decided.
GP8: System is too verbose.	Difficult to test through identified co-operativity problems.
GP9: System provides disorderly discourse.	Great care taken during dialogue design to avoid this problem.
SP7: System does not separate when possible between the needs of novice and expert users.	Difficult to test through identified co-operativity problems.
SP9: System does not initiate repair when it has failed to understand the user.	Repair ability is easy to provide once this has been decided.

Figure 8.25: Why some dialogue design errors were not observed in the user test.

massively present, users tend to suffer in silence during the dialogue and complain afterwards. An example of this was found in the WOZ experiments. The fact that problems GP2 (system provides more information than required) and GP8 (system is too verbose) had occurred became apparent from users' complaints that the system talked too much. The problem was solved by removing superfluous information and constructing more succinct system utterances.

8.3.4 Diagnostic Evaluation Criteria

We have described the methods used for diagnostic evaluation of the WOZ and user test corpora from the Danish Dialogue Project. In particular, we have provided detailed results from the diagnostic evaluation of the user test corpus. We shall now briefly discuss the evaluation criteria from Figure 3.3 which require diagnostic evaluation, i.e. the criteria task domain coverage, robustness, principled restrictions on language and dialogue, and flexibility. Throughout the development process, only ad hoc estimates were made of the extent to which the system conformed to these criteria. No precise and operational metrics were developed for measuring conformance to the criteria most of which, as ordinarily used, are somewhat vague. For this reason, these criteria are also included in the subjective part of the adequacy evaluation (Section 8.5). The exception seems to be task domain coverage. In most cases it will be clear whether the task domain coverage is deficient or not.

WOZ

Considerable work went into ensuring sufficient *task domain coverage* through testing the simulated system on a broad selection of scenarios and repairing deficiencies which had been revealed through the matching and plotting approaches described in Section 8.3.1. The WOZ system was very *robust* because of the wizard. Non-robust system behaviour was not simulated. Users' *language and dialogue* were gradually restricted until the domain communication became completely system-directed. Apart from that, only a minimum of restrictions on language and dialogue were simulated in WOZ7. These additional restrictions were imposed as rejections of user input which clearly could not be handled by the final system. However, rejections were few and rather ad hoc. Missing *flexibility* was a main reason for not implementing those parts of the interaction model which concerned information and change of reservation. Users' had to make a considerable number of tedious and inefficient choices to get their information or change of reservation tasks carried out through system-directed interaction. As regards the reservation task, much work went into defining an acceptable and natural task structure for the users. In addition, an optional introduction and optional information on discount types were introduced to increase flexibility.

User Test

The diagnostic evaluation of the user test corpus showed that the implemented system's *task domain coverage* is functionally acceptable. Usability limitations, on the other hand, still remain exactly at the points of maximum task complexity where system-directed interaction comes close to its limits. When, for instance, four people want to fly out together and only two people want to fly back together, or when a person wants to fly out to airport X and back from airport Y, the system's limitations become apparent. The problem is not functional because, functionally speaking, such cases are dealt with simply through a series of reservations of return tickets and/or one-way tickets. To users, however, this is a counter-intuitive and cumbersome way of doing things. Counter-intuitiveness can be helped through additional system instructions. This, however, makes the entire interaction more cumbersome for *all* users. The tedious splitting-up of complex tasks into simple ones can be avoided by adding a series of extra questions to be posed by the system, making the entire inter-action more cumbersome for the users who want to make simple reservations. Neither of these remedies are particularly attractive. Real solutions can be found only through allowing longer user utterances, more open system questions and mixed initiative interaction.

To allow early error detection by the users, and thereby increase *robustness,* the system provides feedback by echoing the key information in the latest user utter-ance (see SP2 in Figure 8.24, however, for cases of missing feedback). Furthermore, at the end of a reservation task, a summary is provided of the entire reservation made by the user. Functionally speaking, as long as the user can be understood by the system at all, iterative use of the "change" command enables the user to change any-thing that the system has done wrong during the preceding interaction. The system's dialogue is robust in these respects, at least.

The domain communication of the implemented system is completely system-directed, which strongly restricts users' *language and dialogue* but in a natural way. However, the vocabulary and grammar of the system imposed restrictions which were less natural and principled. For instance, conjunctions are not accepted although they are highly natural for users even in system-directed communication. As we have seen, it also turned out that the use of keywords for changing or repeating information was unnatural to users (see SP5 and GP10 in Figure 8.24).

System-directed domain interaction through non-open questions affords little dia-logue *flexibility.* However, as the task of reservation is a well-structured one, system-directedness seems generally acceptable for the purpose of this task, at least up to a certain level of complexity as argued with respect to task domain coverage above. Another example of meeting the complexity boundary is the following. When users have conflicting desiderata, typically concerning hour of departure and an interest in dis-count, one may observe problems in the dialogue because users will have to backtrack to de-select discount if they end up giving priority to the conflicting hour of departure.

8.4   A By-product: User Errors

As a by-product of the diagnostic evaluation of user–system interaction in the user test, the in-depth methodology described in Section 8.3.2 produced a series of inter-action problems which we classified as user errors rather than dialogue interaction design errors. A common topic in the general HCI literature, user errors have received comparatively little treatment in the literature on interactive speech systems. We want to argue that not everything that goes wrong in spoken interaction between user and system is due solely to errors made by the system developers. Users make errors, too. Some might want to disagree. As an extreme viewpoint, it might be maintained that the system must be able to deliver what the user wants no matter how the user behaves. We suspect, however, that not even a mind-reading system could do that. At the other extreme it might be claimed that users just have to get used to the system no matter how stupidly it behaves. But nobody would claim that, we admit. Clearly, a more balanced viewpoint is required. Users make errors during spoken interaction and some interaction problems are the compound effects of interaction design errors and user errors. It follows that diagnostic evaluation of spoken interaction includes user errors within its scope. This raises the tricky issue of how to separate errors made solely by users from compound errors and those from pure errors of dialogue interaction design.

The following discussion of the user errors identified in the user test of the Danish Dialogue System is less principled than the discussion in Section 8.3.3 of dialogue design errors, in the sense that we did not have an independent classification of user error types to depart from. Thus, the typology to be presented below has been established empirically based on the user test itself.

The concept of a "user error" is a complex one, as we shall see. Our initial definition of a user error, and one which might appear plausible to many system developers, was something like the following: a user error is *a case in which a user does not behave in accordance with the full normative model of the dialogue*. In controlled user testing, the full normative model of the dialogue is defined by: (i) explicit designer instructions to users, i.e. the scenarios that users have to carry out in dialogue with the system; (ii) explicit system instructions to users, such as the system's introduction to itself (cf. Figure 2.3); (iii) explicit system utterances during dialogue; and (iv) implicit system "instructions" to users. (i)–(iv) will be illustrated and discussed below. (i) is absent in field testing and in practical system use. In such cases, the full normative dialogue model reduces to (ii)–(iv). (ii) is very important to interactive speech system design and use because interactive speech systems are vastly inferior dialogue partners when compared to humans. This means that humans must be told how to interact with an interactive speech system lest they treat the system as a human dialogue partner. Users, of course, should react appropriately to the system's utterances during dialogue (iii), given their scenarios and the dialogue context. The need to include (iv) follows from the important fact that it is impractical to explicitly inform users about all the types of behaviour that they should avoid during interaction with the system. Rather, users should be made to grasp the general fact that the system is a severely restricted interaction partner which should be treated accordingly.

According to the above definition of "user error", 102 individual user errors were found in the user test corpus which contains a total of 998 user utterances (Figure 8.11). A more thorough analysis of the user errors that were identified on the basis of the above definition revealed, however, that a significant number were *caused* by dialogue design errors. For instance, users responded differently to how they should have responded according to the scenario because of missing system feedback or because a system question was too open and invited users to respond in ways which we had not intended. We shall ignore such cases and focus on the dialogue errors that were made solely by the users. This leaves 62 individual user errors for discussion in what follows.

Each user error was analysed and: (a) characterized with respect to its *symptom*; (b) a *diagnosis* was made; and (c) a *preventive measure* was proposed whenever possible. A single utterance sometimes contained several user errors and sometimes an utterance contained both dialogue design errors and user errors (cf. U6-39 in Figure 8.18 which is analysed in Figures 8.22, 8.23 and 8.26).

Figure 8.26 shows the analysis of a problem detected in Figure 8.17. The analysis led to the classification indicated in the legend to Figure 8.26, i.e. the problem is a user error of type E2: ignoring clear system feedback. Upon diagnostic analysis, and just as in the case of dialogue design error types, user error classification results are

Symptom: S6-38: On which date will the journey start? U6-38: The first weekend of February. S6-39: Friday February 10th. At which time? U6-39: It must be Saturday at 7:20.

Diagnosis: The user ignores the system's date feedback and only tries to change Friday into Saturday.

Preventive measure: People sometimes do not listen sufficiently carefully. They may also care less in experimental settings than in real life. In experiments people may be more attentive if a reward is offered to the best user.

Figure 8.26: A user error from Dialogue T32a. The error is of type E2: ignoring clear system feedback. This error was considered a direct cause of the transaction failure.

Error Types	Error Sub-Types	No. of Cases	Preventive Measure
E1. Misunderstanding of scenario.	a. Careless reading or processing.	14	Use clear scenarios, carefully studied, to reduce errors.
E2. Ignoring clear system feedback.	a. Straight ignorance.	7	Encourage user seriousness to reduce errors.
E3. Responding to a question different from the clear system question.	a. Straight wrong response.	4	Encourage user seriousness to reduce errors.
	b. Indirect response.	3	Disguised dialogue design error.
E4. Change through comments (including 'false' keywords).	a. Cognitive overload.	17	Disguised dialogue design error.
E5. Asking questions.	a. Asking for decision-relevant information.	4	Disguised dialogue design error.
E6. Answering several questions at a time.	a. Natural response 'package'.	10	Disguised dialogue design error.
	b. Slip.	1	None.
E7. Thinking aloud.	a. Natural thinking aloud.	1	None.
E8. Non-cooperativity.	a. Unnecessary complexity.	1	None.

Figure 8.27: The initially identified user error types and sub-types.

inserted in the diagnostic evaluation template to replace the temporary indication of an unclassified problem (cf. Figure 8.17). U6-44 and U6-45 in Figure 8.18 contain two user errors which are similar to the one analysed in Figure 8.26.

Figure 8.27 presents an overview of the user error types that were initially identified in the user test. Two error types (E3 and E6) were divided into sub-types. E1 includes the scenario violations, i.e. violations of explicit designer instructions. E2 and E3a include cases in which users did not pay attention to explicit system utterances (feedback and questions). E3b is closely related to E5 (see below). E3b, E4, E5, E6 and E7 represent violations of explicit system instructions provided in the system's introduction. As we shall see, however, E3b, E4, E5 and E6 turned out to be disguised dialogue design errors. In E8 the user violates implicit system instructions. For each identified user error type in Figure 8.27, one or more sub-types are indicated which briefly characterize the problem. For each sub-type preventive measures, if any, are indicated. In the following each error type is discussed in more detail.

E1: Misunderstanding the Scenario

As remarked earlier, scenario misunderstandings are artefacts of controlled user testing. Nevertheless, controlled user testing is important in system design and it may be worth considering ways of preventing user errors in controlled test environments. It should be noted that scenario misunderstandings cannot give rise to transaction failure. The system cannot be blamed for not knowing that the user was supposed to have asked for something different from what s/he actually did ask for. Transaction failure occurs only when users do not obtain the reservation they actually ask for. In fact, scenario misunderstandings rarely appear to lead to other forms of dialogue interaction problems. They may do so if the user mixes up several possible scenarios and thereby manages to provide inconsistent input. Normally, however, users just carry out a different scenario. This may, however, affect the quality of system evaluation. A scenario which is not being carried out may result in that part of the interaction model remaining untested.

Almost one quarter of the 62 user errors were due to users acting against the instructions in the scenarios. These errors were of three (task-dependent) kinds: (a) users who asked for one-way tickets instead of return tickets; (b) users who were not interested in discount although, according to the scenario, they should have been; and (c) users who tended to miscalculate the date of departure if this date was given only indirectly in the scenario. It seems likely that the main reason for the many scenario misunderstandings was the artificial experimental situation. People care less in an experimental situation than they do in real life and therefore tend not to prepare themselves sufficiently for the dialogue with the system. In addition, unclear scenarios cause errors. E1 thus raises two issues in the preparation of controlled user testing: (i) to reduce the number of errors, scenarios should be made as clear as possible. Nothing is gained by unclear or misleading scenarios. Clear scenarios should not be confused with *simple* scenarios. Scenarios should reflect the types of information real users actually have when addressing the system. This information may be complex and some scenarios should reflect that. This means that users may have to perform some mental processing of the scenario information in order to provide correct answers to the system's questions. (ii) Users should be encouraged to carefully prepare themselves on the scenarios they are to complete in conversation with the system. This should mirror the interest real users have in getting the system to deliver what they want. A practical solution is to promise an award to subjects who stick to their scenarios in conversation with the system. Awards depend on culture, so we will not suggest a good bottle of wine as the sole solution.

Whatever preventive measures are taken, however, scenario misunderstandings are not likely to be entirely absent from controlled user tests but reducing their number is an important goal.

E2: Ignoring Clear System Feedback

The speech recognition capabilities of most telephone-based systems are still fragile. It is therefore important that users listen carefully to the system's feedback to verify that they have been correctly understood. Of the seven transaction failures in the user test, one was caused by a combination of a dialogue design error and a user who ignored clear system feedback. A second transaction failure occurred solely because the user did not pay sufficient attention to the system's feedback which made it clear that the user had been misunderstood (cf. Figures 8.18 and 8.26). Three of the seven detected E2 cases occurred in this dialogue where the user continuously ignored the system feedback on dates. Thus, four of the seven detected cases of ignored system feedback had severe implications for the success of the transactions. Moreover, had the user test included a real recognizer, more cases of system misunderstanding would no doubt have occurred and hence more cases in which users would have had to identify system misrecognitions from the system's feedback.

The notion of a transaction failure that is caused by a "clean" user error may be controversial. It might be argued that transaction failures should be caused by system design errors of one kind or another. On the other hand, it might be said that most user errors of ignoring clear system feedback only arise because the system has misunderstood the user in the first place. This problem does not seem to have any obvious solution. Whatever one chooses to do, this should be made clear in the definition of "transaction failure" adopted because the resulting transaction failure percentage constitutes an important quantitative measure of system performance.

E2 raises the issue of encouraging test subjects to "act" seriously during interaction with the system and be very attentive to what the system says because recognition in interactive speech systems is much more error-prone than the hearing capabilities of normal humans. This would help in reducing the number of user errors caused by ignored system feedback. Nothing is gained by having subjects who care too little about what is going on during the dialogue. Whatever preventive measures are taken,

---

Symptom: S: Where does the journey start? U: Saturday.

Diagnosis: The user responds to a question different from that asked by the system.

Preventive measure: People sometimes do not listen sufficiently carefully. They may also care less in experimental settings than in real life. In experiments people may be more attentive if a reward is offered to the best user.

Figure 8.28: A user error from Dialogue G13a. The error is of type E3: responding to a question different to the clear system question (straight wrong response).

however, the problem of user inattention is not likely to go away completely. This is true of both "artificial" user tests and real-life use of commercial systems.

E3: Responding to a Question Different from a Clear System Question

E3 has at least two sub-types. The first sub-type, E3a, included four cases in which users gave a straight wrong response to a system question. An example is shown in Figure 8.28. In one case the answer was not understood by the system and in three cases it was misunderstood. E3a raises the same issue as E2 of encouraging users to seriously pay attention to the system's utterances. Similarly, E3a errors are not likely to go away completely, neither in "artificial" user tests nor in real-life interaction.

The second sub-type, E3b, concerns *indirect* user responses. An example is shown in Figure 8.29. In human–human conversation, indirect answers of this type would be perfectly all right. An indirect response suggests that the speaker does not possess the information necessary to provide a direct answer. In response to the indirect user answer in Figure 8.29, a human travel agent would list the relevant departures on which discount may be obtained. Our interactive speech system, however, has limited inferential capabilities and is not able to cope with indirect responses. They will be either not understood or misunderstood.

E3b is among the most challenging types of user errors in the test material. Indirect responses are natural to humans in situations in which they do not have sufficient information to produce a direct response. In such cases, we provide instead the information that we actually possess, leaving it to the interlocutor to infer the information asked for. We do this cooperatively, of course, only in cases where the interlocutor can be assumed to have the information needed to perform the inference. The system, posing as a perfect domain expert, may legitimately be assumed to possess the required information. What the user overlooks, however, is that the system does not have *the capability to draw the proper inferences* from the user's information. The E3b cases, therefore, raise the hard issue of the extent to which dialogue designers should consider providing their systems with appropriate inferential skills. There does not currently appear to exist a principled answer to this problem. Furthermore, it may be argued that indirect user responses are not user errors at all. They do not conflict with the system's introduction. At best it might be

---

Symptom: S: At which time? U: It must be as cheap as possible. S: Sorry, at which time?

Diagnosis: The user wants a discount ticket but since s/he has asked for a one-way ticket this is not possible and the system does not offer it. However, the user does not know this and wants to let the hour of departure depend on when there is a cheap departure.

Preventive measure: Probably none. This kind of response is natural to humans in situations in which they do not have sufficient information to provide a direct answer.

Figure 8.29: A user error from Dialogue T13a. The error is of type E3: responding to a question different to the clear system question (indirect response). This problem is a disguised dialogue design error, although in our analysis it was first classified as a user error.

argued that indirect responses conflict with the difficult requirement on users which we have called "implicit instructions" to users (see above). If, however, we are right in the above interpretation of E3b type user contributions, they are, in fact, oblique questions asking for information (see E5 below).

E4: Change Through Comments

E4 gave rise to numerous (almost 30%) user errors in the test. In 16 out of 17 cases, users tried to make corrections through natural sentences rather than by using the keywords prescribed in the system's introduction. An example is shown in Figure 8.18 and analysed in Figure 8.22. In none of these cases was the requested correction understood as intended. Only in one case did the user achieve the intended correction. In this case, the user used a keyword different to "change" but meaning the same, which accidentally was recognized as "change". The theoretical importance of these findings is that of emphasizing the undesirability of including designer-designed user keywords in dialogue design for interactive speech systems. Such keywords will neither correspond to the keywords preferred by all or most users nor to the natural preference among native speakers to reply in spoken sentence form rather than through keywords. It is furthermore our hypothesis that the more cognitive load a user has at a certain stage during dialogue task performance, the more likely it is that the user will ignore the system's instructions concerning the specific keywords to be used.

E4 raises the hard issue of allowing users a more natural form of repair meta-communication.

E5: Asking Questions

E5 is among the most challenging types of user errors in the test data and is closely related to E3b above. Three out of the four E5 cases occurred when the system had asked for an hour of departure. An example is shown in Figure 8.30. What the observed cases show is that reservation dialogue in its very nature, so to speak, is *informed reservation* dialogue. It is natural for users who are making a reservation or, more generally, ordering something, not to always possess the full information needed to decide what to do. In such cases, they ask for information. As the system poses as a perfect domain expert, this is legitimate. What users overlook, despite what was said in the system's introduction, is that the system does not have the skills to process their questions. As with E3b above, it is not clear what the interaction designer should do about this problem in the short term (we shall return to the longer-term perspective in Section 9.2). Current systems are not likely to be able to

Symptom: S: At which time? U: What are the possibilities? S: Sorry, at which time?

Diagnosis: This is a very natural question when the user does not know the exact departure times.

Preventive measure: Allow advanced mixed initiative domain communication. Reservation is often informed reservation.

Figure 8.30: A user error from Dialogue T12a. The error is of type E5: asking questions. In fact, this problem is a disguised dialogue design error, although in our analysis it was first classified as a user error.

understand all possible and relevant user questions in the context of ordering tasks. The optimistic conclusion is that E3b and E5 only constituted seven errors in total in the user test, and that skilled users of the system will learn other ways of eliciting the system's knowledge about departure times. However, a principled solution to the problem only seems possible through enabling the system to conduct rather sophisticated, advanced mixed initiative domain dialogue (see Section 9.2).

E6: Answering Several Questions at a Time

E6 has at least two sub-types. The first sub-type, E6a, gave rise to many (about 16%) user errors in the test. An example is shown in Figure 8.23. Other examples are: a user who answered "the journey starts on Friday at 8:15" when asked for a date of departure; and a user who answered "no, change" when asked if it is correct that the destination is Karup. In seven of the 10 cases only the part of the user's response which answered the system's question was understood. In the remaining three cases the entire user response was misunderstood. What this error type suggests is that: (i) users naturally store information in "packages" consisting of several pieces of information. This means that they are unlikely to consistently split these packages into single pieces of information despite having been told to do so in the system's introduction. Interaction designers should be aware of the existence of such natural information packages and enable their system to understand them. (ii) Users have stereotypical linguistic response patterns, such as prefixing a "change" keyword with a "no". Interaction designers should be aware of these natural stereotypes and enable the system to understand them. The problem posed by the E6 cases appears solvable by today's technology. Our interactive speech system is already able to accept such stereotypes, for example, when information on departure and arrival airports is being provided in the same utterance. However, owing to the present strong limitations on active vocabulary, we have not been able to allow natural information packages and stereotypes throughout the reservation dialogue.

The second sub-type, E6b, illustrates a phenomenon which no feat of spoken interaction design is likely to remove, i.e. the naturally occurring slips of the tongue in spontaneous speech. Slips do not appear to constitute any major problem, however. Only one slip causing an interaction problem occurred in the entire corpus: when asked for the customer number, the user said "four, no sorry, change, change". Only the number was recognized, forcing the user to change it in the following utterance.

E7: Thinking Aloud

E7 illustrates another phenomenon which no dialogue design effort is likely to remove, i.e. the naturally occurring thinking aloud in spontaneous speech. Thinking aloud does not appear to constitute a major problem. Only one case of natural thinking aloud occurred in the entire corpus: when asked for an hour of departure, the user said "well, let me see, at 8:30 at the latest".

E8: Non-cooperativity

E8 illustrates yet another phenomenon which cannot be removed through interaction design, i.e. the deliberately non-cooperative user. Only one case of deliberate user non-cooperativity was detected in the test corpus. The user replied "the ticket should not be sent" to the system's question of whether the ticket should be sent or would be picked up at the airport. This reply would not have been considered non-cooperative if produced in human–human conversation. However, the reply is unnecessarily complex and cannot be handled by our interactive speech system. We know that the particular user who caused the problem was deliberately testing the hypothesis that the system would be unable to handle the input because she said so in the telephone interview following her interaction with the system. Interactive speech system designers have no way of designing dialogues with sufficient robustness to withstand deliberately non-cooperative users. Nor should interactive speech system designers attempt to do so, apart, of course, from ensuring that the system will not break down and that deliberately non-cooperative users cannot cause any harm. When successful, deliberately non-cooperative users will fail to get their task done.

Summary on User Errors

The E1 errors are of only minor importance as they will disappear when the system is used in real life. Furthermore, the evidence suggests that E1 errors do not tend to cause severe dialogue interaction problems. Similarly, E8 errors are of minor importance because users will stop experimenting with the system when they want the task done. E6b and E7 can hardly be prevented but, at least according to our test data, they are infrequent and do not cause severe problems of interaction.

E2 and E3a seem to have a much larger effect on dialogue transaction success. Although they can hardly be completely avoided, it is likely that their number can be reduced by clearly making users aware of the importance of paying attention to system feedback and system questions. Real-life users are likely to be more attentive.

E3b, E4, E5 and E6a are the most challenging error types found in the corpus. They would all be perfectly acceptable in human–human dialogue. However, because of the limited dialogue capabilities of our interactive speech system, it is clearly stated in the system's introduction how users should interact with it in order to prevent these errors. Whereas E3b is less clear, the E4, E5 and E6a errors all violate the system's explicit instructions. The important question is why so many users violate exactly these instructions. A likely explanation is that, at least for many users, it is not *cognitively feasible* to follow the system's explicit instructions. In an extreme example: had we asked users to always use exactly four words in their responses to the system's questions, this would clearly have been cognitively unfeasible. Similarly, several of the things that the system's introduction asks users to do or avoid doing turn out to be unrealistic given the dialogue behaviour that is natural to most people. This reveals a fundamental shortcoming in our initial concept of "user error". It is not sufficient to provide clear and explicit instructions to users on how to interact with the system. *It must also be possible for users, such as they are, to follow these instructions in practice*, as stated in cooperativity problem GP10 in Figure 8.19. The conclusion is that E3b, E4, E5 and E6a are *not* user errors at all but rather constitute more or less difficult problems of dialogue interaction design. A simple revision of our initial definition of "user error" provided at the start of the present section is: a user error is *a case in which a user does not behave in accordance with the full, and cognitively feasible, normative model of the dialogue.*

E3b, E4, E5 and E6a are otherwise very different. E3b and E5 result from a mismatch between generic task type (ordering) and the type of interaction initiative adopted for the application (system-directed domain communication). E4 and E6a belong to a much more general class of human–machine interaction problems. For years, in fact, experts on human error in the field of human factors have been aware of the broad category of errors illustrated by E4 and E6a. The reason why these errors are easy to overlook during design, and until the user and field test data come in, is that, *in principle*, we can all avoid them. For instance, we can all easily say "change" when we want to correct a system misunderstanding. During actual task performance, however, whether the task be one of driving a car or communicating with an interactive speech system, we tend to fall back on our natural skills and what is inherent to the human cognitive processing architecture, more or less ignoring rules or instructions that conflict with those skills and that architecture.

8.5   Adequacy Evaluation

Adequacy evaluation aims at testing how well the system conforms to particular performance measures and meets user needs and expectations. Adequacy evaluation thus includes objective as well as subjective measures. Examples of performance measures which are often included in adequacy evaluations of interactive speech systems are real-time performance and transaction success rate. Adequacy cannot be fully evaluated in a simulated system. However, although perhaps not fully reliable during simulation, the performance measures selected to form part of an adequacy evaluation may still provide valuable information on interaction acceptability and could serve as part of the stop criterion for WOZ.

Transaction success rate, number and nature of interaction problems, and other objective performance measures are not sufficient for measuring adequacy, however. A high transaction success rate does not necessarily guarantee high user satisfaction. User satisfaction is not necessarily achieved by technically excellent systems and cannot be sufficiently measured through objective evaluation. Subjective evaluation techniques, such as questionnaires and interviews, are needed as well. However, it is very difficult to specify in advance the "scoring levels" that should be attained in those questionnaires and interviews.

No methodology exists for synthesizing the results of user evaluations of interactive speech systems (Fraser, 1995). Nevertheless, questionnaires and interviews can be useful in identifying weaknesses that have been overlooked or cannot easily be identified through objective measurements. The difficulties with questionnaires and interviews concern which questions to ask and how, and how to interpret the answers received. Questionnaires also tend to be rigid, in particular if the multiple-choice technique is being used. If, on the other hand, questions are too open, the risk is that people do not tell us what we would like to know. Also, often people do not like to spend time on writing about what they did and did not like about a system. This is much easier to communicate in an interview. In interviews, however, subjects are rarely asked precisely the same questions in precisely the same way. This makes it even more difficult to compare the users' answers. In addition, people tend to express what they like and what they dislike in rather different ways. In spite of problems in evaluating questionnaires and interviews, such evaluation vehicles are still to be recommended (cf. Section 5.3.5).

We did not perform an objective adequacy evaluation of our WOZ data. Transaction success rate was measured in the user test. There is still no standard definition of "transaction success" (Giachin, 1996). In the Danish Dialogue Project we defined successes as reservations carried out according to the scenario specification or according to the user's mistaken interpretation of the scenario. Failures were counted reservations in which the user failed to obtain what was asked for even if this was due to an error committed by the user. Based on this definition, the task transaction success in the user test was 86%. Seven tasks were counted as transaction failures. One of the failures was exclusively caused by a user who did not listen to the system's feedback, and a second transaction failure was caused by a combination of an interaction design error (SG11) and a user error. The five remaining transaction failures were caused by interaction design errors, i.e. violations of the guidelines GG5, SG2, SG4, SG5 and SG11 (cf. Chapter 4). As remarked earlier, it is an open question whether transaction failures caused exclusively by user errors should count as failures.

We also considered using the result of the diagnostic evaluation of number and types of interaction problems as part of the adequacy evaluation. However, the problem is how to specify quantitative criteria in advance. It is not obvious how many and which types of interaction problems could be accepted.

Subjective evaluation was included both in the WOZ experiments and in the user test. In the last three WOZ iterations as well as in the user test, subjects were asked to fill in a questionnaire after their interaction with the simulated system. In this questionnaire users were first asked about their background, including how familiar they were with the task, with voice response systems and with systems that understand speech. They were then asked a number of multiple-choice questions on the interactive speech system. For each question they were asked to tick off one of five boxes on a scale from negative to positive, for instance "difficult" versus "easy". Finally, users were asked to provide free-style comments on whether something ought to be changed in the way in which they had to address the system, what they liked about the system and what they did not like.

The multiple-choice questions and users' responses to them are reflected in Figure 8.31. As the figure also indicates, three new questions were added to the user test questionnaire: How was the systems' speech? What do you think of the language you felt that you had to use? Was the system fast or slow?

In many cases there is no real difference between the WOZ answers and the user test answers. This is true with respect to the properties of satisfactoriness, kindness, simplicity of use, predictability, reliability, desirability, future usefulness and lack of errors, all of which were evaluated positively in the sense that positive evaluations range from 50% upwards. The positive evaluation of the number of errors made by the system (few errors) is encouraging (about 80%). The number of system errors is a quantifiable aspect of robustness (cf. Section 8.3.4). Positive improvements from WOZ7 to the implemented system can be seen for acceptability (to 75%), efficiency (to 70%), usefulness now (to 60%) and ease of task performance (to 80%). There are also improvements in the evaluation of stimulatingness and preference of the system over a human travel agent, but both remain low (45% and 25%, respectively). The main reasons probably are the rigid interaction structure and, in particular for

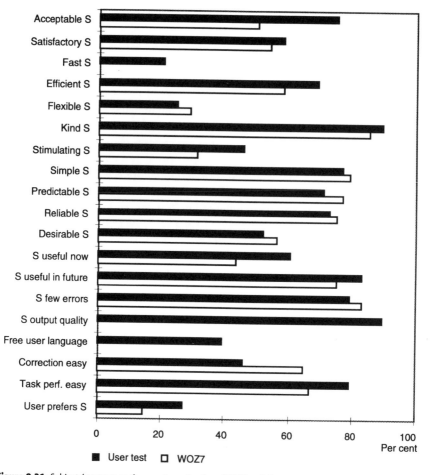

Figure 8.31: Subjects' answers to the questionnaires from WOZ7 and the user test in per cent of maximum positive score. A score of less than 50% indicates a negative opinion of the system. "S" in the left-hand column refers to the system

the latter percentage, the correct impression that the system has limited capabilities and cannot cope with non-routine matters. The preference for a human agent is probably quite common. There is a one-page overview which shows what 19 different newspapers and magazines have written about the Swiss Prisma Voice system for train timetable information. Three in six comments on the system's particular advantages end by stating that humans are still better than machines for the task (van der Linde, personal communication).

There are drops in the positive evaluation of two important parameters, namely on flexibility (to 23%) and ease of making corrections (to 45%). The low evaluation on flexibility is probably due to the rigid, system-directed dialogue structure and the restriction to keywords for meta-communication. The negative development with respect to ease of making corrections may be ascribed to the fact that misunderstandings were not simulated in WOZ7. This meant that hardly any user-initiated meta-communication was required. In the user test the simulated recognizer sometimes misunderstood what the user said. In addition, the use of keywords for making corrections does not form part of the natural human linguistic skills.

Finally, in view of the fact that the user test used a bionic wizard system, it is no surprise that subjects did not find the system fast (20%) and thus did not experience real-time performance. Output quality was rated high (87%). Not surprisingly, in view of the requirement to use keywords in initiating meta-communication and the inadequate vocabulary, subjects did not find that they could use free natural language (40%).

Valuable knowledge from a system design point of view was obtained through the free-style questionnaire answers. Although most subjects wrote only one or two brief remarks, a few subjects had bothered to write detailed comments. In these comments users would sometimes be quite specific about what had annoyed them during interaction with the system, providing useful clues to what might be improved. For instance, one user pointed out that the system should react more quickly when users do not answer. This user would also have liked the possibility of providing the system with a destination without an airport and then be informed on the nearest airport.

We also interviewed users on the telephone immediately after their interaction with the system. During WOZ, the purpose was only to ask whether they believed the system was real and to debrief them on the experiment. In the user test, users were asked the following four questions: How was it to talk to the system? What is your immediate impression of the system (specific problems/advantages)? Do you think the system was real? Would you be interested in trying the system with the real recognizer? Like the free-style comments in the questionnaire, the telephone interviews provided useful information on users' opinions of the system. The opinions expressed in the interviews were in accordance with the multiple-choice answers in the questionnaire but contributed explanations of why the users held those opinions. For instance, a user would have liked the possibility of indicating an arrival hour and then getting the departure time from the system. Other users complained about the rigid dialogue and their difficulties in using the keyword "change".

We did not ask the users to assign priority to their critical comments on the system. However, even if we had done this and modified the system accordingly, there would be no guarantee that users would then be satisfied with the system. User satisfaction is a conglomerate of many parameters, objective as well as subjective (cf. Section 8.1), and users may not even be aware of all the parameters which are important to them.

The adequacy evaluations show reasonable correspondence between the final WOZ results and the results obtained during the user test. The most important complaint from users seems to concern the flexibility of the system.

9. *Next Steps in Interactive Speech Systems*

9.1 Introduction

The advanced interactive speech system technologies that we have been discussing up to this point are more or less at the level of the Danish Dialogue System. It is an interesting, even if somewhat vague, question of how far it will be possible to advance towards fully natural interactive speech systems on the basis of these technologies. What are the issues ahead that will require significant changes of approach? In this chapter, we discuss two such issues. The first issue we have chosen to term the "heterogeneous task" which appears to demand a significant increase in systems' language processing skills and in the theoretical underpinnings of these skills (Section 9.2). The second issue is multimodality. In the future, spoken human-system interaction no doubt will become much more similar to natural human–human spoken interaction than is currently the case. However, as long as the interaction is purely spoken, and hence unimodal, it remains far from the ideal of fully natural human–human communication presented in Section 1.1. Section 9.3 presents a range of multimodal systems which actually or potentially incorporate advanced interactive speech technologies, and discusses ways to develop a systematic understanding of such Advanced Multimodal Interactive Speech Systems (AMISSs).

9.2 Advanced Mixed Initiative Interactive Speech Systems

9.2.1 A Possible Stumbling Block: Heterogeneous Tasks

It is difficult to tell exactly how far it will be possible to go in the development of highly natural, but still unimodal, advanced interactive speech systems on the basis of the technologies discussed in the previous chapters. Based on the evaluation results reported in Chapter 8, we believe that the Danish Dialogue System could be rather straightforwardly developed into a commercial application. As it has a relatively large and quite complex task structure, viable commercial applications could have that as well. Today it would not be difficult to provide the system with an active vocabulary that matches the required domain vocabulary of an estimated 1000–1200 words. It is now possible to go considerably higher than that, depending on the nature of the vocabularies, grammar and parsing strategies required. For instance, stereotypically adding another 1000 names of train stations to an application is less of a problem than adding 1000 common words enabling a rather sophisticated domain communication to take place between user and system.

Larger vocabulary, in combination with a less rigid interaction model, would enable systems that are otherwise technologically similar to the Danish Dialogue System to handle less well-structured tasks through mixed initiative dialogue even if these tasks are relatively large. If the system's active vocabulary allows it to spot that the user jumps to a different, but still task-relevant topic, the flexible interaction model would enable the system to interact on that topic and return to its own agenda later on, making sure that all the information that needs to be exchanged with the user actually does get exchanged. Systems of this kind could afford to ask questions that are considerably more open than those asked by the Danish Dialogue System.

Furthermore, although this will not be straightforward to do, we believe it to be possible to replace the single-word command, user-initiated meta-communication in the Danish Dialogue System with a more natural interaction in which the user can use standard phrases of the language of the interaction to initiate repair. However, user-initiated *clarification* meta-communication would remain a difficult problem (see Sections 4.2 and 8.3). The style of the interaction would still be terse and the users' language would have to be influenced by the system to ensure acceptable speech recognition and "robust parsing", even though we believe that the speech recognition and parsing abilities of the Danish Dialogue System could be considerably improved using available technologies. Prosody would still be a problem. Conceivably, the need for input prosody interpretation grows with (non-stereotypical) vocabulary size and interaction model flexibility, as well as with the introduction of speech act identification as discussed below. Important advances are currently being made in prosody for speech synthesis, as well as in prosody interpretation for semantic disambiguation in language understanding. In Verbmobil, recent demonstrations have shown the exploitation of stress and pauses for semantic disambiguation.

Summarizing, unimodal speaker-independent, continuous speech, interactive speech system technologies are well underway to being able to handle a broad variety of tasks in a reasonably natural way. Tasks may be quite large, and may be well structured or ill structured. Mixed initiative interaction, as such, is not an insurmountable barrier. As we have seen, even the Danish Dialogue System carries out mixed initiative interaction, being system-directed in its domain communication but allowing user-initiated meta-communication. We have also argued that large ill-structured tasks require mixed initiative dialogue (Section 2.4.2). If the task is "homogeneous" in some sense, to be explained below, even if it is relatively large and complex, and no matter whether it is well or ill structured, a flexible interaction model and a medium-size active vocabulary would enable the system to handle the task through mixed initiative domain communication. A medium vocabulary complex information system, for instance, can assume that whatever the user is now contributing to the interaction, that contribution is *either* a request for information *or* an initiation of repair meta-communication. The system might even be able to reason that, if the user wants to know about X, the user would probably want to know about Y as well, and might therefore ask the user whether that is the case, thus conducting natural mixed initiative interaction in the domain.

Several exploratory interactive speech system projects have demonstrated mixed initiative domain communication for small, ill-structured homogeneous tasks (Kanazawa *et al.*, 1994; Smith, 1991). The Sundial system demonstrated the problems involved in carrying out unrestricted mixed initiative dialogue for large, ill-structured homogeneous tasks, one such problem being that users would tend to produce lengthy and verbose utterances at the start of the interaction (Peckham, 1993). The Philips train timetable inquiry system has achieved mixed initiative dialogue for a well-structured homogeneous task that is slightly smaller than Sundial's. Whereas the Sundial dialogues began with a completely open system question, such as "How may I help you?", the Philips system opens with a brief introduction followed by a focused question, i.e. "From where to where would you like to go?". The focused nature of the opening question gives the Philips system much more control of the interaction from the start than was the case in Sundial. Having a much larger active vocabulary than the Danish Dialogue System, the Philips system is able to not only accept partial answers to its opening question but also to accept larger information packages than is asked for, as well as information which is simply different to that asked for. If the user provides information on date or time in response to its opening question, the system will accept this information and ask for the route information again (see Section 1.3.2).

In this section, we discuss what happens if the task is *not* "homogeneous", that is, if the task is not simply an ordering task, or an information task or a task in which the user controls a system through speech, such as an e-mail system being controlled over the telephone, nor is the task an external combination of several such tasks. Rather, the task is *inherently* a combination of several different tasks. Strictly speaking, as we have seen (Section 8.2), even the flight ticket reservation task is not homogeneous in this sense but is heterogeneous: flight ticket reservation, like all or most other ordering tasks, is *informed reservation* (or ordering). To make a rational decision during reservation, the user sometimes needs information, such as on the flights that are available on a certain morning. User requests for information during a reservation task where it is mainly the system which asks the questions, clearly requires mixed initiative interaction. Even then, it may be possible, in practice, to do without mixed initiative interaction. The Danish Dialogue System is purely system-directed in its domain communication. In the user test, users sometimes needed information from the system. It appears that several users found ways around the problem that they could not ask questions, because the test only produced four user questions (Section 8.2). The users probably managed to do so because the flight ticket reservation task is only *weakly heterogeneous,* that is, users typically do not need large amounts of information from the system in order to make their decisions. Moreover, when they do require additional information, this happens at specific points during the interaction rather than anywhere. Typically, users needed precise hours of departure. Instead of asking questions to obtain these, they answered in terms of qualitative time expressions, such as "in the morning" or "around noon". Based on the admittedly limited evidence from the user test, the Danish Dialogue System may perhaps be assumed to work acceptably in practice in its domain even if it does not really cater for the fact that reservation is informed reservation.

The Danish Dialogue System may work in practice *despite* the fact that it is not appropriate to the heterogeneous nature of the task and cannot handle heterogeneity through natural interaction. However, suppose that the ordering task is a different one, i.e. not flight ticket reservation but one for which users regularly need significant amounts of information of a somewhat diverse nature in order to make their decisions. An example could be the purchase of shoes and clothes through advanced spoken interaction. System-directed domain communication would probably be insufficient for such *strongly heterogeneous* tasks. Mixed initiative systems for *homogeneous* tasks as described above would not work either, however. As argued, a fundamental reason why these systems actually do work is that they can assume that the user always wants to, for example, make either a reservation commitment or initiate meta-communication. In informed reservation, the user may intend to do either of those things *or* to be informed. So if the user says, for instance "Are there any late morning flights?" the system must not interpret this utterance as a commitment to making a reservation on a late morning flight. For that matter, the user might eventually decide to fly out in the evening of the previous day. Rather, the system should understand the utterance as a different *speech act* from the speech act of making a commitment to book a late morning flight, namely, as a speech act which requests information.

It would thus appear that to be natural, and sometimes to be possible at all, mixed initiative interaction for heterogeneous tasks requires the system to be able to distinguish among different speech acts when processing the users' input. As argued above, a large class of future advanced interactive speech applications will not need the ability to process different user speech acts. It is quite possible, on the other hand, that another large class of possible future applications *will* need that ability, namely those systems which must handle heterogeneous tasks. The question then becomes: what does it take to handle heterogeneous tasks? Why do heterogeneous tasks appear to be, in principle, more difficult to handle by machine than homogeneous tasks?

The handling by machine of heterogeneous tasks seems to raise at least four additional difficulties. The *first difficulty* concerns the *extent* to which the system must be able to understand users' speech acts. Once a system has to distinguish between user speech acts, where is the stop condition? Does it have to distinguish between speech acts more or less in general or are simpler solutions possible and, if so, why and how?

The *second difficulty* is that the system must do considerably *more advanced linguistic processing* than a system handling a comparable homogeneous task. Word spotting or simple phrase spotting is not enough. These techniques will not capture the difference between (A) and (B) in Figure 9.1.

A:	S: When would you like to leave?
	U: On Saturday at 8:15 AM.
B:	S: When would you like to leave?
	U: Is there a flight on Saturday at 8:15 AM?

Figure 9.1: A user commitment and a user request for information, respectively.

In (A), the user makes a commitment to depart on Saturday at 8:15 AM provided that there is a flight and it is not fully booked. In (B), the user makes no commitment to depart on Saturday at 8:15 AM but merely inquires about flight availability. To detect the difference between (A) and (B), the system must, at least, capture the fact that the user's utterance in (B) is a question, not a statement, as far as its surface language is concerned.

The *third difficulty* may be illustrated as follows. Suppose that the system must handle, in addition to meta-communication, the heterogeneous tasks HT1 and HT2. HT1 may be a reservation task and HT2 may be an information task. As argued earlier, speech act identification by machine is difficult, primarily because speech acts can be indirect as well as direct (Section 2.4.3). In principle, therefore, users may shift from HT1 to HT2 without this being detectable in the surface language they use. In such cases, sufficient grammar and vocabulary will obviously not be enough. To discover such *speech act ambiguities,* the system must first understand that the user's utterance is, for instance, a question as far as its surface language is concerned. Secondly, the system must somehow realize that the user's utterance is a case of *speech act ambiguity* and that it actually may be a reservation commitment. Having detected that, the system would probably ask the user a clarification question. We would like to have indications of how common speech act ambiguities are before putting the search for such sophisticated technical solutions in motion.

The *fourth difficulty* is the question of *how sophisticated* the system's increased linguistic processing skills need to be. What, exactly, is entailed by a system having to spot surface language differences indicating differences between, for instance, questions and statements, and what does it take to identify speech act ambiguity, if necessary? To understand this difficulty, let us expand on the presentation of Speech Acts Theory in Section 2.4.3. Searle (1969) characterizes speech acts in terms of four different types of *felicity conditions,* as illustrated in Figure 9.2.

Felicity conditions	Request	Promise
Preparatory conditions describe the necessary background situation, especially between the speakers, which must exist for the appearance of the speech act.	H is able to perform A. S believes H is able to do A.	S is able to perform A. H wants S to perform A.
Sincerity condition is the psychological state of the speaker.	S wants H to do A.	S intends to do A.
Propositional content condition concerns the textual reference and predication of the speech act.	S predicates a future act A of H.	S predicates a future act A of S.
Essential condition expresses the "point" of the act, i.e., what the utterance "counts as".	Counts as an attempt by S to get H to do A.	Counts as the undertaking by S of an obligation to do A.

Figure 9.2: Felicity conditions of a directive (request) and a commissive (promise). S is the speaker, H is the hearer and A is action. Note that lists of felicity conditions are not exhaustive. For instance, an additional preparatory condition for the request could be that it is not obvious to both S and H that H will do A of his/her own accord in the normal course of events (Schiffrin, 1994).

Systems for heterogeneous tasks, one of which is an information task, will have to interpret requests for information which belong to a sub-type of the request speech act shown in Figure 9.2. What the table suggests is that requests for information can be asked in many different ways when the felicity conditions are taken into account. The user may not simply say, as in (B) above "Is there a flight on Saturday at 8:15 AM?", but also "I would like you to tell me if there is a flight on Saturday at 8:15 AM?" (cf. the sincerity condition), or "Could you tell me if there is a flight on Saturday at 8:15 AM?" (cf. one of the preparatory conditions). Will the system need to understand and distinguish between all these different expressions of the same question or are these differences immaterial?

In view of the above, it is perhaps not surprising that the attempts which have so far been made to make interactive speech systems able to distinguish between speech acts more or less in general, as in, for instance, the Esprit PLUS Project, would seem to have failed through inadequate rule maintenance (Grau *et al.*, 1994). One possibility worth exploring is whether a large class of mixed initiative interactive speech systems for heterogeneous tasks can manage with much less than that. In the following section we present early results on interactive speech systems for heterogeneous tasks, based on explorations of how to extend the Danish Dialogue System to deal with informed reservation, see also Papazachariou *et al.* (1995).

9.2.2   Simulating Heterogeneous Tasks

As argued in Section 2.3, context may be viewed as a collection of all the elements of interactive speech theory, each of which may be analysed with respect to its specific contribution to spoken user–system interaction. Exploitation of context is essential in interactive speech system development for large tasks because such systems are feasible only on the basis of a high degree of control of the environment in which the interaction between user and system takes place. The single most important contextual element is the *task* which imposes strong constraints on most other properties of the system, as illustrated in Figure 9.3.

The problem of extending the Danish Dialogue System to deal with informed reservation may be viewed as the question of how to exploit a specific heterogeneous task context. To prepare the study, we tried to find a suitable corpus, preferably within the ATIS (air travel information systems) domain. It appears, however, that publicly available and technologically realistic, simulated human–machine mixed initiative corpora are hard to find. We considered two mixed initiative corpora which, however, turned out to be inappropriate for our purposes.

The American Express corpus is a corpus of spoken human–human dialogues between customers and a travel agent from the American Express Card (Sidner, 1992). The topics of the dialogues are reservations, information, help to customers in planning their journeys, cancellations and changes of specific reservations. However, as the spoken interactions are conducted freely between humans, they exhibit none of the limitations and constraints that are the constant focus of attention in human–machine interaction model development. The American Express dialogues are far beyond what can be realized by today's machines.

The TRAINS corpus is a simulated human–machine corpus (Gross *et al.*, 1993). It is a collection of 91 planning dialogues (only 16 of which were available via ftp at the

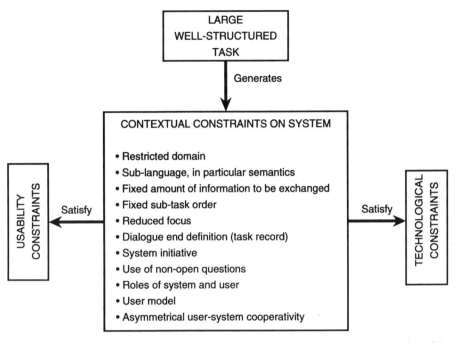

Figure 9.3: The well-structured task context of the Danish Dialogue System generates constraints that may be exploited in system development, thereby helping to satisfy both technological constraints and usability constraints.

time) between a human and a system simulated by a human. The human is a manager whose task it is to construct a plan for the delivery of goods by railway through help from the system. The manager knows only the final goal of a certain delivery and has to obtain all the necessary information from the system in order to successfully plan the necessary stages of delivery. The system is able to provide the necessary information related to the freight problem. It can check the feasibility of the manager's plan but cannot propose any solution. The human who simulated the system maintained all its functional limitations, but his/her linguistic behaviour was completely human and could not be realized in an implemented system.

We therefore decided to collect a mixed initiative corpus ourselves by simulating an extension of the Danish Dialogue System that would allow user initiative to the extent needed by the informed reservation task. Users could take the initiative and ask for information whenever they needed to do so. In such cases, the system would act as the domain expert who has the necessary information on domestic flights, such as departures, arrivals, flight numbers and fares. The corpus was very small, typically including between two and four dialogues per iteration and 13 dialogues in total, all of which were transcribed. Five subjects, all colleagues, participated in the simulations. The subjects knew that the system was simulated and who was acting as the wizard. Only two different scenarios were used throughout the experiments. Four subjects performed both scenarios once. The fifth subject, who was one of the developers, performed one scenario twice and the other scenario three times. The scenarios forced users to ask questions in order to find the optimum solution for the successful completion of their task (Figure 9.4). The simulations focused on domain communication with no particular emphasis on simulation of meta-communication. The wizard followed an interaction model consisting of a set of behavioural rules (cf. Section 5.4) and a graphically presented network of speech acts. Each speech act was accompanied by a list of typical instances of use for the purpose of informed reservation. An assistant operated the tape recorder, listened to the spoken interaction and filled in a reservation task template according to the commitments made by the subject. The filled in template was designed to be read aloud as summarizing feedback. The scenarios are shown in Figure 9.4.

1.	You have to travel from Copenhagen to Aarhus for the weekend. The earliest you can leave is Friday night, but you prefer to pass Friday night with your friends. On the other hand, you have to be in central Aarhus at 9:50 AM on Saturday at the latest. Try to make a reservation which will allow you to manage both plans.
2.	You have to be in Aarhus before noon on Saturday. You prefer to leave on Friday night, but there would be no problem travelling on Saturday morning if only you can be in Aarhus before noon. You prefer to have a cheap ticket, if possible. You are thinking of returning on Sunday evening, not very late. Try to make a reservation that will satisfy all your priorities.

Figure 9.4: The two scenarios used in the informed reservation WOZ experiments with the Danish Dialogue System's reservation task.

During the experiments changes were made to the system's language and behaviour in order to better control the users' language and the topics introduced by them. In the first iteration, more initiative was left to the user than would be possible in an implemented system. The opening system phrase invited the user to take the initiative and the wizard understood even very long user utterances. Having examined the first spoken interactions, we realized that we had to impose additional constraints on the simulated system. In its introduction to the interaction, the system informed the users of its inability to understand lengthy utterances but without defining more exactly what that meant. What it actually did mean was that the wizard would not understand utterances which addressed more than one sub-task and more than two topics. If the user did not adhere to these restrictions, the system would fail to understand them or only understand the first part of what they said. In the last experiment, for instance, the system would not understand the final part of the user utterance in Figure 9.5, which addresses more than one sub-task.

S:	Please state your business.
U:	I'd like to make a reservation for a flight to Aarhus, for this weekend.

Figure 9.5: A user utterance addressing more than one sub-task.

To promote terse user language, the system would, perhaps not very politely, initiate the domain communication phase of the interaction by saying "Please state your business".

The idea which eventually promised feasibility of implementation was the following: at a general level, it is assumed that the user's task goal is to make a reservation rather than using the system as a general-purpose inquiry system. This allowed us to maintain the stereotypical structure of the reservation task as a "backbone" for interaction design. The task context would continue to strongly constrain the interaction behaviour of cooperative users. These may be expected to follow the overall system-directed course of the interaction and to take over the initiative only when they need information from the system in order to be able to proceed in making the commitments needed for reservation. The users' requests for information can be expected to primarily concern sub-tasks which are closely associated with the question in current system focus. Users would not normally ask, for instance, about departure times when the system is addressing the travel destination. In other words, the system will not need to be able to handle arbitrary requests for information at arbitrary points during interaction. This puts a limit on the uncontrolled growth in the focus set that would otherwise have been necessary. Obviously, the idea just described would require further testing before considering implementation.

Moreover, for some sub-tasks, such as number and names of travellers, or points of departure and destination, we would expect no questions at all. For instance, users must be expected to know who is going to travel without having to ask the system – which would not be able to help anyway. The nature of the task thus imposes constraints on the number of sub-tasks for which it may be relevant for users to ask for information. The following are examples of such sub-tasks: users often do not know the precise departure and arrival times and must be informed of these; users may want to know about reduced fare departures before committing to a specific departure time or even departure date; or the departure date may depend on the available departure times. In fact, three of the four user questions asked in the user test of the Danish Dialogue System concerned available departure times. An example is shown in Figure 9.6.

| S3-24b: | At which time? |
| U3-24a: | Which possibilities are there? |

Figure 9.6: Excerpt from dialogue T12a in the user test of the Danish Dialogue System.

When users have part of the initiative during interaction the length of their utterances can be expected to grow compared to system-directed interaction, where elliptical or otherwise brief user answers are typical. Terse system language, interaction which was mainly system-directed and which proceeded through non-open questions which do not offer the initiative to the users, and the system's introduction which instructed users to only ask one question at a time, jointly appeared to ensure limited and manageable growth in user utterance length.

The above assumptions imply that, compared to the Danish Dialogue System, the revised system would need limited extensions of: (i) system focus; and (ii) average user utterance length. As argued in Section 9.2.1, (i) is no longer a major technical difficulty and (ii) does not seem to pose any serious technical difficulties. The need for (only) limited extensions of (i) and (ii) was not contradicted by the simulations.

Let us now see what happened to the core issues of speech acts and heterogeneous tasks in advanced mixed initiative user–system domain interaction (Section 9.2.1). Our hypothesis was that most, if not all, *task-oriented* advanced interactive speech systems, which need to distinguish between speech acts to perform heterogeneous tasks, do not need the ability to distinguish between speech acts in general. This ability will probably be needed in truly conversational systems, such as Verbmobil. Rather, task-oriented advanced interactive speech systems need to be able to distinguish between a small number of speech acts only. In particular, in the informed reservation task context, *only two* different basic types of domain speech act are relevant and must be distinguished by the system, namely, reservation commitments and requests for information (ignoring meta-communication for the sake of the following argument).

This hypothesis was confirmed in the WOZ simulations. In the terms of speech act theory, we found only two basic categories of speech act in human–machine domain communication, namely *directives* and *commissives* (see Section 2.4.3). Although several utterances appeared to express speech acts that do not belong in either of these two categories, the indirect speech acts expressed in context turned out to be either directives or commissives. For example, the corpus contained the surface expressive shown in Figure 9.7.

U:	I would ehm I would like to know which flights there are eh on Friday evening, tonight.

Figure 9.7: Surface expressive from the mixed initiative corpus.

Although this utterance is a surface *expressive* speech act, in the specific context of informed reservation it can only act as an indirect request for information (i.e. a directive). In other situations, such as in communication with friends none of whom is an expert in the field, and when the purpose of communication is not timetable inquiry but social conversation, the same utterance could hardly act as a request for information. It would remain an expressive speech act. Our small corpus did not contain any indirect expressives, commissives or declaratives.

The system must have the linguistic capabilities to distinguish between the user's commissives (or reservation commitments, cf. Figure 9.2) and directives (or requests for information, cf. Figure 9.2), and to detect the shift in initiative that occurs when the user requests domain information instead of simply answering the system's questions. Two general cases may be distinguished.

In the *first general case,* the contents of a user utterance cannot be used to fill a slot in the reservation record, either because the utterance provides no information that is relevant to this purpose, as in "What possibilities are there?", or because the information provided is only partial and hence cannot fill a slot in the record, as in "What departures are there on Saturday morning?". In such cases, the system should treat the user utterance as a request for information no matter whether it is phrased as a question or not. This rule incidentally solves the problem that some requests for information may be hard to detect because their status as questions is mainly expressed through intonation. An example from our experiments is shown in Figure 9.8.

U:	And on Saturday morning before 12?

Figure 9.8: A request for information mainly expressed through intonation.

The system, therefore, should respond in the same way in the two cases shown in Figure 9.9.

S:	When would you like to leave?
U:	Which flights are there on Friday night?
S:	On Friday night there is a flight at 19:30 and another one at 21:30. Would you like one of these?
S':	When would you like to leave?
U':	On Friday night.
S':	On Friday night there is a flight at 19:30 and another one at 21:30. Would you like one of these?

Figure 9.9: Two different user answers requiring the same system response.

Correct interpretation of utterances such as the above does not require any significant improvements in linguistic skills compared to those of the Danish Dialogue System.

In the *second general case,* the user's utterance does provide information that could fill a slot in the reservation record. In this case there are two possibilities. The default possibility is that the utterance fills a slot in the reservation record (Figure 9.10).

S:	When would you like to leave?
U:	On Saturday at 8:15.

Figure 9.10: User information which may fill a slot in a reservation record.

However, the utterance might request information instead, as shown in Figure 9.11.

In such cases, identification of the user's intended action is essential to the successful completion of the reservation task. We analysed the corpus to identify the varieties of expression of the two different speech acts involved. Users made their requests for information in the four different ways shown in Figure 9.12.

S:	When would you like to leave?
U:	Is there a flight at 7.15 AM?

Figure 9.11: User answer requesting information.

a) Direct polar (yes/no) questions.	Is there another flight after that, before noon?
b) Direct WH questions.	When is the earliest flight?
c) Questions that refer to the ability of the system to provide information.	Could you tell me when is the last flight on Friday night?
d) Intonation questions.	And on Saturday morning before 12?

Figure 9.12: Four different ways of making requests for information.

The differences between (a)–(d) can be expressed in terms of the felicity conditions of the speech acts performed, i.e. the preconditions which are responsible for characterizing a speech act as a request for information (Figure 9.2). The direct polar and WH questions (a) and (b) are conventional (elliptical) ways of expressing the essential condition of requests for information. They are the most typical and simple cases of information requests, and, when performed by users in the given context, can only be requests for information. In the same category belongs the intonation question (d). The question about the ability of the system to provide some piece of information (c) refers to one of the preparatory conditions, i.e. that the hearer (the system) is able to provide the information, which is related to the expert role of the system. (c) is an indirect speech act. It indirectly expresses a request for information through reference to the system's abilities.

Searle (1975) argues that the speaker can make an indirect directive (requests for information are directives) by stating either the preparatory conditions that refer to the ability of the hearer, the sincerity condition, the propositional content condition or the essential condition. In our small corpus we only found examples of some of Searle's categories. Successful completion of part of the reservation task was achieved using the three types of (user) expression shown in Figure 9.13.

a) Surface statements.	S: Where are you going? U: To Aarhus.
b) Surface questions about the ability of the speaker to book a flight with specific characteristics.	U: Could I have the Saturday morning flight, at 9:20?
c) Surface questions about the ability of the system to make a particular reservation.	U: Can you give me an earlier flight, between midnight and 9:00?

Figure 9.13: Three different ways of expressing reservation information.

User statements of type (a) are the typical (elliptical) expressions of simple answers. The other two types of user expression (b) and (c) refer to felicity conditions of reservation commitments. The question about the ability of the speaker to book a flight with specific characteristics (b) refers to one of the preparatory conditions of the reservation commitment, and the question about the ability of the system to make a particular reservation (c) refers to another preparatory condition of the reservation commitment.

Comparing the above direct and indirect speech acts for reservation and information, respectively, it appears that none of the reservation utterances refers to the felicity conditions of the requests for information, and vice versa. In other words, there is some evidence that speech act ambiguity is a rare phenomenon, at least for the informed reservation task. This suggests that the system will be able to determine and distinguish the speech acts produced by users in this type of interaction from the semantics of their utterances alone. If true, this means that the system can use the semantics of the users' utterances to identify the cases in which it has to provide information. When the semantics do not refer to the felicity conditions of requests for information, and if the utterance makes it possible to fill a slot in the reservation record, the system may safely accept the utterance as a reservation commitment. In this situation there will be no problem in identifying the utterance in Figure 9.14 as a reservation commitment rather than a request for information.

U:	Could I have the Saturday morning flight at 9:20?

Figure 9.14: A reservation commitment from the mixed initiative corpus.

To summarize, if the system can recognize that the meaning of an utterance refers to either:

- one of the preparatory conditions concerning the ability of the system/expert to provide the information;
- the sincerity condition of requests for information;
- the propositional content condition of requests for information; or
- the essential condition of requests for information

then the system can safely identify the utterance as a request for information.

9.2.3 Conclusion

The following conclusions concerning the four difficulties described in Section 9.2.2 are, of course, tentative and should be tested on larger corpora from several different spoken human–machine interactions concerned with heterogeneous tasks.

The *first conclusion* is that heterogeneous tasks only require the system to identify and distinguish between a small number of speech acts.

The *second conclusion* is that the system, in order to distinguish between speech acts at all, must do considerably more linguistic processing than standard word spotting or phrase spotting of parameters relevant to database lookups and the like. Simply expressed, database lookups only require the system to capture the propositional contents of utterances. But as the propositional contents can be identical across the different speech acts between which the system must be able to distinguish, the system must capture more than the propositional contents of utterances.

The *third conclusion* is that speech act ambiguity does not appear to be an important problem. It can probably be ignored by developers of advanced interactive speech systems for heterogeneous tasks.

The *fourth conclusion* is that, yes, the system must be able to understand felicity condition references in order to identify speech acts.

A final problem is that if non-keyword-based meta-communication is allowed, as was the case in the experiments described above, then the system can no longer simply interpret every speech act which requests information as expressing a request for information at domain level. However, it seems clear that, in any case, non-keyword-based, user-initiated meta-communication will require more sophisticated language processing of the system.

9.3   Intelligent Multimodal Systems Using Advanced Interactive Speech

9.3.1   AMISSs Defined

As argued in Section 1.1, advanced interactive speech systems represent a step towards natural human–computer communication as measured by the ideal standard of the human–human face-to-face communication paradigm. Advanced mixed initiative systems for heterogeneous tasks would constitute another step in that direction. Systems which were able to make natural use of prosody in speech input understanding and speech output generation would represent yet another important step towards natural interactive speech systems. These systems are all *unimodal* interactive speech systems which use nothing but speech to enable users to accomplish their tasks in increasingly natural spoken communication with the system. Natural human–human communication is not unimodal, however, it is *massively multimodal*. Lip movement, facial expression, bodily posture and gesture towards visible objects and other visually accessible information are all key ingredients for representing information in human–human communication. Moreover, humans *combine* these modalities with speech when they communicate, effortlessly generating messages in several modalities simultaneously, such as when speaking about an object and selectively pointing to its features, and effortlessly understanding such combined messages as well, using lip movements and facial expression as additional cues in the understanding process. Such multimodal systems incorporating speech as one of their modalities are becoming an important research topic.

This section briefly addresses the emerging field of multimodal systems which incorporate speaker-independent continuous speech understanding and/or speech generation. We term these systems "Advanced Multimodal Interactive Speech Systems", or AMISSs for short. Such systems are by definition "intelligent", whichever other modalities are used in addition to the speech modalities. Although AMISSs point the way towards the fully natural human–computer communication interface, AMISSs are not necessarily "next steps" in terms of the technologies involved. In many cases, and probably in the first AMISSs to become commercially available, their most advanced system components are the advanced interactive speech components. The additional components typically derive from the Graphical User Interface (GUI) paradigm. More advanced AMISSs include emerging technologies, such as animated speaking faces, input lip movement interpretation, input gesture interpretation, output gesture animation, advanced haptic input devices and 3D graphics output.

In addition to offering increased naturalness of human–machine communication compared to unimodal interactive speech systems, AMISSs promise two additional practical advances. First, AMISSs may augment the capabilities of computer systems viewed as task-oriented tools, enabling the machine to accomplish more types of task than could have been done using speech alone. The important factors involved are *increased expressiveness* and *increased intelligence* through speech or otherwise. By itself, each modality for representing information has limited expressiveness (Section 3.5). In combination, modalities allow the accomplishment of interactive tasks that would not have been possible otherwise. Speech, for instance, is not always appropriate for communicating large amounts of detailed factual information in one turn. Users become inattentive and do not get the details right (cf. Figure 4.26). Static output graphics, on the other hand, is eminently suited for this purpose, as argued in Section 3.5. In combination, speech input/output and static output graphics may serve many tasks which either could not have been done, or could not have been done as well, by each modality taken in isolation. Adding advanced interactive speech to the World Wide Web with its rapidly growing output graphics capabilities, for instance, holds great promise. In this way, multimodality helps alleviate the painstakingly slow progress towards more intelligent computer systems. Still, increased system intelligence is another promise held by AMISSs. It is increased system intelligence when an AMISS permits the user to synchronously input, for instance, a gesture delimiting an area in the graphical output domain and speak a query for car rental companies in that area. In addition, AMISSs may help the partner in communication, whether human or machine, to more easily decode the information being communicated, for instance when the system's output speech is being accompanied by a synchronized graphic "talking face".

Section 9.3.2 provides an admittedly partial and incomplete perspective on AMISSs. We discuss in turn AMISSs that include co-ordinated speech and analogue graphics, speech and facial expression; speech and gesture; speech, typed text and analogue graphics; and combinations of speech, analogue graphics, tables and facial expression. Section 9.3.3 presents early ideas on how to theoretically address the issue of AMISS functionality.

9.3.2   A Perspective on AMISS State of the Art

The following presents a structured view of AMISSs (cf. the surveys in Cole *et al.*, 1996, Chapter 9; Maybury, 1993; Oviatt and Wahlster, 1997). Currently, the sky is the limit for the development of AMISSs. Existing research systems only manage to scratch the surface of an immense and uncharted space of possibilities, and we are far from having a systematic grasp of the functionality of multimodal systems (cf. speech functionality in Section 3.5). Several research systems in progress might have included spoken input and/or spoken output but actually use typed natural language instead. These systems are outside the scope of the present book but are mentioned to illustrate the potential scope of AMISSs technologies. From a generic point of view, AMISSs are of at least two very different types: systems which perform "conversion" between modalities; and systems which exploit the complementarity and, possibly, also the redundancy between different modalities.

Modality "conversion" systems take information represented in one modality (or, potentially, in several modalities) and convert the information for expression in a different modality (or potentially in several different modalities). Examples are systems which simultaneously generate text based on visual scene/event/process understanding, such as traffic scenes or soccer games (Wahlster, 1989), and systems which create animations from text (Badler *et al.,* 1993; Yamada *et al.,* 1992). Although clearly multimodal in some sense, modality "conversion" systems need not be interactive speech systems at all. Their basic function is to perform transformations among modalities, and speech may be one of these. Apart from that, they may be operated interactively using any number of different input/output modalities. Such systems, although highly interesting from several points of view, are not AMISSs proper and we shall disregard them in the remainder of this chapter.

Many modality "conversion" systems lack one of the distinctive advantages of multimodality, namely, interactive task sharing among modalities. Interactive task sharing between different modalities takes place when, for instance, modalities *complement* each other to jointly profit from their respective expressive strengths, or when modalities are partially *redundant,* which increases the likelihood that the message, being redundantly expressed in different modalities, will be understood by the recipient. Humans are very good at integrating complementary sensory inputs and exploiting the redundancy these might have. Current machines are much less adept at fusioning the semantics of several different streams of input information into one coherent message, and have corresponding difficulties in exploiting redundancy (Martin, 1997). Still, a number of systems in progress seek to exploit these basic advantages of multimodality.

Intelligent Multimedia Presentation Systems

The first type of system to be mentioned currently uses typed natural language rather than speech. Intelligent multimedia presentation systems are able to generate co-ordinated multimodal presentations to user requests as required (Rist *et al.,* in press). They currently do so in instructional domains, such as providing support for portable radio operation and maintenance (Feiner and McKeown, 1993), or providing instructions to users on how to operate expresso machines and lawn mowers, or perform modem installation (Wahlster *et al.,* 1993). These systems output 3D ($2^{1}/_{2}$D) analogue graphics and animation (images and compositional diagrams) co-ordinated with (and complementary to) static text. No intelligent multimedia presentation systems using interactive speech appear to have been developed so far, but this is an obvious research challenge.

Speech and Facial Expression

Whether acting as input or output, a speaking face is an image containing a series of complementary and redundant information channels that are relevant to the decoding of the information communicated by the speaker. This leads to the idea of AMISSs which: (a) combine a microphone and a camera to enable the machine to receive facial expression information in combination with spoken input; and/or (b) combine an animated graphical face with speech output to facilitate the comprehension of synthetic speech. Both combinations form natural parts of human–human conversation which becomes artificially curtailed if speech alone is being used for input or output. Current work on systems is investigating synchronous multimodal redundancy to aid the understanding of messages in noisy environments or otherwise (Benoit *et al.,* 1996; Goldschen, 1996). On the input side, work currently being carried out on systems focuses on automatic lip reading while still ignoring most other facial cues. On the output side, work is moving beyond 3D lip movement emulation (Guiard-Marigny *et al.*, 1994) towards whole-face emulation adapted to speech control (Cohen and Massaro, 1990, 1993). The combination of speech and facial expression understanding and/or generation can be viewed as an approximation to natural human–human face-to-face communication which, in principle, can be added to any task-oriented system featuring an input camera and/or an output graphical screen in addition to interactive speech processing (cf. the Waxholm system below).

Speech and Gesture

Another active field of research which addresses the emulation of natural human–human face-to-face conversation is the combination of speech and gesture. Speech and gesture can be combined in several different ways.

Spatial Manipulation

One combination is the integration of speech and gesture as complementary input using standard pointing devices, touch screens or data gloves for gesture. Gesture is understood here as spatial manipulation in the "put that there" paradigm (Bolt, 1980; Hauptmann and McAvinney, 1993). The user indicates a location of interest in the graphical output domain through pointing gesture and tells the system what to do through speech, such as moving an indicated object to an indicated location.

Non-spatial Manipulation

A slightly different, non-spatial manipulation type of natural pointing gesture is used to, for example, indicate a point or area of interest, or point out a route on a map as graphically displayed in the output domain. When combined with spoken input for complementarity, this allows users to ask questions of, or provide input to, the system, such as asking about service facilities in the area indicated on a map (Guyomard *et al.*, 1995). The AMISS that is being developed in the comprehensive MIT GALAXY Project (Goddeau *et al.*, 1994) takes large vocabulary multilingual speech, typed text and mouse pointer events as input, and outputs analogue graphics, typed text and multilingual synthesized speech. GALAXY provides information in close to real-time on air travel, local city navigation and weather using on-line information sources and services, such as airline schedules, yellow pages, metropolitan maps and weather forecasts. By 1994, the travel domain part of the system had been completed. More recently, it has become possible to synchronously combine complementary input speech and mouse pointer events into a graphical map in the output domain, so that users can query specific locations on the map (Seneff, personal communication).

Discourse Gesture

In addition to the forms of gesture discussed above, there is a class of natural discourse gesture which provides "language-like" information complementary to that provided by speech, and from which, presumably, the sign languages for the deaf have arisen. As in the cases of facial expression and lip movements, such gestural combinations with speech represent information relevant to the decoding of the information communicated by the speaker. We are not aware of systems that explore the complementarities and redundancies between discourse gesture and speech as input and/or output but, again, the research challenge is clearly there.

Speech Replacing Gesture

For special user groups, speech may replace gesture. Although Modality Theory predicts that speech is ill suited to providing the detailed spatial information needed for text editing operations (cf. MP1 and MP2 in Figure 3.8), speech input may be the only solution for blind users to perform limited editing operations. Or, rather, this will be the case until the advent of more sophisticated haptic Braille work stations. The French commercial system MEDITOR (Bellik and Burger, 1994) is an AMISS multimodal text editor for the blind. MEDITOR allows blind users to perform a number of common editing tasks on textual documents using continuous speaker-independent speech recognition and speech synthesis, Braille input and output, pointing gesture, and classical keyboard writing. MEDITOR is a command-driven application which is in daily use by many users. The vocabulary is restricted to keywords for editing (about 100) and the grammar is simple (an average of three words per sentence). The computer environment in which MEDITOR has been implemented is the basic workstation used by blind students at the INJA Institute (Institut National des Jeunes Aveugles). It includes a desktop PC, a Braille terminal and a French text-to-speech synthesizer. A speech recognition system has been added.

Augmenting Graphical User Interfaces Through Speech

In Modality Theory, the term "analogue graphics" covers images, maps, compositional diagrams, graphs and conceptual diagrams (see Section 3.5). The AMISS combination of speech input/output with optional mouse and keyboard input, and typed text and analogue graphics output, provides a wealth of application opportunities. In contrast to advanced research systems such as GALAXY, these systems do not require synchronous complementarity between input speech and gesture. Rather, they simply add speech to standard GUIs, thereby significantly augmenting the expressiveness of the communication that is possible between user and system.

The British Telecom Business Catalogue system provides direct access to a subset of the BT Business Catalogue which covers, among other things, telephones, answering machines and telephone systems (Wyard et al., 1995). This near real-time system combines continuous, speaker-independent speech, typed text and mouse pointing input with output text-to-speech, typed text and graphical images in a WWW browser. It is a user initiative system in which users have to express their requests and commands using the technical terms of the catalogue.

The Japanese AMISS TOSBURG II (Kanazawa et al., 1994) combines speech input/output with *non-computerized* static graphical typed text and images output (affixed somewhere on the machine) to enable users to order burger bar food by mentioning the listed food items, the desired food size and their listed number. Although the vocabulary is small and word spotting is used, the system allows mixed initiative dialogue in both domain communication and meta-communication. It needs to be added, though, that trials demonstrated less than 50% success in processing unrestricted user input.

Another Japanese research AMISS, WEATHER (Yi, 1993), combines small vocabulary speech input and text-to-speech output with graphical typed text output. The system provides weather information for nine Japanese cities through mixed initiative dialogue with users. It is reported that in a trial, with 48 inexperienced and five skilled users, 151 dialogues out of 174 were successful.

Combining Speech, Analogue Graphics, Tables and Facial Expression

The Swedish Waxholm is a medium-size vocabulary, real-time multimodal prototype AMISS which provides information on boat traffic and accommodation in the Stockholm archipelago (Bertenstam *et al.*, 1995). It references timetables for a fleet of some 20 boats from the Waxholm company which connects about 200 ports. Besides the dialogue management, and the speech recognition and synthesis components, the system contains output modules that handle graphic information such as images, maps and timetables. This information is presented through user-initiated dialogue. An interesting point about Waxholm is that it combines an increased expressiveness functionality, similar to that of the BT system, TOSBURG II and WEATHER (see above), with an increased redundancy functionality provided by an animated graphical output face image driven by the speech synthesizer. In this way, Waxholm takes yet another step towards natural human–machine communication.

The small sample of systems briefly reviewed above can be seen as a set of state-of-the-art building blocks which can be combined in numerous ways that have yet to be demonstrated, and potentially serving a very large variety of users and tasks which, everything else being equal, would be served in a poorer fashion or not at all by unimodal interactive speech systems.

9.3.3   Speech Functionality in a Multimodal Context

From a theoretical point of view, addressing the issue of speech and multimodality is a venture into very complex territory. In view of the early stage of theoretical research into speech functionality (Section 3.5), it comes as no surprise that no principled, systematic solution is available to the question: under what circumstances should system and interface developers use which multimodal input/output AMISSs combinations for task sharing and in which way? This question is more complex than the speech functionality problem because answering it requires: (i) a more systematic charting of the properties of the non-speech modalities; and (ii) a thorough understanding of how speech works together with other modalities. This section explores the complexity involved based on the list of modality properties presented in Figure 3.8.

Considering the examples of ongoing work on (proper) AMISSs in Section 9.3.2, it appears that most of the increased naturalness and tool versatility of these multimodal combinations can be explained through reference to the modality properties (MPs) in Figure 3.8.

Independently of whether *intelligent multimedia presentation systems* use static text or speech input/output, their superiority to unimodal speech or text-only resides in the fact that these systems add analogue graphics to the linguistic modalities. Linguistic modalities, having interpretational scope (MP1), are unsuited for expressing spatial details such as those needed to understand the details and procedures of radio repair, modem installation and, expresso machine and lawn mower operation. This observation may be generalized to include any combination of linguistic input/output modalities and analogue graphics, whether 2D, $2^1/_2$D, 3D, static or dynamic, or images, compositional diagrams, maps, graphs or conceptual diagrams, thereby generating a huge space of potentially useful multimodal systems. The differences between using static graphic output text and dynamic output speech would have to be explained as well. It is quite likely that static graphic output text would in many cases be preferable to dynamic output speech (MP8), at least when the linguistic output information is complex (MP7). Dynamic speech input/output has the advantage when the operations to be performed by the user require considerable limb and visual activity (MP5). The modality properties in Figure 3.8, focusing on properties of unimodal modalities, do not address the important aspect of intelligent multimedia presentation systems that these systems offer *co-ordinated* complementary linguistic and analogue graphic output.

In the case of *speech and facial expression,* MP1 excludes the possibility that the information provided through facial expression input or output, including lip movement, can be rendered through speech (speech being a linguistic modality). It follows that this complementary and redundant information must be rendered in other ways, for instance graphically. Haptics is hardly an option in this case because of the subtlety of facial expressions. In addition, the current quality of synthetic speech imposes an extra cognitive processing load on the user (MP13), which can be alleviated through the addition of facial expression output.

The advantages offered by the two first cases of *combined input speech and gesture* distinguished above, are negatively explained by MP1 and MP2. These MPs exclude the possibility that, in practice, the information provided for spatial manipulation tasks and spatial indicative tasks can be rendered through speech. An additional MP is needed to positively suggest the obvious, namely that gesture is well suited to input the information in point (Figure 9.15).

The "spatial proximity" qualification expresses the observation that gesture gradually looses its precision when the objects indicated are spatially removed from the gesture. In other words, speech input requires complementary haptic input modalities when there is a need for providing specific spatial information and other information of significant specificity, such as indexical information on specific locations, areas or routes. The advantages of gestural input into the graphical output domain is widely recognized already, and is fundamental to the GUI paradigm. What the combination with speech offers is the *simultaneity of linguistic input* which is due to the fact that speech is hands-free (MP5). This is both faster, more efficient and more natural than having to key in linguistic instructions after having input the gestural information.

In the combined input speech and gesture case, the argument for the camera-captured, graphical representation of input *discourse gesture* proceeds as for the representation of facial expression.

MP19: Input and output gesture is good at providing spatial information, especially in spatial regions of proximity, for spatial manipulation or otherwise.

Figure 9.15: A modality property of gesture.

In the MEDITOR case of *speech replacing gesture*, the prediction following from MP1 and MP2 is that replacement will only be practically feasible for a limited set of editing operations because the difficulties of linguistically expressing complex spatial operations on the typed text will otherwise become too great, and that spoken editing operations are primarily advisable for special user groups, such as the blind.

The advantages of *augmenting* the static typed text and analogue graphics output of *GUIs through speech* follows from MP1, MP2, MP7 and MP8. Speech output just cannot replace analogue graphics and, being dynamic, does not afford the freedom of perceptual inspection needed by users for absorbing the details of larger amounts of linguistic output information. It is much less clear, however, why output speech is needed in such applications in the first place. The limited amount of output speech information provided could always be rendered in typed text instead, once a graphical screen is available. In TOSBURG II, there is no graphical output screen but only a fixed graphical display, so the advantage in terms of augmented expressiveness provided by output speech is self-explanatory. However, both the BT system and the WEATHER system have graphical output screens. In several speech-augmented GUI systems, most of the spoken output has the general form "On the screen you will see the answer to your query", which is not a terribly exciting use of output speech. Indeed, the point of having it at all is not obvious. By contrast, the use of complementary text/speech output in the intelligent multimedia systems is considerably more informative, and GALAXY's spoken output is also quite informative, to the point where it is now being considered to create spin-off unimodal speech systems from the developed applications.

Three advantages of including speech output in GUI systems should be mentioned, however, even before these systems have become more informative than is currently the case through spoken language. One is that input speech tends to generate recognition and understanding errors. Their repair is most naturally performed through spoken dialogue. Of course, the strength of this argument increases with the sophistication of the system's meta-communication abilities. The second reason, as pointed out by the BT designers, is that even limited use of output speech may serve to focus the user's attention when faced with large amounts of typed text and analogue graphics information (Wyard *et al.*, 1995). This is suggested by, but not directly stated in, MP15 and MP16. A third reason is highlighted by MP12: output speech removes the need to include a separate typed text output window that provides the system's response to the user's spoken input.

Several advantages in using input speech for GUI systems follow from Figure 3.8. One is that speech is hands-free (MP5). This means that spoken input may replace keyboard and mouse in, for instance, public kiosk applications (Chhor, 1997) where simplicity and robustness of the hardware is important. It also suggests advantages in terms of speed and effort minimization when control keywords can be spoken instead of having to be clicked on or otherwise pointed to in the graphical output domain using the mouse or other pointing devices. Most importantly, speech is the more natural form of input communication provided that the spoken input is not restricted to specific designer-designed keywords or otherwise. The problem requiring users to address the system through designer-designed typed text output keywords is highlighted by MP17. The BT designers recognize this problem (Wyard *et al.,* 1995), which might also partly account for the low transaction success rate measured on TOSBURG II.

The advantages of *combining speech, analogue graphics, tables and facial expression* (MP8) follow from the discussion of MP2 and MP7 above, and so do the potential drawbacks. Such systems are essentially speech-augmented GUIs with talking output faces. If there is little information for the output speech to provide, the same holds for the talking face.

Summarizing, it seems that modality properties such as those listed in Figure 3.8 are a powerful tool for analysing and predicting the advantages and disadvantages of AMISSs. It is possible that a limited set of modality properties might provide a more or less exhaustive basis for analysing all possible AMISSs. Furthermore, the analysis of AMISSs above suggests the possibility of *componential analysis* of AMISSs into their component AMISSs, which would strongly reduce the complexity of the problem. Componential analysis is illustrated in the discussion of the Waxholm system. The Waxholm system is effectively composed of speech-augmented GUIs and talking output faces (graphical spoken language). The system does not have to be analysed from scratch but can be analysed much more simply as a composite AMISS once its component AMISSs have been correctly analysed in terms of modality properties. We are currently investigating how far it is possible to go on the basis of the two ideas just presented.

References

Ahrenberg, L., Dahlbäck, N. and Jönsson, A.: Coding schemes for studies of natural language dialogue. In *Proceedings of the AAAI 1995 Spring Symposium on Empirical Methods in Discourse Interpretation and Generation*. Menlo Park, CA: AAAI Press, 1995, 8–13.

Allen, J. and Core, M.: *Dialogue Annotation Markup in Several Layers*. Working Report, Discourse Resource Initiative (DRI), Georgetown University, USA, 1997.

Amalberti, R., Carbonell, N. and Falzon, P.: User representations of computer systems in human–computer speech interaction. *International Journal of Man–Machine Studies*, 38, 1993, 547–566.

Anastasi, A.: *Psychological Testing*. New York: Macmillan, 1988.

Andry, F. and Thornton, S.: A parser for speech lattices using a UCG grammar. In *Proceedings of Eurospeech '91*. Grenoble: European Speech and Communication Association (ECSA), 1991, 219–222.

ARISE: http://www2.echo.lu/langeng/en/le3/arise/arise.html

ARPA: *Proceedings of the Speech and Natural Language Workshop*. San Mateo, CA: Morgan Kaufmann, 1994.

Aust, H.: Dialog modelling. In *Compendium of The Fourth European Summer School on Language and Speech Communication: Dialogue Systems*, Budapest, 1996.

Aust, H. and Oerder, M.: Dialogue control in automatic inquiry systems. In *Proceedings of the ESCA Workshop on Spoken Dialogue Systems*. Grenoble: European Speech and Communication Association (ESCA), 1995, 121–124. Also in *Proceedings of TWLT9, 9th Twente Workshop on Language Technology*. Enschede: Universiteit Twente, 1995, 45–49.

Aust, H., Oerder, M., Seide, F. and Stenbiss, V.: The Philips automatic train timetable information system. *Speech Communication*, 17, 1995, 249–262.

Baber, C.: Speech output. In C. Baber and J. M. Noyes (Eds), *Interactive Speech Technology: Human Factors Issues in the Application of Speech Input/Output to Computers*. London: Taylor and Francis, 1993a, 21–24.

Baber, C.: Developing interactive speech technology. In C. Baber and J. M. Noyes (Eds), *Interactive Speech Technology: Noyes Human Factors Issues in the Application of Speech Input/Output to Computers*. London: Taylor and Francis, 1993b, 1–18.

Baber, C. and Noyes, J. M. (Eds): *Interactive Speech Technology: Human Factor Issues in the Application of Speech Input/Output to Computers*. London: Taylor and Francis, 1993.

Badler, N. I., Philips, C. B. and Webber, B. L.: *Simulating Humans: Computer Graphics Animation and Control*. New York: Oxford University Press, 1993.

Bækgaard, A.: *A Generic Dialogue System*. Report 10 from the Danish Project in Spoken Language Dialogue Systems, 1996.

Bækgaard, A., Roman, A. and Wetzel, P.: *Advanced Dialogue Design – DDL Tool and ICM*. Esprit Project 2094 SUNSTAR Deliverable IV.6-2, 1992.

Baggia, P., Gerbino, E., Giachin, E. and Rullent, C.: Spontaneous speech phenomena in naive-user interactions. In *Proceedings of TWLT8, 8th Twente Workshop on Language Technology*. Enschede: Universiteit Twente, 1994, 37–45.

Bahl, L., Jelinek, F. and Mercer, R. L.: A maximum likelihood approach to continuous speech recognition. *IEEE Transactions on Pattern Analysis and Machine Intelligence*, 5(2), 1983, 179–190.

Basson, S., Springer, S., Fong, C., Leung, H., Man, E., Olson, M., Pitrelli, M., Singh, R. and Wong, S.: User participation and compliance in speech automated telecommunications applications. In *Proceedings of the International Conference on Spoken Language Process-

ing (ICSLP '96), Philadelphia. Wilmington, DE: Applied Science and Engineering Laboratories, 1996, 1680–1683.

Bates, M., Boisen, S. and Makhoul, J.: Developing an evaluation methodology for spoken language systems. In *Proceedings of the DARPA Workshop on Speech and Natural Language*, Hidden Valley. USA: Morgan Kaufmann, 1990, 102–108.

Bellik, Y. and Burger, D.: Multimodal interfaces: New solutions to the problem of computer accessibility for the blind. In *Proceedings of CHI '94*, Boston. USA: Association for Computing Machinery, 1994, 267–268.

Benoit, C., Massoro, D. W. and Cohen, M. M.: Modality integration: Facial movement and speech synthesis. In Cole *et al.* (Eds), *Survey of the State of the Art in Human Language Technology*. Sponsors, National Science Foundation, Directorate XIII-E of the Commission of the European Communities, Center for Spoken Language Understanding, Oregon Graduate Institute, 1996, Chapter 9.

Bernsen, N. O.: The structure of the design space. In P. F. Byerley, P. J. Barnard and J. May (Eds), *Computers, Communication and Usability: Design Issues, Research and Methods for Integrated Services*. Amsterdam: North-Holland, 1993a, 221–244.

Bernsen, N. O.: *Types of User Problems in Design. A Study of Knowledge Acquisition Using the Wizard of Oz*. Esprit Basic Research project AMODEUS Working Paper UM/WP 14, in Deliverable D2: Extending the User Modelling Techniques, 1993b.

Bernsen, N O.: Foundations of multimodal representations: A taxonomy of representational modalities. *Interacting with Computers*, 6(4), 1994, 347–371.

Bernsen, N. O.: Why are analogue graphics and natural language both needed in HCI? In F. Paterno (Ed.), *Interactive Systems: Design, Specification, and Verification. Focus on Computer Graphics*. Berlin: Springer, 1995, 235–251.

Bernsen, N. O.: Towards a tool for predicting speech functionality. *Free Speech Journal*, 1996. URL: http://www.cse.ogi.edu/CSLU/fsj/html/home.html. To appear in *Speech Communication*, 1998a.

Bernsen, N. O.: A reference model for output information in intelligent multimedia presentation systems. In G. P. Faconti and T. Rist (Eds). *Proceedings of the ECAI '96 Workshop: Towards a Standard Reference Model for Intelligent Multimedia Presentation Systems: 12th European Conference on Artificial Intelligence*, Budapest, 1996. Revised version to appear in *Computer Standards and Interfaces*, 1998b.

Bernsen, N. O., Dybkjær, H. and Dybkjær, L.: Cooperativity in human–machine and human–human spoken dialogue. *Discourse Processes*, 21(2), 1996, 213–236.

Bernsen, N O., Dybkjær, H., Dybkjær, L. and Zinkevicius, V.: Generality and transferability. Two issues in putting a dialogue evaluation tool into practical use. In *Proceedings of Eurospeech '97*. Grenoble: European Speech and Communication Association (ESCA), 1997, 1911–1914.

Bernsen, N. O. and Ramsay, J.: *Design Structure, Process and Reasoning. The Advancement of a Tool for the Development of Design Spaces*. Esprit Basic Research Project AMODEUS-2 Working Paper RP3-ID-WP28, 1994.

Bertenstam, J., Beskow, J., Blomberg, M., Carlson, R., Elenius, K., Granström, B., Gustafson, J., Hunnicutt, S., Högberg, J., Lindell, R., Neovius, L., Nord, L., de Serpa-Leitao, A. and Ström, N.: The Waxholm system – a progress report. In *Proceedings of the ESCA Workshop on Spoken Dialogue Systems*, Denmark. Grenoble: European Speech and Communication Association (ESCA), 1995, 81–84.

Bilange, E.: A task independent oral dialogue model. In *Proceedings of the 5th Conference of the European Chapter of the Asociation for Computational Linguistics (EACL)*. USA: Association for Computational Linguistics, 1991, 83–88.

Blyth, B. and Piper, H.: Speech recognition: a new dimension in survey research. *Journal of the Market Research Society*, 36(3), 1994, 183–203.

Bolt, R. A.: "Put-That-There": Voice and gesture at the graphics interface. *Computer Graphics*, 14(3), 1980, 262–270.

Bossemeyer, R. W. and Schwab, E. C.: Automated alternate billing services at Ameritech: Speech recognition and the human interface. *Speech Technology Magazine*, 5(3), 1991, 24–30.

Boyce, S. J. and Gorin, A. L.: User interface issues for natural spoken dialogue systems.

In *Proceedings of the International Symposium on Spoken Dialogue (ISSD '96)*. Japan: The Acoustical society of Japan (ASJ), 1996, 65–68.

Brennan, S. E.: Lexical entrainment in spontaneous dialogue. In *Proceedings of the International Symposium on Spoken Dialogue (ISSD '96)*. Japan: The Acoustical Society of Japan (ASJ), 1996, 45–48.

Brill, E.: Transformation-based error-driven learning and natural language processing: A case study in part of speech tagging. *Computational Linguistics*, December, 1995, 543–565.

Brink, L., Lund, J., Heger, S. and Jørgensen, J. N. in collaboration with Andersen, H., Nielsen, E. and Strange, S.: *Den Store Danske Udtaleordbog*. Copenhagen: Munksgaard, 1991.

Buchberger, E.: On the use of prosodic cues in discourse processing. In L. Dybkjær (Ed.), *Proceedings of the Second Spoken Dialogue and Discourse Workshop*, 1995, 58–70.

Bunt, H.: Context and dialogue control. *Think*, 3, 1994, 19–31.

Burnard, L. and Sperberg-McQueen, C. M.: *TEI Lite: An Introduction to Text Encoding for Interchange*. Document No. TEI U 5, 1995. URL: http://www.uic.edu:80/orgs/tei/intros/teiu5.html

Calzolari, N. and McNaught, J.: *EAGLES – Expert Advisory Group on Language Engineering Standards*, 1996. http://www.ilc.pi.cnr.it/EAGLES/home.html

Campbell, R. L.: Will the real scenario please stand up? *SIGCHI Bulletin*, 24(2), 1992, 6–8.

Carberry, S.: *Plan Recognition in Natural Language Dialogue*. Cambridge, MA: MIT Press, 1990.

Carletta, J.: Assessing agreement on classification tasks: The kappa statistics. *Computational Linguistics* 22(2), 1996, 249–254.

Carletta, J., Dahlbäck, N., Reithinger, N. and Walker, M. A. (Eds.): *Standards for Dialogue Coding in Natural Language Processing*. Dagstuhl Seminar Report 167. Schloss Dagstuhl: IBFI, 1997b.

Carletta, J., Isard, A., Isard, S., Kowtko, J. C., Doherty-Sneddon, G and Anderson, A. H.: The reliability of a dialogue structure coding scheme. *Computational Linguistics*, 23 (1), 1997a, 13–31.

Carletta, J., Isard, A., Isard, S., Kowtko, J. C., Doherty-Sneddon, G and Anderson, A. H.: *HCRC Dialogue Structure Coding Manual*. Technical Report HCRC/TR-82, Human Communication Research Centre, University of Edinburgh, 1996.

Carletta, J., Isard, A., Isard, S., Kowtko, J. C., Newlands, A., Doherty-Sneddon, G. and Anderson, A. H.: Dialogue structure coding and its uses in the map task. University of Edinburgh and University of Glasgow, 1995.

Chhor, E. S.: MASK: Multimedia multimodal service kiosk. In K. Varghese and S. Pfleger (Eds), *Human Comfort and Security of Information Systems. Advanced Interfaces for the Information Society*. Berlin: Springer, 1997, 87–92.

Christiansen, H., Larsen, H. L. and Andreasen, T. (Eds): *Proceedings of the Workshop on Flexible Query-Answering Systems*, 1996.

Clark, H. H. and Schaefer, E. F.: Collaborating on contributions to conversation. In R. Dietrich and C. F. Graumann (Eds), *Language Processing in Social Context*. Linguistic Series 54. Amsterdam: North-Holland, 1989, 123–152.

Cohen, M. M. and Massaro, D. W.: Synthesis of visible speech. *Behaviour and Research Methods, Instruments and Computers*, 22(2), 1990, 260–263.

Cohen, M. M. andMassaro, D. W.: Modeling coarticulation in synthetic visual speech. In N. M. Thalmann and D. Thalmann (Eds), *Models and Techniques in Computer Animation*. Tokyo: Springer Verlag, 1993, 139–56.

Cole, R. A., Mariani, J., Uszkoreit, H., Zaenen, A. and Zue, V. W. (Editorial Board), Varile, G. and Zampolli, A. (Managing Editors): *Survey of the State of the Art in Human Language Technology*. Sponsors, National Science Foundation, Directorate XIII-E of the Commission of the European Communities, Center for Spoken Language Understanding, Oregon Graduate Institute, 1996. URL: http://www.cse.ogi.edu/CSLU/HLTsurvey/

Cole, R. A., Novick, D. G., Fanty, M., Vermeulen, P., Sutton, S., Burnett, D. and Schalkwyk, J.: A prototype voice-response questionnaire for the US Census. In *Proceedings of the International Conference on Spoken Language Processing (ICSLP '94)*. Japan: The Acoustical Society of Japan, 1994, 683–686.

comp.speech: http://svr-www.eng.cam.ac.uk/comp.speech/FAQ.Packages.html

Copeland, C., Durand, J., Krauwer, S. and Maegaard, B. (Eds): *The Eurotra Formal Specifications.* Studies in Machine Translation and Natural Language Processing, Vol. 2, 1991.

Dahlbäck, N. and Jönsson, A.: An empirically based computationally tractable dialogue model. In *Proceedings of the Fourteenth Annual Meeting of The Cognitive Science Society,* Indiana. Hillsdale, NJ: Erlbaum, 1992, 785–790.

DARPA: *Speech and Natural Language. Proceedings of a Workshop.* San Mateo, CA: Morgan Kaufmann, 1989.

DARPA: *Speech and Natural Language. Proceedings of a Workshop Held at Hidden Valley, Pennsylvania.* San Mateo, CA: Morgan Kaufmann, 1990.

DARPA: *Speech and Natural Language. Proceedings of a Workshop.* San Mateo, CA: Morgan Kaufmann, 1991.

DARPA. *Proceedings of the Speech and Natural Language Workshop.* San Mateo, CA: Morgan Kaufmann, 1992.

Day, D. S.: *Alembic Workbench User's Guide.* Bedford, MA: MITRE Corporation, 1996.

DISC: http://www.elsnet.org/disc/

Dobler, S. and Ruehl, H.-W.: Speaker adaptation for telephone based speech dialogue systems. In *Proceedings of Eurospeech '95.* Grenoble: European Speech and Communication Asociation (ESCA), 1995, 1139–1141.

Dybkjær, L. (Ed.): *Proceedings of the Second Spoken Dialogue and Discourse Workshop,* Dublin, Ireland. Denmark: Roskilde University, 1995.

Dybkjær, L., Bernsen, N. O. and Dybkjær, H.: *Evaluation of Spoken Dialogues. User Test with a Simulated Speech Recogniser.* Report 9b from the Danish Project in Spoken Language Dialogue Systems. Roskilde University, 1996.

Dybkjær, L. and Dybkjær, H.: *Wizard of Oz Experiments in the Development of the Dialogue Model for P1.* Report 3 from the Danish Project in Spoken Language Dialogue Systems, Roskilde University, 1993.

Dybkjær, H. and Heid, U.: *Towards Annotated Dialogue Corpora.* Final report of the Elsnet transition phase dialogue annotation action, 1996. URL: http://www.mip.ou.dk/nis/publications/papers/elsnet-da-96/elsnet-da-96.html

Eckert, W. and McGlashan, S.: Managing spoken dialogues for information services. In *Proceedings of Eurospeech '93,* Berlin. Grenoble: European Speech and Communication Association (ESCA), 1993, 1653–1656.

Ericsson, K. and Simon, H.: Verbal reports as data. *Psychological Review,* 67, 1985, 215–251.

Fanty, M., Sutton, S., Novick, D. G. and Cole, R.: Automated appointment scheduling. In *Proceedings of the ESCA Workshop on Spoken Dialogue Systems,* Denmark. Grenoble: European Speech and Communication Association (ESCA), 1995, 141–144.

Feiner, S. K. and McKeown, K. R.: Automating the generation of coordinated multimedia explanations. In M. T. Maybury (Ed.), *Intelligent Multimedia Interfaces.* Cambridge, MA: MIT Press, 1993, 117–138.

Fischer, M., Maier, E. and Stein, A.: Generating cooperative system responses in information retrieval dialogue. In *Proceedings of the International Workshop on Natural Language Generation (INLGW '94),* 1994, 207–216.

Flammia, G. and Zue, V.: N.b.: A graphical user interface for annotating spoken dialogue. In J. Moore and M. Walker (Eds), *Empirical Methods in Discourse Interpretation and Generation. Papers from the 1995 AAAI Symposium,* USA: Stanford University, 1995, 40–46.

Forssten, B.: Speech technology: A one-shot possibility. In *Proceedings of Voice '94,* 1994.

Franco, V.: Automation of operator services at AT&T. In *Proceedings of Voice '93,* 1993.

Francony, J.-M., Kuijpers, E. and Polity, Y.: Towards a methodology for Wizard of Oz experiments. In *Proceedings of the Workshop on Empirical Models and Methodology for Natural Language Dialogue Systems.* Sweden: Linköping University, 1992.

Fraser, N. M.: Quality standards for spoken language dialogue systems: A report on progress in EAGLES. In *Proceedings of the ESCA Workshop on Spoken Dialogue Systems,* Denmark. Grenoble: European Speech and Communication Association (ESCA), 1995, 157–160.

Fraser, N. M. and Gilbert, G. N.: Effects of system voice quality on user utterances in speech dialogue systems. In *Proceedings of Eurospeech '91,* Genova. Grenoble: European Speech and Communication Association (ESCA), 1991a, 57–60.

Fraser, N. M. and Gilbert, G. N.: Simulating speech systems. *Computer Speech and Language*, 5, 1991b, 81–99.

Fraser, N. M. and Thornton, S.: Vocalist: A robust, portable spoken language dialogue system for telephone applications. In *Proceedings of Eurospeech '95*, Madrid. European Speech and Communication Association (ESCA), 1995, 1947–1950.

Gasterland, T., Godfrey, P. and Minker, J.: An overview of cooperative answering. *Journal of Intelligent Information Systems*, 1, 1992, 123–157.

Giachin, E.: Spoken language dialogue. In Cole *et al.* (Eds), *Survey of the State of the Art in Human Language Technology*. Sponsors, National Science Foundation, Directorate XIII-E of the Commission of the European Communities, Center for Spoken Language Understanding, Oregon Graduate Institute, 1996, Chapter 6.4.

Gibbon, D., Moore, R. and Winski, R. (Eds): *Handbook of Standards and Resources for Spoken Language Systems*. New York: Mouton de Gruyter, 1997.

Goddeau, D., Brill, E., Glass, J., Pao, C., Phillips, M., Polifroni, J., Seneff, S. and Zue, V. W.: Galaxy: A human–language interface to on-line travel information. In *Proceedings of the International Conference on Spoken Language Processing (ICSLP '94)*, Yokohama. Japan: The Acoustical Society of Japan (ASJ), 1994, 707–710.

Goldschen, A. J.: Modality integration: Facial movement and speech recognition. In Cole *et al.* (Eds), *Survey of the State of the Art in Human Language Technology*. Sponsors, National Science Foundation, Directorate XIII-E of the Commission of the European Communities, Center for Spoken Language Understanding, Oregon Graduate Institute, 1996, Chapter 9.

Grau, B., Sabah, G. and Vilnat, A.: Control in man–machine dialogue. *Think*, 3, 1994, 32–55.

Gregersen, F. and Pedersen, I. L. (Eds): *The Copenhagen Study in Urban Sociolinguistics*. 2 Vols. Copenhagen: C.A. Reitzel, 1991.

Grice, P.: Logic and conversation. In P. Cole and J. L. Morgan (Eds), *Syntax and Semantics*, Vol. 3: *Speech Acts*. New York: Academic Press 1975, 41–58. Reprinted in Grice, P.: *Studies in the Way of Words*. Cambridge, MA: Harvard University Press, 1989.

Grice, P.: Further notes on logic and conversation. In P. Cole (Ed.), *Syntax and Semantics* Vol. 9: *Pragmatics*. New York: Academic Press, 1978, 113–128. Reprinted in Grice, P.: *Studies in the Way of Words*. Cambridge, MA: Harvard University Press, 1989.

Gross, D., Allen, J. F. and Traum, D. R.: *The Trains 91 Dialogues*. TRAINS Technical Note 92-1, University of Rochester, New York, 1993.

Grosz, B. J., Pollack, M. E. and Sidner, C. L.: Discourse. In Michael I. Posner (Ed.), *Foundations of Cognitive Science*. Cambridge, MA: MIT Press, 1989, 437–468.

Grosz, B. J and Sidner, C. L.: Attention, intentions, and the structure of discourse. *Computational Linguistics*, 12(3), 1986, 175–204.

Grote, B., Hagen, E., Stein, A. and Teich, E.: Speech production in human–machine dialogue: A natural language generation perspective. In E. Maier, M. Mast and S. LuperFoy (Eds), *Dialogue Processing in Spoken Language Systems*. Lecture Notes in Artificial Intelligence 1236. Berlin: Springer, 1997, 70–85.

Guiard-Marigny, T., Adjoudani, A. and Benoit, C.: A 3-D model of the lips for visual speech synthesis. In *Proceedings of the 2nd ESCA/IEEE Workshop on Speech Synthesis*, New York. Grenoble : European Speech and Communication Association (SCA), 1994, 49–52.

Guyomard, M. and Siroux, J.: Experimentation in the specification of an oral dialogue. In H. Niemann, M. Lang, and G. Sagerer (Eds), *Recent Advances in Speech Understanding and Dialog Systems*. NATO ASI Series, Vol. F46. Berlin: Springer, 1988, 497–501.

Guyomard, M., Le Meur, D., Poignonnec, S. and Siroux, J: Experimental work on the dual usage of voice and touch screen for a cartographic application. In *Proceedings of the ESCA Workshop on Spoken Dialogue Systems*, Denmark. Grenoble: European Speech and Communication Association (ESCA), 1995, 153–156.

Hansen, P. M., Holtse, P., Nielsen, H. and Petersen, N. R.: Speech synthesis - Teaching a computer spoken language. *Teleteknik* 1-2, 1993, 52–65.

Haton, J.: Knowledge-based approaches in acoustic-phonetic decoding of speech. In H. Niemann, M. Lang and G. Sagerer (Eds), *Recent Advances in Speech Understanding and Dialog Systems*. NATO ASI Series, Vol. F46. Berlin: Springer, 1988, 51–70.

Hauptmann, A. G.: Speech and gestures for graphic image manipulation. In *Proceedings of CHI' 89*. New York: The Association for Computing Machinery, 1989, 241–245.

Hauptmann, A. G. and McAvinney, P.: Gestures with speech for graphic manipulation. *International Journal of Man–Machine Studies*, 38(2), 1993, 231–49.

Hauptmann, A. G. and Rudnicky, A. I.: Talking to computers: An empirical investigation. *International Journal of Man–Machine Studies*, 28, 1988, 583–604.

Hazen, T. J. and Zue, V. W.: Recent improvements in an approach to segment-based automatic language identification. In *Proceedings of the International Conference on Spoken Language Processing (ICSLP '94)*, Yokohama. Japan: The Acoustical Society of Japan (ASJ), 1994, 1883–1886.

Heisterkamp, P.: Ambiguity and uncertainty in spoken dialogue. In *Proceedings of Eurospeech '93*, Berlin. Grenoble: European Speech and Communication Association (ESCA), 1993, 1657–1660.

Hirschberg, J., Nakatani, C. H. and Grosz, B. J.: Conveying discourse structure through intonation variation. In *Proceedings of the ESCA Workshop on Spoken Dialogue Systems*, Denmark. Grenoble: European Speech and Communication Association (ESCA), 1995, 189–192.

Hirschmann, L., Robinson, P., Burger, J. and Vilain, M.: The MUC coreference annotation: Status and plans. In *Proceedings of the SALT Club Workshop on Evaluation in Speech and Language Technology*. UK: Speech and Language Technology (SALT), 1997, 87–88.

Hirschmann, L. and Thompson, H. S.: Overview of evaluation in speech and natural language processing. In Cole *et al.* (Eds), *Survey of the State of the Art in Human Language Technology*. Sponsors, National Science Foundation, Directorate XIII-E of the Commission of the European Communities, Center for Spoken Language Understanding, Oregon Graduate Institute, 1996, Section 13.1.

Hovy, E. and Arens, Y.: *When is a Picture Worth a Thousand Words? Allocation of Modalities in Multimedia Communication*. Paper presented at the AAAI Symposium on Human–Computer Interfaces, 1990.

IBM: http://www.software.ibm.com/is/voicetype/

Ide, N. (Ed.): CES. *The Corpus Encoding Standard*. http://www.cs.vassar.edu/~ide/CES/CES1.html

Ide, N. and Véronis, J. (Eds): *Text Encoding Initiative. Background and Context*. Dordrecht: Kluwer, 1995.

Iwanska, L.: *Summary of the IJCAI-95 Workshop on Context in Natural Language Processing,*. USA: Wayne State University, 1995. http://zeus.cs.wayne.edu/summary/index.html

Jekat, S., Klein, A., Maier, E., Maleck, I., Mast, M. and Quantz, J.: *Dialogue acts in VERBMO-BIL*. Verbmobil Report 65, Universität Hamburg, DFKI Saarbrücken, Universität Erlangen, TU Berlin, 1995.

Johansson, S.: The encoding of spoken texts. In N. Ide and J. Véronis (Eds), *Text Encoding Initiative. Background and Context*. Dordrecht: Kluwer, 1995, 149–158.

Jones, C. and Carigliano, R.: Dialogue analysis and generation: A theory for modelling natural English dialogue. In *Proceedings of Eurospeech '93*, Berlin. Grenoble: European Speech and Communication Association (ESCA), 1993, 951–954.

Jones, K. S. and Galliers, J. R.: *Evaluating Natural Language Processing Systems. An Analysis and Review*. Berlin: Springer Verlag, 1996.

Jönsson, A.: *Dialogue Management for Natural Language Interfaces. An Empirical Approach*. Ph.D. thesis, Linköping Studies in Science and Technology No. 312, 1993.

Kamp, H. and Reyle, U.: *From Discourse to Logic*. Dordrecht: Kluwer, 1993.

Kamp, Y.: *Introduction to Continuous Speech Recognition*. Fourth European Summer School in Logic, Language and Information, Essex, UK, 1992.

Kanazawa, H., Seto, S., Hashimoto, H., Shinchi, H. and Takebayashi, Y.: A user-initiated dialogue model and its implementation for spontaneous human–computer interaction. In *Proceedings of the International Conference on Spoken Language Processing (ICSLP '94)*, Yokohama. Japan: The Acoustical Society of Japan, 1994, 111–114.

Kitano, H.: FDmDialog: A speech-to-speech dialogue translation system. *Machine Translation*, 5(4), 1991, 301–338.

Klausen, T. and Bernsen, N. O.: CO-SITUE: Towards a methodology for constructing scenarios. In E. Hollnagel and M. Lind (Eds), *Proceedings of the Fourth European Meeting on Cognitive Science Approaches to Process Control (CSAPC '93): Designing for Simplicity,* Copenhagen: Symbion Conference Service, 1993, 1–16.

Kompe, R., Kiessling, A., Niemann, H., Noeth, E., Batliner, A., Schachtl, S., Ruland, T. and Block, H.: Improving parsing of spontaneous speech with the help of prosodic boundaries. In *Proceedings of ICASSP '97,* Munich. USA: The Institute of Electrical and Electronic Engineers, 1997, 811–814.

Kuhn, T., Niemann, H., Schukat-Talamazzini, E. G., Eckert, W. and Rieck, S.: Context-dependent modeling in a two-stage HMM word recognizer for continuous speech. In J. Vandewalle, R. Boite, M. Moonen and A. Oosterlinck (Eds), *Signal Processing VI: Theories and Applications,* Vol. 1. Amsterdam: Elsevier Science, 1992, 439–442.

Lamel, L., Bennacef, S., Bonneau-Maynard, H., Rosset, S. and Gauvain, J. L.: Recent developments in spoken language systems for information retrieval. In *Proceedings of the ESCA Workshop on Spoken Dialogue Systems,* Denmark. Grenoble: European Speech and Communications Association (ESCA), 1995, 17–20.

Lavie, A., Waibel, A., Levin, L., Gates, D., Gavaldà, M., Zeppenfeld, T., Zhan, P. and Glickman, O.: Translation of conversational speech with JANUS-II. In *Proceedings of the International Conference on Spoken Language Processing (ICSLP '96),* Philadelphia. Wilmington, DE: Applied Science and Engineering Laboratories, 1996, 2375–2378.

Leech, G., Myers, G. and Thomas, J. (Eds): *Spoken English on Computer. Transcription, Markup and Application.* New York: Longman, 1995.

Life, A., Salter, I., Temem, J. N., Bernard, F., Rosset, S., Bennacef, S. and Lamel, L.: Data collection for the MASK kiosk: WOZ vs. prototype system. In *Proceedings of the International Cionference on Spoken Language Processing (ICSLP '96),* Philadelphia. Wilmington, DE: Applied Science and Engineering Laboratories, 1996, 1672–1675.

Lindberg, B. and Kristiansen, J.: *Real-time Continuous Speech Recognition within Dialogue Systems.* Report 8 from the Danish Project in Spoken Language Dialogue Systems, Aalborg University, 1995.

Lindberg, B., Kristiansen, J. and Andersen, B.: *SUNCAR Functional Description.* Esprit Project 2094 SUNSTAR, STC.WPIV.008, 1992.

Litman, D.: *Plan Recognition and Discourse Analysis: An Integrated Approach for Understanding Dialogues.* Technical Report TR 170, University of Rochester, NY, 1985.

Llisterri, J.: *Preliminary Recommendations on Spoken Texts.* Eagles Document EAG-TCWG-SPT/P, 1996.

Luzzati, D. and Néel, F.: Dialogue behaviour induced by the machine. In *Proceedings of Eurospeech '89,* Paris. Grenoble: European Speech and Communications Association (ESCA), 1989, 601–604.

MacDermid, C.: Features of naive callers' dialogues with a simulated speech understanding and dialogue system. In *Proceedings of Eurospeech '93,* Berlin. Grenoble: European Speech and Communications Association (ESCA), 1993, 955–958.

MAIS: http://guagua.echo.lu/langeng/en/mlap94/mais.html

Mann, W. C. and Thompson, S. A.: Rhetorical structure theory: A theory of text organisation. In L. Polanyi (Ed.), *The Structure of Discourse.* Norwood, NJ: Ablex, 1987a, 85–96.

Mann, W. C. and Thompson, S. A.: Rhetorical structure theory: Description and construction of text structures. In G. Kempen (Ed.): *Natural Language Generation. New Results in Artificial Intelligence, Psychology and Linguistics.* NATO ASI Series E No. 135. the Netherlands: Martinus Nijhoff, 1987b, Chapter 7.

Mariani, J. and Krauwer, S.: Is speech language? In *Proceedings of the 16th International Conference on Computational Linguistics (COLING '96),* Copenhagen. Copenhagen: Center for Sprogteknologi, 1996, 996.

Martin, J.-C.: Towards "intelligent" co-operation between modalities. The example of a system enabling multimodal interaction with a map. In *Proceedings of the IJCAI '97 Workshop on Intelligent Multimodal Systems,* Nagoya. Japan: The Japanese Society for Artificial Intelligence (JSAI), 1997, 63–69. http://www.limsi.fr/Individu/martin/ijcai/article.html

Martin, P. M., Crabbe, F., Adams, S., Baatz, E. and Yankelovich, N.: SpeechActs: A spoken language framework. *IEEE Computer,* 29(7), 1996, 33–40.

Maulsby, D., Greenberg, S. and Mander, R.: Prototyping an intelligent agent through Wizard of Oz. In *Proceedings of INTERCHI '93*. New York: The Association for Computing Machinery, 1993, 277–284.

Maybury, M. T. (Ed.): *Intelligent Multimedia Interfaces*. Cambridge, MA: MIT Press, 1993.

MAX: Reference Card for MAX. ECHO (European Commission Host Organisation), Luxembourg, 1991.

Mazor, B., Braun, J., Ziegler, B., Lerner, S., Feng, M.-W. and Zhou, H.: OASIS – a speech recognition system for telephone service orders. In *Proceedings of the International Conference on Spoken Language Processing (ICSLP '94)*, Yokohama. Japan: The Acoustical Society of Japan (ASJ), 1994, 679–682.

McEnery, A. and Wilson, A. *Corpus Linguistics*. Edinburgh, UK: Edinburgh University Press, 1996.

McGlashan, S., Fraser, N. M., Gilbert, G. N., Bilange, E., Heisterkamp, P. and Youd, N. J.: Dialogue management for telephone information services. In *Proceedings of the Third Conference on Applied Natural Language Processing*. Morristown, NJ: Association for Computational Linguistics, 1992, 245–246.

Miller, G.: *Experimental Design and Statistics*. London: Methuen, New Essential Psychology, 1984.

Moran, T. and Carroll, J.: *Design Rationale: Concepts, Techniques and Use*. Hillsdale, NJ: Lawrence Erlbaum, 1996.

Morel, M. A.: Computer–human communication. In M. M. Taylor, F. Néel, and D. G. Bouwhuis (Eds), *The Structure of Multimodal Dialogue*. Amsterdam: North-Holland, 1989, 323–330.

Music, B. and Offersgaard, L.: *The NLP Module*. Report 7 from the Danish Project in Spoken Language Dialogue Systems, Centre for Language Technology, Copenhagen, 1994.

Naito, M., Kuroiwa, S., Takeda, K., Yamamoto, S. and Yato, F.: A real-time speech dialogue system for a voice activated telephone extension service. In *Proceedings of the ESCA Workshop on Spoken Dialogue Systems*, Denmark. Grenoble: European Speech and Communication Association (ESCA), 1995, 129–132.

Newell, A. F., Arnott, J. L., Dye, R. and Cairns, Y.: A full-speed listening typewriter simulation. *International Journal of Man–Machine Studies*, 35, 1991, 119–131.

Niemann, H., Brietzmann, A., Ehrlich, U., Posch, S., Regel, P., Sagerer, G., Salzbrunn, R. and Schukat-Talamazzini, G.: A knowledge based speech understanding system. *International Journal of Pattern Recognition and Artificial Intelligence*, 2(2), 1988, 321–350.

Nielsen, J.: *Usability Engineering*. New York: Academic Press, 1993.

Niimi, Y. and Kobayashi, Y.: Modeling dialogue control strategies to relieve speech recognition errors. In *Proceedings of Eurospeech '95*, Madrid. Grenoble: European Speech and Communication Association (ESCA), 1995, 1177–1180.

Nofsinger, R. E.: *Everyday Conversation*. Newbury Park, CA: Sage, 1991.

Novick, D. G. and Sutton, S.: Building on experience: Managing spoken interaction through library subdialogues. In *Proceedings of TWLT11, 11th Twente Workshop on Speech and Language Technology*. Enschede: Universiteit Twente, 1996, 51–60.

Noyes, J.: Speech technology in the future. In C. Baber and J. M. Noyes (Eds), *Interactive Speech Technology: Human Factors Issues in the Application of Speech Input/Output to Computers*. London: Taylor and Francis, 1993, 189–208.

Operetta: http://www.vocalis.com/pages/products/operetta.htm

Ortel, W. C. G.: Observed long-term changes in customer calling patterns in a telephone application using automatic speech recognition. In *Proceedings of Eurospeech '95*, Madrid. Grenoble: European Speech and Communication Association (ESCA), 1995, 269–272.

Ostler, N.: Working dialogue systems: Summary. Electronic mail on Elsnet-list, 15 August 1996.

Oviatt, S. and Wahlster, W.: Introduction to this special issue on multimodal interfaces. *Human–Computer Interaction*, 12(1/2), 1997, 1–5.

Papazachariou, D., Bernsen, N. O., Dybkjær, L. and Dybkjær, H.: Identification of speaker actions in mixed initiative dialogue. In L. Dybkjær (Ed.), *Proceedings of the Second Spoken Dialogue and Discourse Workshop*, 1995, 50–57.

Peckham, J.: Speech understanding and dialogue over the telephone: An overview of progress in the SUNDIAL project. In *Proceedings of Eurospeech '91*, Genova. Grenoble: European Speech and Communiaction Association (ESCA), 1991, 1469–1472.

Peckham, J.: A new generation of spoken dialogue systems: Results and lessons from the SUNDIAL project. In *Proceedings of Eurospeech '93*, Berlin. Grenoble: European Speech and Communication Association (ESCA), 1993, 33–40.

Peckham, J. and Fraser, N. M.: Spoken language dialogue over the telephone. In H. Niemann, R. de Mori and G. Hanrieder (Eds), *Progress and Prospects of Speech Research and Technology*. Sankt Augustin: Infix, 1994, 192–203.

Peckham, J. and Fraser, N. M.: *Speech Understanding and Dialogue*. Cambridge, MA: MIT Press (forthcoming).

Peng, J.-C. and Vital, F.: Der sprechende Fahrplan. *Output* 10, 1996, 92–96.

Ponamalé, M., Bilange, E., Choukri, K. and Soudoplatoff, S.: A computer-aided approach to the design of an oral dialogue system. In W. Webster and R. Uttamsingh (Eds). *AI and Simulation. Theory and Application. Proceedings of the SCS Eastern Multiconference*, Tennessee. San Diego, CA: Society for Computer Simulation, 1990, 229–232.

Povlsen, C.: *Sublanguage Definition and Specification*. Report 4 from the Danish Project in Spoken Language Dialogue Systems. Centre for Language Technology, Copenhagen, 1994.

Rabiner, L. R.: Mathematical foundations of hidden Markov Models. In H. Niemann, M. Lang and G. Sagerer (Eds), *Recent Advances in Speech Understanding and Dialog Systems*, NATO ASI Series F: Computer and Systems Sciences, Vol. 46. Berlin: Springer, 1988, 183–206.

Richards, M. A. and Underwood, K.: Talking to machines. How are people naturally inclined to speak. In E. D. Megaw (Ed.), *Contemporary Ergonomics*. London: Taylor and Francis, 1984, 62–67.

Rist, T. *et al.* (Eds): Special Issue on Intelligent Multimedia Presentation Systems. *Computer Standards and Interfaces*, 1997–1998 (to appear).

Roach, P. and Arnfield, S.: Linking prosodic transcription to the time dimension. In G. Leech, G. Myers, and J. Thomas (Eds), *Spoken English on Computer. Transcription, Markup and Application*. New York: Longman, 1995, 149–160.

Russell, S. and Norvig, P.: *Solution Manual for Artificial Intelligence: A Modern Approach*. Englewood Cliffs, NJ: Prentice Hall, 1995.

Sadek, M., Sadek, D., Ferrieux, A., Cozannet, A., Bretier, P., Panaget, F. and Simonin, J.: Effective human–computer cooperative spoken dialogue: The AGS demonstrator. In *Proceedings of the International Conference on Spoken Language Processing (ICSLP '96)*, Philadelphia. Wilmington, DE: Applied Science and Engineering Laboratories, 1996, 546–549.

Salber, D. and Coutaz, J.: A Wizard of Oz platform for the study of multimodal systems. In *INTERCHI '93 Adjunct Proceedings*, Amsterdam. New York: The Association for Computing Machinery, 1993a, 95–96.

Salber, D. and Coutaz, J.: Applying the Wizard of Oz technique to the study of multimodal systems. In L. Bass, J. Gornostaev and C. Unger (Eds), *Proceedings of Human Computer Interaction, 3rd International Conference EWHCI'93, East/West Human Computer Interaction*. Lecture Notes in Computer Science 753. Berlin: Springer, 1993b, 219–230.

Schiffrin, D.: *Approaches to Discourse*. Oxford: Blackwell, 1994.

Schneider, D. K., Drozdowski, T. M., Glusman, G., Godard, R., Block, K. and Tennison, J.: *The Evolving TecfaMOO Book – Part I: Concepts*, 1996. URL: http://tecfa.unige.ch/moo/book1/ tm.html

Schneidermann, B.: *Designing the User Interface*. Reading, MA: Addison-Wesley, 1987.

Searle, J. R.: *Speech Acts. An Essay in the Philosophy of Language*. Cambridge: Cambridge University Press, 1969.

Searle, J. R.: Indirect speech acts. In P. Cole and J. L. Morgan (Eds), *Syntax and Semantics*, Vol. 3: *Speech Acts*. New York: Academic Press, 1975.

Searle, J. R.: *Expression and Meaning. Studies in the Theory of Speech Acts*. New York: Cambridge University Press, 1979.

Searle, J. R.: Conversation. In H. Parret and J. Verschueren (Eds), *(On) Searle on Conversation*. Amsterdam: John Benjamin's Publishing Company, 1992, 7–29.

Sidner, C.: *The American Express Corpus*. Stanford, CA: SRI, Stanford Research Institute, 1992.

Simpson, A. and Fraser, N.: Black box and glassbox evaluation of the SUNDIAL system. In *Proceedings of Eurospeech '93*, Berlin. Grenoble: European Speech and Communication Association (ESCA), 1993, 1423–1426.

Smith, R. W.: *A Computational Model of Expectation-Driven Mixed-Initiative Dialogue Processing*. Ph.D. Thesis, Department of Computer Science, Duke University, Durham, NC, 1991.

Smith, R. W. and Hipp, D. R.: *Spoken Natural Language Dialog Systems: A Practical Approach*. New York: Oxford University Press, 1994.

Sommerville, I.: *Software Engineering*, 4th edition. Reading, MA: Addison-Wesley, 1992.

SPEECHtel: http://www.vocalis.com/pages/products/spchtel.htm

Sperber, D. and Wilson, D.: Précis of relevance, communication and cognition with open peer commentary. *Behavioral and Brain Sciences*, 10(4), 1987, 697–754.

Stein, A. and Maier, E.: Structuring collaborative information-seeking dialogues. *Knowledge-Based Systems*, 8(2/3), 1994, 82–93.

Strik, H., Russel, A., Heuvel, H., Cucchiarini, C. and Boves, L.: Localising an automatic inquiry system for public transport information. In *Proceedings of the International Conference on Spoken Language Processing (ICSLP '96)*, Philadelphia. Wilmington, DE: Applied Science and Engineering Laboratories, 1996, 853–856.

Sutton, S., Novick, D., Cole, R., Vermeulen, P., Villiers, J., Schalkwyk, J. and Fanty, M.: Building 10,000 spoken dialogue systems. In *Proceedings of ICSLP '96*, 1996, 709–712.

Thompson, H.: *HCRC Map Task Editorial Conventions and Markup Structure*. Edinburgh, UK: HCRC, University of Edinburgh, 1992.

Traum, D. R. and Dillenbourg, P.: Miscommunication in multi-modal collaboration. In *Workshop Notes of the AAAI Workshop on Detecting, Repairing, and Preventing Human-Machine Miscommunication*. USA: American Association for Artificial Intelligence (AAAI), 1996, 37–46.

Traum, D. R. and Heeman, P. A.: Utterance units in spoken dialogue. In *Proceedings of the ECAI '96 Workshop on Dialogue Processing in Spoken Language Systems*, Budapest. Germany: European Coordinating Committee for Artificial Intelligence (ECCAI), 1996, 84–91.

Tutiya, S.: *Chiba Map Task Dialog Corpus Home Page*. http://cogsci.l.chiba-u.ac.jp/MapTask/, 1996.

Vocalis Operetta: http://www.vocalis.com/pages/products/operetta.htm

Vossen, P. H.: Evaluating speech input and output in a CAD system using the hidden-operator method. In *Proceedings of Eurospeech '91*, Genova. Grenoble: European Speech and Communication Association, 1991, 69–72.

Wahlster, W.: One word says more than a thousand pictures. On the automatic verbalization of the results of image sequence analysis systems. *Computers and Artificial Intelligence*, 8, 1989, 479–492.

Wahlster, W.: Verbmobil – Translation of face to face dialogues. *Machine Translation Summary IV*, 1993.

Wahlster, W., André, E., Finkler, W., Profitlich, H.-J. and Rist, T.: Plan-based integration of natural language and graphics generation. *Artificial Intelligence*, 63, 1993, 387–427.

Waibel, A.: Interactive translation of conversational speech. *IEEE Computer*, 29(7), 1996, 41–48.

Whittaker, S. and Stenton, P.: Cues and control in expert–client dialogues. In *Proceedings of the 26th Annual Meeting of the ACL*. Morristown, NJ: Association for Computational Linguistics (ACL), 1988, 123–130.

Wyard, P., Appleby, S., Kaneen, E., Williams, S. and Preston, K.: A combined speech and visual interface to the BT Business Catalogue. In *Proceedings of the ESCA Workshop on Spoken Dialogue Systems*, Denmark. Grenoble: European Speech and Communication Associations (ESCA), 1995, 165–168.

Yamada, A., Yamamoto, T., Ikeda, H., Nishida, T. and Doshita, S.: Reconstructing spatial images from natural language texts. In *Proceedings of the 14th International Conference on Computational Linguistics (COLING '92)*. Nantes: ICCL, 1992, 1279–1283.

Yi, J.: Analysis of user's responses in a speech dialogue system. In *Proceedings of International Symposium on Spoken Dialogue (ISSD). New Directions in Human and Man-Machine Communication*, Tokyo. Tokyo: Waseda University, 1993, 37–40.

Young, S.: Speech recognition evaluation: A review of the ARPA CSR Programme. In *Proceedings of the SALT Club Workshop on Evaluation in Speech and Language Technology,* Sheffield. UK: Speech and Language Technology (SALT) Club, 1997, 197–205.

Yourdon, E.: *Managing the System Life Cycle. A Software Development Methodology Overview.* New York: Yourdon Press, 1982.

Zhan, P., Ries, K., Gavaldà, M., Gates, D., Lavie, A. and Waibel, A.: JANUS-II: Towards spontaneous Spanish speech recognition. In *Proceedings of the International Conference on Spoken Language Processing (ICSLP '96),* Philadelphia. Wilmington, DE: Applied Science and Engineering Laboratories, 1996, 2285–2288.

Zoltan-Ford, E.: How to get people to say and type what computers can understand. *International Journal of Man–Machine Studies,* 34, 1991, 527–547.

Zue, V. W.: Toward systems that understand spoken language. *IEEE Expert,* 9(1), 1994, 51–59.

Index

Acceptance test 68, 193
Acoustic models 32, 35, 53–4, 80
  see also Speech
Ad hoc generated phrases and jumps
    198–9
Advanced multimodal interactive speech
    systems (AMISS)
  all modalities combined 250
  componential analysis of 252
  defined 244–5
  facial expression 246–7
  gesture 247–8
  graphical user interfaces 248–9
  modality conversion 245–6
  multimedia presentation 246
Air travel information systems (ATIS) 13,
    23, 236
Alembic workbench 188, 189
Ambiguity, *see* Manner *and* Meta-
    communication
AMISSs, *see* Advanced multimodal
    interactive speech systems
AMODEUS-2 project ix
Annotation, *see* Corpus annotation
Aphodex system 12
Appointment scheduling systems, *see*
    Verbmobil
APSGs, *see* Augmented phrase structure
    grammars
Architecture
  of Danish Dialogue System 10, 162–4
  logical 10
ARISE project 15
ARNE-3 WOZ tool 22
ARPA, *see* DARPA
Aspects of interaction 90–1
  see also Background knowledge,
    Informativeness, Manner, Partner
    asymmetry, Relevance, Repair and
    clarification, *and* Truth and
    evidence
  see also Guidelines
Assertions 45
Assistant, *see* Wizard-of-Oz method
ATIS, *see* Air travel information systems

Attentional state 32, 35, 40, 41
  simulated by wizard 139
  see also Expectations *and* Focus
AudioTool 190
Augmented phrase structure grammars
    (APSG) 9, 50–1

Background knowledge 91, 106–9
  domain 109–10
  is non-Gricean 121–3
  novices and experts 108
  users' 107
  user expectations 108–9
  user inferences 107
  see also Guidelines *and* Aspects
Banking systems 21
Barge-in 17–18
  talk-in 49
Best practice and interactive speech
    systems
  in development and evaluation 7, 26–7,
    61
Bigram 54
Blackbox evaluation 14, 23, 172, 174–5,
    191
Bottom-up test 171, 173
Braille systems 248
Brevity, *see* Manner
British Telecom business catalogue system
    248–9, 251

CDHMM, Compact density hidden Markov
    models, *see* Hidden Markov models
CES, *see* Corpus encoding standard
Chiba tools 188
Circuit-fix-it-shop system 11, 39
Clarification, *see* Repair and clarification
Coded speech 32, 37
Codes, *see* Markup
Coding 178, 185–8
  consistency 185
  coverability 185
  intercoder reliability 185